TAJIKISTAN

T0289854

INDUSTRIAL AND BUSINESS DIRECTORY

International Business Publications, USA
Washington, DC, USA - Tajikistan

TAJIKISTAN
INDUSTRIAL AND BUSINESS DIRECTORY

Editorial content: International Business Publications, USA
Editor-in-Chief: Dr. Igor S. Oleynik
Editor: Natasha Alexander
Managing Editor: Karl Cherepanya

Published by
International Business Publications, USA
P.O.Box 15343, Washington, DC 20003
Phone: (202) 546-2103, Fax: (202) 546-3275, E-mail: rusric@erols.com

UPDATED ANNUALLY

Databases & Information: Global Investment Center, USA
Cover Design: International Business Publications, USA

We express our sincere gratitude to all government agencies and international organizations which provided information and other materials for this *directory*

2006 International Business Publications, USA
ISBN 0-7397-0711-6

This guide provides basic information for starting or/and conducting business in the country. The extraordinary volume of materials covering the topic, prevents us from placing all these materials in this guide. For more detailed information on issues related to any specific investment and business activity in the country, please contact Global Investment Center, USA
Please acquire the list of our business intelligence and marketing reports and other business publications. We constantly update and expand our business intelligence and marketing materials. Please contact the center for the updated list of reports on over 200 countries.

in the USA: **Global Investment Center, USA.**
                P.O.Box 15343, Washington, DC 20003
                Phone: (202) 546-2103, Fax: (202) 546-3275, E-mail: rusric@erols.com

For additional analytical, marketing and other information please contact
Global Investment Center, USA

Printed in the USA

For additional analytical, business and investment opportunities information,
please contact Global Investment & Business Center, USA
at (202) 546-2103. Fax: (202) 546-3275. E-mail: rusric@erols.com

TAJIKISTAN

INDUSTRIAL AND BUSINESS DIRECTORY

TABLE OF CONTENTS

**For additional analytical, business and investment opportunities information,
please contact Global Investment & Business Center, USA
at (202) 546-2103. Fax: (202) 546-3275. E-mail: rusric@erols.com**

**For additional analytical, business and investment opportunities information,
please contact Global Investment & Business Center, USA
at (202) 546-2103. Fax: (202) 546-3275. E-mail: rusric@erols.com**

For additional analytical, business and investment opportunities information,
please contact Global Investment & Business Center, USA
at (202) 546-2103. Fax: (202) 546-3275. E-mail: rusric@erols.com

**For additional analytical, business and investment opportunities information,
please contact Global Investment & Business Center, USA
at (202) 546-2103. Fax: (202) 546-3275. E-mail: rusric@erols.com**

**For additional analytical, business and investment opportunities information,
please contact Global Investment & Business Center, USA
at (202) 546-2103. Fax: (202) 546-3275. E-mail: rusric@erols.com**

STRATEGIC & BUSINESS PROFILES

COUNTRY OVERVIEW

President: Emomili Rakhmonov
Prime Minister: Abdujalil Samadov
Independence: September 9, 1991 (from Soviet Union)
Population : 6.0 million
Location/Size: Central Asia/143,100 sq. miles, slightly smaller than Wisconsin
Major Cities: Dushanbe (capital)
Languages: Tajik (official), Russian
Ethnic Groups: Tajiks (64.9%), Uzbek (25%), Russian (3.5%), other (6.6%)
Religions: Sunni Muslim (80%), Shi'a Muslim (5%), other (15%)
Defense : Army (2,500), CIS Forces (mostly Russian) (25,000), National Guard (NA), Security Forces (NA)

ECONOMIC OVERVIEW

Currency: Ruble
Gross Domestic Product (Purchasing Power Equivalent) : $6.9 billion
Real GDP Growth Rate : -21%
Inflation Rate (Consumer Prices) (1993 Average): 38% per month
Merchandise Exports : $263 million to non-FSU
Merchandise Imports : $371 million from non-FSU
Major Export Products: Cotton, aluminum, fruits
Major Import Products: Fuel, chemicals, machinery

Current issues: Tajikistan has experienced three changes of government since it gained independence in September 1991. The current president, Emomali RAHMONOV, was elected in November 1994, yet has been in power since 1992. The country is suffering through its fourth year of a civil conflict, with no clear end in sight. Underlying the conflict are deeply rooted regional and clan-based animosities that pit a government consisting of people primarily from the Kulob (Kulyab), Khujand (Leninabad), and Hisor (Hissar) regions against a secular and Islamic-led opposition from the Gharm, Gorno-Badakhshan, and Qurghonteppa (Kurgan-Tyube) regions. Government and opposition representatives have held periodic rounds of UN-mediated peace talks and agreed in September 1994 to a cease-fire which has been periodically extended. Russian-led peacekeeping troops are deployed throughout the country, and Russian-commanded border guards are stationed along the Tajikistani-Afghan border.

GEOGRAPHY

Location: Central Asia, west of China
Geographic coordinates: 39 00 N, 71 00 E
Map references: Commonwealth of Independent States
Area:
total : 143,100 sq km
land: 142,700 sq km
water: 400 sq km

For additional analytical, business and investment opportunities information, please contact Global Investment & Business Center, USA at (202) 546-2103. Fax: (202) 546-3275. E-mail: rusric@erols.com

Area - comparative: slightly smaller than Wisconsin

Land boundaries:
total: 3,651 km
border countries: Afghanistan 1,206 km, China 414 km, Kyrgyzstan 870 km, Uzbekistan 1,161 km
Coastline: 0 km (landlocked)
Maritime claims: none (landlocked)
Climate: midlatitude continental, hot summers, mild winters; semiarid to polar in Pamir Mountains
Terrain: Pamirs and Alay Mountains dominate landscape; western Fergana Valley in north, Kofarnihon and Vakhsh Valleys in southwest

Elevation extremes:
lowest point: Syrdariya 300 m
highest point: Qullai Kommunizm 7,495 m

Natural resources: significant hydropower potential, some petroleum, uranium, mercury, brown coal, lead, zinc, antimony, tungsten

Land use:
arable land : 6%
permanent crops: 0%
permanent pastures: 25%
forests and woodland: 4%
other: 65% (1993 est.)

Irrigated land: 6,390 sq km (1993 est.)
Natural hazards: NA

Environment - current issues: inadequate sanitation facilities; increasing levels of soil salinity; industrial pollution; excessive pesticides; part of the basin of the shrinking Aral Sea suffers from severe overutilization of available water for irrigation and associated pollution

party to: none of the selected agreements
signed, but not ratified: none of the selected agreements

Geography - note: landlocked

PEOPLE

Population: 5,945,903

Age structure:
0-14 years: 42% (male 1,263,725; female 1,234,730)
15-64 years : 53% (male 1,578,940; female 1,599,458)

For additional analytical, business and investment opportunities information,
please contact Global Investment & Business Center, USA
at (202) 546-2103. Fax: (202) 546-3275. E-mail: rusric@erols.com

65 years and over: 5% (male 114,118; female 154,932) (July 1997 est.)

Population growth rate: 1.18%
Birth rate: 27.93 births/1,000 population
Death rate: 7.74 deaths/1,000 population
Net migration rate: -8.42 migrant(s)/1,000 population **Environment - international agreements:**

Sex ratio:
at birth : 1.05 male(s)/female
under 15 years: 1.02 male(s)/female
15-64 years: 0.99 male(s)/female
65 years and over: 0.74 male(s)/female
total population: 0.99 male(s)/female

Infant mortality rate: 109.5 deaths/1,000 live births

Life expectancy at birth:
total population: 64.68 years
male : 61.55 years
female: 67.97 years

Total fertility rate: 3.58 children born/woman

Nationality:
noun: Tajikistani(s)
adjective: Tajikistani

Ethnic groups: Tajik 64.9%, Uzbek 25%, Russian 3.5% (declining because of emigration), other 6.6%
Religions: Sunni Muslim 80%, Shi'a Muslim 5%
Languages: Tajik (official), Russian widely used in government and business
Literacy:
definition: age 15 and over can read and write
total population: 98%
male: 99%
female: 97%

GOVERNMENT

Country name:
conventional long form : Republic of Tajikistan
conventional short form: Tajikistan
local long form: Jumhurii Tojikistan
local short form: none
former : Tajik Soviet Socialist Republic
Data code: TI
Government type: republic
National capital: Dushanbe

For additional analytical, business and investment opportunities information,
please contact Global Investment & Business Center, USA
at (202) 546-2103. Fax: (202) 546-3275. E-mail: rusric@erols.com

Administrative divisions: 2 oblasts (viloyatho, singular - viloyat) and one autonomous oblast* (viloyati avtonomii); Viloyati Avtonomii Badakhshoni Kuni* (Khorugh - formerly Khorog), Viloyati Khatlon (Qurghonteppa - formerly Kurgan-Tyube), Viloyati Leninobod (Khujand - formerly Leninabad)
note: the administrative center name follows in parentheses
Independence: 9 September 1991 (from Soviet Union)
National holiday: National Day, 9 September (1991)
Constitution: new constitution adopted 6 November 1994
Legal system: based on civil law system; no judicial review of legislative acts
Suffrage: 18 years of age; universal

Executive branch:
Tajikistan

President	**Emomali RAHMONOV**
Prime Minister	**Oqil OQILOV**
First Dep. Prime Min.	**Hajji Akbar TURAJONZODA**
Dep. Prime Min.	**Khayrinisso MAVLONOVA**
Min. of Agriculture	**Voris MADAMINOV**
Min. of Culture	**Rajabmad AMIROV**
Min. of Defense	**Sherali KHAYRULLOYEV,** *Col. Gen.*
Min. of Economy & Trade	**Hakim SOLIYEV**
Min. of Education	**Abdujabbor RAHMONOV**
Min. of Emergency Situations	**Mirzo ZIYOYEV**
Min. of Energy	**Jurabek NURMAHMADOV**
Min. of Finance	**Safarali NAJMUDDINOV**
Min. of Foreign Affairs	**Talbak NAZAROV**
Min. of Grain Products	**Bekmurod UROQOV**
Min. of Health	**Nusratullo FAIZULLOYEV**
Min. of Internal Affairs	**Khomiddin SHARIPOV**
Min. of Industry	**Zayd SAIDOV**
Min. of Justice	**Halifabobo HAMIDOV**
Min. of Labor, Employment, & Social Welfare	**Zokir VAZIROV**
Min. of Land Improvement & Water Economy	**Abduqohir NAZIROV**
Min. of Security	**Khayriddin ABDURAHIMOV**
Min. of State Revenue & Tax Collections	**Ghulomjon BOBOYEV**
Min. of Transport	**Abdurahim ASHUROV**
Chmn.. State Committee on Construction &	**Ismat ESHMIRZOYEV**

Architecture	
Chmn., State Committee for Environmental Protection & Forestry	**Abduvohid KARIMOV**
Chmn., State Committee on Land Resources & Reclamation	**Davlatsho GULMAHMADOV**
Chmn., State Committee for Oil & Gas	**Salamsho MUHABBATOV**
Chmn., State Committee on Protection of State Borders	**Saidamir ZUHUROV,** *Col. Gen.*
Chmn., State Committee for Radio & Television	**Asadullo RAHMONOV**
Chmn., State Committee on Religious Affairs	**Murodullo DAVLATOV**
Chmn., State Committee on State Property	**Sherali GULOV**
Chmn., State Committee on Statistics	**Mirgand SHABOZOV**
Chmn., National Security Council	**Amirkul AZIMOV**
Prosecutor General	**Bobojon BOBOKHONOV**
Director, Drug Control Agency	**Rustam NAZAROV,** *Lt. Gen.*
Chmn., National Bank	**Murodali ALIMARDONOV**
Ambassador to the US	**Khamrokhon ZARIPOV**
Permanent Representative to the UN, New York	**Rashid ALIMOV**

Legislative branch: unicameral Supreme Assembly or Majlisi Oli (181 seats; members are popularly elected to serve five-year terms)
elections : last held 26 February and 12 March 1995 (next to be held NA 2000)
election results: percent of vote by party - NA; estimated seats by party - Communist Party and affiliates 100, People's Party 10, Party of People's Unity 6, Party of Economic and Political Renewal 1, other 64

Judicial branch: Supreme Court, judges are appointed by the president

Political parties and leaders: People's Party of Tajikistan [Abdumajid DOSTIYEV]; National Revival Bloc [Abdumalik ABDULLOJONOV]; Tajik Communist Party [Shodi SHABDOLOV]; Democratic Party [Jumaboy NIYAZOV, chairman]; Islamic Renaissance Party or IRP [Mohammed Sharif HIMMATZODA, chairman]; Rebirth (Rastokhez) [Takhir ABDUZHABOROV]; Lali Badakhshan Society [Atobek AMIRBEK]; Tajikistan Party of Economic and Political Renewal or TPEPR; Citizenship, Patriotism, Unity Party [Bobokhon MAHMADOV]; Adolatho "Justice" Party [Abdurahmon KARIMOV, chairman]

Political pressure groups and leaders: Tajikistan Opposition Movement based in northern Afghanistan [Seyed Abdullah NURI, chairman]

International organization participation: CIS, EBRD, ECE, ECO, ESCAP, FAO, IBRD, ICAO, IDA, IDB, IFAD, IFC, ILO, IMF, Intelsat, IOC, IOM, ITU, NACC, OIC, OSCE, UN, UNCTAD, UNESCO, UNIDO, UPU, WFTU, WHO, WIPO, WMO, WTrO (observer)

Diplomatic representation in the US: Tajikistan does not have an embassy in the US, but has a mission at the UN: address - 136 East 67th Street, New York, NY 10021, telephone - [1] (212) 472-7645, FAX - [1] (212) 628-0252; permanent representative to the UN is Rashid ALIMOV

Diplomatic representation from the US:
chief of mission: Ambassador R. Grant SMITH
embassy : interim chancery, Oktyabrskaya Hotel, 105A Prospect Rudaki, Dushanbe 734001
mailing address: use embassy street address
telephone : [7] (3772) 21-03-56
FAX: Telex (787) 20116

Flag description: three horizontal stripes of red (top), a wider stripe of white, and green; a gold crown surmounted by seven five-pointed gold stars is located in the center of the white stripe

ECONOMY

Economy - overview: Tajikistan had the next-to-lowest per capita GDP in the former USSR, the highest rate of population growth, an extremely low standard of living, and rampant inflation. Agriculture dominates the economy, with cotton being the most important crop. Mineral resources, varied but limited in amount, include silver, gold, uranium, and tungsten. Industry is limited to a large aluminum plant, hydropower facilities, and small obsolete factories mostly in light industry and food processing. The Tajik economy has been gravely weakened by four years of civil conflict and by the loss of subsidies from Moscow and of markets for its products, which has left Tajikistan dependent on Russia and Uzbekistan and on international humanitarian assistance for much of its basic subsistence needs. Moreover, constant political turmoil and the continued dominance by former communist officials have impeded the introduction of meaningful economic reforms. The regime made initial efforts to stabilize the economy and promote reform in 1996.
GDP: purchasing power parity - $5.4 billion (1996 estimate as extrapolated from World Bank estimate for 1994)
GDP - real growth rate: -17%
GDP - per capita: purchasing power parity - $920
GDP - composition by sector:
agriculture: NA%
industry: NA%
services: NA%
Inflation rate - consumer price index: 65%
Labor force:
total: 1.9 million
by occupation: agriculture and forestry 52%, manufacturing, mining, and construction 17%, services 31% (1995)
Unemployment rate: 2.4% includes only officially registered unemployed; also large numbers of underemployed workers and unregistered unemployed people (December 1996)

Budget:
revenues: $NA
expenditures : $NA, including capital expenditures of $NA
Industries: aluminum, zinc, lead, chemicals and fertilizers, cement, vegetable oil, metal-cutting machine tools, refrigerators and freezers
Industrial production growth rate: -20%
Electricity - capacity: 4.44 million kW
Electricity - production: 16.8 billion kWh
Electricity - consumption per capita: 2,135 kWh (1995 est.)

Agriculture - products: cotton, grain, fruits, grapes, vegetables; cattle, sheep, goats

Exports:
total value: $768 million
commodities : cotton, aluminum, fruits, vegetable oil, textiles
partners: FSU 78%, Netherlands
Imports:
total value: $657 million
commodities: fuel, chemicals, machinery and transport equipment, textiles, foodstuffs
partners : FSU 55%, Switzerland, UK
Debt - external: $635 million (of which $250 million to Russia) (1995 est.)
Economic aid:
recipient : ODA, $22 million
note: commitments, $885 million (disbursements $115 million) (1992-95)
Currency: the Tajikistani ruble (TSR) = 100 tanga; Tajikistan introduced its own currency in May 1995
Exchange rates: Tajikistani rubles (TJR) per US$1 - 350 (January 1997), 284 (January 1996)
Fiscal year: calendar year

COMMUNICATIONS

Telephones: 303,000

Telephone system: poorly developed and not well maintained; many towns are not reached by the national network
domestic: cable and microwave radio relay
international: linked by cable and microwave radio relay to other CIS republics, and by leased connections to the Moscow international gateway switch; Dushanbe linked by Intelsat to international gateway switch in Ankara (Turkey); satellite earth stations - 1 Orbita and 2 Intelsat

Radio broadcast stations: 1 state-owned radio broadcast station
Radios: NA
Television broadcast stations: 1
note : 1 Intelsat earth station provides TV receive-only service from Turkey
Televisions: NA

TRANSPORTATION

For additional analytical, business and investment opportunities information,
please contact Global Investment & Business Center, USA
at (202) 546-2103. Fax: (202) 546-3275. E-mail: rusric@erols.com

total: 480 km in common carrier service; does not include industrial lines

Highways:
total: 32,752 km
paved: 21,119 km (note - these roads are said to be hard-surfaced, meaning that some are paved and some are all-weather gravel surfaced)
unpaved: 11,633 km (1992 est.)

Pipelines: natural gas 400 km (1992)
Ports and harbors: none
Airports: 59
Airports - with paved runways:
total : 14
over 3,047 m: 1
2,438 to 3,047 m: 5
1,524 to 2,437 m: 7
914 to 1,523 m: 1
Airports - with unpaved runways:
total: 45
914 to 1,523 m: 9
under 914 m : 36

MILITARY

Military branches: Army, Air Force, Presidential National Guard, Security Forces (internal and border troops)
Military manpower - military age: 18 years of age
Military manpower - availability:
males age 15-49: 1,393,416
Military manpower - fit for military service:
males : 1,143,159
Military manpower - reaching military age annually:
males: 60,832
Military expenditures - dollar figure: 180 billion rubles (1995); note - conversion of defense expenditures into US dollars using the current exchange rate could produce misleading results
Military expenditures - percent of GDP: 3.4%

TRANSNATIONAL ISSUES

Disputes - international: boundary with China in dispute; territorial dispute with Kyrgyzstan on northern boundary in Isfara Valley area; foreign support to Islamic fighters based in northern Afghanistan in Tajikistan's civil war

Illicit drugs: limited illicit cultivation of cannabis and opium poppy, mostly for domestic consumption; increasingly used as transshipment point for illicit drugs from Southwest Asia to Russia and Western Europe

For additional analytical, business and investment opportunities information, please contact Global Investment & Business Center, USA at (202) 546-2103. Fax: (202) 546-3275. E-mail: rusric@erols.com

NARCOTICS

Tajikistan is not a major producer of narcotics, but is a major transit country for heroin and opium from Afghanistan. The opium/heroin moves through Tajikistan through Central Asia and on to Russian and European markets, and it generally does not enter the United States. The volume of drugs following this route via multiple methods of transportation is significant and growing. Although there were dramatic gains in the total volume of drugs seized, the Government of Tajikistan (GOT) continued to have difficulty combating drug trafficking and other narcotics-related problems in a coordinated manner. Drug abuse of heroin, opium, and cannabis in Tajikistan is a growing problem. Tajikistan's medical infrastructure is highly inadequate and cannot address the population's growing need for addiction treatment and rehabilitation. The GOT remained committed during the year to implementing a counternarcotics strategy and cooperative programs with the UN Office for Drug Control and Crime Prevention (UNODCCP). It has also participated in the UN Six Plus Two counternarcotics initiative, signing the Regional Action Plan, which it helped to draft. Tajikistan is a party to the 1988 UN Drug Convention.

STATUS OF COUNTRY

Geography and economics have made Tajikistan an attractive transit route for illegal narcotics. Its border with opium-producing Afghanistan, which is dominated by mountainous terrain, is thinly guarded, difficult to patrol, and easily crossed without inspection at a number of points. The disruption of normal economic activity during the 1992-1997 civil war gave rise to a warlord class whose leaders continue to jostle for control of the lucrative narcotics trade. With the average monthly income in the country remaining below U.S. $10, the temptation to become involved in narcotics-related transactions remains high for many segments of society. In-country cultivation of narcotic crops is minimal, and the GOT is unaware of any processing or precursor chemical production facilities.

COUNTRY ACTIONS AGAINST DRUGS

Policy Initiatives. The Presidential Office's Drug Control Agency (DCA), created in 1999 with UNODCCP support, continued to implement a number of programs with the UNODCCP designed to strengthen Tajikistan's drug control capacity. The programs are part of a "Security Belt" strategy to stem drug trafficking from Afghanistan. The DCA aims to centralize the GOT's counternarcotics efforts and support drug treatment and rehabilitation efforts. The GOT appears to be giving counternarcotics law enforcement a higher priority than in the past, but it remains subject to pressure from regional power centers, benefiting from trafficking. The GOT's resources for counternarcotics efforts remain limited.

Accomplishments. Despite a slow start due to a lack of resources and infighting with other government security organs, the DCA became fully operational in April 2000. It recruited and trained a capable staff, well regarded by the UNODCCP. During 2001, it continued to raise its profile in the country and increased its public outreach efforts. The

DCA also extended its links with international organizations and foreign states while expanding its cooperation with other Tajik security agencies.

Law Enforcement Efforts. During the first ten months of 2001, Tajikistan officials reported seizing 8.1 tons of illegal narcotics, including 3,780 kilograms of heroin and 3,590 kilograms of opium. Heroin seizures increased sharply over the previous year's ten-month totals (1.9 MT), while opium seizures fell sharply from 4.8 MT last year to 3.6 MT this year. Given the ten-to-one ratio between heroin and opium, opium equivalent seizures rose sharply. Russian Border Guard personnel were responsible for more than half the seizures. Although Tajik and Russian border forces are Tajikistan's first and main line of defense against illegal narcotics trafficking, they remain unequal to the task. Given low pay and high incentives for corruption, they are at times, in fact, part of the problem.

Corruption. Influential figures from both sides of Tajikistan's civil war, many of whom now hold government positions, are widely believed to have a hand in the drug trade. While it is impossible to determine how pervasive drug corruption is within government circles, salaries for even top officials are low and often seem inadequate to support the lifestyles many officials maintain. Even when arrests are made, the resulting cases are not always brought to a satisfactory conclusion. As a matter of policy, however, Tajikistan does not encourage or facilitate illicit production or distribution of narcotic or psychotropic drugs or other controlled substances. While accusations of drug-related corruption are routinely made by political figures against their enemies, there is no direct evidence of senior officials of the GOT engaging in, encouraging, or facilitating illicit production or distribution of such drugs or substances.

Agreements and Treaties. Tajikistan is a party to the 1988 UN Drug Convention, the 1961 UN Single Convention on Narcotic Drugs, as amended by the 1972 Protocol, and the 1972 UN Convention on Psychotropic Substances. It has signed the Central Asian Counternarcotics Protocol with the UNODCCP and neighboring Central Asian countries. Tajikistan is a party to the World Customs Organization's International Convention on Mutual Administrative Assistance for Prevention, Investigation, and Repression of Customs Offenses (the Nairobi Convention), Annex X on Narcotics Cases. Tajikistan signed the UN Convention against Transnational Organized Crime in December 2000.

Cultivation/Production. Opium poppies and, to a lesser extent, cannabis, are cultivated in limited amounts, most in the northern Aini and Pendjikent districts. Opium cultivation has been limited by law enforcement efforts and because it has been cheaper and safer to cultivate opium poppies in neighboring Afghanistan until the events following September 11.

Drug Flow/Transit. An estimated 80 percent of the narcotics produced in Afghanistan are smuggled across the border into Tajikistan's Shurobod, Moskovski, and Pyanj districts, according to GOT statistics. While the GOT may be overestimating the percentage of Afghanistan's drug production that transits Tajikistan, the total volume of drugs is certainly high. One UN estimate put the amount of heroin from Afghanistan going through the country at roughly 30 to 50 tons a year. Hashish from Afghanistan also transits Tajikistan en route to Russian and European markets.

Domestic Programs (Demand Reduction). The DCA expanded its initiatives aimed at increasing drug awareness, primarily among school children. However, the number of young addicts continues to grow—over 60 percent of Tajikistan's drug addicts fall into the 18-30 age group. The DCA also significantly expanded its public advocacy efforts in mass media outlets.

U.S. POLICY INITIATIVES AND PROGRAMS

Bilateral Cooperation. The USG is committed to providing counternarcotics and law enforcement training to Tajikistan. Because security restrictions precluded the USG from providing training in Tajikistan, the USG provided law enforcement training at venues outside the country.

The Road Ahead. The UNODCCP will remain the principal agency supporting counternarcotics efforts in Tajikistan. The United States will continue to provide law enforcement training, encourage similar support from Western European countries, and promote regional cooperation as essential to improve counternarcotics performance for all countries in the region. It is unclear what effect U.S. operations and the removal of the Taliban in Afghanistan will have on the cross-border drug trade, but every effort will be made to assure the effects are positive.

IMPORTANT INFORMATION FOR UNDERSTANDING TAJIKISTAN

PROFILE

OFFICIAL NAME: Republic of Tajikistan

GEOGRAPHY

Area: 143,100 sq. km.
Capital: Dushanbe.
Terrain: Pamir and Alay mountains dominate landscape; western Ferghana valley in north, Kofarnihon and Vakhsh Valleys in southwest.
Climate: Mid-latitude continental, hot summers, mild winters; semiarid to polar in Pamir mountains.

PEOPLE

Nationality: Tajikistani.
Population : 6.1 million .
Population growth rate : 1.5%.
Ethnic groups: Tajik 67%, Uzbek 23%, Russian 3.5%, other 6.5%.
Religion: Sunni Muslim 80%, Shi'a Muslim 5%, other 15%.
Language: Tajik (sole official language as of 1994), Russian widely used in government and business, 77% of the country, however, is rural and they speak mostly Tajik.
Education: *Literacy* (according to Tajikistan official statistics, 2000)--99%. The Tajik education system has suffered greatly since independence.
Health: *Life expectancy*--60.95 years men; 67.38 years women. *Infant mortality rate*--117.42 deaths/1,000 live births .
Work force: No recent data available.

GOVERNMENT

Type: Republic.
Independence: September 9, 1991 (from Soviet Union).
Constitution: November 6, 1994.
Branches: *Executive*--Chief of state: President Emomali RAHMONOV since November 6, 1994; head of state and Supreme Assembly chairman since November 19, 1992; head of government: Prime Minister Oqil OQILOV since January 20, 1999. Cabinet: Council of Ministers appointed by the president, approved by the Supreme Assembly. Elections: president elected by popular vote for a 7-year term; election last held November 6, 1999 (next to be held NA 2006); prime minister appointed by the president. Election results: Emomali RAHMONOV elected president; percent of vote: Emomali RAHMONOV 96%, Davlat USMONOV 4%. *Legislative*--Bicameral Supreme Assembly or Majlisi Oli (181 seats; next election 96 seats; members are elected by popular vote to serve 5-year terms). Elections held February 26 and March 12, 1995 (next were held

For additional analytical, business and investment opportunities information, please contact Global Investment & Business Center, USA at (202) 546-2103. Fax: (202) 546-3275. E-mail: rusric@erols.com

February 27 and March 23, 2000). Election results: percent of vote by party, NA. Estimated seats by party: Communist Party and affiliates 100; People's Party 10; Party of People's Unity 6; Party of Economic and Political Renewal 1; Islamic Rebirth Party 2; other 62. *Judicial*--Supreme Court, judges are appointed by the president. Political parties and leaders: Democratic Party or TDP [Mahmadruzi SKANDDAROV, chairman]; Islamic Rebirth Party [Said Abdullo NURI]; National Unity Party--evolved from the People's Party and Party of People's Unity; Party of Justice and Development Rahmatullo ZOIROV]; People's Democratic Party of Tajikistan or PDPT [Abdulmajid DOSTIEV]; Rastokhez (Rebirth) Movement [Tohiri ABDUJABBOR]; Tajik Communist Party or CPT [Shodi SHABDOLOV]; Tajikistan Party of Economic and Political Renewal or TPEPR [leader NA].

Suffrage: 18 years of age, universal.

Defense: military manpower (availability): 1,253,427 .

Flag: three horizontal stripes of red (top), a wider stripe of white, and green; a gold crown surmounted by seven gold, five-pointed stars is located in the center of the white stripe.

ECONOMY

GDP nominal: $955 million.

GDP per capita : $154/per capita.

GDP : Real growth rate: 8.3%.

Inflation rate: 33%.

Natural resources: Hydropower, some petroleum, uranium, gold, mercury, brown coal, lead, zinc, antimony, tungsten.

Unemployment rate: 54.1% , under-employment also is high; 80% live under the poverty line .

Agriculture: *Products*--cotton, grain, fruits, grapes, vegetables; cattle, sheep, goats.

Industry: *Types*--aluminum, zinc, lead, chemicals and fertilizers, cement, vegetable oil, textiles, metal-cutting machine tools, refrigerators and freezers.

Trade: *Exports*--$792 million : aluminum (49%), electricity (23%), cotton (12%), gold, fruits, vegetable oil, textiles. *Partners*--Europe 43%, Russia 30%, Uzbekistan 13%, Asia 12%, other CIS 2% . *Imports*--$839 million (2000.): electricity, petroleum products, aluminum oxide, machinery and equipment, foodstuffs. *Partners*--Other CIS 41%, Uzbekistan 27%, Russia 16%, Europe 12%, Asia 4% .

External debt total : $1.2 billion. Bilateral external debt: total --$509 million: Uzbekistan $130 million, Russia $288 million, U.S. $22 million, Turkey $26 million, Kazakhstan $19 million, Pakistan $16 million; multilateral debt: total--$365 million: World Bank $153 million, IMF $113 million, ADB $19 million .

Debt/GDP ratio : 129.

GEOGRAPHY

At 36'40' northern latitude and 41'14' eastern longitude, Tajikistan is nestled between Kyrgyztsan and Uzbekistan to the north and west, China to the east, and Afghanistan to the south. Tajikistan is home to some of the highest mountains in the world including the Pamir and Alay ranges. Ninety-three percent of Tajikistan is mountainous with altitudes ranging from 1,000 feet to 27,000 feet, with nearly 50% of Tajikistan's territory above

10,000 feet. Earthquakes are of varying degrees and are frequent. The massive mountain ranges are cut by hundreds of canyons and gorges at the bottom of which run streams which flow into larger river valleys where the majority of the country's population lives and works. The principal rivers of Central Asia, the Amu Darya and the Syr Darya, both flow through Tajiksitan, fed by melting snow from mountains of Tajikistan and Kyrgyztsan. Flooding sometimes occurs during the annual Spring thaw.

PEOPLE

Contemporary Tajiks are the descendants of ancient Eastern Iranian inhabitants of Central Asia, in particular the Soghdians and the Bactrians, and possibly other groups, with an admixture of western Iranian Persians and non-Iranian peoples, Mongols, and Turkic peoples, and reports of Alexander the Great's army. Until the 20th century, people in the region used two types of distinction to identify themselves: way of life--either nomadic or sedentary--and place of residence. By the late 19th century, the Tajik and Uzbek peoples, who lived in proximity for centuries and often used--and continue to use--each other's languages, did not perceive themselves as two distinct nationalities. The division of Central Asia into five Soviet Republics in the 1920s imposed artificial labels on a region in which many different peoples lived intermixed.

HISTORY

The current Tajik Republic hearkens back to the Samanid Empire (A.D. 875-999), that ruled what is now Tajikistan as well as territory to the south and west, as their role model and name for their currency. During their reign, the Samanids supported the revival of the written Persian language in the wake of the Arab Islamic conquest in the early 8th century and played an important role in preserving the culture of the pre-Islamic persian-speaking world. They were the last Persian-speaking empire to rule Central Asia.

After a series of attacks beginning in the 1860s during the Great Game, the Tajik people came under Russian rule. This rule waned briefly after the Russian Revolution of 1917 as the Bolsheviks consolidated their power and were embroiled in a civil war in other regions of the former Russian Empire. As the Bolsheviks attempted to regain Central Asia in the 1920s, an indigenous Central Asian resistance movement based in the Ferghana Valley, the "Basmachi movement," attempted to resist but was eventually defeated in 1925. Tajikistan became fully established under Soviet control with the creation of Tajikistan as an autonomous Soviet socialist republic within Uzbekistan in 1924, and as one of the independent Soviet socialist republics in 1929.

STRATEGIC INFORMATION AND US-TADJIK RELATIONS

POLITICAL DEVELOPMENTS

Tajikistan is a nation undergoing profound political and economic change. It is a newly independent nation still in the process of stabilizing its internal political situation as well as its relations with neighboring states. Although the 1992 civil war, which was caused by regional economic and political differences, largely subsided by March 1993, there

---

continues to be sporadic fighting along the Tajik border with Afghanistan between remnants of the Tajik opposition and Russian border guard forces.

In June 1997 a peace agreement was signed between the government and the United Tajik Opposition (UTO) under which the government promised to lift the ban on all parties of the United Tajik Opposition in order that fair and democratic elections can take place. The signing of the peace agreement opened a new window of opportunity for economic reforms. In spite of this major step for the peace process, Tajikistan is still plagued by occasional outbreaks of violence led by regional warlords and disgruntled UTO guerilla leaders.

In August 1998, four United Nations military observers were killed in the eastern part of the country, and in November 1998, an armed rebellion in Khujand, in the northern part of the country, led by Colonel Mahmud Khudoiberdiyev and former premier Abdumalik Abdullojonov was defeated by government troops after intense fighting. The Tajik peace process suffered an additional blow when, in May 1999, UTO leaders pulled out of the National Reconciliation Commission following the government's refusal of the opposition's demand for greater influence in the power sharing coalition.

Tajikistan is located at a crossroads of major world civilizations--Russia, Turkey, Iran, India-Pakistan, and China--and has been influenced by each. Russia, China and India share an interest in restraining Islamic fundamentalism, while Iran and Pakistan vie to reinforce Tajikistan's Islamic identity. Russia and Tajikistan's fellow Central Asian neighbors--Kazakhstan, Kyrgyzstan, and Uzbekistan--have been concerned about drug and gun running across the borders as well as Islamic fundamentalism, and have mostly supported Tajikistan's secular regime. Russia has been concerned to safeguard the 90,000 ethnic Russians still residing in Tajikistan, and Uzbekistan, to safeguard the 1.5 million ethnic Uzbeks residing there.

Discrimination against ethnic Russians in Tajikistan has increased and fuels a continuing exodus. The only political violence in Dushanbe has been a number of killings of ethnic Russians, usually soldiers, which has been of little comfort to Russian civilians.

Tajikistan's neighbors in the region, in particular Uzbekistan and the Russian Federation, maintain great influence over the course of internal Tajik politics. Russia, which already has 25,000 armed troops in Tajikistan (largely Russian CIS peacekeeping forces), tentatively agreed in April 1999 to the establishment of a military base which would help increase the stability in Tajikistan. Due to the geography of the region and the whims of Soviet planners, Tajikistan is largely at the mercy of Uzbekistan for all overland and rail transport. Tajikistan has moved to reduce its energy dependency on Uzbekistan by signing a tripartite agreement on trade, economic, and cultural relations with Turkmenistan and Iran. Turkmenistan provides Tajikistan with reduced cost fuel and natural gas as part of the agreement.

The government of President Emomali Rakhmonov is dominated by Tajiks from the southern Kulyab region who were victorious in the 1992-93 civil war. The November 1994 Presidential election, while peacefully conducted, was marred by fraud and intimidation, as were the February 1995 parliamentary elections. Tajikistan also adopted

**For additional analytical, business and investment opportunities information,
please contact Global Investment & Business Center, USA
at (202) 546-2103. Fax: (202) 546-3275. E-mail: rusric@erols.com**

a new constitution in November 1994, which, while not a perfect document, is still judged to be a significant improvement over the Soviet-era version.

Political relations with the United States are on a cordial footing in spite of the temporary suspension of Embassy operations in Dushanbe in the fall of 1998. This decision was made due to concerns about threats to U.S. facilities worldwide, turmoil in Tajikistan, and a limited ability to secure the safety of personnel in their facility. This suspension is temporary and the State Department intends to resume operations as soon as a suitable new site is identified and a more secure facility for the Embassy can be built.

ECONOMIC SITUATION

Tajikistan is in a very slow transition from a command economy to a more market-oriented economy. Difficulties abound with the disruption of established trade routes, civil unrest, natural disasters, and an absence of the traditional Soviet-era inputs that came from Moscow for over seventy years.

The collapse of the trade and payment system, the deterioration of the terms of trade, and the absence of union transfers from Moscow, which had been the main method of funding Soviet Republics during the Soviet period, have inflicted significant damage to Tajikistan's economy. The move from a command economy under the Soviet system to a more open and market-oriented economy has been an onerous task, replete with legislative, institutional, and cultural obstacles.

These obstacles have been compounded by civil war and natural disasters. As a result of political instability, Tajikistan has been late in receiving the international monetary assistance and foreign investment that other former Soviet Republics have already received. On the economic front, the government of Tajikistan now appears to be ready to do the work necessary to receive international donor support and to return Tajikistan to the standard of living experienced prior to the outbreak of the civil war.

With the assistance of the IMF, Tajikistan has established a three-stage economic reform process designed to carry the country into the next century. The first stage (mid-1995/1997) focused on improvement in the legal infrastructure, reforms in the agricultural sector, privatization of small-scale enterprises, and creation of favorable conditions to attract foreign investors. The second stage (1998- 2000) presently focuses on the privatizing of large-scale enterprises, and establishing efficiently- functioning banking, credit and taxation systems. The third stage (2001+) will focus on the further modernization of the economy, the formation of an efficient infrastructure and the implementation of large scale socio-economic programs.

There appears to be a good degree of political will behind the reforms and their implementation. Progress has been slow, but steady. Partially to reward the government's implementation of some economic reforms and to encourage more, international financial organizations such as the IMF and the World Bank have begun an infusion of credit to Tajikistan which should straighten the path of economic reform. On June 15, 1999, the World bank approved three credits worth a total of $31.7 million with $20 million being used to support the privatization of farms.

For additional analytical, business and investment opportunities information, please contact Global Investment & Business Center, USA at (202) 546-2103. Fax: (202) 546-3275. E-mail: rusric@erols.com

BASIC STRATEGY OF ECONOMIC REFORM

The basic strategy of the economic reform plan is to move the economy from a command economy to a socially-oriented, market-oriented one which provides for economic growth and the welfare of the population. The current program envisages a set of measures for deepening economic changes and for finding a way out of the crisis to promote stabilization and economic growth.

THE FIRST STAGE OF ECONOMIC REFORM

The first stage of economic reform entails legislative reform. The following laws were adopted in 1995 and 1996 to provide a legal basis for reform:
- On Credit Insurance;
- On Money Circulation;
- On the National Budget for 1996;
- On Copyrights;
- A decree "On Support of Small Business" was also adopted instead of the Law of the Republic of Tajikistan for the Protection of Private Entrepreneurs.

PRIVATIZATION

The Government of Tajikistan has outlined plans to accelerate the pace of privatization and to form a securities market in 1997. While most of the small retail enterprises have already been privatized, only 11 percent of medium and large enterprises have been privatized. In most cases the government has maintained a share of more than 40 percent of privatized enterprises. While leveraged buyout has been the preferred method of privatization, the program has reportedly been plagued by corruption.

The current share of the private sector in GDP is approximately 20-30%. Obstacles to the growth of the private sector include difficult entry and exit rules, lack of finance, limited access to business information, strict labor regulations and an incomplete legal framework.

Enterprise restructuring began in 1991 but stalled as a result of the war and political instability and has yet to gain momentum. A Law on Bankruptcy was passed in June 1992 but few companies have been forced into bankruptcy. The 1995 decree on "The Identification of Bankrupt Enterprises" represents an effort to speed up rehabilitation and restructuring of inefficient enterprises.

Agricultural reform - The goal of the government's plans for agricultural reform is to release a sufficient amount of land to individual farmers so as to reinvigorate agricultural production and generate more commercial activity. At present the agrarian sector is still controlled by large collective farms (kolkhozes) and state farms (sovkhozes). All kolkhozes will be transformed into farms which will be governed by individuals or a group of private farmers having the right of inheritance leasing, which permits the lessor to designate an heir to control the property being leased. One of the difficulties of this type of reform is choosing deserving candidates for land use and giving equitable compensation to those farmers who will be deprived of land.

The government reorganized "Glavkhlopkoprom" (a state organization called "The Main Cotton Industry" which controls all the ginning and part of the selling of cotton fiber) at the end of 1997. The organization was replaced by half a dozen firms which are intermediaries for receiving crop loans from international banks and assisting individual kolkhozes to buy inputs and sell their cotton. The intermediary firms see this as a temporary stage, with some of the kolkhozes already dealing directly with suppliers and buyers. Smaller producers and traders are already dealing directly, but such activity is impeded by the lack of effective international banking facilities.

Concerning other agricultural products, the government has started to liberalize of the marketing system by reducing the share of production being purchased by the state order and giving producers the right to sell the remainder of their products not sold to the state. This creates a more commercial atmosphere.

EU TAJIKISTAN

POLITICAL SITUATION

Following the break-up of the former Soviet Union, **Tajikistan became an independent Republic on 9 September 1991.** Largely unprepared for this new reality, Tajikistan soon faced an acute social and economic crisis as the previous interdependent central planning system disintegrated. The situation was severely aggravated by the ensuing civil war. The country experienced the emergence of various political platforms presenting divergent policies to deal with the rapidly deteriorating situation. The failure to maintain stability was largely caused by the struggle between different regional and political affiliations for the redistribution of power in the country after the collapse of the previous political system. The crisis was further compounded by ideological differences.

As a consequence, **civil war erupted in May 1992,** with the heaviest fighting taking place in the latter half of the year. The armed conflict continued for the next four years with varying degrees of intensity. The fighting resulted in many casualties, widespread human suffering and economic collapse. During the hostilities, an estimated **50.000 people lost their lives.** Hundreds of thousands fled the turmoil with an estimated **600.000 internally displaced persons. 60.000 Tajiks took refuge across the border in Afghanistan.** After the worst of the fighting subsided in early 1993, many internally displaced persons began to return to their communities. At the same time, a large number of refugees also returned to Tajikistan. By the end of 1996, 43.000 refugees had been repatriated to their homes, leaving an estimated 20.000 remaining in Afghanistan and many more in other neighbouring countries and the Russian Federation.

A complex process of inter-Tajik peace negotiations under the auspices of the United Nations began in April 1994. The **peace talks concluded on 27 June 1997** with signing in Moscow by President Emomali Rakhmonov and the leader of the Union of Tajik Opposition (UTO) M. Said Abdullo Nuri of the *General Agreement on the Establishment of Peace and National Accord in Tajikistan (General Agreement).* The *General*

For additional analytical, business and investment opportunities information, please contact Global Investment & Business Center, USA at (202) 546-2103. Fax: (202) 546-3275. E-mail: rusric@erols.com

Agreement incorporates the previous protocols and documents that were signed during the negotiations. The *General Agreement* provides a comprehensive foundation for the National reconciliation process and set up a power-sharing arrangement in Dushanbe between the neo-communist government and Islamic rebels.

In practical terms, the *General Agreement* provides for a transitional of 12-18 months during which all the provisions contained therein are to be implemented, thus creating the necessary political, legislative and security environment under which all provisions are to be implemented, thus creating the necessary political, legislative and security environment under which new parliamentary elections which should have been held in the second half of 1998. Some positive results have been achieved but general elections foreseen in the second half of 1998 have been postponed to the second half of 1999.

Following the civil war the government implemented the Peace agreement and started working on Tajikistan recovery. A high price has nevertheless been paid to the war: GDP is now at only 25% of its 1991 level, poverty is rife (83% of population is below poverty level). The key elements of the Peace Agreement between the Government and the United Tajik Opposition have been implemented. A constitutional referendum, formation of a coalition government (involving representatives of the United Tajik Opposition) and presidential and parliamentary elections in 1999 and 2000, although not fully in conformity with international standards, were important benchmarks in this process. Notwithstanding these achievements, many problems and challenges remain. The judiciary is weak and does not contribute to eradicating corruption. Even if the security situation is improved, it is now safe to travel in most of the country, the government is still not in full control of the full territory, where local ex-warlords are still in charge, often also of criminal activities such as drugs smuggling.

The **past years have seen a certain tendency among the government to renege on earlier agreements**: the guaranteed share of 30% in government posts for the Islamist opposition is not fully respected (especially at regional and local level), former opposition fighters included in the regular forces have almost all been dismissed, and under the pretext of the fight against terrorism there has been increasing pressure on the –legal- Islamic Renaissance Party (IRP led by Said Nuri) and Islamic clergy in the North of the country. For example the head of the Democratic Party of Tajikistan Iskandarov was removed from his post of Director of state enterprise "Tojikgaz"; several members of the (IRP), including a senior leader Shamsuddinov, have been sentenced to 16 to 25 years in prison in the past months.

Also, opposition parties other than the Social Democrats, who were finally registered in December 2002 after years of obstruction, still have difficulty in obtaining official registration, which would give them the right to participate in elections. Some IRP candidates for the Parliamentary by-elections were refused on futile grounds in October 2002. The extension of the limit of the presidential term in office is a concern following controversial constitutional referendum held on 22 June 2003. The opposition warned that this extension may give President Rakhmonov (and his Democratic Party) the possibility of remaining in office until 2020. Although the OSCE did not formally monitor the referendum, they welcomed the calm atmosphere in which the voting took place but noted shortcomings in the electoral framework.

The next parliamentary elections will be held in February 2005. Following international pressure, the Tajik government agreed to improve the electoral law which will be changed soon. OSCE/ODIHR as well as major foreign partners will study carefully the entire process from the preparation of the new law, to the campaign and the holding of the elections.

A number of **positive developments** can however be noted: exit visas were abolished; the prison system has been transferred from the Ministry of Interior to the Ministry of Justice after many problems; a National Commission for Human Rights has been created; the President has expressed a clear commitment to fight corruption within law-enforcement agencies, which poses a threat to the rule of law; his January 2003 and January 2004 reshuffles of a number of Ministries and local bodies is seen in the light of the fight against (all too conspicuous) corruption. It can also be seen as an attempt to boost performance of government services. **Tajikistan remains the only country in Central Asia with a legal Islamist opposition.** The Tajik authorities modified recently the criminal law **abolishing death penalty for women**. However the rate at which death penalties are delivered (about 5 per month) and executed is still very high. The EU protested the sudden execution of the Nazriev brothers in June 2002, who received their sentence for attempting to assassinate the Mayor of Dushanbe in February 2000.

Despite some early improvement in the media situation (three independent radio stations received a broadcasting license, charges of slander of the President and sedition against critical journalist Dodojon Atovullo were dropped), **many media restrictions remain in place**; most journalists exercise self-censorship when reporting about the government or vested interests. In addition several legal changes concerning the media have been introduced over the past several months. These changes effectively give the government control over the media and increase the potential for abuse and corruption. In September 2003, the law on television and radio was revised and a special inspection body created. This body has sweeping authority over all aspects of broadcast media and can unduly influence the licensing procedure. In December 2003, the Tajik parliament approved additional amendments to the law, including enacting "technical standards" which are financially beyond the means of most Tajik media outlets. Moreover, all production studios must now be licensed to ensure the quality of their programming – thus essentially allowing the government to also control the content of programs. In addition, President Rakhmonov issued a decree in November 2003, creating a national plan for information security. This decree contains broad provisions that could easily be abused to limit freedom of the press, particularly in the run-up to next year's elections. Following this drawback the EU issued a statement on 24 January 2004.

ECONOMIC SITUATION

Following independence in 1991, economic conditions in Tajikistan deteriorated sharply. The break-up of the Soviet Union accounted partly for these developments: the budget transfers from the Central Union budget stopped and inter-republic trade and payments arrangements collapsed. In the political uncertainty following the separation from the Soviet Union, and civil unrest between different groups, the civil war resulted in much destruction of infrastructure base and large population displacement. The economic damage from the civil war is estimated at about US$ 7 billion. Natural disasters in 1992 and 1993 aggravated the economic conditions. The GDP fell an

For additional analytical, business and investment opportunities information, please contact Global Investment & Business Center, USA at (202) 546-2103. Fax: (202) 546-3275. E-mail: rusric@erols.com

estimated at least 60% in five years. Current account and fiscal deficits reached unsustainable levels, and hyperinflation emerged. As the civil war started tapering off, the government was able to start efforts for economic recovery. In 1997, after the signing of a peace accord sustained economic programs began.

The IMF's Post-Conflict Facility and Enhanced Structural Adjustment Facility (ESAF) came into effect (1998-2001). The ESAF program was later transformed into a **Poverty Reduction and Growth Facility (PRGF).** To restore the economy, the authorities worked with the multilateral and bilateral donor organizations implementing country assistance strategies, Structural Adjustment Credits, and projects for rehabilitation of Social Sector, infrastructure, emergency flood and power sectors. They adopted, with the support of the international community, a **Poverty Reduction Strategy Paper (PRSP)** and a **Public Investment Programme (PIP)**, which serve as a basis for dialogue between the authorities and the international community of donors. These documents were aimed at macroeconomic stabilization and introduced structural reforms designed to assist the transition to market economy. The broad hallmarks of the initial programs were price and trade liberalizations, privatisation of state enterprises, land reform, improvements in the social safety net, and legal and institutional reforms. Fight against poverty remains a key element of the Tajik authorities' policy. It is an essential component of EU assistance strategy for the country. Tajikistan is one of the countries included in the CIS-7 Initiative supported by the Bretton Woods Institutions.

Tajikistan applied to join the WTO in 2001. No documents have been submitted by Tajikistan since then. Tajikistan needs to continue the reform process, and, in parallel, prepare the necessary documentation for Geneva, as well as submit a first market access offer on goods and services. A delegation from Tajikistan (at Ministerial level) was to table its memorandum on foreign trade regime in the beginning of February 2003.

Macroeconomic performance has improved significantly. Since the end of the civil war, economic growth averaged about 7.5% in 1997-2001. This strong economic growth accelerated in the last three years (9.2% growth on average since 2001 and 8.6% year on year in the first half of 2003), supported by increased production of key commodities (mainly aluminium and cotton) and strong domestic demand fuelled by increasing remittances from Tajiks working abroad. Moreover, there have been improvements in fiscal management, reducing the fiscal deficit from 3.8% of GDP in 1998 to 0.1% of GDP in 2001 and a surplus of 1.% of GDP in 2003. Public expenditure discipline is very severe : the civil service force was cut by 5% in the first quarter of 2003 and the Tajik government is committed to continue this policy allowing the release of the third "tranche" of the PRGF. The exchange rate has been relatively stable, although concerns persist over inflation (average annual rate still around 10%) and the consistency of monetary policy. The recent bilateral debt rescheduling agreements have reduced the debt stock to US$ 985 million (82% of GDP) in 2002 and to 73% of GDP in 2003. The government also decided to limit public financed investments to 3% of GDP (US$ 40 million for 2003) and not to allow non-concessional sovereign borrowings under the IMF programme. Tajikistan has a liberal foreign trade regime. Most prices are liberalized, except for public utility services.

However some concerns remain. There is a **lack of transparency in three key areas of the economy such as agriculture, banking and energy sectors.** Further

For additional analytical, business and investment opportunities information, please contact Global Investment & Business Center, USA at (202) 546-2103. Fax: (202) 546-3275. E-mail: rusric@erols.com

privatisation of agriculture and of major state owned enterprises remain also a key political issue in Tajikistan. The **process of land reform and farm privatisation** has accelerated since mid-1998. Half of all arable land is now in private hands. To further the privatisation process, land lease procedures need to be simplified, it is a pre-condition for increased productivity of the sector and to reduce poverty in rural areas where 70% of the population lives. To reach sustainable development, the rural sector requires infrastructure in road networks, communication, and extension services which are currently missing. **Banking reform** is lagging behind and has an impact on the efficiency of the rural sector. One of the necessary components of private agriculture activity is the availability of financing. Low public confidence in the banking sector continues to constrain the capacity of the economy. In particular in managing the revenue sent by the Tajik workers abroad in particular in Russia. **Most prices are liberalised, except for public utility services**. The utilities sectors, and especially the energy sector, are responsible for large quasi-fiscal losses. The prices of electricity and natural gas have remained low. The energy sector also has not been able to increase tariff collections rates to financially acceptable levels. Recently, Government increased tariff collection rates and adjusted tariffs to cost recovery which is a first step. Further efforts should be put into this sector.

Privatisation of state enterprises has been largely completed for small firms. Almost a quarter of medium to large enterprises have been sold. The Government has adopted Medium Term Privatisation Strategy in conjunction with the World Bank to **accelerate the privatisation process especially of the bigger enterprises**. Privatisations in the communications and the transport sectors are being planned. Progress is also being made in simplifying the legal and regulatory framework for development of the private sector and the proper functioning of markets. The Government is also determined to fight corruption.

Inflows of foreign direct investment are still low, with net FDI amounting to about $45m in 2001 (up from $22m in 2000). The government is optimistic about raising cumulative investment to around $448 million by end-2004, from $320m in April 2002.

Poverty reduction has become a central concern of government policy. 83% of the Tajik population lives below poverty level as defined by the World Bank. Many social indicators have fallen from their pre-war levels. Malnutrition is a problem. Primary health services reach fewer people. Rural-urban income disparities have increased. Unemployment remains high. Social protection of the vulnerable population is inadequate. In adopting the PRSP, the Tajik authorities try to promote a cohesive targeted approach towards alleviating poverty. **The PRSP emphasizes economic growth through macroeconomic stabilization, low inflation and stable exchange rates.** The agricultural sector, due its size and its large share of the poor, is the sector in which to make the most gains against poverty. Private initiatives both in agricultural rural areas and in other economic sectors will make gains in productivity most rapidly. During the transition period to a larger role of the private sector in the economy, the budget will directly target the most vulnerable groups of the society by cash compensations. At the same time, all the implementing policies will take into consideration the protection of the poor. The targeted key areas are in health, education, social protection and in agriculture, key domains for EU assistance.

EU-TAJIKISTAN BILATERAL RELATIONS

LEGAL FRAMEWORK

The legal framework for EU-Tajikistan bilateral relations is the **Trade and Cooperation Agreement (TCA)** of 1989 between the EU and the former Soviet Union, which was endorsed by Tajikistan by exchange of letter in 1994. For a long time dormant because of Tajikistan's internal problems, the TCA was revived at the Commission's initiative in the wake of 11 September 2001. Since December 2001, three joint committees took place in the framework of the TCA dealing with trade, economic and cooperation issues.

Backed up by a Council decision in December 2001, the Commission opened negotiation with Tajikistan for a **Partnership and Cooperation Agreement (PCA) which was initialled on 16 December 2003 in Brussels**. The signature of the PCA will take place soon after the formal EC procedures are completed. The PCA will heighten EC profile and EU interests in Tajikistan. It will reinforce Tajik stability and the fight against drugs and terrorism. The Tajik PCA is the last one negotiated with a CIS partner, it brings EU relations with Tajikistan in line with relations with the other Central Asian countries. With ratification in 25 member States, the new PCA will probably not be fully operational before 2006/2007. An Interim Agreement will therefore be sought for dialogue in the period between signature and full ratification.

On 26 March 2003, President Rakhmonov paid an official visit to Brussels, he met President Prodi, Mr. Solana, and Mr. Pat Cox.

BILATERAL TRADE

EU-Tajikistan trade relations are extremely limited. In 2002 the EU imported €68 million worth of Tajik goods, compared to €60 million in 2001, €44 million in 2000 and €55 million in 1999. Over 60% of the imports were of raw materials. EU exports to Tajikistan totalled €32 million in 2002 similar to the figures for the three previous years (€34 million in 2001 for example). Over a third of these exports were of agricultural products; machinery and transport materials accounted for around a quarter of the total. There are no trade defence measures, in either direction, between the EU and Tajikistan.

Generalised System of Preferences - GSP. Around one third of total Tajik imports to the EU are eligible for GSP benefits and 90% of these goods benefit from preferential rates.

EC ASSISTANCE

The Community's strategy towards the Central Asian region is set out in the Commission's Strategy Paper for Central Asia 2002-2006.

Tajikistan is by far the most significant per capita beneficiary of European Community assistance in Central Asia. From 1992 to 2002, the **Community budget has provided to Tajikistan more than €350 million most of it in grant form.** The EU is present in Tajikistan with no less than **four assistance instruments**: humanitarian assistance through ECHO, the Food Security Programme, exceptional macro-financial and, as of now, with Tacis. Food Security Programme and Tacis operations were suspended in 1997 for security reasons, but have now been resumed.

MACRO-FINANCIAL ASSISTANCE

The EC has provided Tajikistan with macro-financial assistance in the form of a **loan of €60 million (disbursed in March 2001) and a total available grant amount of up to €35 million, disbursed in successive annual tranches**. Three grant tranches, totaling €21 million, have already been released while Tajikistan has reduced its outstanding debt to the Community by €16 million to the present €44 million. A Commission staff mission assesses every year the progress made by Tajik authorities in fulfilling the structural conditionality attached to each grant tranche of up to EUR 7 million. This conditionality is in line with the IMF conditionality, and includes conditions in the most important areas of structural reform such as an increase in tax revenues as a ratio to the GDP, strengthening of banking regulation, enhancement of monetary policy (no issuing of directed credits), continued restructuring and privatisation of large state-owned enterprises and governance (concerning most importantly government's policy towards the cotton sector). The remaining two grant tranches are scheduled to be released in 2004 and 2005, they will be released following EC staff missions, the next one will take place at the time of your visit in Dushanbe.

HUMANITARIAN ASSISTANCE (ECHO)

In 2002, **ECHO signed contracts worth €10 million** to help alleviate the effects of the 1999-2001 drought. Improved rainfall in 2002 contributed to higher crop yields. But according to the UN 30% of the rural population still require emergency food aid. Most of the population lack access to medical care and clean drinking water. It is clear that the impact of humanitarian assistance has slightly improved in the past 12 months. Nevertheless, widespread needs remain unmet. The EC is still providing humanitarian assistance but will progressively phase out from Tajikistan. It is foreseen a progressive withdrawal of Echo activities in the coming years. **ECHO activities will decrease from €10 million in 2003, to €8 million in 2004, €6 million in 2005 and €3 million in 2006.** Particular attention will be paid to linking relief, rehabilitation and development assistance (LRRD) during ECHO phasing out. Given Tajikistan's high vulnerability to natural disasters such as floods, earthquakes and landslides, **the first disaster preparedness Action Plan for Central Asia (DIPECHO) was launched in March 2003. Of the €3m available for Central Asia, around €2.4 is being spent by EC partner organisations throughout Tajikistan.**

FOOD SECURITY

The Food Security Programme, which was active even during the civil war, focuses on the poorest of the population through budget support combined with technical assistance to the Ministries of Agriculture and the ministry of Social Protection. The resumption of the EC Food Security Programme (FSP) is now effective since 2002. Funds which were blocked in the Central Bank for more than 5 years are now being used, some of them to finance irrigation works. The Commission is now studying a new €8 million new grant allocation in favor of Tajikistan. €7.5 million of this assistance will be provided in the form of a foreign exchange facility, the counter-value funds of which will be targeted to support the state budget and €0.5 million will take the form of technical assistance. The situation in Tajikistan is aggravated by the limited capacity of the authorities to set up and run an effective social safety net. A comprehensive reform of the whole social system is required with an emphasis on public expenditure management. As improvements in access to land (through farm restructuring and land reform) have been delayed by the political situation our objective will be to support the restructuring of state and collective farms into private entities and to facilitate the access to land use.

TACIS

In December 1997, one of the EC Tacis experts was kidnapped and his wife was tragically killed. For these unfortunate reasons **European Community technical assistance provided by EC Tacis and Food Security programmes was suspended**. However, following a subsequent improvement in domestic circumstances, the European Commission decided in December 2001 to resume its technical assistance and to allocate new funds to Tajikistan. In December 2002 it took the decision to allocate €10.7 million to Tajikistan mainly for social sectors such as vocational education, and to the ministry of Labour and Social Protection. The Commission allocated €9.7 million from the 2003 budget. As ECHO is phasing out particular attention is paid to linking relief, rehabilitation and development (LRRD). In this context Tacis put particular emphasis on poverty alleviation. Two regions are targeted Khatlon region along the Vakhsh River in southern Tajikistan and the enclaves in northern Tajikistan.

Apart from focusing on poverty alleviation, and community and rural development centred on the most vulnerable groups, the EC addresses the issue of regional cooperation in Central Asia, in particular in the field of drug trafficking, and of border management. Tajikistan provided support to the EC Central Asia Action Plan against drug (CADAP). More than €25 million were already committed in December 2003 for this regional priority and these funds are now being used. The EC expects that real progress will be achieved in this field.

For additional analytical, business and investment opportunities information,
please contact Global Investment & Business Center, USA
at (202) 546-2103. Fax: (202) 546-3275. E-mail: rusric@erols.com

STRATEGIC INFORMATION FOR CONDUCTING BUSINESS

U.S. AND MULTILATERAL INSTITUTIONS ACTIVE IN TAJIKISTAN

STATUS OF U.S.-TAJIK COMMERCIAL AGREEMENTS

On November 24, 1993 a trade agreement and a bilateral assistance treaty went into effect. Within the bilateral assistance treaty, Tajikistan has been granted MFN (Most Favored Nation) trading status which allows for lower tariffs on exports from Tajikistan to the United States. However, Tajikistan is not a member of the Generalized System of Preferences (GSP), which provides preferential duty-free entry to over 4,000 products from designated beneficiary countries. For further information on GSP, please (202) 395-6971.

Overseas Private Investment Corporation (OPIC). OPIC has signed a bilateral agreement with Tajikistan authorizing it to provide loan guarantees and insurance to U.S. companies establishing business ventures in the country. OPIC's Project Development Program provides U.S. businesses with up to 50% financing for evaluations to determine commercial viability of projects in Tajikistan. For more information on OPIC's activities in Tajikistan, contact James Gale, regional Director (Tel.: 202- 336-8629; Fax 202-408-5145; E-mail jgale@opic.gov).

Export-Import Bank (EXIM). Although closed for certain routine trade finance transactions, Ex-Im Bank will consider structured financing arrangements such as Ex-Im Bank's project finance program, asset-based aircraft leases, and other financing arrangements that offer a reasonable assurance of repayment, including reliable access to adequate foreign exchange.

U.S. Trade and Development Agency Program (TDA). TDA is authorized to operate in Tajikistan. TDA provides funding for U.S. firms to carry out feasibility studies, consultations, and other planning services related to major projects in developing countries. For more information on TDA funding for Tajikistan, contact Daniel Stein, Regional Director or KelleyAnn Szalkowski, Country Manager (Tel: 703-875-4357; Fax: 703-875-4009).

International Monetary Fund(IMF)/World Bank: Tajikistan joined the IMF and the World Bank in 1993. The World Bank provides financing to Tajikistan for capital infrastructure projects, such as roads and railways, telecommunications, and power facilities. The Multilateral Investment Guarantee Agency (MIGA), an agency of the World Bank that provides investment insurance for noncommercial risks to firms of member countries, including the United States, is also active in Tajikistan.

In June 1998 the IMF announced a three-year $128 million arrangement under an Enhanced Structural Adjustment Facility (ESAF). $48 million were disbursed in 1998. In December 1997 the Fund had already agreed to provide $20 million in financial assistance. The Fund supported the Consultation Group helping with the stabilization efforts. In May 1996, the IMF also approved a $22 million Stand- by Arrangement. Consequently, total IMF commitment to date amounts to $170 million.

European Bank for Reconstruction and Development (EBRD): U.S. companies investing in Tajikistan are eligible to receive EBRD loans. The EBRD provides counseling, loans, equity investments, and debt guarantees. By the end of 1998, The EBRD had approved investments totaling ECU 13.3 million in Tajikistan. Its first investment project was a SME credit line involving two local private banks. The EBRD has implemented several other projects in Tajikistan such as a project to resurface the runway at Dushanbe airport, one for a packaging plant in Khujand and one for the Obi-Zulol Water Bottling Plant.

Firms seeking involvement in EBRD-funded projects can call the U.S. Government points of contact: Gene Harris, Senior Commercial Officer, in the U.S. Executive Director's Office, in London at 44-71- 558-4027 or fax at 44-71-588-4026 or email at harrisg@ebrd.com.

Central Asian-American Enterprise Fund (CAAEF): The Central Asian-American Enterprise Fund was incorporated in July 1994 to promote the development of emerging private sectors in the five Central Asian countries of Kazakhstan, Uzbekistan, Turkmenistan, Kyrgyzstan, and Tajikistan. The Fund has been capitalized by the U.S. Government at $150 million. The Fund is managed by a private board of directors, and has the authority to make debt and equity investments and offer technical assistance to promote new private enterprises in the Central Asian states. The Fund concentrates mainly on promoting small- and medium-size companies and gives preference to projects in infrastructure sectors such as food processing, textile manufacturing, distribution and transportation, and consumer goods production.

In Tajikistan, the Fund has made three investments: a Pepsi bottler, a carbide plant, and a food company. For more information, contact Brian K. Mercer, Chief Financial Officer (Tel: 202-737-7000; Fax: 202- 737-7077; E-mail: us@caaef.com).

Asian Development Bank (ADB): Tajikistan became the 57th member of the ADB in April 1998. ADB is a development finance institution consisting of over 50 member countries and is engaged in promoting economic and social progress in the Asian and Pacific region. The ADB's principal functions are to make debt and equity investments for the economic and social advancement of developing member countries, to provide technical assistance for the preparation and execution of development projects, to conduct advisory services, and to promote investment of public and private capital for development purposes. As a member of the ADB, Tajikistan is eligible for the full range ADB financing programs. In December 1998, the ADB approved its first project, the Post-Conflict Infrastructure Program Loan amounting to $20 million, and two technical assistance grants totaling $1.65 million.

Primary sectors of ADB lending include energy and power, telecommunications, transportation, and the environment. Firms seeking involvement in ADB-funded projects can call Denny Barnes, Senior Commercial Officer in the U.S. Executive Director's Office, in Manila at +63-2-890-9364 or by fax at 63-2-890-9713; E-mail:dbarnes@doc.gov.

THE WORLD BANK IN TADJIKISTAN

Tajikistan declared independence from the former Soviet Union (FSU) in September 1991, and shares borders with Uzbekistan, the Kyrgyz Republic, China and Afghanistan. Seventy percent of the country's 5.8 million population resides in rural areas. Ethnically, the population is divided among several groups including: Tajiks (62 percent); Uzbeks (23 percent); Russians (8 percent); Tatars (1.4 percent) and Kyrgyz (1.3 percent). The population is large relative to the available arable land. Tajikistan's 143,000 square kilometers are mostly mountainous; 7 percent of its land is arable with 85 percent irrigated. A system of glacier fed rivers provides 3,900 megawatts of hydroelectric power. With a GNP per capita of US$330 in 1996, Tajikistan is the poorest of the FSU republics.

Tajikistan's economy is based on its primary commodities of cotton and aluminum. The country's highly mechanized and irrigated agricultural sector takes advantage of the country's vast and inexpensive water supply. The sector also accounts for 25 percent of output and 50 percent of employment, a higher share than in most FSU republics. The country's main agricultural products are cotton, silk, fruits and vegetables. Industry accounts for 35 percent of output, 12 percent of employment. The country has considerable development potential in gold and silver. The other major component of the industrial sector is textile production which accounts for about one-third of industrial output. While the Tursunzade aluminum smelter is a dominant feature of the country's landscape, its contribution to employment is relatively small. It also requires considerable subsidies and is a source of serious environmental problems in the region. However, the political and social costs of closing the plant would be substantial.

Although aluminum and cotton are unquestionably at the heart of the economy, the structure is such that links between the production of these commodities and other sectors of the economy are comparatively small, reflecting the severity of past policy distortions. For example, although cotton accounts for about 50 percent of total crop production, only 10-15 percent of cotton fiber produced is used by the local textile industry.

Despite Tajikistan's present economic crisis, it has considerable potential for development. Its land, is very fertile and has demonstrated a capacity to produce competitively for international markets. Tajikistan also has an established but idle industrial base with assets that can be deployed more efficiently and productively.

Tajikistan has been wracked by political instability and civil war since its independence. The collapse of the trade and payments system among the FSU countries triggered a precipitous decline in output. Civil war, floods and mud slides took more than 50,000 lives, displaced 850,000 persons and inflicted extensive damage to the country's

For additional analytical, business and investment opportunities information, please contact Global Investment & Business Center, USA at (202) 546-2103. Fax: (202) 546-3275. E-mail: rusric@erols.com

infrastructure. These external shocks further contributed to inflation, an unprecedented drop in output, loss of control over public finances, rapid deterioration of the financial sector, widening trade deficit and an explosive buildup of external debt.

Recent economic and social indicators reflect the adverse impact of events on the country since its independence. Between 1991 and 1996, output fell by 40 percent, with agriculture and industry the most severely affected. In 1995, output plummeted by 8 percent. Most industrial firms have been operating at less than one-third of their capacity because fuel and other essential imports have been in short supply. Agricultural production is only at about 30 percent of its 1991 level.

The financial sector also deteriorated rapidly due to the poor performance of state-owned enterprises, which are unable to repay most of their loans. Inflation has been rampant, reaching 635 percent in 1995 and 42 percent in 1996. Inflation prior to May 1995 was linked to inflation in Russia. Also, faster than targeted credit and excessive monetary expansion in Tajikistan after the launch of the Tajik ruble also had adverse effects on inflation. In addition, both the state budget and current account deficits have been unsustainably large due to the legacy of dependence on transfers from Moscow during the Soviet era. Budget deficits on an accrual basis averaged over 27 percent of GDP between 1992-1994. For 1995 and 1996, the deficit declined to about 11 percent of GDP. At present, external debt amounts to about $850 million, over 80 percent of which is owed to the CIS countries-mainly Russia, Uzbekistan, and Kazakstan.

In an effort to embark on economic reforms, the government approved an economic program in 1995 that emphasizes stabilization of the economy and the initiation of structural changes that would halt the economic decline and increase foreign exchange earnings as well as budget revenues. The program's near-term strategic priorities are to: reform the agricultural sector and complete small and initiate large-scale privatization; restore production and business activity; create conditions for attracting foreign investments; and maintain a minimum level of social protection.

The Government's reform program has been supported by an IMF stand-by arrangement (May 1996), and IDA Credit in the form of a policy-based Agricultural Recovery and Social Protection (ARSP). Implementation of these programs were satisfactory until late 1996 when renewed violence caused the government to increase its defense expenditures significantly. They were financed by a combination of budget arrears and monetary expansion. Since the Peace Accord was signed in June 1997, there has been tangible progress on several economic issues. Since July 1997, the government has made substantial progress on getting the macroeconomic framework back on track. Inflation is slowing down as a result of stopping credit expansion and controlling the budget deficit.

THE WORLD BANK PROJECTS

Since Tajikistan joined the Bank and the International Development Association (IDA) in June 1993, the Bank's assistance has focused mainly on policy dialogue and support for the government's external assistance policy. Privatization of state-owned enterprises, farm restructuring and financial sector reform have been on the government's agenda for structural change.

Given the widespread poverty, in the country, the government and the Bank Group have agreed that the primary objective of the economic program should be poverty reduction and that this objective will be best achieved in the near-term by focusing on structural reforms, macroeconomic stability, strengthening the social safety net and fostering employment intensive growth. The rationale for this emphasis rests on the massive increase in unemployment and underemployment, accompanied by a decline in household incomes and an increase in poverty since 1991.

In May 1996, the World Bank provided its first credit, a US$5 million International Building Technical Assistance to help Tajikistan initiate privatization and undertake reforms in the financial sector. In September 1996, the World Bank approved a US$50 million Agricultural Recovery and Social Protection Credit to facilitate key agricultural reforms while helping to cushion the social costs of reform. In addition, a third credit, in the amount of US$12 million for a Pilot Poverty Alleviation Project, approved by the Bank in April 1997, will help to revive local economic activity and strengthen community-based social infrastructure and services.

The recent peace agreement between the Government and the opposition on the Terms of a Peace Accord signal a new era in Tajikistan. The Bank Group is responding to the new environment by increasing the number of operation to be implemented in 1998 and 1999.

THE WORLD BANK GROUP ACTIVITIES IN TAJIKISTAN[1]

The World Bank Group, which consists of the International Bank for Reconstruction and Development (IBRD), the International Development Association (IDA), International Finance Corporation (IFC) and the Multilateral Investment Guarantee Agency (MIGA) has one overarching goal: helping its borrowers reduce poverty. The IBRD and IDA make loans to borrower governments for projects and programs that promote economic and social progress by helping raise productivity so that people may live better lives. Along with these loans, the World Bank provides policy advice and technical assistance.

The IBRD was established in 1945 and is now owned by the governments of 180 countries. The IDA was established in 1960 to provide assistance to poorer developing countries that can not meet the IBRD terms. IDA provides credits to poorest countries - mainly those with an annual per capita gross national product of $785 (in 1996 US dollars) or less. By this criterion, about seventy countries are eligible. These are concessional credits: 40 years repayment period, 10 years grace period and interest rate zero.

The Republic of Tajikistan became a member of the World Bank on June 4, 1993. On October 15, 1996 the World Bank Field Office in Dushanbe was established. Since 1994 seven projects have been approved by the World Bank for a total commitment of USD 142 million. In addition, some nearly USD 1.0 million have been made available to Tajikistan for institutional building and post-conflict assistance on a grant basis.

---

[1] Source: The World Bank Group

Furthermore, IFC contributed USD 15.5 million for the development of a gold mining project. At present, there are two additional projects under active preparation.

A summary of the World Bank activities in Tajikistan as well as brief project description are presented below.

I. THE FRAMEWORK FOR BANK ASSISTANCE-- THE COUNTRY ASSISTANCE STRATEGY

The Bank Group's initial assistance strategy for Tajikistan (September 1996) was intended to provide support for meeting Tajikistan's immediate needs. The Bank program began with 3 operations that were intended to a) strengthen institutional capacity to plan and implement a medium-term program of structural reform, b) support the government's efforts to stabilize the economy; and c) moderate the impact of the economy collapse on vulnerable groups.

The second Country Assistance Strategy (July 1998), which covers the period FY99-FY01, focuses on poverty reduction, post-conflict rehabilitation, economic reform and institutional building. The development of the program is linked to the security situation and paced to government's progress with the reform process. Specifically, the CAS addresses the following issues: a) reducing inefficiency by transferring publicly owned enterprises to the private sector; b) restructuring farms under private ownership and investing in rural infrastructure as a means of creating rural growth and livelihoods; c) improving coverage, access and quality of social services; d) targeting assistance to the poorest groups; and e) enhancing institutional capacity. Because most of the poor are in rural areas, a primary theme of the Country Assistance Strategy (CAS) is transferring agricultural assets from public to private hands, enhancing incentives, and investing in rural infrastructure. This would be complemented by investments in health, education, and social funds.

NON-LENDING ACTIVITIES

Emphasis on Institutional Building, Aid Coordination and Policy Dialogue

A. Country Economic and Sector Work and Policy Dialogue

Two economic reports (1994 and 1996) were produced by the Bank since Tajikistan joined the Bank. Two additional reports (Country Economic Memorandum and Public Expenditures Review) are planned for FY99.
Two sector notes (poverty note, health note) were completed and a third note (education) is being prepared.

Policy dialogue with the Government is a continuous process. It is carried out during Bank missions, Government visits to Washington and by the Field Office on a regular basis.

B. Institutional Building

Institutional Development Fund Grants (FY94-FY98). The Bank approved three IDF grants (totaling US$ 827,000) for:
establishment of an external assistance management unit (approved in August 1993 and completed in 1996, US$ 442,000) in collaboration with UNDP;
public procurement reform (approved in June 1996, US$ 178,000). The government is in

the process of identifying consultants to carry out the work; and
public debt management (approved in April 1997, US$ 207,000.). Government has
already identified a consultant who is expected to begin his work in August 1997.

Post-Conflict Program Grant (FY98). The Bank also approved (in March 1998) a
Post-Conflict Program Grant to the CNR in the amount of USD 165,000. The grant is
provided from a new facility established by the World Bank specifically for post-conflict
countries. Its objective is to support the CNR sub-commission on military issues in the
design and preparation of a program for the reintegration of demobilized soldiers. The
CNR is expected to set-up a Reintegration Center with an overall coordinating role and
to contract to external partners some of the activities to be implemented.

Training activities. Over the past 18 months, about 140 Tajiks have or will have
attended 40 World Bank Group (essentially EDI) training courses. The topics include
social policy reform, health, agriculture and procurement. Other donors and agencies
tend to provide similar training. There is room for coordination between the donor
community so as to reduce the degree of overlap, particularly with respect to the
selection of candidates.

C. Aid Coordination--Consultative Group Meeting

The World Bank organized the first CGM for Tajikistan in Tokyo on October 31, 1996.
Indications of pledges amounting to US$185 million in 1997 were received to help
support the balance-of-payments, the investment program and technical assistance
needs of Tajikistan. The second CG Meeting was held on May 20, 1998 in Paris. A total
of US$280 million of potential commitments for 1998 and 1999 were indicated by the
participants. All commitments of assistance are subject to negotiation and signing of
agreements between the Government and the concerned parties. The government,
through the ACU, is currently in the process of following up on the CGM.

LENDING ACTIVITIES

Emphasis on Poverty Alleviation and Policy Reform

A. Two Completed Operations

1. Agricultural Recovery and Social Protection Credit (FY97). This credit of US$ 50
million was approved by the Bank in September 1996 and was fully disbursed. The main
objectives of the credit were:
To support Government's efforts to: (a) stabilize the economy; (b) ease the foreign
exchange shortage so that critical imported inputs can be acquired; (c) reform agriculture
policy in areas including the pricing and marketing of agricultural commodities, land
reform, trade, and privatizing state enterprises; and (d) enhance the social safety net
and improve its targeting. Restoring macroeconomic stability and implementing
structural reforms in agriculture would be help arrest the collapse in production and
employment.

Status: The credit had been fully disbursed by April 1997 (USD 30 million disbursed in
1996 and USD 20 million in 1997). The government used the proceeds of the credit to
finance the overall budget, with particular emphasis on the social safety net in 1996.
About US$15 million was used to fund the SSN during the fourth quarter of 1996.

2. Post-Conflict Rehabilitation Credit (FY98). The PCRC was designed as a budget support project to help the Government support the peace process in Tajikistan. Total amount of credit is $10 million, of which $7 million are intended to be used by the Government to reduce its compensation arrears, and the rest $3 million will go for implementing the peace accord (expenses on refugees, CNR, etc.). This operation was approved by the World Bank Board of Directors on December 16 1997 and became effective on December 19, 1997. The whole amount of the credit was disbursed to the Government in one tranche.

B. Five Ongoing Operations

1. **Institutional Building Technical Assistance (FY96).** This US$ 5 million credit was approved by the Bank in May 1996. The project consists of three components:

Technical assistance to the SPC: The project provides financing for consultants, training and office equipment to help prepare and implement a comprehensive privatization program. The technical assistance to the SPC will help with design and implementation in the following four sub-components: (i) privatization of small enterprises; (ii) privatization of medium and large enterprises; (iii) mass privatization; and (iv) public information in support of privatization. Training SPC staff in all aspects of privatization will be an on-going activity of each sub-component.

Technical Assistance to the Ministry of Agriculture (MOA): The proposed project supports the Government's farm restructuring program and demonopolization of the cotton processing and marketing channels. It provides consultancy services, training and office equipment to help the MOA to: (i) identify and propose changes in existing laws that are needed to ensure secure land access rights and full transferability to access rights, specify implementation mechanisms for the farm restructuring program and develop voluntary farmer associations; (ii) identify options for revising the legal framework in cotton processing and marketing, work toward design and implementation of a strategy for demonopolizing the state cotton marketing entity and ginneries and provide options for reforming the cotton sector; (iii) train MOA staff in all aspects of farm restructuring and demonopolization of the state cotton marketing entity.

Assistance to the Financial Sector: The major objective of technical assistance for the financial sector s to help upgrade a number of key operations crucial for the success of banking reform. The project supports banking reform by providing technical assistance and training for the NBT and other banks to facilitate transition to a market-based financial system. Technical assistance under this component will be closely coordinated with assistance provided by the IMF and USAID and will consist of the following sun-components: (i) revising the current legal framework for banks; (ii) preparing and implementing new accounting and auditing procedures for banks, based on internationally accepted accounting principles; (iii) developing audit reports for the four sectoral banks; (iv) developing effective supervision of the banking system; and (v) introducing efficient payment mechanisms.

Status: All 3 components--privatization, banking and farm restructuring--are under implementation. All the legal aspects of the privatization component (law on privatization, regulations on valuation, segmentation, and investment funds) are now in place. The database on PEs is being established. The banking component (Arthur Andersen) is on schedule, with the legal component completed. Work on land reform and cotton

For additional analytical, business and investment opportunities information,
please contact Global Investment & Business Center, USA
at (202) 546-2103. Fax: (202) 546-3275. E-mail: rusric@erols.com

marketing restructuring (under SOFRECO) begun in May, after some delays related to the security situation.

2. Pilot Poverty Alleviation Project (FY97). The project (US$ 12 million) was approved by the Bank in April 1997 and became effective in July 1997. The project consists of two components:

Expanding Existing Poverty Alleviation Programs of International Non-Governmental Organizations (NGOs) (US$7.5 million) will help to improve the living standards of the most vulnerable through:

The Shelter and Housing Rehabilitation Program, (US$3.2 million), carried out by Save the Children Federation of the United States, which will assist 2,000 poor and previously displaced families in the self-help reconstruction of their homes in the five districts most devastated by the recent civil war, Bokhtar, Vakhsh, kabodien and Shaartuz of the Khatlon region.

The Micro-Credit program (US$ 1.0 million), carried out by the Save the Children of the United States, which will provide access to credit and mobilize savings for 3,750 poor women in the Bokhtar, Vakhsh, Vose, Kurgan-Tube and Kolkhozabad districts of the Khatlon region.

The Program of Support to female-Headed Households (US$1.0 million), carried out by the Save the Children of the United Kingdom, which will provide a total of 3,700 female-headed households (2,100 of them in Vakhsh, and 1,600 in Aini, Penjikent, Dushanbe, and Shaartuz) will access to and ownership of agricultural assets such as livestock, seed and tools, as well as technical advise, and start-up grants for day-care centers and schools.

Agricultural Reform Program (US$0.7 million), carried out by the Aga Khan Foundation, which will help to increase food crop production and productivity, and establish and support private farm management in the Gorno-Badakhshan region.

Future sponsored activities (US$1.6 million) which will provide funding for the above or other NGO programs, and/or additional micro-projects. Tajikistan Social Investment Fund (US$4.2 million) will help to channel new funds to many poor communities through:

Development of the Tajikistan Social Investment Fund (TASIF) (US$1.6 million) which will provide funds for operational support, training, and technical assistance to TASIF staff on participatory community development, contracting, bidding procedures, project management, supervision, and evaluation.
70 Microprojects (US$ 2.6 million) which will primarily improve water supply and sanitation, irrigation canals, local roads, and reconstruct kindergartens, schools, and health facilities.

3. Post-Conflict Emergency Reconstruction Project Credit (FY98). The main objective of the PCERP is to support Tajikistan's recovery from the civil conflict. The amount of this credit is $10 million. The project was approved by the World Bank Board of Directors on January 29, 1998; its implementation started in March 1998 and is expected to be completed in two years, in Spring 2000. It will help the Government in reconstruction of the physical infrastructure and economic assets in war-affected areas (namely Karategin Valley) and has the following components:

Agricultural Support: the emergency purchase and distribution of seed and fertilizer to private farmers for the Spring 1998 planting season (US$0.6 million equivalent, or 6 percent of base cost);

Bridges and Roads: the repair or reconstruction of an estimated 15 destroyed or damaged bridges, and completion of a 4 kilometer by-pass road for the town of Darband to replace the current non-functional road (US$5.1 million equivalent, or 51 percent of base cost);

Small Community Works: the reconstruction, repair and/or rehabilitation of destroyed, damaged or dilapidated schools, health care facilities, and other community facilities, and the implementation of other programs of small works benefiting local communities in the Karategin-Tavildara Valley area (US$2.3 million equivalent, or 23 percent of base cost); and

Other Infrastructure Works: the repair and rehabilitation of war-damaged infrastructure in the power and agriculture sectors (US$1.9 million equivalent, or 20 percent of base cost).

4. STRUCTURAL ADJUSTMENT CREDIT (FY98)

This policy-based operation of US$50 million (SDR 37.1 million) is designed to focus on privatization, banking sector reform and protecting the social safety net. The operation is underpinned by the analytical work being undertaken under IBTA. Being an adjustment operation, this credit is conditional on having a satisfactory macroeconomic framework.

The project was approved by the Board on July 30, 1998. Specifically the credit will assist in the following:

Privatization of Enterprises. (i) Prepare the necessary legal framework for accelerated privatization and development of the private sector; (ii) develop a comprehensive Privatization Action Plan for 1998; (iii) accelerate privatization of small-scale and large-scale enterprises; (iv) accelerate conversion of large-scale enterprises to open joint-stock companies; (v) protect shareholder rights by establishing a centralized share registry; (vi) sell state-owned unfinished construction; (vii) accelerate privatization of the state-owned trucking fleet; and (viii) restructure the cotton marketing agency, Glavkhlopkoprom, and the Tajik Aluminum Plant.

Financial Sector Reform. (i) Strengthen the banking sector's legal framework; (ii) provide banks with additional mechanisms to protect themselves against borrower defaults by improving the current Law on Collateral; (iii) ensure that banks manage risk well by improving regulations and supervision; (iv) improve information on banks for shareholders, management, creditors, regulators, and the public; (v) improve the payments system to reduce risk and transaction costs; and (vi) restructure the banking sector and promote savings.

Enhancing Budgetary Provisions for the Social Safety Net, Health and Education. Protect social expenditures by ensuring that education, health and the social safety net receive a reasonable share of the budget.

Status: First tranche (US$ 20 million) was disbursed on August --, 1998. The reforms supported by the second tranche are being implemented.

5. Emergency Flood Assistance Project (FY99). This project was designed to help the Government overcome the consequences of the natural disasters which took place in the country between January and May 1998 (heavy snows and rains, which caused floods, landslides, etc.). The project focuses on rehabilitation of the infrastructure (mainly roads and bridges) in the flood-affected areas. The project, which amounts to US$5 million, was approved by the World Bank on August --, 1998.

IFC

1. Zeravshan Gold Company (IFC, FY97-98). This is the largest foreign joint venture and the first mining project in the country. IFC financial involvement (loan/equity/quasi-equity) amounts to US$ 15.55 million. After a difficult start, the company is operating satisfactorily, with gold exports actually taking place.

B. Two Planned Operations (FY99)

1. Farm Privatization Support Project. Main objective is to support the Government program for land reform and restructuring of the state and collective farms in a systematic and transparent manner and to provide models for wider geographical replicability. The proposed project will have the following components:

provision for essential pre-privatization support services necessary to sustain privatized agriculture, which are: (a) land registration services, (b) farm information and advisory services, and (c) rehabilitation of critical irrigation and drainage infrastructure; and

provision of post privatization support services which are credit and community based social services.

2. Institutional Building Technical Assistance II. (to be defined)

US ASSISTANCE TO TAJIKISTAN

	FY 1998 Actual	FY 1999 Estimate	FY 2000 Request
FREEDOM Support Act	$12,150,000	$11,870,000	$12,000,000
P.L. 480 Title II	4,049	--	--

Tajikistan is a small, but unstable, new state in the center of Asia that is emerging from five years of civil war between regional and ideological factions. The United States is the largest bilateral donor, and a key supporter of the 1997 Peace Accord and an independent and stable Tajikistan. The fragile peace and potential disintegration of Tajikistan threatens regional stability and deflects attention within the region from critical economic and political reforms. The humanitarian situation is dire.

THE DEVELOPMENT CHALLENGE.

Tajikistan is the poorest of the new Central Asian states and the only one in which underlying ethnic, regional, economic and ideological strains led to open warfare and major population displacements. The June 27, 1997 Peace Accord opened a new phase in Tajikistan's short history, formally ending a civil war begun in 1992 which left at least 50,000 dead and 700,000 displaced and a legacy of hatred and suspicion which makes reconstruction tenuous and difficult.

The most important task for Tajikistan is to carry out the Peace Accord. USAID's role is to provide support for the reconciliation process and to rebuild institutional capacity. However, in the fall of 1998, relocation of the U.S. Ambassador and all U.S. employees from Dushanbe to Almaty, Kazakhstan limited USAID's capacity to support the Peace Accord and development change. The security situation had deteriorated to the point where it was unsafe to continue a U.S. physical presence. Official travel was severely curtailed. Neither USAID officers nor contractors have easy access to development partners or clients. USAID must now find ways to provide effective assistance from its regional office in Almaty, Kazakhstan.

By the end of FY 1998, progress had slowed and little if any prospects were on the horizon for improvement. While most of the Tajik refugees who fled to Afghanistan had returned by early 1998, the government and opposition groups continued to face internal obstacles to a sustained peace settlement. On the more positive side, however, proposals for amendments to the constitution are under review and parliamentary elections tentatively planned for mid-1999. These may well be the most important elections within the region.

Likewise, progress on economic reform faltered in 1998. Macroeconomic stability suffered, and the Tajik ruble continued its decline, albeit at a slower pace. By October 1998, the Government of Tajikistan (GOT) was implementing International Monetary Fund (IMF) fiscal austerity policies, and the macroeconomic situation had made up some lost ground. Whereas progress in privatization remained slow, there have been some hopeful signs, such as changes proposed to the antiquated Russian tax laws.

The focus for U.S. assistance remains humanitarian in nature. Private voluntary organizations (PVOs), such as the World Food Program, Mercy Corps, CARE, Save the Children, and the Aga Khan Foundation (AKF), have been innovative in using U.S. assistance and the transition from strictly humanitarian relief to humanitarian-focused economic development which lays a foundation for sustainable development. USAID assistance to other international organizations (e.g., United Nations Mission of Observers in Tajikistan (UNMOT), UNDP, and IBRD is anticipated in order to secure a favorable environment for USAID intervention and to maximize impact. Assistance to the Tajikistan Social Investment Fund's poverty alleviation program provides an opportunity for USAID to support community mobilization around water use issues, institute measures to prevent water-borne diseases, and address policy issues related to water charges and consumer use.

USAID increased its support for the peace process through reconstruction, assistance to civil society development, and constitutional and electoral reform. USAID also continued to provide advice and training on privatization and bank supervision with plans to expand this modest effort, the security situation permitting. Some short-term technical assistance and training is underway in economic restructuring, democratization, and health and family planning. USAID participant training programs both expose Tajik citizens to alternative approaches and systems for managing their country and develop the human resources needed for development once there is greater political stability.

OTHER DONORS.

While the U.S. had taken the lead in responding to the humanitarian crises following the civil war, the IMF and the World Bank (IBRD) provided substantial resources to support macroeconomic stability and reform. Thus far, $22 million has been received from the IMF and $60 million from the IBRD. Their assistance has dropped in recent years, with IBRD currently financing only a $12 million Poverty Alleviation Project. However, at the end of FY 1998, each organization came forward with $10 million to support the peace process. United Nations High Commission of Refugees (UNHCR) has provided significant assistance during the refugee repatriation period, with the United Nations Development Program (UNDP) moving into the field with increasingly significant resources beginning in FY 1995. The European Union (EU), individual EU countries, Turkey, Russia and Iran have also assisted Tajikistan, as has the International Red Cross, supported in part by U.S. Government contributions. Large numbers of Private Voluntary Organizations, including several from the United States, are active and effectively managing their programs in Tajikistan.

FY 2000 PROGRAM.

USAID's involvement in Tajikistan assumes continued progress in the inter-Tajik peace process, which is essential for achieving national reconciliation and holding elections that meet international standards. Under economic restructuring, USAID will focus on two objectives: growth and development of private enterprise and evolution of a commercial legal and regulatory structure. There may also be some assistance to build the private banking sector. Tajikistan is one of the lowest rated countries in the region in terms of macroeconomic policy, and economic growth will be limited until they move forward on reforms.

The size and nature of USAID's programs will be determined by the political and security situation of Tajikistan. USAID will continue to support the development of non-governmental organizations (NGOs), with a focus on those that contribute to the peace process through reconciliation and local community development. USAID is combining humanitarian and economic development efforts by moving forward with a competitive grant process to identify and support the most cost-effective local government activities in communities where there are also opportunities to build reconciliation in the post war period. These grants will be implemented by private voluntary and international organizations.

USAID will continue to support independent electronic media, focussing on how media stations can contribute to public understanding of the peace initiatives, upcoming elections, and proposed constitutional changes. After the election of the new parliament, USAID expects to direct assistance toward building the institutional capacity of the parliament. These elections, scheduled for mid-1999, are considered to be among the most significant and competitive in the region. USAID intends to increase support for this important undertaking. In the social sector, USAID will continue to work closely with other donors, PVOs and NGOs. Special initiatives in reproductive health, infectious disease, and health partnerships will be programmed in a manner which promotes citizen and community involvement as well as achieves needed improvements in health.

TAJIKISTAN FY 1999 PROGRAM SUMMARY*
(in Thousand of Dollars)

Strategic Objectives	Economic Restructuring	Democratic Transition	Social Stabilization	Cross-cutting / Special Initiatives	Total
Privatization	--	--	--	--	--
Fiscal Reform	--	--	--	--	--
Private Enterprise	1,650	--	--	--	1,650
Financial Reform	1,150	--	--	--	1,150
Energy	--	--	--	--	--
Environmental Management	--	--	--	--	--
Citizens' Participation	--	1,800	--	--	1,800
Legal Systems	--	--	--	--	--
Local Government	--	--	--	--	--
Crises	--	--	1,400	--	1,400
Social Benefits	--	--	--	--	--
Environmental Health	--	--	--	--	--
Cross-cutting / Special Initiatives	--	--	--	6,000	6,000
TOTAL	2,800	1,800	1,400	6,000	12,000
*Freedom Support Act (FSA) funds					
USAID Mission Director: Glenn Anders					

For additional analytical, business and investment opportunities information, please contact Global Investment & Business Center, USA at (202) 546-2103. Fax: (202) 546-3275. E-mail: rusric@erols.com

SELECTED PROJECTS

ACCELERATED DEVELOPMENT AND GROWTH OF PRIVATE ENTERPRISES, 110-S001.3

STATUS: Continuing
PROPOSED OBLIGATION AND FUNDING SOURCE: FY 2000: $1,650,000 Freedom Support Act
INITIAL OBLIGATION: FY 1995; **ESTIMATED COMPLETION DATE:** FY 2002

Summary: Prior to 1996, the policy environment was not conducive to concentrated technical assistance in the area of economic restructuring. In the wake of the ongoing civil war, training and exchange were the best mechanisms for Tajiks to observe developments elsewhere and to gain international experience. To encourage reform, USAID engaged Tajik counterparts in necessary private sector reforms through training courses and modest, targeted technical assistance.

The objective of this activity is to achieve accelerated development and growth of private enterprises. USAID has sent hundreds of Tajiks to U.S. and other Central Asian countries for short-term training in a variety of economic reform areas. Specialized in-country training has also been effective. Tajiks trained under these programs now form a professional cadre of reform-minded officials who are taking the lead in crafting long-term economic stabilization and structural adjustment programs.

An area of USAID training support that has been well received in Tajikistan is commercial law reform. As in the other countries of Central Asia, the Government of Tajikistan (GOT) has indicated its support for the development of a core set of commercial legislation that will serve as the legal backbone for the nation's emerging private sector. USAID has already demonstrated its capacity to provide expertise in this area through its comprehensive commercial law assistance activities in Kazakhstan and Kyrgyzstan.

Although continued political instability led to the suspension of USAID activity at the end of the year, the security situation permitting, new technical assistance is planned that will constitute a critical element of the peace process. Success in this area will be achieved with an increase in the share of GDP being generated by private enterprises to 75% in 2001.

Entrepreneurs and those involved in private sector development stand to benefit from this initiative. More broadly, the citizens of Tajikistan would benefit from economic reform that leads to sustainable economic growth.

Key Results: Accelerated development and growth of private enterprise hinge on progress toward the following: 1) continued GOT adherence to conditionality of international financial institutions; 2) the dollar volume of joint venture funds invested increasing to $11 million in FY 2001; 3) the share of GDP generated by private enterprise growing to 50% by FY 2001; and 4) the percentage of total capital investment in the private sector also growing to 75% by FY 2001.

Performance & Prospects: During FY 1998, the Central Asian-American Enterprise Fund (CAAEF) made eight loans totaling $730,468 to private businesses in Tajikistan. Winrock Farmer-to-Farmer and USAID-funded International Executive Service Corps advisors have assisted Tajik enterprises in preparing business plans and loan/equity proposals for CAAEF and have acted as consultants on post-investment management.

Subject to continued commitment by the Government of Tajikistan to economic reforms, as well as increased security and political stability in the country, USAID plans to undertake a modest commercial law assistance initiative in FY 1999 and FY 2000 to help the GOT develop a market-oriented commercial infrastructure, including key reforms in the law.

The program will initially focus on drafting the following laws: bankruptcy; collateral law; banking; and foreign investment; areas designed to promote the transfer of productive assets to the private sector and strengthen the rights of private investors. Practical constraints to business formation and operation (*e.g.*, licensing and registration procedures) will also be addressed. In addition to commercial law reform, the activity will provide in-country training to key officials involved with the implementation of a market-friendly regulatory regime, *i.e.*, judges, lawyers, and prosecutors. Work under this strategic objective will promote the rule of law and thereby the solidification of the peace process.

Possible Adjustments to Plans: The most immediate concern is the direction that the country takes with regard to the civil war and violence. USAID closely monitors this issue and will adjust the program accordingly. USAID is interested in restarting efforts in commercial law.

One of the key foci in the coming years will be the Fergana Valley, for it is one of the most dynamic regions for private enterprise growth in Central Asia. Plus, parts of the Valley have been untouched by the civil war. If the opportunity presents itself, USAID will strengthen the IESC activities in this region.

Other Donors Programs: USAID will continue to work closely with the various governmental entities involved in private sector development and economic restructuring issues. The World Bank and IMF are also directly engaged in this effort. USAID coordinates closely with these two institutions on their activities and in some instances, such as in the recent placement of a privatization advisor in Dushanbe, directly supports their programs. Activities are also coordinated with those of other donors such as the European Union and UNDP, as they are interested in economic reform issues.

Principal Contractors/Grantees/Implementing Agencies: USAID assistance activities are implemented through private U.S. firms, such as ARD/Checchi, and U.S. PVOs, IESC and CAAEF.

Selected Performance Measures:

For additional analytical, business and investment opportunities information,
please contact Global Investment & Business Center, USA
at (202) 546-2103. Fax: (202) 546-3275. E-mail: rusric@erols.com

	Baseline	Target
GOT adherence to conditions of international financial institutions	Yes	Yes
Dollar value of joint venture funds invested (millions)	$3	$11
Share of GDP generated by private enterprise	20% (1996)	50%
Percentage of total capital investment in the private sector	20%	75%

A MORE COMPETITIVE AND MARKET RESPONSIVE PRIVATE FINANCIAL SECTOR, 110-S001.4

STATUS: Continuing
PROPOSED OBLIGATION AND FUNDING SOURCE: FY 2000: $1,150,000 Freedom Support Act
INITIAL OBLIGATION: FY 1998; **ESTIMATED COMPLETION DATE:** FY 2000

Summary: Before 1996, the policy environment was not conducive to concentrated technical assistance in the area of economic restructuring. In the wake of the civil war, training and exchanges were the best mechanisms for Tajiks to observe developments elsewhere and to gain international experience. To encourage reform, USAID engaged Tajik counterparts in necessary private sector reforms through training courses and modest, targeted technical assistance.

The objective of this activity is to create a more competitive and market responsive private financial sector. USAID has sent hundreds of Tajiks to the U.S. and other Central Asian countries for short-term training in a variety of economic reform areas. Specialized in-country training has also been effective. Tajiks trained under these programs now form a cadre of reform-minded officials who are taking the lead in crafting long-term economic stabilization and structural adjustment programs.

USAID's targeted training and technical support has sought to maximize its impact on key economic reforms. For example, in early FY 1997, a USAID privatization advisor played a crucial role in initiating privatization reforms that are now being undertaken as part of a comprehensive World Bank program. In early 1998, a USAID bank supervision consultant began an assignment with the Tajik Central Bank. The activity was designed to help the Central Bank establish the capability to effectively supervise the commercial banking sector in Tajikistan through design and training of a modern bank supervision unit. The project appeared to get off to a very rapid start, with the resident advisor quickly establishing credibility with his counterparts.

After only a few weeks, the advisor had already undertaken an on-site commercial bank examination. In addition, the Chairman of the Central Bank requested weekly meetings with the USAID advisor to review progress in implementing the advisor's ambitious work plan. Although continued political instability led to the suspension of USAID activity at

For additional analytical, business and investment opportunities information,
please contact Global Investment & Business Center, USA
at (202) 546-2103. Fax: (202) 546-3275. E-mail: rusric@erols.com

the end of FY 1998, further technical assistance is planned for 1999 and beyond and will constitute a critical element of the peace process.

Despite problems related to ongoing political instability in Tajikistan, during the 1996-1998 period, the Government of Tajikistan showed increased commitment to economic reforms. Success in this activity will be achieved if there are increases in the ratio of private sector deposits in Tajikistan's banking system to GDP. To date, however, baseline data have not been gathered.

The direct beneficiary of this activity would be the Central Bank of Tajikistan. More importantly, the citizens of Tajikistan would benefit from economic reform that leads to sustainable economic growth, a critical element of the peace process.

Key Results: This was a new activity in FY 1998. Baseline data and targets will have to be completed. Achievement of financial sector reform will depend upon progress as measured by the following indicators: 1) increases in private sector deposits in Tajikistan's banking system as a percentage of GDP; 2) a positive USAID assessment of regulatory readiness of the Central Bank of Tajikistan; 3) increases in the number of banks converted to international accounting standards by FY 2001; and 4) consideration/adoption of appropriate official laws and regulations.

Performance and Prospects: The political and security situation permitting, USAID's efforts in FY 2000 will continue to be targeted at achieving key results in the legal/regulatory structure of the commercial banking sector, increasing the number and quality of financial services available, and improving Central Bank access to information about the banking system and its capability to enforce prudent norms in the banking sector. These core efforts will likely be complemented by a progressive emphasis on use and strengthening of international accounting standards in the banking sector. USAID will coordinate its Central Bank assistance closely with the IMF and with the advisory assistance from the World Bank. USAID's successful work in banking system development in Kazakhstan and Kyrgyzstan provides a significant advantage in continuation of the program in Tajikistan.

Possible Adjustments to Plans: The most immediate concern is the direction that the country takes with regard to the civil war and violence. USAID closely monitors this issue and will adjust the program accordingly. Based upon an expressed need, USAID may begin to work in the area of accounting conversion for private enterprise, with limited training and technical assistance. This would complement an existing privatization program of the World Bank.

Other Donor Programs: USAID will continue to work closely with the various governmental entities involved in private sector development and economic restructuring issues. The World Bank and IMF are also directly engaged in this effort. USAID has coordinated closely with these two institutions on their activities. Activities are also coordinated with those of other donors such as EU and UNDP, which are interested in economic reform issues.

Principal Contractors, Grantees, or Implementing Agencies: The private U.S. firm of Arthur Andersen has been the primary implementing agency.

Selected Performance Measures: This was a new activity in FY 1998. Baseline data and targets will have to be completed. The indicators to be tracked are listed below:

	Baseline	Target
Private sector deposits in banking system as a percentage of GDP	NA	NA
USAID assessment of regulatory readiness of Central Bank	NA	NA
Number of banks converted to international accounting standards	NA	NA
Consideration/adoption of appropriate official laws and regulations	NA	NA

INCREASED CITIZEN'S PARTICIPATION IN POLITICAL AND ECONOMIC DECISION-MAKING, 110-SOO2.1

STATUS: Continuing
PROPOSED OBLIGATIONS AND FUNDING SOURCES: FY 2000: $1,800,000
Freedom Support Act
INITIAL OBLIGATION: FY 1995; **ESTIMATED COMPLETION DATE**: FY 2002

Summary: Efforts to bring about political consensus in Tajikistan have proven to be long, arduous and fragile. Nonetheless, provided that the security situation permits international organizations to operate in Tajikistan, opportunities do exist to promote reconciliation through assistance to the election process, enhancement of information flows about the peace process and the upcoming elections, and assistance in increasing the participation of Tajik citizens in the rehabilitation process. The aftermath of civil war and the economic decline have, in a number of instances, left vacuums that can be filled in part by local community groups working together to help in rehabilitating the country. In FY 1999, USAID initiated substantial assistance for the upcoming parliamentary elections. In addition, modest NGO, judicial and media support activities will continue, but with more emphasis on the peace process.

Key Results: Three key intermediate results were concluded to be necessary to achieve the Strategic Objective. NGO participation in civil society must be strengthened, information on domestic economic policies and politics must become more widely available and the Government must become more responsive and accountable to citizens and citizens' organizations.

Performance and Prospects: To date, over 1072 NGOs and local community group representatives have participated in USAID training courses, and USAID has made some 90 small NGO seed grants totaling approximately $239,370 (through Counterpart Consortium and ISAR). USAID assistance through the International Center for Not-for-profit Law (ICNL) helped to facilitate the drafting of revisions to the Public Association Law which was passed by the parliament over this past year. The judicial association of Tajikistan, with the assistance of ABA/CEELI, has played an active role in promoting an independent judiciary as the Council for National Reconciliation considers constitutional amendments. The association adopted an ethics code to which all judges must adhere -- an important step toward transparency and accountability. ABA/CEELI recently convened a successful workshop with Tajik officials on corruption law and intends to follow-up in the near future. Assistance to independent media continues to be required given the government's use of the media law against media outlets and given future demands of the peace process. USAID is supporting the Internews production of Pairachi Zindagi ("The Path of Life"), a first step in supporting more independent media outlets, critical to fostering greater citizen participation.

USAID is looking to continue these successes with the eventual return of American staff to our partner offices (i.e., Internews and ABA). In addition, the upcoming elections in the summer of 1999 in Tajikistan challenge the GOT and our partners to support electoral reforms necessary to convene fraud-free elections. USAID and its partners are working closely with GOT (through legislation reform, election administration training, and voter registration system development) to develop conditions conducive for elections that meet international standards.

Possible Adjustments to Plans: In addition to an increase in election-related assistance this year, USAID anticipates a more intensive strategic focus on conflict/crisis management and the peace process in the upcoming years. In particular, USAID intends to work more closely with other donor partners on cross-sectoral integration and synergies in our programming.

Other Donor Programs: USAID is working closely with UNMOT and the OSCE on coordinating election-related assistance, as well as on specific joint projects. The international community, including USAID, is paying particular attention the country's all-important first post-conflict elections. Joint activities include co-sponsoring a constitutional reform workshop and an upcoming election law seminar. The OSCE and UNMOT have indicated an interest in providing additional commodities to support USAID's voter registration system development activity. Other donors, including the EU and various UN agencies, are also involved in a variety of activities that promote democracy and the peace efforts. Donors meet regularly to discuss areas of common concern, and this coordination will continue.

Principal Contractors, Grantees or Agencies: Several USAID-funded American NGOs, such as the American Bar Association/CEELI, Internews, and the International Foundation for Electoral Systems (IFES), are playing a role in promoting democracy and the peace effort in Tajikistan. The Counterpart International, Aid to Artisans, and the International Center for Not-for-profit Law, which together form the Counterpart Consortium, also participate in local NGO development. Initiative for Social Action and

For additional analytical, business and investment opportunities information,
please contact Global Investment & Business Center, USA
at (202) 546-2103. Fax: (202) 546-3275. E-mail: rusric@erols.com

Renewal in Eurasia (ISAR) will also participate in the development of local environmental NGOs.

Selected Performance Measures:

	Baseline	Target
Number of NGOs involved in advocacy	9/9	60/40
Average daily minutes of local news programming	5 (1996)	14
Number of Parliamentary hearings and committee meetings addressing legislative/policy issues	0 (1994)	5

IMPROVED RESPONSE TO AND MANAGEMENT OF HUMANITARIAN CRISES, 110-S003.1

STATUS: Continuing
PROPOSED OBLIGATION AND FUNDING SOURCES: FY 2000 $1,400,000 Freedom Support Act
INITIAL OBLIGATION: FY 1993; **ESTIMATED COMPLETION DATE:** FY 2000

Summary: The U.S. has been a lead donor in providing humanitarian assistance following the 1992 civil war. In FY 1996 and FY 1997, there was a marked shift away from strictly humanitarian assistance toward a program emphasizing economic growth. However, events in 1998, including the worsening of the already fragile political situation, a number of serious security incidents, and set-backs in implementation of the 1997 peace accords, have now required that programming needs to take into account the relative instability of the domestic situation. The closing of the U.S. Embassy in Dushanbe and the withdrawal of USG employees has reinforced this view.

Therefore, support for the peace process has assumed a greater priority for USAID in Tajikistan. Seventy-five percent of the available development resources in 1998 were directed towards this end. USAID expects that the program emphasis on reinforcing the peace process will continue through FY 2000. USAID has therefore chosen to target social development activities that involve members of the local community, contribute to the development of indigenous organizations, encourage sustainability, and provide a strong link to longer-term development within an environment of peace and social harmony.

Key Results: In 1998, USAID's Tajikistan Social Investment Fund (TASIF) started to implement micro projects. The major participants involved in implementing micro projects are: a) the community or group that benefits directly from the micro project in terms of increased job opportunities and income and improved access to services; b) the sponsoring agency, that is, the local government, NGO or community group; and c) the implementing agency.

The implementing agency is an NGO, local government or other community group. More than 40 micro-projects have been implemented already. USAID is also supporting activities that have proven successful in increasing employment and income in the agricultural and agro-processing sector through community participation. USAID supports activities to increase community access to primary health care. USAID actively supported citizen-sponsored government action to meet the challenges facing Tajikistan and coordinated with the Ministries of Health, Education, Agriculture, Finance and the State Committee for Emergencies; helped pass a decree to prohibit the reconstruction of houses in flood plains working closely with flood-affected populations and local and international NGOs; and integrated a peace component into a rehabilitation project for war-affected schools.

Performance & Prospects: Development-oriented humanitarian programs introduced since 1996 have achieved increasingly noteworthy results. A USAID-supported small loan program for farmers permits loan repayment in kind directly to local institutions such as hospitals and orphanages, thereby benefitting not only farmers but vulnerable groups. Other programs have improved access to basic health services for 260,000 people, and established 62 village health committees covering approximately 85,000 beneficiaries. A revolving pharmaceutical fund established with USAID support has enabled 17,000 patients to purchase or receive needed medications.

USAID has provided critically needed funding to the United Nations Mission of Observers in Tajikistan (UNMOT) as a key contribution to maintaining personnel and peacekeeping activities at a critical time in the implementation of the peace process. USAID also provided support for UNDP/UNOPS activities, particularly a UNDP rural reconstruction project for war affected areas. In 1998, USAID initiated assistance to a project of the Aga Khan Foundation (AKF) to support establishment of private farmers in a war-affected area, to promote community-based peace and confidence-building measures in the Gharm region, and supported World Bank assistance to their Poverty Alleviation Project to improve access to social and economic services.

Possible Adjustments: It is expected that assistance through the year 2000 will continue to focus on economic and social development activities which support the peace process.

Other Donor Programs: Donor coordination in Tajikistan is excellent and is regarded as among the most effective in the former Soviet Union. Various donor groups meet weekly to discuss programs and exchange information on important developmental and security issues affecting Tajikistan. Lead organizations include the United Nations (UNDP/UNOPS, UNICEF, WHO, etc.), bilateral donors including various European organizations, and a variety of American and international PVOs. Both the World Bank and the UNDP support initiatives that rely largely on local and foreign non-governmental organizations to deliver badly needed goods and services to many areas of Tajikistan.

Principal Contractors, Grantees, or Implementing Agencies: Groups that have received USAID funds include Save the Children, Relief International, CARE, World Food Program, Mercy Corps International, and AKF.

Selected Performance Measures:

	Baseline	Target
Humanitarian/crises activities	50%	10% (2000)
Reconciliation/development programs	50%	90% (2000)

STRATEGIC INFORMATION AND US-TADJIK RELATIONS

POLITICAL DEVELOPMENTS

Tajikistan is a nation undergoing profound political and economic change. It is a newly independent nation still in the process of stabilizing its internal political situation as well as its relations with neighboring states. Although the 1992 civil war, which was caused by regional economic and political differences, largely subsided by March 1993, there continues to be sporadic fighting along the Tajik border with Afghanistan between remnants of the Tajik opposition and Russian border guard forces.

In June 1997 a peace agreement was signed between the government and the United Tajik Opposition (UTO) under which the government promised to lift the ban on all parties of the United Tajik Opposition in order that fair and democratic elections can take place. The signing of the peace agreement opened a new window of opportunity for economic reforms. In spite of this major step for the peace process, Tajikistan is still plagued by occasional outbreaks of violence led by regional warlords and disgruntled UTO guerilla leaders.

In August 1998, four United Nations military observers were killed in the eastern part of the country, and in November 1998, an armed rebellion in Khujand, in the northern part of the country, led by Colonel Mahmud Khudoiberdiyev and former premier Abdumalik Abdullojonov was defeated by government troops after intense fighting. The Tajik peace process suffered an additional blow when, in May 1999, UTO leaders pulled out of the National Reconciliation Commission following the government's refusal of the opposition's demand for greater influence in the power sharing coalition.

Tajikistan is located at a crossroads of major world civilizations--Russia, Turkey, Iran, India-Pakistan, and China--and has been influenced by each. Russia, China and India share an interest in restraining Islamic fundamentalism, while Iran and Pakistan vie to reinforce Tajikistan's Islamic identity. Russia and Tajikistan's fellow Central Asian neighbors--Kazakhstan, Kyrgyzstan, and Uzbekistan--have been concerned about drug and gun running across the borders as well as Islamic fundamentalism, and have mostly supported Tajikistan's secular regime. Russia has been concerned to safeguard the 90,000 ethnic Russians still residing in Tajikistan, and Uzbekistan, to safeguard the 1.5 million ethnic Uzbeks residing there.

Discrimination against ethnic Russians in Tajikistan has increased and fuels a continuing exodus. The only political violence in Dushanbe has been a number of killings of ethnic Russians, usually soldiers, which has been of little comfort to Russian civilians.

For additional analytical, business and investment opportunities information, please contact Global Investment & Business Center, USA at (202) 546-2103. Fax: (202) 546-3275. E-mail: rusric@erols.com

Tajikistan's neighbors in the region, in particular Uzbekistan and the Russian Federation, maintain great influence over the course of internal Tajik politics. Russia, which already has 25,000 armed troops in Tajikistan (largely Russian CIS peacekeeping forces), tentatively agreed in April 1999 to the establishment of a military base which would help increase the stability in Tajikistan. Due to the geography of the region and the whims of Soviet planners, Tajikistan is largely at the mercy of Uzbekistan for all overland and rail transport. Tajikistan has moved to reduce its energy dependency on Uzbekistan by signing a tripartite agreement on trade, economic, and cultural relations with Turkmenistan and Iran. Turkmenistan provides Tajikistan with reduced cost fuel and natural gas as part of the agreement.

The government of President Emomali Rakhmonov is dominated by Tajiks from the southern Kulyab region who were victorious in the 1992-93 civil war. The November 1994 Presidential election, while peacefully conducted, was marred by fraud and intimidation, as were the February 1995 parliamentary elections. Tajikistan also adopted a new constitution in November 1994, which, while not a perfect document, is still judged to be a significant improvement over the Soviet-era version.

Political relations with the United States are on a cordial footing in spite of the temporary suspension of Embassy operations in Dushanbe in the fall of 1998. This decision was made due to concerns about threats to U.S. facilities worldwide, turmoil in Tajikistan, and a limited ability to secure the safety of personnel in their facility. This suspension is temporary and the State Department intends to resume operations as soon as a suitable new site is identified and a more secure facility for the Embassy can be built.

ECONOMIC SITUATION

Tajikistan is in a very slow transition from a command economy to a more market-oriented economy. Difficulties abound with the disruption of established trade routes, civil unrest, natural disasters, and an absence of the traditional Soviet-era inputs that came from Moscow for over seventy years.

The collapse of the trade and payment system, the deterioration of the terms of trade, and the absence of union transfers from Moscow, which had been the main method of funding Soviet Republics during the Soviet period, have inflicted significant damage to Tajikistan's economy. The move from a command economy under the Soviet system to a more open and market-oriented economy has been an onerous task, replete with legislative, institutional, and cultural obstacles.

These obstacles have been compounded by civil war and natural disasters. As a result of political instability, Tajikistan has been late in receiving the international monetary assistance and foreign investment that other former Soviet Republics have already received. On the economic front, the government of Tajikistan now appears to be ready to do the work necessary to receive international donor support and to return Tajikistan to the standard of living experienced prior to the outbreak of the civil war.

With the assistance of the IMF, Tajikistan has established a three-stage economic reform process designed to carry the country into the next century. The first stage (mid-

For additional analytical, business and investment opportunities information,
please contact Global Investment & Business Center, USA
at (202) 546-2103. Fax: (202) 546-3275. E-mail: rusric@erols.com

1995/1997) focused on improvement in the legal infrastructure, reforms in the agricultural sector, privatization of small-scale enterprises, and creation of favorable conditions to attract foreign investors. The second stage (1998- 2000) presently focuses on the privatizing of large-scale enterprises, and establishing efficiently- functioning banking, credit and taxation systems. The third stage (2001+) will focus on the further modernization of the economy, the formation of an efficient infrastructure and the implementation of large scale socio-economic programs.

There appears to be a good degree of political will behind the reforms and their implementation. Progress has been slow, but steady. Partially to reward the government's implementation of some economic reforms and to encourage more, international financial organizations such as the IMF and the World Bank have begun an infusion of credit to Tajikistan which should straighten the path of economic reform. On June 15, 1999, the World bank approved three credits worth a total of $31.7 million with $20 million being used to support the privatization of farms.

BASIC STRATEGY OF ECONOMIC REFORM

The basic strategy of the economic reform plan is to move the economy from a command economy to a socially-oriented, market-oriented one which provides for economic growth and the welfare of the population. The current program envisages a set of measures for deepening economic changes and for finding a way out of the crisis to promote stabilization and economic growth.

THE FIRST STAGE OF ECONOMIC REFORM

The first stage of economic reform entails legislative reform. The following laws were adopted in 1995 and 1996 to provide a legal basis for reform:
- On Credit Insurance;
- On Money Circulation;
- On the National Budget for 1996;
- On Copyrights;
- A decree "On Support of Small Business" was also adopted instead of the Law of the Republic of Tajikistan for the Protection of Private Entrepreneurs.

PRIVATIZATION

The Government of Tajikistan has outlined plans to accelerate the pace of privatization and to form a securities market in 1997. While most of the small retail enterprises have already been privatized, only 11 percent of medium and large enterprises have been privatized. In most cases the government has maintained a share of more than 40 percent of privatized enterprises. While leveraged buyout has been the preferred method of privatization, the program has reportedly been plagued by corruption.

The current share of the private sector in GDP is approximately 20-30%. Obstacles to the growth of the private sector include difficult entry and exit rules, lack of finance, limited access to business information, strict labor regulations and an incomplete legal framework.

Enterprise restructuring began in 1991 but stalled as a result of the war and political instability and has yet to gain momentum. A Law on Bankruptcy was passed in June 1992 but few companies have been forced into bankruptcy. The 1995 decree on "The Identification of Bankrupt Enterprises" represents an effort to speed up rehabilitation and restructuring of inefficient enterprises.

Agricultural reform - The goal of the government's plans for agricultural reform is to release a sufficient amount of land to individual farmers so as to reinvigorate agricultural production and generate more commercial activity. At present the agrarian sector is still controlled by large collective farms (kolkhozes) and state farms (sovkhozes). All kolkhozes will be transformed into farms which will be governed by individuals or a group of private farmers having the right of inheritance leasing, which permits the lessor to designate an heir to control the property being leased. One of the difficulties of this type of reform is choosing deserving candidates for land use and giving equitable compensation to those farmers who will be deprived of land.

The government reorganized "Glavkhlopkoprom" (a state organization called "The Main Cotton Industry" which controls all the ginning and part of the selling of cotton fiber) at the end of 1997. The organization was replaced by half a dozen firms which are intermediaries for receiving crop loans from international banks and assisting individual kolkhozes to buy inputs and sell their cotton. The intermediary firms see this as a temporary stage, with some of the kolkhozes already dealing directly with suppliers and buyers. Smaller producers and traders are already dealing directly, but such activity is impeded by the lack of effective international banking facilities.

Concerning other agricultural products, the government has started to liberalize of the marketing system by reducing the share of production being purchased by the state order and giving producers the right to sell the remainder of their products not sold to the state. This creates a more commercial atmosphere.

THE FOREIGN ECONOMIC ACTIVITY.

With the export and import operation in the Republic of Tajikistan are engaged 749 entities of the foreign economic activity officially registered in the Ministry of economy and the foreign economic relations including 515 collective farms and state farms. According to the information of the state statistical agency at the Government of the Republic of Tajikistan, the trade economic partners of Tajikistan are 71 countries of the world , from them 10 countries of CIS. In January-August of 2000, the foreign trade turnover of the Republic of Tajikistan including electrical energy and natural gas made 265,9 million dollars of USA, and has exceeded the level of the last year to 11% or to 92,0 million dollars. There are exported goods for January - August of 2000 on the amount of 522,9million dollars that in 19% is more than in January - August of 1999. There are imported goods to the Republic on the amount 443,0 million dollars that in 2% is more than the last year. For the countries of the CIS in the foreign trade turnover is 66% or 636,8 million dollars and for remote countries is 34%. The deficit of the balance of trade with the countries of the CIS turned out negative and made 94,4 million dollars. In export a little advantage belongs to the countries of the CIS and makes 52% or 271,2

For additional analytical, business and investment opportunities information, please contact Global Investment & Business Center, USA at (202) 546-2103. Fax: (202) 546-3275. E-mail: rusric@erols.com

million dollars. In import a considerable share are occupied by the countries of CIS-83% or 365,6 million dollars.

The share of the electrical energy in the foreign trade turnover made 16%. For January-August of 2000 its export made 2855,3 million kilowatt / hours on 85,0 million dollars. The import of the natural gas made 474,9 million cubic metre on the amount of 23,0 million dollars. In the export of the republic 54,5% takes aluminum. For January - August of 2000 it has been sent outside the country 179,7 thousand tones on the amount 285,2 million dollars , from them a considerable part on the amount of 160,0 million dollars are sent to the remote countries. An average cost for one tone in comparison with the last year has increased up to 22% and made 1587 dollars. The export of cotton-fibre has made 36,9 thousand tones on the amount 41,4 million dollars and has decreased with the comparison of the last year on 17,5% or 8,7 mill. dollars. The deliveries to the remote countries has decreased on 27% and to the countries of the CIS has increased up to 86%.

ECONOMIC INDICATORS

I. MACROECONOMIC INDICATORS			
	1999, in actual prices	1999 in % to 1998 (in comparable prices	To the right 1998 to 1997
ECONOMIC INDICATORS			
Operative gross domestic product, milliard roubles	1345	103.7	105
Volume of industrial output, million roubles	852126	105.0	108
Production of national consumer goods, million roubles	218230	90.0	118
Transportation of goods (including private enteprisers), thousand tones	7151,2	88.1	X
Transfered by road of general use, thousand tones	3720,6	83,9	130
Goods turnover by road of general use	1404,1	87,7	X
Including by road of general use, mill. tone. kms	1330,8	87,1	83,1
Million passengers have been carriaged (including private enteprisers)	145,8	105,9	
Million people are transfered by road of	120,9	105,5	108

general use			
Turnover of passengers	1436.8	96,1	X
Turnover of passengers by road of general use	1138,0	82,2	98,4
Gross production of agriculture	412942	103,8	106
Including: * public sector * population (farm economy)	139852 273090	87,6 114,6	96,5 116
Volume of animal production in agricultural undertaking , tone			
- meat	9742	86,9	73
- milk	42315	100,3	107
- hundred eggs	3691	98,1	84
Million roubles at the expense of all financial resources	102900,3	X	X
Million roubles are put into the operation of:			
- main funds,	56168,0	X	X
- dwelling houses	135469	138	74
- comprehensive schools, educational sites	3295	126	66
- hospitals, bunks	240	65	7
-policlinics, visits per shift	308	60	73
- clubs,	150	-	-
SOCIAL INDICATORS			
Retail turnover through all the channels of realisation, million roubles	566479,6	104,0	108
Including:			
-through registered companies	28804,6	82,4	105
Fee paying services through all the channels of realisation: through considered rate	142296,0 30674,2	117,8 83,1	116 113
Foreign trade turnover , hundred $	1353496,4	103	87

- through countries CIS and	830410,0	128	86
- remote countries	522077,4	79	89
Export total - hundred dollars	688669,1	115	80
- through countries CIS	314984,5	155	74
- through remote countries	373684,6	95	83
Import total – hundred dollars	663827,3	93	95
- through countries CIS	515434,5	116	93
- through remote countries	148392,8	56	99
A number of registered unemployed makes hundred people (for December , 1)	53,3	84,4	
An average monthly wages of one employee for January - November			
- Nominal wages	11503	138,8	179
- Real wages	X	110,3	121

MAJOR ECONOMIC AND INDUSTRIAL SECTORS

AGRICULTURE

The agricultural sector is the major employer (45% of the work force) and the most important economic activity in Tajikistan. Agricultural production makes a significant contribution to the balance of payments. Agriculture and agribusiness have helped lead the way towards economic recovery for the country since independence. Agriculture is more mechanized in Tajikistan than in neighboring countries although the country now faces shortages of spare parts and adequate maintenance.

Although the agricultural sector is one of the most modernized in the NIS, total output has been declining sharply during the last five years. Cotton yields, for example, are suffering from a lack of fertilizers, pesticides and herbicides.

The main crop production areas lie in the irrigated valleys of the tributaries of the Amu and Syr Darya rivers. About 9.6 million hectares of land are under cultivation, mainly in the hands of state and collective farms. Cotton, which is the major cash crop accounting for about two thirds of the gross production value of the agriculture sector, takes up 35 percent of the cultivated area. There are unconfirmed reports that the government intends to permit forward sales of cotton for the first time. The state cotton procurement agency, Glavkhlopoprom, has indicated that some of the cotton should be sold from foreign shipment points like Riga, Latvia, and that letters of credit should be used rather than pre- payment terms. The introduction of forward trading would serve to boost foreign confidence in Tajik cotton.

Agriculture in Tajikistan offers virtually unlimited opportunities for investment in terms of capital, joint ventures and the transfer of know-how. This includes improved management techniques, better irrigation practices, the use of basic agricultural chemicals, and more efficient harvesting and distribution. In addition, there are many opportunities to increase the added value of products through more quality control, processing and packaging. The first loan signed by the Dushanbe office of the Central Asian-American Enterprise Fund was for a cannery on the outskirts of Dushanbe. A visit by BISNIS in May 1996 revealed an intense interest in both northern and southern Tajikistan for food processing ventures and food packaging ventures to take advantage of the country's rich agricultural output and export the products to Russia, the NIS, and surrounding countries.

Cotton Production - The 1998 cotton harvest of approximately 350,000 tons fell below 1997's 358,000 tons, due to inadequate inputs, reduced acreage and poor weather. Productivity also dropped in terms of kilograms per hectare. In 1996, a total of 95,000 tons of cotton, with an estimated value of $146 million, was exported to more than 18 countries. The state cotton procurement agency Glavkhlopkoprom was recently liquidated and some of its functions were taken over by the Ministry of Agriculture.

Tursunzade consumes nearly 40 percent of the total power output in the country, employs 12,000 workers and indirectly supports a community of 100,000. The only downstream industries at present are a cable and foil plant. Aluminum is one of the two main exports. The government is seeking foreign investment in the aluminum plant itself as well as opportunities for downstream projects. There have been instances of fighting near the plant as different factions have tried to assert control over the plant's production and lucrative exports.

The Government of Tajikistan has decided to include the plant in its privatization program. The government would retain a controlling block of shares, while the remaining assets could be purchased by foreign investors. The plant has, however, accumulated an estimated $120 million in debt to foreign creditors which is likely to make it less attractive to foreign investors.

The Republic of Tajikistan is an agrarian country. Early in nineties, the total floorspace of an agricultural arable of Tajikistan exceeded 4,3 million hectares. 82% of an arable lands (over 660 thousand hectares) had been irrigating. Crop-growing had been giving over 65% of gross production. The basic article of Tajik export is cotton. There had been producing up to 1 million tone of seed-cotton in Tajikistan before. In 1997, more than 360 thousand tones of cotton were collected in the Republic. The Tajik cotton is highly valued in the world. Both fine-fibre and average-fibre grades of cotton, which go to various needs, are grown in the Republic of Tajikistan. The Tajik cotton fibre is divided into seven categories from which the first, second and the third kinds refer to fine-fibre, deduced from the cotton of Gossypium barbadense L's kind. The other four kinds of the fibre are from the Gossypium brisytum L's type, which was deduced by Soviet scientists.

For additional analytical, business and investment opportunities information, please contact Global Investment & Business Center, USA at (202) 546-2103. Fax: (202) 546-3275. E-mail: rusric@erols.com

According to impurity, the fibre is divided into five classes: the supreme, good, average, usual and weed, depending on which there changes also the price from +5 up to -55 percents in Liverpool cotton exchange. After demobilisation of the cotton market, the cotton-growing economies have received the right to dispose independently the collected crop i.e. to sell a production inside the Republic or export it outside the Republic. There acts a cotton exchange in the Republic of Tajikistan, on which there are carried out bargains on purchase and sale of cotton fibre and other cotton production. During the last years, there are widely spread so-called future bargains in the Republic of Tajikistan. According to the contracts, the foreign firms provide crop-growing economies means for future crop as the petroleum Products, tractors, chemical weed-killers, fertilisers and money to cotton-growers for their labour.

The greatest investors and buyers, working actively with Tajik producers of cotton are: the Switzerland firm "Paul Reinkhard", Trade Department of Switzerland bank "A credit Swiss Fest Boston". The Tajik cotton is also exported to Hungary, Austria, Italy, Poland, Cyprus and USA. There is also grown grain and other crops: potatoes, fruit, grape, vegetable and water-melons. There were developed meat and milk cattle breeding, meat and wool sheep farming and silkworm breeding.

MINING AND MINERALS

Underneath Tajikistan's ever-present mountains lie a wide array of natural resources, many of which have not yet been exploited because of their geographical location or geological depth. For its size, Tajikistan is relatively blessed with silver and gold deposits. Total silver ore deposits are estimated at 60,000 tons and the largest, in Bolshoi Kanemansur, is around 38,000 tons. There are more than 30 known gold deposits, of which only a few have been prospected. Several potentially important coal deposits have been identified but have not yet been exploited. May of the mineral deposits are suitable for relatively inexpensive open-pit mining, but they are found in mountainous regions where extreme weather conditions prevail and transportation routes are difficult or non-existent. There is some coal extraction at the Yagnob mine in the Leninabad Region, while a number of other coal deposits have not yet been exploited.

A large antimony deposit has been discovered in the Khovland district southeast of Dushanbe. Japan has tentatively agreed to provide financing for the mine with an initial sum of $2 million earmarked for planning and feasibility study.

ALUMINUM

During the Soviet era, Tajikistan was famous for its aluminum smelter. The largest enterprise in Tajikistan, the Tursunzade Aluminum Smelter (Tadaz) is in the south-west of the country. It has an overall capacity of over 520,000 tons a year and

For additional analytical, business and investment opportunities information,
please contact Global Investment & Business Center, USA
at (202) 546-2103. Fax: (202) 546-3275. E-mail: rusric@erols.com

accounting for 53 percent of total exports making it one of the largest in the world. Tajikistan produced 131,900 tons of aluminum and earned $210 million in export revenues. However, This is small compared with 450,000 tons in 1990. The aluminum is exported to countries including the Netherlands, Finland, England, Hungary, South Korea, Turkey and Belgium. Among NIS countries, Russia and Turkmenistan are the largest importers of Tajik aluminum. An estimated 5,000 tons of aluminum was consumed domestically to produce kitchenware and other household necessities.

Tursunzade consumes nearly 40 percent of the total power output in the country, employs 12,000 workers and indirectly supports a community of 100,000. It has a capacity of 520,000 tons and accounts for more than 30 percent of total exports. By 2005 Tursunzade plans to increase its production levels to 346,000 tons. The only downstream industries at present are a cable and foil plant. Aluminum is one of the two main exports. The government is seeking foreign investment in the aluminum plant itself as well as opportunities for downstream projects. There have been instances of fighting near the plant as different factions have tried to assert control over the plant's production and lucrative exports.

The Government of Tajikistan has decided to include the plant in its privatization program. The government would retain a controlling block of shares, while the remaining assets could be purchased by foreign investors. The plant has, however, accumulated an estimated $120 million in debt to foreign creditors, which is likely to make it less attractive to foreign investors.

SILVER AND GOLD

Tajikistan produced 1.5 tons of gold during the first eight months of 2000, a 15 percent increases over the same period in 1999 and worth about $35.8 million. Tajikistan has big plans for its silver sector. The country has plans to establish a joint venture with Indian companies to develop the Bolshoi Kinimansur silver deposit. The Indian companies plan to inject US $ 100 million into the deposit, which is home to 53,000 tons of silver.

ENERGY

Tajikistan is the world's third largest producer of hydroelectric power after the U.S. and Russia. Hydroelectric generation accounts for 76 percent of total energy output in the country. Energy consumption per capita is among the lowest in the NIS. An estimated 3.8 billion kWh of electricity was exported to other Central Asian countries in 1996, generating approximately $177 million in export earnings. The primary consumer was Uzbekistan, which consumed 3.4 billion kWh at a cost of nearly $170 million. Tajikistan is also an importer of electricity and in 1996 imported electricity worth $135 million, which amounted to almost 3 billion kWh, the bulk of which came from Uzbekistan.

The hydroelectric power station at Norwalk is one of the largest in Central Asia. Another major power station, a legacy of Soviet ‘gigantism', is the Rogun dam which is under construction. Rogun is designed to have a capacity of 3,6000 megawatts, which would produce an average annual output of 13.3 billion kilowatt hours. The Government

For additional analytical, business and investment opportunities information,
please contact Global Investment & Business Center, USA
at (202) 546-2103. Fax: (202) 546-3275. E-mail: rusric@erols.com

of Tajikistan is anxious to identify foreign financing to finish the construction of the Rogun complex to address the country's critical energy shortages that result in only a few hours a day of electricity in the winter and has shut down much of the country's industry. Upon completion, the Rogun Dam would have an estimated annual output of 13.3 billion kWh.

Tajikistan also consumes significant quantities of oil, natural gas and coal but is self-sufficient for less than 50 percent of its total energy needs. Tajikistan imported more than $64 million of oil products in 1996, of which 35 percent was supplied by Turkmenistan, with 22 percent supplied by Uzbekistan and 21 percent by Kazakhstan. Indigenous oil and gas production provides six percent of demand, the remainder coming from imports.

In the past, Tajikistan relied on Uzbekistan for its supply of natural gas but payment arrears and political difficulties have resulted in frequent shut-offs and drastically reduced supplies. The government has identified several gas fields for development and is seeking foreign investors.

INDUSTRY AND POWER ENGINEERING.

During the decades, past after 1924, as a result of social-economic transformations, Tajikistan has turned into advanced agro-industrial state. Active population makes 34,4% of all inhabitants of the Republic (67,8% of which are men). 97,7% of the population are literates. 55% of them have secondary education and 7,5% Higher Education.

INDUSTRY.

On a boundary of nineties, about 400 industrial enterprisers acted in Tajikistan, in which there were occupied about 215 thousand workers, engineers and employees. The branch of heavy industry had about 40% of industrial production; light and food industry - 60%. The main branches of heavy industry are: electric power engineering, mining industry, non-ferrous metallurgy (enterprisers in Tursunzade and Isfara), engineering (enterprisers in Dushanbe and Khujand), metal processing, manufacture of building materials (Nurek), chemical industry (enterprisers in Dushanbe, Kurgan-Tube, Yavan). The basis of non-ferrous metallurgy are the factories in Tursunzade (in Gissar valley) and in Isfara (Leninabad region). There are extracted and concentrated ores of non-ferrous and rare metals, such as: lead-ore, zinc, bismuth, stibium, mercury, tungsten, molybdenum and gold. The brown coal is extracted in Shurab (Leninabad region).

There are also extracted oil (in the north and south regions of Tajikistan) and natural gas (in Gissar and Vaksh valley). The main branches of light industry are: food, cotton - cleaning, boot and shoe industry, silk and carpet industry. During last years, there is observed a volume of production's manufacture in industry. The growth in industry manufacture is mainly reached due to Tajik aluminium factory. The production's volume of this factory makes 108,9%.

POWER ENGINEERING.

Tajikistan, according to indexes of hydropower resources, takes the first place in the world and by absolute indexes (300 milliard kilowatt/hour per year) the eighth. The Republic could be the largest exporter of hydropower energy in the region, in case of using it outside the country. The basis of electric power engineering of Tajikistan make hydroelectric power stations: the Nurek hydroelectric power station (2700) enters into 30 the most powerful hydro stations of the world.

According to the level of dam's height, Nurek is the world leader - 300metres above sea level. Except for Nurek's hydroelectric power station, there also exists Golovnaya and Baipazin (in Vaksh river) and Kairakum hydroelectric power station in Sirdarya river. There also acted a hydroelectric power station near Khorog in GBAO. In 1989, a construction of the large hydroelectric power station in Vaksh-Rogumskaya river started. The Sangtuda hydroelectric power station is also under construction. There act the large thermal power stations in Dushanbe and Yavan.

TRANSPORT AND TELECOMMUNICATIONS

MOTOR TRANSPORT.

In Tajikistan despite the absence of good roads , motor transport is the most popular kind of movement. About 90% from the total volume of passengers carriages (537386,9 thousand persons within 8months of 2000) and more than 80% of internal cargo carriage (1350,5 thousand ton cargo within 8 months of 2000)are the duty of motor car. The network of highways of general use makes in Tajikistan about 13 thousand kilometers. And moreover the road network is distributed unevenly at the territory of the republic and its structure depends on population density, geographical factors. There is a developed rail network with a good surface in the valley of Sirdarya river (the north of the republic) of Kulob region, Gissar and Vaksh valleys. In the mountainous Badakhshan and in Garm group of regions and Zerafshan valley because of the complex mountain relief, the road network is less developed and has a bad surface.. Because of the climatic conditions and technical characteristics two more important arterial roads " Dushanbe-Aini" and "Kalaikhumb- Khorog" are opened for transport only six months in a year.

For additional analytical, business and investment opportunities information, please contact Global Investment & Business Center, USA at (202) 546-2103. Fax: (202) 546-3275. E-mail: rusric@erols.com

AIR TRANSPORT.

111,2 thousand passengers and 1,1 thousand ton of cargoes are carried by air transport within 8 months of 2000. The air transport has a great value for the republic which has not yet a direct way to sea and developed network of motor roads. At the present time the air transport considers as a "bridge" connecting it with the external world. The air company " Tojikiston" that acts independently since October 1992 and have a state status was created on the base of the air technique inherited from the soviet "Air company". There work more than 3 thousand persons in the company. At the beginning of 1998 the park of the air company of "Tajikistan" consisted of 14 planes TY-154M, 11units - TY-154A, 12-liners YAK-40, 3-AN-28. The other air vessels At the present time the air company is in the scheduled service to Moscow(four times in a week), Alma-Ata (three times), Novosibirsk (one time), Bishkek(one time), Samara(one time), Ashkhabad (once in a week) to Khujand and Khorog daily. There also carries out a charter flights to Karachi, Mashhad, Dubai and Shardgu.

Railway transport.

Because of the complex relief conditions the railways didn't develop in the republic. The total extent of the railways makes altogether 474 kms. The basic part of these roads is located in the south part of the country connecting the capital of the state with the industrial zones of Gissar, Vaksh valley and the external world. In Tajikistan within 8 months of the current year, 322,6 thousand persons and 409,1 ton of cargo have been carried by railway transport.

TELECOMMUNICATION.

At the present time the total capacity of the local telephone stations of the Republic of Tajikistan make 247thousand numbers, serviced by 80 urban stations (202thousand numbers) and by majority of small stations located in the rural areas (45 thousand numbers). The national density of telecommunication services is equal to 4,1 telephone for 100 persons. According to this information Tajikistan occupies the last place among the countries of the CIS and the Central Europe.

Until very recently Tajikistan hadn't hot automatic line with remote countries. Beginning from 1994 the Ministry of Finance provides to those who wish the service by means of connecting the subscriber to the state station of satellite communication. It became possible after opening in Dushanbe the 60-channel ground station of communication satellite and the modern digital automatic telephone station on 2,5 thousand numbers. All this equipment was

delivered to Tajikistan by Turkish government. Because of the high cost of the direct communication satellite, nowadays a limited circus of subscribers use this service-they are missions of international organizations, diplomatic structures and a large commercial organizations.

For additional analytical, business and investment opportunities information, please contact Global Investment & Business Center, USA at (202) 546-2103. Fax: (202) 546-3275. E-mail: rusric@erols.com

The overwhelming majority of users of international communication have to book a coupon beforehand in the post department and call the subscriber through the (switchboard) operator. The new kinds of communication services have appeared in Dushanbe recently, they are mobile communication, mobile radio-link and radio paging. The operator of the mobile radio-link in Dushanbe since 1996 is joint enterprise " Tajik Tel", radio paging is provided by joint enterprise "Jakhon Page". Since June 1995 there acts an Electronic mail(E-mail) in the republic. In December 1998 Internet-link has appeared.

The national company "Telecomm Technology" became its parent. Nowadays almost all international organizations, large banks, commercial structures, the President apparatus of the Republic of Tajikistan, a number of ministries, departments, the largest highest educational establishments and private persons use the services of the company "Telecomm Technology". At the present time the company introduces Internet-link in a larger industrial- developed region of the republic - Sogd (the former Leninabad) region and this year is also going to open Internet - unit in Khatlon region that allows to cover all large regions of the country with Internet- link. Besides the company "Telecomm Technology" the Internet providers in Dushanbe are the companies "Tajiktelecomm", "Babilon-T" and " Intercom".

INVESTMENT AND BUSINESS CLIMATE

BASIC STRATEGY OF ECONOMIC REFORM

Economic Strengths: Tajikistan is blessed with abundant natural resources that could make the country an important producer of gold and other precious metals. It is currently a major-hydro-electric power producer, with a potential to increase capacity considerably. A relatively strong agricultural sector allows export opportunities for high quality cotton and processed food products. Tajikistan maintains a skilled industrial labor force at competitive wage rates, and has the potential to be a major exporter of aluminum. With mountains, valleys, lakes, and numerous rivers, the eco-tourism industry in Tajikistan is just waiting to be developed.

The basic strategy of the economic reform plan is to move the economy from a command economy to a socially-oriented, market-oriented one which provides for economic growth and the welfare of the population. The current program envisages a set of measures for deepening economic changes and for finding a way out of the crisis to promote stabilization and economic growth.

THE FIRST STAGE OF ECONOMIC REFORM

The first stage of economic reform entails legislative reform. The following laws were adopted in 1995 and 1996 to provide a legal basis for reform:
- · On Credit Insurance;
- · On Money Circulation;
- · On the National Budget for 1996;
- · On Copyrights;

- · A decree "On Support of Small Business" was also adopted instead of the Law of the Republic of Tajikistan for the Protection of Private Entrepreneurs.

AGRICULTURAL REFORM

The goal of the government's plans for agricultural reform is to release a sufficient amount of land to individual farmers so as to reinvigorate agricultural production and generate more commercial activity. In the past agrarian sector has been controlled by large collective farms (kolkhozes) and state farms (sovkhozes). All kolkhozes will be transformed into farms, which will be governed by individuals or a group of private farmers having the right of inheritance leasing, which permits the lesser to designate an heir to control the property being leased. The issue of land use certificates is planned, by the Land Reform Committee, to affect 120 large state-owned farms and more than 9,000 farmers by September 2001. However, the farms can choose whether to reorganize as collective farms or to be broken up into privately held farms. One of the difficulties of this type of reform is choosing deserving candidates for land use and giving equitable compensation to those farmers who will be deprived of land.

Around 55 percent of all agricultural land was estimated to be in private hands by the end if 2000, up from 25 percent in 1997. However, this process of transitioning state-owned farms into privatized farms has not always run smoothly. Farmers have remained very dependent on the old Kolkhoz and Sovkhoz management for key and use of former collective assets, such as tractors. Also, old collectivized farm debts place an extra weight upon privatized farms in the cotton industry.

The government reorganized "Glavkhlopkoprom" (a state organization called "The Main Cotton Industry" which controlled all the ginning and part of the selling of cotton fiber) at the end of 1997, was replaced by half a dozen firms which are intermediaries for receiving crop loans from international banks and assisting individual kolkhozes to buy inputs and sell their cotton. The intermediary firms see this as a temporary stage, with some of the kolkhozes already dealing directly with suppliers and buyers. Smaller producers and traders are already dealing directly, but such activity is impeded by the lack of effective international banking facilities.

Concerning other agricultural products, the government has started to liberalize of the marketing system by reducing the share of production being purchased by the state order and giving producers the right to sell the remainder of their products not sold to the state. This creates a more commercial atmosphere.

FOREIGN INVESTMENT AND TRADE ENVIRONMENT

The Tajik Government welcomes foreign investment, and Tajikistan offers genuine opportunities for those willing to consider innovative forms of financing for trade and investment which usually involve significant risk. Numerous barriers to U.S. exports and trade are more a result of geography and the general economic crisis than any deliberate targeting of U.S. goods and services which are highly regarded and desired in the country. Tajikistan's geographical isolation, devastated economy and, most importantly, lack of currency, largely crimp its ability to trade effectively, even with neighboring NIS states.

Great interest in U.S. products is hindered by the lack of banking transfers or cash payments with which to purchase them. Another hindrance is a business culture which emphasizes personal contacts over competitive bidding, a concept American companies are frequently slow to acknowledge. In general, legislation encourages foreign investment but contradictory decrees and an expanded tax burden make doing business in Tajikistan a labyrinthine process.

There were almost 200 registered joint ventures in Tajikistan in 1996, a minority of which are currently operational. Seventy percent of existing joint ventures are involved in production, and the remainder are mostly in trading and services. The two largest joint ventures are with British mining companies, Zarafshan and Darvoz. There is one Italian joint venture, Giavoni, with Carrera jeans which started in 1995, and one South Korean cotton processing joint venture, Koobal.

There were six registered Tajik- American joint ventures and four American representative offices, Interfur and Karakum Oil Ltd. being the most active. Due to financial and bureaucratic problems, 229 joint ventures and foreign companies closed in 1996. Among these, 19 involved some level of American capital: 13 Tajik-American joint ventures, 2 American companies, and 4 Tajik-American joint ventures with British, Russian, and Ukrainian capital. At present there are only seven companies with American capital officially present in Tajikistan. Most joint ventures are located where the raw materials are found, and therefore, many are in the northern part of the country.

INVESTMENT BARRIERS

There are difficulties with repatriation of profits and capital, due to a lack of legislation protecting foreign profits; currency convertibility problems; and prohibition on land ownership (only leases are allowed). Foreign investors have equal access to government contracts, although the Bilateral Investment Treaty between Tajikistan and the U.S. is still in the process of negotiation.

ATTRACTING FOREIGN INVESTMENT

As prescribed in the law "On Foreign Investments in the Republic of Tajikistan," foreign investors and enterprises with foreign investments are allowed to conduct business in the free economic zones, despite the fact that the law "On Free Economic Zones" has not been adopted yet.

Major efforts have been done to inform potential foreign investors of business opportunities in Tajikistan through the intermediary of the internet:

- The State Property Committee of the Republic of Tajikistan has put together a list a major investment projects as well as comprehensive information on the privatization process in Tajikistan.
http://privatization.tajikistan.com/

For additional analytical, business and investment opportunities information, please contact Global Investment & Business Center, USA at (202) 546-2103. Fax: (202) 546-3275. E-mail: rusric@erols.com

- The External Resources Management Division (ERMD) within the Office of the Prime Minister of the Republic of Tajikistan provides information related to economic life and business opportunities in Tajikistan.
http://www.glasnet.ru/~ermdtaj/index.htm

BEST PROSPECTS FOR U.S. EXPORTS AND INVESTMENT

U.S.-Tajikistan trade has been small since Tajikistan's independence. U.S. exports to Tajikistan amounted to $12 million in 1998 down from $18.5 million in 1997. U.S. imports went up from $9 million in 1997 to $33 million in 1998, $30 million being import of aluminum.

Non-Agribusiness Sectors - Mining and related equipment, medical and pharmaceutical supplies, textile machinery, telecommunications, oil/gas extraction equipment and eco-tourism.

Agribusiness and Related Sectors - Canning/food processing equipment, grain/flour, fertilizers, and farm equipment (ginning and harvesting equipment and tractors).

In the agribusiness sector excellent opportunities exist in the food processing and packaging industry, particularly for packaging of tomato paste and dried fruit, as well as bottling of juices and wine. Currently, 40-50 percent of fruits and vegetables harvested goes to waste due to the lack of preservatives and portion technology for producing smaller packaging.

In the mining sector, there are significant reserves of rare and non-ferrous metals, as well as silver and gold quarries. Western technology is needed to develop these deposits. Tajikistan has made public its desire to seek foreign partners to rapidly develop its gold deposits and is actively courting foreign mining firms. In addition, the Government of Tajikistan has made strenuous efforts to attract foreign investment to the hydroelectric energy industry, with some projects already under construction.

As part of its effort to attract foreign investment to the mining sector, a September 1995 Presidential decree created the Committee on Precious Metals and Semi-Precious Stones ("Tajikdrag- metsamotzvety"). The goal of this committee is to develop and coordinate state policy on the extraction, processing, and use of precious metals and stones. The committee is based upon a combination of the previous government structures regulating gold extraction and production and "Pamirquartzsamotzvety".

There are no quantitative restriction on imports, but there is a list of commodities which can only be imported after the Ministry of Economy and Foreign Economic Relations has examined the contract. This list includes trucks, oil and oil products, fertilizers, wheat, flour, rice, tea, sugar, and vegetable oil. There is also a list of commodities which need government permission to import, including natural gas, uranium and other radioactive substances, narcotic and psychotropic substances, weapons and other military equipment, ammunition, cipher equipment, and electric power.

Standards - Standards, testing, labeling, and certification for export goods are in accordance with the standards of the Russian Federation. Quality certificates for import goods are checked by three government agencies: the Trade Industrial Agency, the State Committee on Standards, and the State Veterinary Control. Phyto-sanitary control was recently introduced. Ecological requirements for import goods are in the process of development.

VAT and fees - All companies, regardless of ownership or forms of property are subject to the value added tax (VAT) of 20 percent. In cases where other CIS republics have higher VAT rates Tajikistan imposes a reciprocal VAT.

Intellectual Property Rights - Tajikistan joined the World Intellectual Property Organization's permanent committee in the field of industrial property protection in 1994, thereby recognizing all international conventions in this area. The departments of copyright at the Ministry of Culture and Information and the National Center for Patents and Information have been charged with the administration of intellectual property rights in the country.

BANKING IN TAJIKISTAN

While banks in Tajikistan have not been rated by the major rating agencies and it is not as easy to transfer money in and out of the country as it may be in other NIS countries, there are signs that the banking sector is improving. In the past year, the National Bank of Tajikistan (NBT) has instituted measures to reform and improve the sector. These measures include raising capital requirements and signing reorganization agreements with larger banks. In addition, international technical assistance is aimed at improving the regulation of the sector and increasing working capital available from banks to businesses.

CAPITAL REQUIREMENTS

As in most NIS countries, many Tajikistani "banks" started operating with little capital. The NBT has taken an active role in closing down such banks by gradually raising the minimum capital requirements in order to establish a more sound and reliable banking system. The board of the NBT set the present minimum capital requirement for existing banks on April 17, 1998 (in its instruction No. 79). The minimum capital requirement will be raised gradually to: US$500,000 as of January 1, 1999; US$750,000 as of July 1, 1999; and US$1 million as of January 1, 2000. Banks created in 1998 have been required to meet the US$1 million statutory minimum from the time of their establishment.

The NBT declared bankrupt and closed certain banks that have failed to meet the 1998 requirements. These banks included Bahtovar, Toribank, and Ziroat. Two others, Ilhom and Rishta, were transformed into branches of Agroinvestbank. In addition, as a result of the more stringent requirements, the NBT has not been receiving any applications for banking activity licenses or the establishment of new banks.

REORGANIZATION AGREEMENTS

The NBT signed reorganization agreements with four large commercial banks: Agroinvestbank, Tajikbankbusiness, Sberbank, and Vnesheconombank. According to the guidelines set out in the agreements, these four banks had until November 30, 1998, to increase their statutory capital, reduce expenditures, try harder to collect earlier-issued loans, pay back overdue debts and loans, and liquidate unprofitable branches.

Another important requirement of the agreements (with these banks) is the transition to International Accounting Standards (IAS). All other banks in Tajikistan have until December 31, 1998, to convert to IAS. The transition has been facilitated by the requirement, as of November 1, 1996, that all banks prepare parallel financial statements in accordance with IAS.

CORRESPONDENT RELATIONSHIPS AND MONEY TRANSFER

Almost all Tajikistani banks have correspondent relationships with Western banks, with the three largest banks having the most relationships of this type. For instance, Orienbank has relationships with around 50 foreign banks, including one with a U.S. bank (Citibank in New York). Vnesheconombank has correspondent relationships with 35 Western banks, but no direct relationships with U.S. banks. Sberbank's corresponding relationships are limited to Russian banks.

An ordinary money transfer usually takes two to three days, while an urgent transfer can take up to one and a half days. Usually, a bank charges a commission of 0.1 percent. Vnesheconombank charges US$50 for a transfer plus a 0.1 percent commission; Orienbank's commissions range from US$40 to US$150.

Regional branches of banks usually do not perform money transfers themselves; instead they send transfer instructions to their headquarters in Dushanbe. This procedure can add one to three days to the transfer process. However, some banks have authorized their branches to make transfers themselves. Tajikbankbusiness granted such a right to its branch in Khojand.

There are no monetary amount restrictions for currency transfers by individuals or legal entities. However, the transfer must be justified: for individuals, the client must have written confirmation from the local tax authorities that the individual is a law-abiding taxpayer; for legal entities, proof of existence of a contract or another legal document is required.

OUTSIDE ASSISTANCE

Financial assistance by multilateral institutions, such as the World Bank, the International Monetary Fund, and the European Bank for Reconstruction and Development (EBRD), kicked off the reform of the banking system in Tajikistan in 1994. The EBRD has granted lines of credit totaling US$4 million to Orienbank, enabling it to lend to private sector small and medium-sized enterprises or to privatizing state-owned companies. Loans range in size from US$10,000 to US$250,000.

CHOOSING A BANK

Investors and depositors should exercise caution when choosing a bank in Tajikistan, especially considering that the major rating agencies have not rated any banks in Tajikistan. Currently, all banks in Tajikistan that have been issued a license by NBT to carry out banking operations and that have met and can meet the minimum capital requirements could be considered reliable. However, the existence of a correspondent account with a foreign bank should not be considered a sure sign of a bank's reliability. As a guideline, one should first consider those banks already using IAS and meeting the future US$1 million minimum capital requirement. A potential client can utilize financial statements prepared in accordance with IAS to assess the future viability of the bank considered.

PROCEDURES FOR ESTABLISHING A JOINT VENTURE

Registering a joint venture conservatively takes about three weeks of hard work by a local representative savvy to the machinations of the Tajikistan bureaucracy. There is no restriction on the percentage of foreign ownership in a joint venture and there are no prohibitions against a foreign enterprise establishing wholly owned subsidiary in Tajikistan. However, several bureaucratic hoops must be negotiated.

I. First, a joint venture must register with the Ministry of Finance. In order to register with the Ministry, the following steps and documents are required:

A) Application by the Tajik partner;
B) Copies of the charter and agreement of the future joint venture, certified by a local notary;
C) Bank certificates confirming the foreign and Tajik partners' solvency;
D) Registration fee to be paid at the Foreign Economic Bank into the Republican Hard Currency Fund.

Following review by a special commission of the Ministry of Finance which is to take place within a two week period, a certificate is issued which permits the joint venture to open a bank account.

II. Second, a joint venture must register with the State Statistical Committee. The following documents and steps are required before issuance of the Statistical Committee certificate:

A) Certificate from the Ministry of Finance;
B) Copy of the charter and agreement;
C) Registration fee.

III. Third, the joint venture should inform the local regional, district, or city executive committee by official letter of its existence.

IV. Fourth, the joint venture should register with local tax authorities.

V. Fifth, any joint venture for a foreign firm planning to engage in foreign economic activity must register with the Ministry of Foreign Economic Relations as a "participant in foreign economic activity." The following steps and documents are necessary to complete the process:

A) An application;
B) Copy of charter and agreement certified by notary;
C) Certificate of the State Statistical Committee;
D) Certificate of the Ministry of Finance;
E) Three copies of a registration form;
F) Registration fee paid to the Foreign Economic Bank Republic Hard Currency Fund.

A special commission of the Ministry of Foreign Economic Relations will study all the submitted documentation and, subject to approval, will register the joint venture and issue a license of "participant of foreign economic activity."

ESTABLISHING AN OFFICE

To register a branch office or representative of a foreign firm, the following documents must be presented to the Ministry of Foreign Economic Relations:

A) Application describing the objectives of opening the branch or establishing representation and a description of the firm;
B) Copy of the charter, which should be certified by an original stamp from a consulate of the Republic of Tajikistan (or Russian Consulate) in the firm's country of registration;
C) Extract on the firm from the trade register of the firm's home country;
D) Letter-guarantee from the firm's bank;
E) Registration paid to the Foreign Economic Bank Republic Hard Currency Fund.

A special commission of the ministry of Foreign Economic Relations will examine the submitted documents and, subject to approval, register and issue the license for a branch or representative office.

EXPORT AND CURRENCY LIBERALIZATION

President Rahmonov of Tajikistan signed a decree in February 1996 liberalizing currency and export operations. All export customs duties were canceled effective March 1, 1996. This move was designed to stimulate exports in order to reduce the trade deficit and attract foreign exchange that has been fleeing the country. Local exporters may freely use their currency profits but payments on export-import operations of Tajik enterprises with foreign partners cannot be held in offshore banks. All export articles shall be sold at world market prices or at those determined by the Republican Commodity Exchange.

As a result of this decree, all hard currency profits of Tajik exporters are free of any taxes except those of cotton and aluminum, with sales taxes of 5 and 25 percent respectively. The government of Tajikistan hopes by this decree to encourage exporters to return their hard currency earnings to Tajikistan instead of hiding them abroad. The government stipulates that exporters may use them for their own purposes. However,

For additional analytical, business and investment opportunities information,
please contact Global Investment & Business Center, USA
at (202) 546-2103. Fax: (202) 546-3275. E-mail: rusric@erols.com

the government would prefer they be used for purposes meeting the interests of Tajikistan and developing further production.

Perhaps the most important feature of the decree is the cancellation of the obligation for exporters to sell 30 percent of their hard currency profits to the gold-currency fund to the Tajik National Bank. This onerous requirement had encouraged Tajik enterprises to hide their profits abroad. Now all foreign exchange will be sold and purchased through the Republican Currency Exchange.

The government estimates that it will lose about one billion Tajik rubles in customs duties but hopes to offset the losses through better regulation of taxes and the introduction of taxes on profits on exporting cotton and aluminum.

BUSINESS TRAVEL TO TAJIKISTAN

COUNTRY DESCRIPTION: Tajikistan, a newly independent country in central Asia, has been undergoing profound political and economic changes since the break-up of the Soviet Union. After the civil war in 1992, sporadic fighting continued, largely in remote areas, the comprehensive peace accords were signed in June 1997, some armed clashes involving renegade forces still take place. Tourist facilities are undeveloped, and many goods and services taken for granted in other countries are unavailable.

ENTRY REQUIREMENTS: A passport and visa are required. Entry into Tajikistan at points along the Gorno-Badakhshan border requires special authorization in advance. Without a visa, travelers cannot register at hotels and may be required to leave the country immediately. In the U.S., the Russian Embassy, Consular Division, 1825 Phelps Place NW, Washington, D.C. 20008, telephone (202) 939-8907, or the Russian Consulates in New York, San Francisco or Seattle issue visas for Tajikistan. Tajik visas granted by these offices are valid for a stay of three days in Tajikistan. Visas issued for other CIS countries (except Turkmenistan) are also valid for up to a three-day stay in Tajikistan. If travelers plan a longer stay, they may apply for a longer visa at the Ministry of Foreign Affairs after arriving in the country.

Note: Travelers who intend to visit Tajikistan should obtain double entry Russian, Kazak and Uzbek visas prior to departure, depending on intended transit points. There is no Uzbek embassy in Tajikistan.

INTERNAL TRAVEL: Travel to, from, and within Tajikistan is difficult and unreliable. Flights may be cancelled or substantially delayed. Return commercial charter flights are frequently overloaded with merchandise. International train connections are dangerous because of criminals operating on board.

AVIATION SAFETY OVERSIGHT: As there is no direct commercial air service at present, or economic authority to operate such service, between the U.S. and Tajikistan, the U.S. Federal Aviation Administration (FAA) has not assessed Tajikistan's civil aviation authority for compliance with international aviation safety standards for oversight of Tajikistan's air carrier operations. For further information, travelers may contact the Department of Transportation within the U.S. at 1-800-322-7873, or visit the FAA internet home page at http://www.faa.gov/avr/iasa/index.htm. The U.S. Department of Defense (DOD) separately assesses some foreign air carriers for suitability as official providers of air services. For information regarding the DOD policy on specific carriers, travelers may contact DOD at 618-256-4801.

ROAD CONDITIONS AND TRAFFIC SAFETY: Road travel can be made difficult by checkpoints, where police or soldiers are armed and known to shoot if vehicles do not stop. Some checkpoints, operated by independent armed groups that have targeted foreigners in the past, exist on the road east of Dushanbe. For this reason, road travel to the East is strongly discouraged. Vehicles with Tajik license plates have frequently been refused permission to enter Uzbekistan, so a change of vehicles at the border may be required. Road travel should be done only in daylight hours, and on routes known to the traveler or with a reliable escort.

AREAS OF INSTABILITY: Due in part to the actions of those opposed to the implementation of the June 1997 peace accords,the situation in the capital and its environs remains insecure. In November 1997 two French citizens were taken hostage by a semi-independent armed group operating to the east of Dushanbe. One was released after two weeks, but the other was killed during a rescue attempt. The group that took these hostages has reportedly been eliminated, but the general security situation is not stable. Also in the fall of 1997, there were a number of explosions, some on public transport, in which some local persons were killed or injured. In August 1997 there was an outbreak of fighting between government factions within Dushanbe and to the south

and west. Smaller clashes between paramilitary gangs took place in Dushanbe in September 1997 and May 1998 as well. In July 1998, four United Nations personnel were murdered in the Karotegin Valley. The identity of the murderers is still unknown.

To date, Americans have not been targeted but bystanders have been hurt in some of these attacks. Because of this unpredictability, U.S. travelers should avoid demonstrations, crowds, and places where military personnel congregate. Americans should remain inside during hours of darkness. Security forces are visible in the capital and the southern half of the country. U.S. citizens should check with the U.S. Embassy Almaty in Kazakhstan for current information before traveling outside of Dushanbe, and should observe strict security precautions while moving about, at their work sites, and at their homes. The situation in Leninabad Province, in the northern part of the country, and in Gorno Badakhshan, in the east has been generally quiet.

MEDICAL FACILITIES: The medical infrastructure of Tajikistan is significantly below western standards. Many trained medical personnel have left the country. Medical equipment and medicines are scarce, and significant disease outbreaks are possible due to population shifts and the breakdown in immunization activity. There have been outbreaks of typhoid in the Dushanbe area and in the south, and the risk of cholera and water-borne illnesses is high.

U.S. medical insurance is not always valid outside the United States. Travelers have found that supplemental medical insurance with specific overseas coverage, including air evacuation, has proved useful. The government of Tajikistan requires visitors who remain in country for more than 90 days to present a medical certificate showing that they are AIDS-free, or to submit to an AIDS test in Tajikistan. This testing requirement has not been implemented, but could be at any time. Because of the lack of medical supplies, submitting to an AIDS test in Tajikistan could be risky. Further information on

For additional analytical, business and investment opportunities information, please contact Global Investment & Business Center, USA at (202) 546-2103. Fax: (202) 546-3275. E-mail: rusric@erols.com

health matters can be obtained from the Centers for Disease Control and Prevention's (CDC) international travelers' hotline, tel: 1-800-232-3228; fax:

1-800cdc-faxx, or via the CDC home page on the Internet:http://www.cdc.gov.

CRIME INFORMATION: Tajikistan is a country with a struggling economy and widespread unemployment, which have resulted in a high rate of street crime. There has been a recent surge in pickpocketings, muggings, and armed robberies in the homes of persons perceived as having money, including foreigners. Travelers should not travel alone or on foot after dark. The loss or theft abroad of a U.S. passport should be reported immediately to the local police and the nearest U.S. Embassy or Consulate.

The Department of State's pamphlet A Safe Trip Abroad provides useful information on guarding valuables and protecting personal security while traveling abroad. Additional information on the region can be found in the brochure Tips for Travelers to Russia and the Newly Independent States. Both publications are available from the Superintendent of Documents, U.S. Government Printing Office, Washington D.C. 20402, and via the internet athttp://www.access.gpo.gov/su_docs.

Currency Regulations: Tajikistan is a cash-only economy. International banking services are not available. Credit cards and traveler's checks are not accepted. Travel with large amounts of cash can be dangerous. Tajikistan has introduced its own currency, the Tajik ruble, which is convertible.

DRUG PENALTIES: U.S. citizens are subject to the laws of the country in which they are traveling. Penalties for possession, use, or trafficking in illegal drugs in Tajikistan are strict, and convicted offenders can expect jail sentences and fines.

REGISTRATION AND EMBASSY LOCATION: U.S. citizens are urged to register with the Consular Section of the U.S. Embassy Almaty, Kazakhstan and obtain updated information on travel and security within Tajikistan.

The U.S. Embassy in Almaty is located at 99/97A Furmanov Street, telephone 7(3272)63-39-05. Limited information is available in Dushanbe at telephone 7(3772)21-03-56.

For additional analytical, business and investment opportunities information, please contact Global Investment & Business Center, USA at (202) 546-2103. Fax: (202) 546-3275. E-mail: rusric@erols.com

IMPORTANT BUSINESS AND INVESTMENT CONTACTS FOR TAJIKISTAN

CONSULTING

Finconsult LLC
(Tax and Law consulting/Audit)
Mr. Firuz Afruz, General Manager
Tel: +992 (372) 210819/210863
Fax: +992 (372) 210819
Email: finconsult.tajik@runbox.com

Lex, LLC
(Legal and consulting firm)
Mr. Ravshan Rashidov, Director
21 Rudaki Avenue
Dushanbe, Tajikistan 734025
Tel: +992 (372) 278365
Email: lex_tj@mail.ru
www.lex.tj

MARKETING
Asia-Plus Media Holding
Mr. Umed Babakhanov, Director
35/1 Bohtar Street
Dushanbe, Tajikistan
Tel: +992 (372) 217220
Services: News and analytical information. Television and radio broadcast. Advertising services.

Tajik Agency for Standartization, Metrology, Certification and Trade Inspection (TajST)
42/2 Negmat Karabaev Street
Dushanbe, Tajikistan 734018
Tel: +992 (372) 340865/346869
Fax: +992 (372) 510174
Email: tjstandart@tajik.net

National Patent and Information Center
14A Ayni Street
Dushanbe, Tajikistan 734012
Tel: +992 (372) 214682/214760
Services: Registration of trademarks, issuance of patents for invention. Consultation on intellectual property rights.

Zerkalo, Center for Sociological Research
37 Foteh Niyozi Street, Office 28
Dushanbe, Tajikistan 734025
Tel: +992 (372) 235557

Email: zerkalo@tjinter.com

Services: Sociological and marketing research.
MULTIPLIERS
Association for Support and Development of Entrepreneurship
Mr. Davlat Jumaev, General Director
20 Rudaki Avenue
Dushanbe, Tajikistan
Tel: +992 372 215693
Email: davlat@tojikiston.com

Chamber of Commerce of Tajikistan
Mr. Sharif Saidov, Chairman
21 Valamatzade Street
Dushanbe, Tajikistan
Tel: +992 (372) 215284
Fax: +992 (372) 211480
Email: chamber@tjinter.com
http://tpp.tojikiston.com

Enterprise Development Center
73 Tolstoy Street
Dushanbe, Tajikistan
Tel: +992 (372) 243228
Fax: +992 (372) 247047
Email: dushanbe@pragma-tj.net
www.casme.net

INTERNATIONAL FINANCIAL INSTITUTIONS
Asian Development Bank
Ms. Kazuko Motomura, Country Director
Tajikistan Resident Mission
107-5, Nozim Hikmat Street
Dushanbe, 734001, Tajikistan
Tel: + 992 (372) 235314/235315/210558
Fax: + 992 (372) 244900

European Bank for Reconstruction and Development (EBRD)
Mr. Fernand Pillonel, Head of Mission
85/22 Internatsionalnaya Street
Dushanbe, Tajikistan
Tel: +992 (372) 240235
Fax: +992 (372) 210763

The World Bank Tajikistan Field Office
International Finance Corporation
Mr. Olim Khomidov, Investment Officer
91-10 Shevchenko Street
Dushanbe, Tajikistan

Tel: +992 (372) 210756/210381/216743
Fax: +992 (372) 510042
Email: dzoirova@worldbank.org

EXPRESS MAIL AND LOGISTICS
DHL Worldwide Express
105 Rudaki Avenue, Floor 1
Dushanbe, Tajikistan 734025
Tel/fax: +992 (372) 210280

UPS
14A Ayni Street
Dushanbe, Tajikistan 734042
Tel/fax: +992 (372) 235414
Tekstilkontrakttorg, LLC
143 Nazarshoev Street
Dushanbe, Tajikistan 734012
Tel: +992 (372) 278497
Services: Warehouse/delivery/distribution services

Tajikistan Railways Corporation (State Unitary Enterprise)
Mr. Amonullo Khukumov, Chairman
35 Akademik Nazarshoev Street
Dushanbe, Tajikistan 734012
Tel: +992 (372) 215033/218854
Services: railway transportation, freight management

Globalink
Mr. Manuchehr Kasymov, Manager
25 Behzod Street, Office 2 and 5
Dushanbe, Tajikistan
Tel: +992 (372) 217767
Fax: +992 (372) 217790
Email: globalink@tajnet.com
www.globalink-logistics.com
Services: Logistics

TAJIKISTAN: LOCAL COMMERCIAL BANKS

Agroinvestbank, JSC
21 Saadi Sherozi Street
Dushanbe, Tajikistan 734018
Tel: +992 (372) 332656/365065
Fax: +992 (372) 211206/219208
Email: info@aib-tj.com
www.aib-tj.com

Eskhata Bank, JSC
Mr. Nasimjon Shokirov, Chief of Branch
Dushanbe Branch Office

For additional analytical, business and investment opportunities information,
please contact Global Investment & Business Center, USA
at (202) 546-2103. Fax: (202) 546-3275. E-mail: rusric@erols.com

16 Negmat Karaboyev Street
Dushanbe, Tajikistan
Tel: +992 (372) 331853/331854/331855
Fax: +992 (372) 219898

Orien Bank, JSC
Mr. Hasan Asadulloev, Chairman
95/1 Rudaki Avenue
Dushanbe, Tajikistan 734001
Tel: +992 (372) 235361
Fax: +992 (372) 210803
www.orienbank.com

Tojiksodirotbonk, JSC
Mr. Izatullo Lalbekov, Chairman of Executive Board
4 Dehlavi Street
Dushanbe, Tajikistan
Tel: +992 (372) 213219/216949/214738
Fax: +992 (372) 215952
Email: info@sodirotbonk.com
www.sodirotbonk.com

Tajprombank, JSC
Mr. Jamshed Ziyaev, Chairman
12/3 Dekhlavi Street
Dushanbe, Tajikistan 734025
Tel: +992 (372) 212720
Fax: +992 (372) 215757

TELECOMMUNICATIONS SECTOR CONTACTS

STATE AGENCIES

Ministry of Communications
Mr. Said Zuvaydov, Minister
57 Rudaki Avenue
Dushanbe, Tajikistan 734025
Tel: +992 (372) 212384
Fax: +992 (372) 219636

MOBILE COMMUNICATIONS OPERATORS

TT-Mobile, JSC (GSM Operator)
Mr. Saidakbar Shukurov, General Director
57 Rudaki Avenue
Dushanbe, Tajikistan
Tel: +992 (372) 218144
Fax: +992 (372) 217074
Email: ttmobile@mlt.tj
www.mlt.tj

For additional analytical, business and investment opportunities information,
please contact Global Investment & Business Center, USA
at (202) 546-2103. Fax: (202) 546-3275. E-mail: rusric@erols.com

Indigo Tajikistan, JSC (GSM Operator)
Mr. Bahriddin Najmuddinov, General Director
23 Mirzo Tursunzade Street
Dushanbe, Tajikistan 734025
Tel: +992 (372) 232121
Fax: +992 (372) 232123
Email: bahriddin@tajnet.com
www.indigo.tj

Babylon-Mobile (GSM Operator)
Mr. Behzod Fayzullaev, General Director
8 Ismoili Somoni Street
Dushanbe, Tajikistan
Tel: +992 (372) 245570
Fax: +992 (372) 210777
Email: babilon-t@tojikiston.com
www.babilon.tj

INTERNET SERVICE PROVIDERS

Babylon-T, LLC
Mr. Behzod Fayzullaev, General Director
8 Ismoil Somoni Street
Dusbanbe, Tajikistan
Tel: +992 (372) 245570
Fax: +992 (372) 210777
Email: babilon-t@tojikiston.com
www.babilon.tj

CompuWorld, LLC
Mr. Vasiliy Krasnov, Executive Director
77 Rudaki Avenue, Office 11
Dushanbe, Tajikistan 734002
Tel: +992 (372) 244644/244642
Fax: +992 (372) 214643
Email: info@cwtaj.com
www.cw.tj/isp

Doro, LLC
Mr. Alisher Mamatkulov, Director of Department for Internet Systems
115 Shevchenko Street
Dushanbe, Tajikistan
Tel: +992 (372) 233099
Fax: +992 (372) 230256
Email: info@doroltd.com
www.doroltd.com

Eastera, LLC
21 Rudaki Avenue

For additional analytical, business and investment opportunities information,
please contact Global Investment & Business Center, USA
at (202) 546-2103. Fax: (202) 546-3275. E-mail: rusric@erols.com

Dushanbe, Tajikistan 734025
Tel: +992 (372) 270101/277682/213627
Email: eastera@tajik.net
www.eastera.net

Telecomm Technologies, JSC
Mr. Shavkat Khalilov, Director
35/1 Bokhtar Street, 9th Floor
Dushanbe, Tajikistan 734002
Tel: +992 (372) 211422, 231388
Email: khalilov@tajnet.com
www.tajnet.com

Tajik Telecom, JSC
Mr. Gulmahmad Kayumov, General Director
57 Rudaki Avenue
Dushanbe, Tajikistan
MKF Networks, JSC
Mr. Nurullo Fozilov, Director
63 Pushkina Street
Dushanbe, Tajikistan
Tel: +992 (372) 233399/214570
Fax: +992 (372) 215676
Email: nur@mkfnet.com
www.mkf.tj

TELECOM SERVICE COMPANIES
All Systems TJ, LLC (Communications Company)
Mr. Edward Pustovalov, Executive Director
29 Shotemur Street
Dushanbe, Tajikistan
Phone: +992 (372) 218847
Fax: +992 (372) 218143
Email: allsys@tajik.net

T-Runk, JSC (Communications Company) Motorola Representative
Mr. Vitaliy Khinenzon, Executive Director
57 Rudaki Avenue, Office 337
Dushanbe, Tajikistan
Email: vvh@vitra.tajik.net

KEY CONTACTS IN DUSHANBE

Organization	Office	Address	Main Phone #s:	Fax, Telex, E-mail	Key staff/ Title [E-mail]
ACIE / ACCELS (American Councils for	Dushanbe	105 Rudaki Ave., apt.13-14	21-17-95 (tel/fax) 21-21-03 (tel/fax)	oseas@amc.tajik.net fsa@flex.tajik.net	Matluba Mamadjanova, Director

For additional analytical, business and investment opportunities information,
please contact Global Investment & Business Center, USA
at (202) 546-2103. Fax: (202) 546-3275. E-mail: rusric@erols.com

Organization	City	Address	Tel	Fax/Email	Contact
International Education)					
ACTED (Agency for Technical Cooperation and Development)	Dushanbe	15 Rajabovs St.	21-92-89 24-65-83 27-03-67	51-01-12 (sat. tel/fax) 00 873 762 048 184 dushanbe@acted.org	Frederic Roussel, Regional Coordinator Central Asia [frederic.roussel @acted.org] Stephane Nicolas, Country Director [stephane.nicolas @acted.org]
ADRA (Adventist Development & Relief Agency)	Dushanbe	43 Shors St. First Soviet District	34-69-95	21-47-06 (tel/fax) adratad@tajik.net 21-05-18 (tel/fax)	Vladimir Kononkov, Country Director [Off: 21-47-05; adratjcd@tajnet.com]
(Academy for Educational Development/ USAID/CAR Global Training Project)	Dushanbe	40 Rudaki Ave., room 300-303	21-07-87 21-82-49 21-05-22 21-05-26 21-05-28	51-01-02 (sat. fax/tel) acie@tajik.net center@bic.tajik.net	Shamsuddin Karimov, Director [global@tajnet.com]
AAH (UK) (Action Against Hunger)	Dushanbe	8 Firdausi St.	24-14-09 21-51-73	901 5043 (tel/fax), 873 762 060 558 (sat ph.) aah_tajikistan@tajnet.com, aah@aah.td.silk.org	Philippe Mougin, Head of Mission
AKDN (The Aga Khan Development Network)	Dushanbe	6 Hakimzoda St.	24-65-00 21-51-18 21-70-87 (tel/fax)	51-00-66 (sat.tel/fax) 00 873 762 716 155 (sat. ph) 00 873 762 716 156 (sat. fax) akftjk@atge.automail.com	Hakim Feerasta, Resident Representative
AKHP (The Aga Khan Humanities)	Dushanbe	75 Tolstoy St.	23-58-23 24-52-97 24-07-02	Shamsova@tajik.net	Rafique Keshavjee, Director [akhum@atge.automail.com]

AKF (Aga Khan Foundation)	Dushanbe	6 Hakimzade St.	24-34-42 (Reception) 21-84-06 21-80-01	51-00-61 (sat.fax) 00 873 762 560 066 (sat. Fax) akfdushanbe@atge.automail.com	Mirza Jahani, Chief Executive Office [Off: 21-84-06; sat.ph:873 762 560 065; mirzajahani@atge.automail.com]
MSDSP (Mountain Societies Development Support Program)	Dushanbe	II passage, 14 Azizbekova St.	21-87-48 21-56-63 21-38-93 (tel/fax)	00 873-761-241-347 / 00 873 761-241-345 msdsp@akdn.td.silk.org	Mahmadamin Mahmadaminov, General Manager [msdspdushanbe@atge.automail.com]
AKFED (Aga Khan Fund for Economic Development)	Dushanbe	3 Hakimzade St.	21-67-33 24-23-41	24-65-65 (tel/fax)	Matthew Scanlon, Project Development Manager [scanlon@tajnet.com]
CAAEF (Central Asian-American Enterprise Fund)	Dushanbe	31 Kirova, apt. 1	21-60-13 21-56-01 21-50-14	51-00-88 (sat. tel/fax) nazar@caaef.tajnet.com	Benjamin Rayan, Vice President
C A D (Children's Aid Direct)	Dushanbe	9 Samad Gani (Mikhailova) St.	21-66-05	24-83-27 (tel/fax) cad@cad.tajnet.com	Dr. Julian Edwards, Country Representative
CADA (Central Asian Development Agency)	Dushanbe	40 Rudaki Ave., room 307	21-22-10	51-00-52 (sat. fax) cadmin@tajik.net	David Lovett, Director [Off: 21-22-10; david.lovett@tajik.net]
CARE International	Dushanbe	25 Bekhzod St. 1st and 2nd floor	21-17-83 21-00-91 21-78-71 21-75-42 24-43-06	21-17-78 (fax) 51-00-36 (sat. line) care@care.tajnet.com	Genevieve Abel, Country Director
CCCID (Coordinating Child Center for International Development)	Dushanbe	20/1 Behzod St., apt.5,7	27-34-94 24-41-82	21-46-91 (fax/tel) cid@cid.td.silk.org	Ibod Sharifi, Country Coordinator

COUNTERPART CONSORTIUM (NGO Capacity Building Program)	Dushanbe	20 Huseinzoda (Kirova) St.	21-75-59 21-65-14 21-82-65	office@counterpart-tj.org 21-75-59 (fax/tel) 21-82-65 (tel/fax) 21-65-14 (tel/faxl) 51-01-31(sat. tel/fax)	Randall Olson, Country Director [rolson@counterpart-tj.org; tajdar@aol.com]
EBRD (European Bank for Reconstruction and Development)	Dushanbe	29 Shotemur St., apt. 36, 38	21-07-63(tel/fax)	ahrorovan@ebrd.tojikiston.com usmanovm@ebrd.tojikiston.com	Muzafar Usmanov
ECHO (European Community Humanitarian Office)	Dushanbe	25 Tursunzade St. 3d floor	21-60-83 (tel/fax) 23-16-15 (tel/fax)	00 873 762 140 758 (sat.tel) 00 873 762 140 760 (sat. fax) echo@tajnet.com echo@tjk.tajik.net	Peter Burgess, ECHO Correspondent
EF (Eurasia Foundation)	Dushanbe	18 Rudaki Ave., 2nd Floor	21-69-86	21-69-86 (tel/fax) eurofnd@tajik.net	Tatiana Falko, Country Representative in Tajikistan [tatiana@ef.td.silk.org]
FOCUS (Disaster Preparedness and Mitigation Project)	Dushanbe	15 Mahmadali Kurbonov St.	21-96-11, 21-98-30 23-02-20	21-98-30 / 23-02-20 (tel/fax) 21-96-11 (fax/tel) focus.dsh@tajnet.com	Goulsara Pulatova, Program Director
GAA (German Agro Action)	Dushanbe	20/1 Behzod St.	21-54-79 21-33-68	21-21-68 (fax) intlwork@tajik.net gaadu@tajnet.com	Beate Schoreit, Program Coordinator [intlwork@tajik.net]
GTZ (German Technical Assistance Agency)	Dushanbe	21 Rudaki Ave.	21-71-26	51-00-37 (sat. fax) gtztad@tajik.net	Karlfried Metzler, Head of Office [metzlergtz@nursat.kz]
Global Partners	Dushanbe	184 Zainabbibi St	21-07-95	21-07-95 (fax) gp@tajik.net	Greg Gamble, Country Director [greg.gamble@tajik.net]

ICRC (International Committee of Red Cross)	Dushanbe	14/3 Aini St.	21-68-23 21-73-37 21-86-60 27-53-24	51-00-51 (sat.fax) 00 873 762 376 763 dushanbe.dus@icrc.org	Elisabeth Knecht, Head of Delegation
IFRC (International Federation of Red Cross and Red Crescent Societies)	Dushanbe	120 Omar Khayom St.	24-00-33 24-42-96 24-59-81	24-85-20 (fax) 901-50-06 (cell. fax) 00 873 682 284 630 (sat. phone) ifrcdsb@ifrc.org rroom@ifrc.tojikiston.com	Charlotta Relander, Head of Delegation
IFES (International Foundation for Election Systems)	Dushanbe	25 Behzod St. 3d floor	21-80-52 21-70-98	21-25-80 (fax) ifes@tajik.net	Philip Griffin, Project Manager
IMF (International Monetary Fund)	Dushanbe	23/2 Rudaki Ave., apt. 34 (National Bank)	21-24-80	51-01-21 (sat. tel/fax) resrep@imf.tajik.net	Munira Salieva, Assistant/Interpreter
Inter News	Dushanbe	92 Rudaki Ave., apt. 24	21-43-12 (tel/fax) 24-25-51	24-54-83 (tel/fax) bahodoor@intaj.tajnet.com	Roshan Khadivi, Country Director
International Education Foundation	Dushanbe	school 21, apt. 35-36	21-63-26	21-08-88 (fax)	Aliresa Rojanian, Country Representative [alireza@rojanian.td.silk.org]
IOM (International Organization for Migration)	Dushanbe	5 Zakariyoi Rozi	21-03-02 (tel/fax) 24-71-96 (tel/fax)	51-00-62 (sat. fax) iomdushanbe@iom.tajnet.com	Igor Bosc, Chief of Mission [ibosc@iom.tajnet.com]
MCT (Mercy Corps Tajikistan)	Dushanbe	1 &2 Firdausi St.	21-08-60 21-08-64 21-08-79 24-06-89	51-01-33 (sat.tel/fax) mct@mct.tajnet.com	Kurt Gibson, Country Director [kurt@mct.tajnet.com]
MERLIN (Medical Emergency Relief International)	Dushanbe	8 Karamova St.	21-47-64	51-01-20 (tel/fax)	Paul Handley, Programme Coordinator
Mission Ost	Dushanbe	7 Baumana St.	21-60-34 24-50-90	00 873 762 521 694 (sat.ph.) miseast@miseast.taji	Graeme Glover, Country Director

For additional analytical, business and investment opportunities information, please contact Global Investment & Business Center, USA at (202) 546-2103. Fax: (202) 546-3275. E-mail: rusric@erols.com

				k.net	
MSF (Holland) (Medecins Sans Frontieres)	Dushanbe	21 Guliston St.	21-44-25 24-52-34 24-34-49 24-75-40	51-00-71 (tel/fax) msfdush@tajnet.com	Penny Harrison, Country Manager
ORA International	Dushanbe	17 Academician Rajabov St. apt 11	21-64-42 27-46-10	21-64-42 (fax/tel) oradush@tajik.net	Jeff Paulsen, Director
OSI (Open Society Institute/SOROS Foundation)	Dushanbe	65 Tolstoy St.	21-19-58 21-32-60 24-22-41 51-01-42	21-19-58 (fax/tel) 51-01-42 (sat. fax/tel) osi@osi.tajik.net	Zuhra Halimova, Executive Director
OSCE (Organization for Security and Cooperation in Europe)	Dushanbe	12 Zikrullo Khojaev St.	24-33-38 21-40-63 24-58-79	00 873-682-322-495 (sat. phone) 00 873-382-322-012 (sat.phone) 00 873-382-322-014 (sat. fax) 00 873-682-322-497 (sat. fax) 24-91-59 (tel/fax) sand@osce.tajik.net	Marc Gilbert, Ambassador, Head of Mission
PSF CI (Pharmaciens Sans Frontieres Comite International)	Dushanbe	122 Proletarsky St.	24-34-40 24-64-33	51-01-32 (sat. fax) 00 873 761 607 714 psf@psf.tojikiston.com psf@psfkh.khorugh.tajik.net	Bruno Clary, General Co-ordinator [Off: 24-64-33; t/f :51-01-32; bruno@psf.tojikiston.com]
RI (Relief International)	Dushanbe	70 Rudaki Ave., apt.76	21-07-17	21-86-53 (tel/fax) ritaj@ri.org	Bahriddin Sharipov, Programme Assistant Gulnoza Khairullaeva, Office Manager
SCOLASIA/MAISONS DOUCES	Dushanbe	11 Shota Rustavely St., apt. 4	23-29-11	21-78-04 (tel/fax) scolasi@attglobal.net	Yves Rocquencourt, Director of Scolasia project Isabelle Clevenot, Head of Mission
STAR	Dushanbe	9 Gertsen	27-56-58	admin@star.edu.tj	Dr. John

(Society in Tajikistan for Assistance and Research)	be	St.			Hayward, English Language School Director [els@star.edu.tj]
SCF/UK (Save the Children Fund/UK)	Dushanbe	18 Fazliddin Shahobov St.	24-12-07 24-10-70 24-70-84	51-00-75 Fax/phone office@scftajikistan.tajnet.com	Mandal Urtnasan Program Manager
SC/US (Save the Children Fund/US)	Dushanbe	53 Ibn Simo St.	21-07-71 24-02-06 24-33-88	51-00-79 savetfo@tajnet.com	Akm Jamaluddin Field Office Director
SNI (Shelter Now International)	Dushanbe Dushanbe	5 Lufti St. 7 Lutfi St	24-65-80 21-64-43 21-48-35 24-64-08	51-01-51 (sat. tel/fax) rano@shelter.tajnet.com	Mark Baltzer, Regional Director [Off: 24-49-47; nolanmmb@yahoo.com]
UMCOR (United Methodist Committee on Relief)	Dushanbe	108 Lahuti St., 2nd floor	21-70-48	51-01-60 (fax) umcor@tajnet.com	Eric Blender, Head of Mission [Off: 21-42-39]
UNDP (United Nations Development Program)	Dushanbe	39 Aini St.	21-06-70 21-06-80 21-06-86 21-06-94	51-00-21 (fax) 51-00-84 (sat.tel) 00 873-382-420-321(sat.tel) 00 873-382-420-322 (sat.fax) registry.tj@undp.org	Matthew Kahane, Resident Representative[Off: 21-06-79]
UNFAO (Food & Aqriculture Organization)	Dushanbe	39 Aini St.	21-06-80 21-06-70 21-18-49	51-00-21(sat.fax)	Halka Otto, Coordinator [halka.otto@undp.org]
UNFPA (Population Fund)	Dushanbe	39 Aini St.	Switchboard: 21-18-09 21-06-80 21-06-86	51-01-54 (tel/fax) unfpa.tj@undp.org 00 873 761 242 425 (sat.phone)	Matthew Kahane, UNFPA Representative [matthew.kahane@undp.org] Zuhra Akhmedova, National Programme Officer

					[unfpa.tj@undp.org]
UNHCR (United Nations High Commissioner for Refugees)	Dushanbe	106 Druzhba Narodov Pst.	21-83-78 24-62-65 24-61-84	00 873 682 285 930 (satphone) 51-00-39 (fax/tel) tjkdu@unhcr.ch	Nicolas Kaussidis Head of Liaison Office
UNICEF (United Nations Children Fund)	Dushanbe	14/1 Hamza Hakim-Zade St.	24-72-61 24-91-08 51-01-49	51-00-81 (sat. fax/tel)	Yukie Mokuo Elena Kazandzi, Assistant Operations Officer
UNIFEM (United Nations Development Fund for Women)	Dushanbe	25 Behzod St.	23-09-61	21-70-31 (fax/tel)	Shuhrat Rajabov, Project Assistant [shuhrat@unifem.tojikiston.com]
		room 7			Jahongir Munzim, Project Assistant [jahongir@unifem.tojikiston.com]
	Training Centre	270 Huvaidulloev St., 2nd floor	35-86-43 / 23-09-61	21-70-31 (fax/tel)	Nargis Nurullo-Khoja, Training Centre Manager [nargis@unifem.tojikiston.com]
UNTOP (United Nations Tajikistan Office for Peace-Building)	Dushanbe	7 Gorki St.	21-01-10 21-01-27 21-01-47	21-01-59 (fax)	Vladimir Sotirov, Representative of the Secretary-General, Head of UNTOP [sotirov@un.org]
UNOCHA (Office for Humanitarian Affairs)	Dushanbe	39 Aini St.	21-78-27 21-06-08	51-00-21 (fax/tel) ochatj@undp.org	Valentin Gatsinski, Humanitarian Affairs Officer
UNOPS (United Nations Office for Project Services)	Dushanbe	25 Behzod St. 3d floor	21-06-86 21-06-82 21-08-96 21-09-34 23-09-16	9-01-5019 (fax) bcomnas@cs.com	

USAID/CAR (US Agency for International Development)	Dushanbe	10 Pavlova St.	21-03-48 / 50	usaid@usaid-tj.org	Michael Harvey, Country Program Officer USAID Tajikistan in Almaty
VI (Vision International Healthcare Ltd.)	Dushanbe	155 Rudaki Ave., apt. 6	24-33-47	zdreform@tajik.net	Mr. Masouddi, Acting Director
WHO (World Health Organization)	Dushanbe	106 Druzhba Narodov St.	21-48-71 21-01-08	21-48-71(tel/fax) lotjk@who.tajik.net 91 901 50 41 (mobile ph.)	Luybomir Ivanov, Head of WHO Office [Off: 21-01-08; lyubomirivanov@tajnet.com]
WFP (United Nations World Food Program)	Dushanbe	Tolstoy St.	24-39-50/23-38-75 21-09-19 21-57-15 21-09-07	51-00-87 (sat. fax/tel) 00 873 716 351 997 (sat. ph) 00 873 716 351 999 (sat. fax) wfp.dushanbe@wfp.org	Ardag Megdessian, Representative / Country Director
World Bank / IBRD (International Bank for Reconstruction and Development)	Dushanbe	105 Rudaki Ave.	21-07-56 21-03-81 21-15-18 21-67-43	51-00-42 (sat. fax)	Mustapha Rouis, Country Manager [Mrouis@worldbank.org]

LAWYERS IN DUSHANBE AND NEAR-BY REGIONS

Office of judicial consultation of the **Tsentralny district**, #46A N. Karabayev Pr., Dushanbe; phone: 33-96-01:

1. Odinayev, Saidalimsho Khukumatovich — 10 yrs, criminal
2. Burkhanova, Svetlana Pavlovna — 24 yrs, civil and criminal
3. Komilov, Saidakram Saidovich — 19 yrs, criminal
   home phone: 36-24-38
4. Yunusova, Alexandra Pavlovna — 19 yrs, civil
   home phone: 33-22-69
5. Yatimov, K. — criminal and civil
6. Sharipova, B. — civil and criminal

For additional analytical, business and investment opportunities information, please contact Global Investment & Business Center, USA at (202) 546-2103. Fax: (202) 546-3275. E-mail: rusric@erols.com

Office of judicial consultation of the **Zheleznodorozhny (Railway) district**, phone in Dushanbe: 27-85-04

1. Kurbanov, Saidkomil	11 yrs, criminal
2. Khushvakhtova, Gulniso Abdullayevna phone: 27-01-39	8 yrs, criminal
3. Urinbayev, Gani Odilovich	9 yrs, criminal
4. Kurbonov, M.	civil and criminal
5. Ms. Nusratova	civil and criminal
6. Ms. Rasulova	criminal
7. Mr. Yorov	civil and criminal

Office of judicial consultation of the **Frunzensky district**, #57 Ismoili Somoni Pr., Dushanbe, phone: 36-18-30

1. Khametova Nailya Ismoilovna	11 yrs, criminal
2. Ubaydov, Nodirsho Saydulloevich	11 yrs, civil and criminal
3. Beknazarov, S.	
4. Mr. Anandiyev	

Office of judicial consultation of **the October district**, #91 Rudaki Pr., Dushanbe, phone 21-76-51, 24-12-97:

1. Boboyeva, Zebo	14 yrs, civil and	criminal
2. Boturov, Bakhtiyor Mirzomuradovih	9 yrs, civil and criminal	
4. Faiziyev, Akbar	20 yrs, civil and	criminal
5. Ms. Soliyeva	civil and	criminal
6. Mr. Badriddinov	criminal	
7. Karimov, N.	civil and criminal	

Chairman of the Presidium of Collegiate of Lawyers of the Republic of Tajikistan - Amirbekov, Naim Amirbekovich, phone: 21-24-03;, address: #12 Parhar St., Dushanbe

Vice chairman of the Presidium of Collegiate of Lawyers of the Republic of Tajikistan – Asozoda, Mirzo, phone in Dushanbe: 27-84-77

Commercial Law Project, Dushanbe, 4 Govorov St., Dushanbe, Akbar Muratov, speaks English, phone: 21-17-79, 24-22-84, 24-03-52 e-mail: Akbar79@hotmail.com

"Contract" judicial company - #54 Ostrovsky St., Dushanbe, phones: 21-14-10, 21-27-38, 23-09-20; fax: 23-43-40; e-mail: uristcontract@tojikiston.com
(the company can invite a Russian/English translator/interpreter)

F.D. and Partners, Dushanbe, phone: 21-53-75,

For additional analytical, business and investment opportunities information,
please contact Global Investment & Business Center, USA
at (202) 546-2103. Fax: (202) 546-3275. E-mail: rusric@erols.com

fax: 21-98-25, e-mail: f.d.and.partners@tajnet.com – Nodir Toirov (lawyer/consultant – civil cases), Saadi Umarov (assistant)

"Open Door" (NGO engaged in judicial practice: civil and adoption cases), 12-3 Kommunalnaya St., Dushanbe, phone: 23-34-75 or 21-35-16; pager: 001 for "Open Doors";
e-mail: opendoor@tajik.net, Director – Abubakr Inomov

ABA/CEELI (American Bar Association/Central and East European Law Initiative) – 72 Tolstoy St., Dushanbe, phone: 24-15-05, 24-68-62, 21-15-02, fax: 24-26-80.
near-by regions:
Office of judicial consultation of **Leninskiy District:**
Ms. Umarova   civil and criminal

Office of judicial consultation of **Kofarnihon district**,
phone: 2-44-81, 2-41-05
1. Mr. Asatullayev   civil and criminal
Office of judicial consultation of **Ghissar district**
Mr. Rajabov   civil and criminal
Office of judicial consultation of **the City of Tursunzade**
1. Mr. Khojankulov   civil and criminal
Office of judicial consultation of **the City of Kughan-Tyube, Khatlon Region**
1. Ms. Amonova   civil and criminal
2. Mr. Nuritdinov   civil and criminal

TAJIKISTAN INDUSTRY: LARGEST COMPANIES
ALPHABETICAL LISTING

1   ADRASMAN LEAD and ZINC WORKS

Ownership: *state*
Industry: *Ore mining industry*
Number of Employees:
CEO: **Yevgeny N.Bondarevsky**
Address: 735780, Republic Tadjikistan, Leninabad
Reg., Kairakkum, pos. Adrasman,
Leninabad

Gertsen St., 72

Phone: **27-30**
Products: **unwrought lead 3,800 tons**
silver 27.2 tons

2   ADRASMAN LOW-VOLTAGE ELECTRIC EQUIPMENT WORKS

Ownership: *state*
Industry: *Electrical engineering*
Number of Employees: *529.00*
CEO: **Amon E.Eshbaev**
Address: 735780, Republic Tadjikistan,

Reg., Kairakkum, pos. Adrasman,
Leninabadskaya St., 9

Phone: **3-34-38**
Products: **low-voltage apparatus**

3   AGROINDUSTRIAL GRAIN PROCESSING PRODUCTION COMPANY

Ownership: *state*
Industry: *Food & food processing*
Number of Employees:
CEO: **Sobir Rakhimov**
Leninsky
Address: 735140, Repiblic Tadjikistan, Khatlon
Reg., Kurgan-Tyube, Sverdlov St., 43

Phone: **(37744) 2-25-24, 2-25-54**
Products: **flour, mixed fodder**

4   AINI GINNERY

Ownership: *state*
Industry: *Textile industry*
Number of Employees: *650.00*
CEO: **Lyambir Z.Shoyev**
Address: 735100, Republic Tadjikistan,

Dist., pos. Novabad

Phone: **31-18-83**
Products: **cotton 7,514 tons**
seeds 14,291 tons
lint 1,859 tons

5   ANZOBSKY ORE CONCENTRATING MILL

Ownership: *state*
Industry: *Ore mining industry*
Number of Employees: *985.00*
CEO: **Ivan F.Glazunov**
Address: 735522, Republic Tadjikistan, Leninabad
Reg., Aini Dist., pos. Zeravshan-2
Leninabad

Solprom

Phone: **24-43, 1-69**
Products: **antimony concentrate**
mercury concentrate

6   ASHTI SALT WORKS n2

Ownership: *state*
Industry: *Mining industry (building mateirlas)*
Number of Employees: *190.00*
CEO: **Azamdzhon Karimov**
Address: 735790, Republic Tadjikistan,

Reg., Ashti Dist., pos. Shaidon,

St., 1

Phone: **2-20-51, 2-11-67**
Products: **salt 28,454 tons**

For additional analytical, business and investment opportunities information, please contact Global Investment & Business Center, USA at (202) 546-2103. Fax: (202) 546-3275. E-mail: rusric@erols.com

7   BAIRAZA HYDROELECTRIC STATION

Ownership: *state*
Industry: *Power industry*
Number of Employees: *10.00*
CEO: **A. N.Kozlov**
Address: 735300, Republic Tadjikistan, Nurek, post
box 43

Phone: **(37738) 2-17-35, ext. 3-60**
Products: electric power supply 2,289 mln kWh

8   BAKERY "NONPAZ"

Ownership: *state*
Industry: *Food & food processing*
Number of Employees: *178.00*
CEO: **Muzafarkhon Kamolov**
Address: 735360, Repiblic Tadjikistan, Khatlon
Reg., Kulyab, Lenin St., 100

Phone: **(37713) 3-27-43, 3-27-40, 3-22-46**
Products: **bakers' wares 6,415 tons**
confectionery 362 tons
corn sticks

9   BUSTON GINNERY

Ownership: *state*
Industry: *Textile industry*
Number of Employees: *383.00*
CEO: **Abdurasul Khikmatov**
Address: 735800, Republic Tadjikistan, Leninabad
Reg., Matchinsky Dist., pos. Buston,
Dushanbe,
Navoi St., 1

Phone: **2-20-68**
Products: cotton 7,320 tons
kWh
seeds 13,626 tons
lint

**10   CENTRAL ELECTRIC POWER
TRANSMISSION NETWORK**

Ownership: *state*
Industry: *Power industry*
Number of Employees: *1,237.00*
CEO: **Umar A.Ashrapov**
Address: 734045, Republic Tadjikistan,

Kalinin St., 1/3

Phone: **(3772) 36-46-43, 36-62-13**
Products: electric power supply 96 mln

**11   CLOSED JOINT-STOCK COMPANY
"BOFANDA"**

Ownership: *joint-stock*
Industry: *Textile industry*
Number of Employees: *480.00*
CEO: **Tursunpulot Khodzhimatov**
Address: 735790, Republic Tadjikistan, Leninabad
Reg., Ashti Dist., pos. Shaidon, S.Niyazov
St., 13

Phone: **2-25-00**
children
Products: **carpets 54 ths sq m**
floor coverings
vests

12   CLOTHING FACTORY "FIRUZA"

Ownership: *state*
Industry: *Clothing industry*
Number of Employees: *550.00*
CEO: **Amadkhon Amonov**
Address: 735360, Repiblic Tadjikistan, Khatlon
Reg., Kulyab, Kalinin St., 40

Phone: **(37713) 3-26-91, 3-37-96, 3-42-43**
Products: **articles of apparel and clothing
accessories**   trousers for

bed-linen

**13   CLOTHING FIRM "GULISTAN"
WORKS**

Ownership: *state*
Industry: *Clothing industry*
Number of Employees: *1,668.00*
research
CEO: **Valentina R.Krayushkina**
Address: 734025, Republic Tadjikistan, Dushanbe,
Tegron St., 21

14   COMPUTING APPARATUS REPAIR

Ownership: *state*
Industry: *High-tech products, PC,*

& design services
Number of Employees: *132.00*
CEO: **Mikhail E.Uryadov**

Dushanbe,
Phone: **(3772) 22-31-42, 22-55-96, 22-56-09**
Products: **bathrobes 0.3 ths pcs**
suits 317.7 ths pcs

processing

Address: 734030, Republic Tadjikistan,

Aini St., 259

Phone: **(3772) 25-27-03, 25-26-49**
Products: **repair of automatic data**

machines

15 CONFECTIONERY FACTORY "MAISHAT"
Ownership: *joint-stock*
Industry: *Food & food processing*
Number of Employees: *80.00*
CEO: **Rustam R.Abdullo-zade**
Address: 735700, Republic Tadjikistan, Leninabad
Dushanbe,
Reg., Khudzhand, Teatralnaya St., 1

Phone: **(37922) 6-01-70**
Products: **confectionery 1,430 tons**
preserved fruit 100 ths tins
milk and dairy products

16 CONFECTIONERY FACTORY "SHIRIN"
Ownership: *joint-stock*
Industry: *Food & food processing*
Number of Employees: *644.00*
CEO: **Saida F.Mirazorova**
Address: 734009, Republic Tadjikistan,

Dzh.Rasulov Ave., 10

Phone: **(3772) 36-17-70, 36-95-57**
Products: **sugar confectionery**

17 DUSHANBE AGRARIAN PRODUCTION COMPANY "NONPAZ"
Ownership: *state*
Industry: *Food & food processing*
Number of Employees: *1,146.00*
CEO: **Davon Ibragimov**
Address: 734013, Republic Tadjikistan, Dushanbe,
Dushanbe,
P.Lumumba St., 28

Phone: **(3772) 22-87-66**
Products: **bakers' wares**
pasta

18 DUSHANBE AGROINDUSTRIAL PRODUCTION COMPANY
Ownership: *state*
Industry: *Food & food processing*
Number of Employees: *275.00*
CEO: **Umed Dusmatov**
Address: 734032, Republic Tadjikistan,

Firdousi St., 8

Phone: **(3772) 31-44-44**
Products: **bakers' wares 7,038 tons**

19 DUSHANBE BRICK YARD PRODUCTION COMPANY
Ownership: *state*
Industry: *Building materials industry*
Number of Employees: *300.00*
CEO: **Gies K.Nazirov**
Address: 734002, Republic Tadjikistan, Dushanbe,
Dushanbe,
Surkhob St., 5

Phone: **(3772) 24-77-56**
Products: **building bricks 17,801 ths pcs**

20 DUSHANBE CABLE PLANT "TADZHIKKABEL"
Ownership: *state*
Industry: *Electrical engineering*
Number of Employees: *271.00*
CEO: **Fakhriddin A.Alekberov**
Address: 734033, Republic Tadjikistan,

GSP, Oktyabrya St., 210

Phone: **(3772) 33-49-63, 33-49-43, 33-21-54**
Products: **cables**

21 DUSHANBE CHEESE PLANT
Ownership: *joint-stock*

22 DUSHANBE CLOTHING PRODUCTION COMPANY "CHEVAR"

Industry: *Food & food processing*
Number of Employees: *93.00*
CEO: Khairali M.Saidov
Address: 734011, Republic Tadjikistan, Dushanbe,
40 let Tadzhikistana St., 35
Dushanbe,

Phone: (3772) 22-22-71, 22-52-54
Products: butter 124 tons
cheese 692 tons
milk and dairy products

23 DUSHANBE COMPANY "GULDAST" "TADZHIKATLAS"

Ownership: *state*
Industry: *Clothing industry*
Number of Employees: *426.00*
CEO: Karomat Sharipova
Address: 734067, Republic Tadjikistan, Dushanbe,
Dushanbe,
Gagarin St., 19

Phone: (3772) 24-57-07, 24-57-20, 24-27-46
Products: dresses 41.1 ths pcs
dresses of silk 24.8 ths pcs

25 DUSHANBE CONFECTIONERY FACTORY "LAZZAT" (JOINT-STOCK COMPANY)

Ownership: *joint-stock*
Industry: *Food & food processing*
Number of Employees: *52.00*
CEO: Alexander Ya.Dorovskikh
Dushanbe,
Address: 734015, Republic Tadjikistan, Dushanbe,
1-i Pr. Afzali, 17

Phone: (3772) 27-73-31
Products: sugar confectionery 112.7 tons

27 DUSHANBE EXCAVATOR REPAIR WORKS

Ownership: *state*
Industry: *Metal-working industry*
Number of Employees: *82.00*
CEO: Galina V.Solovyeva
Address: 734033, Republic Tadjikistan, Dushanbe,
Borbad St., 23-a
Dushanbe,

Phone: (3772) 33-50-41, 33-67-79
Products: welded metal structures 898 tons
repair of motor vehicles

Ownership: *state*
Industry: *Clothing industry*
Number of Employees: *1,196.00*
CEO: Igor A.Fraidin
Address: 734010, Republic Tadjikistan,

Dzh.Rasulov Ave., 71/7

Phone: (3772) 33-38-26, 33-31-67
Products: industrial clothing
suits 256 ths pcs

24 DUSHANBE COMPANY

Ownership: *state*
Industry: *Textile industry*
Number of Employees: *958.00*
CEO: Rano O.Umarova
Address: 734018, Republic Tadjikistan,

N.Karabaev St., 8

Phone: (3772) 33-39-94
Products: fabrics of silk 3,064.8 ths m
twisted threads of silk 38.2 ths m
folk handicraft articles

26 DUSHANBE DAIRY

Ownership: *state*
Industry: *Food & food processing*
Number of Employees: *439.00*
CEO: Mirzo M.Kamildzhanov
Address: 734043, Republic Tadjikistan,

Dzh.Rasulov Ave., 9

Phone: (3772) 36-96-77, 36-95-87
Products: butter 226 tons
cheese 29 tons
milk and dairy products

28 DUSHANBE EXPERIMENTAL PLANT "SISTEMAVTOMATIKA"

Ownership: *state*
Industry: *Medical equipment industry*
Number of Employees: *65.00*
CEO: Vladimir I.Gavrilov
Address: 734024, Republic Tadjikistan,

Druzhby narodov Ave., 62

Phone: (3772) 23-04-83, 27-09-39
Products: instruments and apparatus
maintenance of instruments and
automated equipment

For additional analytical, business and investment opportunities information,
please contact Global Investment & Business Center, USA
at (202) 546-2103. Fax: (202) 546-3275. E-mail: rusric@erols.com

29 DUSHANBE FERROCONCRETE STRUCTURES and BUILDING ARTICLES PLANT n1

Ownership: *state*
Industry: *Building materials industry*
Number of Employees: *288.00*
CEO: **President**
Address: 734029, Republic Tadjikistan, Dushanbe, Dushanbe,

K.Tsetkin St., 2

Phone: **(3772) 36-72-05**
Products: **pre-cast ferroconcrete 25.2 ths cu m**
pipes

concrete

30 DUSHANBE FERROCONCRETE STRUCTURES and BUILDING ARTICLES PLANT n2

Ownership: *state*
Industry: *Building materials industry*
Number of Employees: *132.00*
CEO: **Takhir K.Mukhitdinov**
Address: 734065, Republic Tadjikistan,

9-i km Kofarnikhon Shosse

Phone: **(3772) 25-10-77, 25-07-84, 25-05-54**
Products: **pre-cast ferroconcrete**
articles of concrete, not reinforced concrete

31 DUSHANBE FERROCONCRETE STRUCTURES and BUILDING ARTICLES PLANT n3

Ownership: *state*
Industry: *Building materials industry*
Number of Employees: *216.00*
CEO: **Rasul K.Kasymov**
Address: 734055, Republic Tadjikistan, Dushanbe, Dushanbe,

Borbad St., 36
Ordzhonikidzeabad

Phone: **(3772) 31-22-51, 31-26-97**
Products: **pre-cast ferroconcrete**
wall panels

m

32 DUSHANBE FERROCONCRETE STRUCTURES and BUILDING ARTICLES PLANT n6

Ownership: *state*
Industry: *Building materials industry*
Number of Employees: *178.00*
CEO: **Victor V.Fundurakin**
Address: 734063, Republic Tadjikistan,

p/o Guliston, 9-i km

Shosse

Phone: **(3772) 29-85-06**
Products: **pre-cast ferroconcrete 6.2 ths cu**

33 DUSHANBE FERROCONCRETE STRUCTURES and PRE-CAST PARTS PLANT

Ownership: *state*
Industry: *Building materials industry*
Number of Employees: *467.00*
CEO: **Victor M.Nasyrov**
Dushanbe,
Address: 734060, Republic Tadjikistan, Dushanbe, Lomonosov St., 377/1

Phone: **(3772) 33-11-63**
Products: **pre-cast ferroconcrete 16.8 ths cu m**
articles of concrete, not reinforced

concrete

34 DUSHANBE FOLK DECORATIVE HANDICRAFT COMPANY "DILOROM"

Ownership: *state*
Industry: *Textile industry*
Number of Employees: *938.00*
CEO: **Lyutfiya R.Bakoyeva**
Address: 734018, Republic Tadjikistan,

Sherozi Ave., 11

Phone: **(3772) 33-63-78, 33-25-91**
Products: **articles of apparel and clothing accessories** fabrics of cotton

fabrics of silk

35 DUSHANBE FOOD PROCESSING ENTERPRISE

Ownership: *state*
Industry: *Food & food processing*

36 DUSHANBE FURNITURE PLANT

Ownership: *state*
Industry: *Consumer goods, furniture, household & cultural goods*

For additional analytical, business and investment opportunities information, please contact Global Investment & Business Center, USA at (202) 546-2103. Fax: (202) 546-3275. E-mail: rusric@erols.com

Number of Employees: *300.00*
CEO: **Akhmad Kh.Radzhabov**
Address: 734002, Republic Tadjikistan, Dushanbe, Dushanbe,

Shotemur St., 60

Phone: **(3772) 27-27-83, 27-47-32**
Products: **beer 1,082 ths dal**
non-alcoholic beverages 216 ths dal
mineral waters

37   DUSHANBE GRAIN PROCESSING PLANT

Ownership: *state*
Industry: *Food & food processing*
Number of Employees: *243.00*
CEO: **Rakhmetdin Sh.Davlyatov**
Address: 734029, Republic Tadjikistan, Dushanbe,
Vose St., 12
Dushanbe,

Phone: **(3772) 25-19-69, 25-18-91**
Products: **wheat flour 110,390 tons**

39   DUSHANBE JOINT-STOCK LEATHER FOOTWEAR COMPANY "RAFIK"

Ownership: *joint-stock*
Industry: *Footwer & tanning industry*
Number of Employees: *3,928.00*
CEO: **Arkady P.Rokhman**
Dushanbe,
Address: 734005, Republic Tadjikistan, Dushanbe,
Charm-Garon St., 10-a

Phone: **(3772) 22-84-84, 22-32-80**
Products: **footwear 2,005 ths pairs**

41   DUSHANBE LEATHER HABERDASHERY FACTORY "CHARMDUZ"

Ownership: *state*
Industry: *Footwer & tanning industry*
Number of Employees: *143.00*
CEO: **Leonid D.Khovansky**
Dushanbe,
Address: 734060, Republic Tadjikistan, Dushanbe,
Dzh.Rasulov Ave., 71/7

Phone: **(3772) 33-49-26, 33-78-11**
Products: **suitcases 7.5 ths pcs**
satchels 18.9 ths pcs
bags 118.6 ths pcs

Number of Employees: *537.00*
CEO: **Yury D.Volchinsky**
Address: 734012, Republic Tadjikistan,

Korgar St., 130

Phone: **(3772) 22-49-43**
Products: **furniture**

38   DUSHANBE JEWELLERY PLANT

Ownership: *state*
Industry: *Consumer goods, furniture, household & cultural goods*
Number of Employees: *401.00*
CEO: **Isak Burkhanov**
Address: 734033, Republic Tadjikistan,

Shestopalov St., 7

Phone: **(3772) 33-25-18, 33-15-78**
Products: **articles of jewellery**
metal haberdashery
fittings

40   DUSHANBE KNITTING MILL

Ownership: *state*
Industry: *Textile industry*
Number of Employees: *743.00*
CEO: **Davlyat S.Boboyev**
Address: 734005, Republic Tadjikistan,

40 let Tadzhikistana St., 123

Phone: **(3772) 27-48-96, 27-55-66**
Products: **knitted linen**

42   DUSHANBE MEAT PROCESSING PLANT

Ownership: *state*
Industry: *Food & food processing*
Number of Employees: *562.00*
CEO: **Bakhtier Kh.Gadoyev**
Address: 734005, Republic Tadjikistan,

Fuchik St., 4

Phone: **(3772) 22-64-76, 22-36-74**
Products: **meat 2,558 tons**

43 DUSHANBE OILERY and FAT PLANT

Ownership: *state*
Industry: *Food & food processing*
Number of Employees: *917.00*
CEO: Said Kh.Radzhabov
Address: 734009, Republic Tadjikistan, Dushanbe, Dzh.Rasulov Ave., 9

Dushanbe,
Phone: (3772) 36-95-35
Products: **vegetable oil 11.2 ths tons**
hydrogenated fat 3.5 ths tons
household soap 5 ths tons

44 DUSHANBE PAINTS and VARNISHES PLANT "RANGINKAMON"

Ownership: *state*
Industry: *Chemical, pharmaceutical & micribiology industry*
Number of Employees: *290.00*
CEO: Khairullo A.Abdulloyev
Address: 734008, Republic Tadjikistan,

Rudaki Ave., 205

Phone: (3772) 24-85-51, 24-28-53
Products: **paints and varnishes 996 tons**
floor oil paints
pottery articles

45 DUSHANBE PILOT-PRODUCTION and EXPERIMENTAL PLANT "REMSTROIDORMASH"

Ownership: *state*
Industry: *Metal-working industry*
Number of Employees: *141.00*
CEO: Odildzhon M.Abdullaev
Address: 734036, Republic Tadjikistan, Dushanbe, 40 let Tadzhikistana St., 45

Phone: (3772) 33-48-09, 33-27-42
Products: **structural aluminium 172 tons**
welded metal structures 6.7 tons

46 DUSHANBE PILOT-PRODUCTION and EXPERIMENTAL PLANT "SELEKTSIONNAYA TEKHNIKA"

Ownership: *state*
Industry: *Machine building industry*
Number of Employees: *10.00*
CEO: Sadullo S.Giyasov
Address: 735100, Republic Tadjikistan, pos. Leninsky, kolkhoz "Leningradsky"

Phone: 27-54-76
Products: **warehousing equipment**

47 DUSHANBE PIPE APPLIANCES PLANT NAMED AFTER ORDZHONIKIDZE

Ownership: *state*
Industry: *Metal-working industry*
Number of Employees: *1,328.00*
CEO: Aktam A.Akbarov
Dushanbe,
Address: 734036, Republic Tadjikistan, Dushanbe, Dzhami Pr., 2/1

Phone: (3772) 31-07-67
Products: **appliances for pipes, boilers, etc** equipment
gate valves of steel
cast articles of pig iron

48 DUSHANBE PLANT "STROMMASH"

Ownership: *state*
Industry: *Machine building industry*
Number of Employees: *98.00*
CEO: Fazlidin T.Abdusamiev
Address: 734008, Republic Tadjikistan,

Rudaki St., 204

Phone: (3772) 24-27-42, 24-57-92
Products: **oxygen 61 ths cu m**
non-standard machinery and

343.7 tons

49 DUSHANBE PLANT "TADZHIKTEKSTILMASH"

Ownership: *state*
Industry: *Machine building industry*
Number of Employees: *1,400.00*
CEO: Rufik M.Biktimirov
Dushanbe,
Address: 734042, Republic Tadjikistan, Dushanbe,

50 DUSHANBE PLANT "TORGMASH"

Ownership: *state*
Industry: *Machine building industry*
Number of Employees: *493.00*
CEO: Vladimir G.Koknaev
Address: 734000, Republic Tadjikistan,

Navruz St., 161

For additional analytical, business and investment opportunities information, please contact Global Investment & Business Center, USA at (202) 546-2103. Fax: (202) 546-3275. E-mail: rusric@erols.com

Shapkin St., 7

Phone: (3772) 23-44-57, 22-31-72
Products: winding machinery and spare parts
200 pcs
electric cabinets

trade equipment

Phone: (3772) 22-33-73
Products: trade equipment and spare parts
electric ovens 23,911 pcs
textile spinning machines 152 pcs

51   DUSHANBE PRINT-SHOP n18
Ownership: *state*
Industry: *Publishing & printing*
Number of Employees:
CEO: Rasima I.Osipova
Address: 734017, Republic Tadjikistan, Dushanbe, Dushanbe,
Nosir-Khisrav St., 6

Phone: (3772) 24-56-14
Products: printed matter

52   DUSHANBE PRINTING WORKS
Ownership: *state*
Industry: *Publishing & printing*
Number of Employees: *382.00*
CEO: Vladimir Sh.Mansurov
Address: 734063, Republic Tadjikistan,
Aini St., 126

Phone: (3772) 25-10-46
Products: printed matter

53   DUSHANBE SILK MILL
Ownership: *state*
Industry: *Textile industry*
Number of Employees: *1,986.00*
CEO: Abdurakhman T.Khabibov
Address: 734007, Republic Tadjikistan, Dushanbe,
Akhmadi Donish St., 5

Dushanbe,
Phone: (3772) 27-02-36, 27-45-57, 29-07-61
Products: threads of silk, unbleached 70 tons
fabrics of silk
twisted threads of silk

54   DUSHANBE SOUVENIR FACTORY "ARMUGON"
Ownership: *joint-stock*
Industry: *Consumer goods, furniture, household & cultural goods*
Number of Employees: *96.00*
CEO: Bagrad A.Mardoyants
Address: 734014, Republic Tadjikistan,
Druzhby narodov Ave., 78

Phone: (3772) 27-09-91, 27-24-88
Products: folk handicraft articles

55   DUSHANBE SPECIALIZED ENGINEERING DESIGN BUREAU
Ownership: *state*
Industry: *Machine building industry*
Number of Employees: *174.00*
CEO: Abdurakhim K.Avganov
Dushanbe,
Address: 734018, Republic Tadjikistan, Dushanbe,
N.Karabaev St., 54

Phone: (3772) 34-82-77
kWh
Products: designing
non-standard machinery and equipment

56   DUSHANBE THERMOELECTRIC STATION
Ownership: *state*
Industry: *Power industry*
Number of Employees: *748.00*
CEO: Alisher I.Arifov
Address: 734054, Republic Tadjikistan,
40 let Tadzhikistana St., 39

Phone: (3772) 27-67-19, 23-38-32
Products: electric power supply 680 mln
heating 3,245 ths Gcal

57   DUSHANBE TOBACCO FACTORY
Ownership: *state*

58   DUSHANBE TOWN ELECTRIC POWER TRANSMISSION NETWORK

Industry: *Tobacco industry*
Number of Employees: *235.00*
CEO: Kamar D.Mirazorov
Address: 734002, Republic Tadjikistan, Dushanbe, Telman St., 31
Dushanbe,

Phone: (3772) 27-46-64, 24-60-07, 24-60-13
Products: cigarettes 2,607 mln pcs

59 DUSHANBE WINE PLANT

Ownership: *state*
Industry: *Food & food processing*
Number of Employees: *260.00*
CEO: Abduvose A.Bakiev
Address: 734013, Republic Tadjikistan, Dushanbe, Druzhby narodov Ave., 106
Dushanbe,

Phone: (3772) 22-89-89, 23-08-82, 22-31-54
Products: vodka 258 ths dal
wine 110 ths dal
brandy

61 DUSHANBE WOOD-WORKING PLANT

Ownership: *state*
Industry: *Forestry & timber processing industry*
Number of Employees: *294.00*
CEO: Ulyashbai F.Muminov
Address: 734029, Republic Tadjikistan, Dushanbe,
Dushanbe,
Zebunisso St., 5

Phone: (3772) 25-18-81, 25-16-16
Products: window assemblies 25.5 ths sq m
door assemblies 14.7 ths sq m
wood sawn lengthwise

63 DUSHANBEPRESSURE PIPES and FERROCONCRETE ARTICLES PLANT

Ownership: *state*
Industry: *Building materials industry*
Number of Employees: *221.00*
CEO: Alexander V.Kiryushin
Address: 734050, Republic Tadjikistan, Dushanbe, 9-i km Ordzhonikidzeabad Shosse

Phone: (3772) 25-18-13, 25-24-23, 25-25-91
Products: pre-cast ferroconcrete
chutes
power transmission line supports

Ownership: *state*
Industry: *Power industry*
Number of Employees: *380.00*
CEO: Dzhamshed M.Mansurov
Address: 734060, Republic Tadjikistan,

1-i Ostrovsky pr.

Phone: (3772) 22-69-21, 22-67-64, 22-67-91
Products: electric power supply

60 DUSHANBE WOOD-WORKING PLANT

Ownership: *state*
Industry: *Forestry & timber processing industry*
Number of Employees: *121.00*
CEO: Oleg Kh.Sabirov
Address: 734063, Republic Tadjikistan,

9-i km Ordzhonikidzeabad Shosse

Phone: (3772) 25-27-10, 25-24-38
Products: window assemblies 9.4 ths sq m
door assemblies 3.5 ths sq m
floor panels

62 DUSHANBE WOOD-WORKING PLANT

Ownership: *state*
Industry: *Forestry & timber processing industry*
Number of Employees: *74.00*
CEO: Akram N.Uzakov
Address: 734005, Republic Tadjikistan,

Fuchik St., 88

Phone: (3772) 22-36-17, 22-48-00
Products: window assemblies 4.9 ths sq m
door assemblies 1.9 ths sq m
PVC pipes

64 DZHILIKUL FISHING FARM

Ownership: *state*
Industry: *Fishing & fish processing*
Number of Employees: *90.00*
CEO: Vladimir S.Bulychev
Address: 735218, Repiblic Tadjikistan, Khatlon Reg., pos. Dzhilikul

Phone: 5-52-99
Products: live fish 600 tons
smoked fish 190 tons

65   DZHILIKUL FISHING FARM

Ownership: *state*
Industry: *Fishing & fish processing*
Number of Employees: *89.00*
CEO: **Valery D.Golikov**
Address: 735207, Repiblic Tadjikistan, Khatlon
Reg., Dzhilikul Dist., s. Pakhtakor, uch.
Dushanbe,
40

Phone: **5-52-99, 82-48**
Products: fish

67   FACTORY "ZARDUZ"

Ownership: *state*
Industry: *Textile industry*
Number of Employees: *462.00*
CEO: **Khalimdzhon Okhundzhanov**
Address: 735702, Republic Tadjikistan, Leninabad
Reg., Khudzhand, Lenin St., 223

Phone: **(37922) 6-78-02, 6-37-85, 6-47-48**
Products: **textile haberdashery 240 mln pcs**
articles of apparel and clothing
accessories 100 mln pcs

69   FERMENTED TOBACCO PLANT

Ownership: *state*
Industry: *Tobacco industry*
Number of Employees: *85.00*
CEO: **President**
Address: 734024, Republic Tadjikistan, Dushanbe,
Dushanbe,
Shapkin St., 157

Phone: **(3772) 23-29-24**
Products: **fermented tobacco 1,186 tons**

cellophane

71   FIRM "DOVUD"

Ownership: *joint-stock*
Industry: *Scrap & waste processing*
industry
Number of Employees: *96.00*
CEO: **President**
Dushanbe,
Address: 734000, Republic Tadjikistan, Dushanbe,
Dzh.Rasulov Ave., 60

Phone: **no data**

66   ENTERPRISE "TADZHIKENERGOREMONT"

Ownership: *state*
Industry: *Electrical engineering*
Number of Employees: *268.00*
CEO: **Vyacheslav M.Palatov**
Address: 734011, Republic Tadjikistan,

Sherozi Ave., 26

Phone: **(3772) 23-16-58, 27-37-09**
Products: **repair of power equipment**
spare parts for power machinery

68   FARKHOR GINNERY

Ownership: *state*
Industry: *Textile industry*
Number of Employees:
CEO: **Rakhmonzon Tetaboev**
Address: 735390, Repiblic Tadjikistan, Khatlon
Reg., pos. Farkhor, Lenin St., 25

Phone: **2-35-91, 2-20-95, 3-35-92**
Products: **cotton 6,048 tons**
seeds 10,361 tons
lint

70   FIRM "BORCHOMA"

Ownership: *state*
Industry: *Pulp & paper industry*
Number of Employees: *133.00*
CEO: **Karim S.Kadyrov**
Address: 734060, Republic Tadjikistan,

pos. Rokhi-Nav, 208

Phone: **(3772) 33-48-94, 33-50-64, 33-50-38**
Products: **articles of plastics**
packing containers of paperboard
articles of polyethylene and

72   FIRM "NAFISA"

Ownership: *joint-stock*
Industry: *Textile industry*
Number of Employees: *1,702.00*
CEO: **Ismon O.Obidov**
Address: 734024, Republic Tadjikistan,

Popov St., 11

Phone: **(3772) 27-30-77**
Products: **stockings 4,260 ths pairs**

Products: processing of metal scrap 40,234 tons

panty hoses
socks

73 FISHING FARM "CHUBEK"

Ownership: *state*
Industry: *Fishing & fish processing*
Number of Employees: *80.00*
CEO: **Rustam Salimov**
Address: 735370, Repiblic Tadjikistan, Khatlon Reg., Moskovsky Dist., kishlak Tudaboen Leninabad

Phone: 2-24-92
Products: live fish 90 tons
chilled fish 8 tons
m

74 GAFUROV FERROCONCRETE STRUCTURES PLANT n7

Ownership: *state*
Industry: *Building materials industry*
Number of Employees: *164.00*
CEO: **Nematzhon Domulloyev**
Address: 735690, Republic Tadjikistan, Reg., Khodzhent Dist., Gafurov

Phone: 3-29-28, 3-26-56, 3-21-08
Products: pre-cast ferroconcrete 26,763 cu concrete 1,331 cu m

75 GAFUROV MEAT PROCESSING PLANT

Ownership: *state*
Industry: *Food & food processing*
Number of Employees: *390.00*
CEO: **Abdurazak Latipov**
Address: 735690, Republic Tadjikistan, Leninabad Leninabad Reg., Khodzhent Dist., Gafurov, 119-i Gogolya kvartal

Phone: 3-15-49
Products: hides
dal
meat 2,657 tons
sausages

76 GAFUROV WINE PLANT

Ownership: *state*
Industry: *Food & food processing*
Number of Employees:
CEO: **Mullodzhon Oglukov**
Address: 735690, Republic Tadjikistan, Reg., Khodzhent Dist., Gafurov, St., 63-a

Phone: 3-39-36, 3-12-54
Products: wine of fresh grapes 368.1 ths
vodka

77 GANCHI BRICK YARD

Ownership: *state*
Industry: *Building materials industry*
Number of Employees: *240.00*
CEO: **Maruf Khakimov**
Address: 735620, Republic Tadjikistan, Leninabad Reg., pos. Ganchi Leninabad

Phone: 7-76
Products: building bricks 15,844 ths pcs

78 GANCHI CLOTHING and KNITWEAR FACTORY

Ownership: *state*
Industry: *Textile industry*
Number of Employees: *471.00*
CEO: **Kurbonali Boboyev**
Address: 735620, Republic Tadjikistan, Reg., pos. Ganchi

Phone: no data
Products: knitted outerwear 687 ths pcs

79 GISSAR COMPANY "GIDROSTROIMATERIALY"

Ownership: *state*

80 GISSAR GINNERY

Ownership: *state*
Industry: *Textile industry*

Industry: *Oil refining & gas processing*
Number of Employees: *800.00*
CEO: **Abdurakhmon Tabarov**
Address: 735020, Republic Tadjikistan, pos. Gissar

Phone: **(37739) 2-59-52**
Products: **linoleum 355.6 ths sq m**
          roll roofing materials 1,811 ths sq m
          building bricks

Number of Employees: *10.00*
CEO: **President**
Address: 735020, Republic Tadjikistan, Gissar
         Dist., pos. Sharora

Phone: no data
Products: **cotton 1,035 tons**
          seeds 1,831 tons
          lint

81   GISSAR GRAIN INTAKE PLANT
Ownership: *state*
Industry: *Food & food processing*
Number of Employees: *64.00*
CEO: **Razok K.Kadyrov**
Address: 735020, Republic Tadjikistan, pos.
         Gissar, K.Marks St., 4

Phone: **(37739) 2-62-10, 2-65-15**
Products: **wheat flour 44 ths tons**
          bran 11 ths tons

82   GISSAR TEXTILE MILL
Ownership: *state*
Industry: *Textile industry*
Number of Employees: *20.00*
CEO: **President**
Address: 735020, Republic Tadjikistan, pos.
         Gissar, K.Marks St., 54

Phone: **(37739) 2-61-67**
Products: **fabrics, unbleached 3,207 ths m**

83   GISSAR TRAINING and PRODUCTION POWER
WORKS
Ownership: *joint-stock*
Industry: *Food & food processing*
Number of Employees:
CEO: **President**
Address: 735020, Republic Tadjikistan, pos. Gissar

Region,

Phone: no data
Products: **lids for preserves 15,801 ths pcs**
          crown corks 3,724 ths pcs
kwh
          folders

84   GORNO-BADAKHSHAN ELECTRIC
TRANSMISSION NETWORK
Ownership: *joint-stock*
Industry: *Power industry*
Number of Employees: *570.00*
CEO: **Safar M.Dzhumaev**
Address: 736100, Republic Tadjikistan,
         Gorno-Badakhshan Autonomous

         Khorog, Gulmamad St., 75

Phone: **(377910) 28-10, 29-15**
Products: **electric power supply 93,500 ths**

85   GRAIN INTAKE PLANT
Ownership: *state*
Industry: *Food & food processing*
Number of Employees: *126.00*
CEO: **Miron K.Sakhibov**
Address: 735320, Repiblic Tadjikistan, Khatlon
Leninabad
         Reg., pos. Dangara

Phone: **2-28, 2-20, 2-19**
Products: **mixed fodder 31 ths tons**

86   GRAIN INTAKE YARD
Ownership: *state*
Industry: *Food & food processing*
Number of Employees: *20.00*
CEO: **Nemat Rakhmankulov**
Address: 735500, Republic Tadjikistan,

         Reg., Pendzhikent

Phone: **(37775) 2-34-74**
Products: **cereal meal 4,974 tons**
          rice meal 947 tons

87   GRAIN PROCESSING PLANT
Ownership: *state*

88   ILIYCHEVSKY FEED MILL
Ownership: *state*

Industry: *Food & food processing*
Number of Employees: *513.00*
CEO: K. T.Turaev
Address: 735400, Republic Tadjikistan,
Kofarnikhon, Rabochaya St., 19

Phone: 2-37-31, 2-24-93
Products: wheat flour 142 ths tons
bran 40 ths tons
semolina

Industry: *Food & food processing*
Number of Employees: *37.00*
CEO: Amir Kh.Khudoidodov
Address: 735131, Repiblic Tadjikistan, Khatlon
Reg., Iliychevsky Dist., s. Obi-Kiik

Phone: 2-11-61, 2-12-58
Products: mixed fodder

89 INDUSTRIAL and COMMERCIAL FIRM "ISMAIL"

Ownership: *state*
Industry: *Consumer goods, furniture, household & cultural goods*
Number of Employees: *10.00*
Leninabad
CEO: Ismail Gulov
Address: 735400, Republic Tadjikistan,
Kofarnikhon, Guliston St., 2

Phone: 2-28-19, 2-44-23
Products: kitchen furniture
stools 86.6 ths rbls 865 pcs
dinner-tables

90 INDUSTRIAL and TRADING FIRM "SIMO"

Ownership: *state*
Industry: *Footwer & tanning industry*
Number of Employees: *262.00*
CEO: Abdullo Khusainov
Address: 735500, Republic Tadjikistan,

Reg., Pendzhikent, K.Marks St., 72

Phone: (37775) 2-50-07, 2-50-52, 2-51-69
Products: footwear 500 ths pairs

91 ISFARA BAKERY

Ownership: *state*
Industry: *Food & food processing*
Number of Employees: *125.00*
CEO: Abdurakhim T.Timurkhanov
Address: 735920, Republic Tadjikistan, Leninabad
Leninabad

Reg., Isfara, Lenin St., 62

Phone: 2-15-63, 2-45-43
Products: bakers' wares

92 ISFARA BUILDING MATERIALS PLANT

Ownership: *state*
Industry: *Building materials industry*
Number of Employees: *508.00*
CEO: Abdullo Gafurov
Address: 735920, Republic Tadjikistan,

Reg., Isfara Dist., pos. Khonobad

Phone: 2-32-04, 2-18-51, 2-31-03
Products: gypsum, building bricks

93 ISFARA CANNERY

Ownership: *state*
Industry: *Food & food processing*
Number of Employees: *941.00*
CEO: Atakhon Abdukadyrov
Address: 735920, Republic Tadjikistan, Leninabad
Reg., Isfara, Lenin St., 143
Leninabad

Phone: 2-12-71, 2-13-81, 2-17-64
Products: preserved vegetables 6,657 ths tins

94 ISFARA CHEMICALS PLANT

Ownership: *state*
Industry: *Chemical, pharmaceutical & micribiology industry*
Number of Employees: *1,609.00*
CEO: Ilyes Aslamov
Address: 735920, Republic Tadjikistan,

Reg., Isfara Dist., pos. Novobad

Phone: no data
Products: household chemicals
paints and varnishes
mineral fertilizers

95 ISFARA CONFECTIONERY FACTORY

Ownership: *state*
Industry: *Food & food processing*
Number of Employees: *106.00*
CEO: **Abdugafar Kadyrov Sh.Shomirsaadov**
Address: 735920, Republic Tadjikistan, Leninabad Leninabad

Reg., Isfara, Abdullaev St., 2

Phone: **2-36-02, 2-41-89**
Products: caramel

96 ISFARA CREAMERY

Ownership: *state*
Industry: *Food & food processing*
Number of Employees: *79.00*
CEO: **Abdusamad**

Address: 735920, Republic Tadjikistan,

Reg., Isfara Dist., pos. Istaravshan

Phone: **2-54-00, 2-13-76**
Products: **butter 465.4 tons**
milk 2,138.6 tons
fermented milk products

97 ISFARA FERROCONCRETE STRUCTURES and BUILDING ARTICLES PLANT n5

Ownership: *state*
Industry: *Building materials industry*
Number of Employees: *310.00*
CEO: **Ibragim Mukhamadov**
Address: 735920, Republic Tadjikistan, Leninabad Leninabad

Reg., Isfara, Zavodskaya St., 20

Phone: **2-47-31, 2-32-69, 2-28-80**
Products: pre-cast ferroconcrete
structural components for house
construction 3.3 ths sq m

98 ISFARA FURNITURE PLANT

Ownership: *state*
Industry: *Consumer goods, furniture, household & cultural goods*
Number of Employees: *52.00*
CEO: **Abdulafiz Abdusattarov**
Address: 735920, Republic Tadjikistan,

Reg., Isfara, Lenin St., 49

Phone: **2-15-43, 2-48-07**
Products: furniture
tables
beds
supports for power transmission lines

99 ISFARA HYDROMETALLURGICAL PLANT

Ownership: *state*
Industry: *Metallurgy*
Number of Employees: *10.00*
CEO: **Abduzhabar R.Kataev**
Address: 735920, Republic Tadjikistan, Leninabad Leninabad

Reg., Isfara, Lenin St., 132-a

Phone: **2-42-84**
Products: **barium metal 9,812 kg**
chemical products 6,555 tons
precious metals

100 ISFARA MEAT PROCESSING PLANT

Ownership: *state*
Industry: *Food & food processing*
Number of Employees: *122.00*
CEO: **Farkhad A.Abdullaev**
Address: 735920, Republic Tadjikistan,

Reg., Isfara, Lenin St., 71

Phone: **2-42-98, 2-43-38**
Products: **meat 545.5 tons**

101 ISFARA MEDICAL PREPARATIONS and FEED PROTEIN PLANT

Ownership: *state*
Industry: *Chemical, pharmaceutical & micribiology industry*
Number of Employees: *125.00*
CEO: **Bakhram S.Boboyev**
Address: 735920, Republic Tadjikistan, Leninabad

102 ISFARA MINERAL PAINTS PLANT "NILUFOR"

Ownership: *state*
Industry: *Chemical, pharmaceutical & micribiology industry*
Number of Employees: *244.00*
CEO: **Domullo Kadyrov**
Address: 735920, Republic Tadjikistan,

Leninabad

Reg., Isfara, Ashurbibi Azimov St., 86

Phone: 2-88-77, 2-48-39
Products: crude alcohol 286.7 ths dal

Reg., Isfara, Lenin St., 55

Phone: 2-48-46, 2-14-83
Products: dry ochre 5,980 tons
silicate paints
paints and varnishes

103   JOINT-STOCK COMPANY "BOFANDA"
Ownership: *joint-stock*
Industry: *Textile industry*
Number of Employees: *2,281.00*
CEO: Saidullo M.Makhsumov
Address: 734011, Republic Tadjikistan, Dushanbe,
Leninabad

Sherozi Ave., 6

Phone: (3772) 27-76-91, 22-36-73, 29-94-36
Products: yarn of cotton 6,371 tons

104   JOINT-STOCK COMPANY "FAIZ"
Ownership: *joint-stock*
Industry: *Textile industry*
Number of Employees: *1,055.00*
CEO: Khamdam F.Khodzhibaev
Address: 735610, Republic Tadjikistan,

Reg., Ura-Tyube, Fabrichnaya St., 14

Phone: 2-20-24, 2-10-84
Products: socks for men 7 ths pairs
socks for children
panty hoses for children

105   JOINT-STOCK COMPANY "KOLINKHO"
Ownership: *joint-stock*
Industry: *Textile industry*
Number of Employees: *5,429.00*
CEO: Yakhye N.Azlmov
Address: 735750, Republic Tadjikistan, Leninabad
Leninabad

Reg., Kairakkum, Tekstilshchikov St., 1

Phone: 2-20-01, 2-12-17
Products: carpets and other textile floor
coverings 8,297.5 ths sq m
8,000 ths pcs

yarn in skeins

106   JOINT-STOCK ENTERPRISE "LACHP"
Ownership: *joint-stock*
Industry: *Building materials industry*
Number of Employees: *495.00*
CEO: Mirzokhalim Mirzokarimov
Address: 735702, Republic Tadjikistan,

Reg., Khudzhand, Lenin St., 262

Phone: (37922) 6-45-94
Products: cans 100 mln pcs
twisted yarn 4,014.5 tons   bottles

paperboard boxes

107   KAIRAKKUM AGROINDUSTRIAL PRODUCTION COMPANY
Ownership: *state*
Industry: *Food & food processing*
Number of Employees: *442.00*
CEO: Abduzhalil M.Khamidov
Address: 735750, Republic Tadjikistan, Leninabad
Leninabad

Reg., Kairakkum

Phone: 2-28-41
Products: wheat flour 93,206 tons
pasta 7,701 tons
bran

108   KAIRAKKUM FISHING INDUSTRY ENTERPRISE
Ownership: *state*
Industry: *Fishing & fish processing*
Number of Employees:
CEO: Tatyana I.Divitskaya
Address: 735750, Republic Tadjikistan,

Reg., Kairakkum

Phone: 2-15-30, 2-17-34
Products: fish 497 tons
live fish 298 tons
smoked fish

109   KAIRAKKUM MECHANICAL REPAIR

110   KAIRAKKUM MINE

WORKSHOP

Ownership: state
Industry: *Metal-working industry*
Number of Employees: 60.00
CEO: Valery I.Shtorts
Leninabad
Address: 735750, Republic Tadjikistan, Leninabad
        Reg., Kairakkum, Lenin St., 108

Phone: 2-15-64, 2-13-22
Products: welded metal structures 447 tons
          repair of building machinery

Ownership: state
Industry: *Ore mining industry*
Number of Employees:
CEO: Rakhim N.Nurmatov
Address: 735750, Republic Tadjikistan,

        Reg., Kairakkum

Phone: no data
Products: precious metals

111   KAIRAKKUM SUBSIDIARY ENTERPRISE

Ownership: state
Industry: *Building materials industry*
Number of Employees: 397.00
CEO: Kamil Kh.Kabanov
Address: 735750, Republic Tadjikistan, Leninabad
        Reg., Kairakkum, Kovrovshchikov St., 3

Phone: 2-11-32, 2-12-09, 2-23-46
Products: pre-cast ferroconcrete

112   KALININABAD FERROCONCRETE STRUCTURES PLANT n1

Ownership: state
Industry: *Building materials industry*
Number of Employees: 202.00
CEO: Yevgeny I.Ababkov
Address: 735147, Repiblic Tadjikistan, Khatlon
        Reg., Kalininabad

Phone: (37744) 6-13-57
Products: pre-cast ferroconcrete

113   KALININABAD FERROCONCRETE STRUCTURES PLANT n8

Ownership: state
Industry: *Building materials industry*
Number of Employees: 150.00
CEO: Akhmatkul V.Khalikov
Address: 735147, Repiblic Tadjikistan, Khatlon
        Reg., Kalininabad

Phone: (37744) 6-13-44, 2-55-05, 2-13-57
Products: pre-cast ferroconcrete 7.7 ths cu m
          welded metal structures 639 tons
          bars and rods for use in construction

114   KALININABAD GRAVEL SIZING MILL

Ownership: state
Industry: *Mining industry (building mateirlas)*
Number of Employees: 50.00
CEO: Ivan I.Skuneman
Address: 735147, Repiblic Tadjikistan, Khatlon
        Reg., Kalininabad

Phone: (37744) 2-12-83
Products: crushed stone 22.2 ths cu m
          natural sands 12.8 ths cu m

115   KANIBADAM BAKERY

Ownership: state
Industry: *Food & food processing*
Number of Employees: 159.00
CEO: Ikram A.Abdullaev
Address: 735900, Republic Tadjikistan, Leninabad
Leninabad
        Reg., Kanibadam, Lenin St., 533

Phone: 2-27-94, 2-28-57
Products: bakers' wares

116   KANIBADAM BRAKE EQUIPMENT PLANT

Ownership: state
Industry: *Metal-working industry*
Number of Employees: 1,682.00
CEO: Yusuf Akhmedov
Address: 735900, Republic Tadjikistan,

        Reg., Kanibadam, Lenin St., 257

Phone: 2-22-55, 2-21-75, 2-23-24
Products: metal-working tools
          machining attachments
          consumer goods

117   KANIBADAM CANNERY

Ownership: joint-stock
Industry: Food & food processing
Number of Employees: 730.00
CEO: Gaffar Aliev
Address: 735900, Republic Tadjikistan, Leninabad
          Reg., Kanibadam, Madaniyat St., 19
Leninabad

Phone: 2-45-11
Products: preserved vegetables 4,232 ths tins
          preserved fruit 13,501 ths tins

118   KANIBADAM CLOTHING PRODUCTION COMPANY "KHUSNORO"

Ownership: state
Industry: Clothing industry
Number of Employees: 1,791.00
CEO: Nematzhon U.Umatov
Address: 735907, Republic Tadjikistan,

          Reg., Kanibadam, Aini St., 260

Phone: 2-28-25, 2-27-20
Products: industrial clothing
          dresses, bathrobes 696.7 ths pcs

119   KANIBADAM FERROCONCRETE STRUCTURES PLANT n2

Ownership: state
Industry: Building materials industry
Number of Employees: 100.00
CEO: Ibragim B.Islamov
Leninabad
    Address: 735900, Republic Tadjikistan, Leninabad
          Reg., Kanibadam

Phone: 2-52-91
Products: pre-cast ferroconcrete 4.3 ths cu m
          ferroconcrete articles
          concrete

120   KANIBADAM GINNERY

Ownership: state
Industry: Textile industry
Number of Employees: 951.00
CEO: Israil Z.Obidzhanov
Address: 735903, Republic Tadjikistan,

          Reg., Kanibadam, Aini St., 64

Phone: 2-27-80, 2-58-86
Products: cotton 17,499 tons
          seeds 32,492 tons
          lint 2,641 tons

121   KANIBADAM OILERY and FAT PLANT MILL

Ownership: state
Industry: Food & food processing
Number of Employees:
CEO: Karim Kenzhaev
Address: 735900, Republic Tadjikistan, Leninabad
          Reg., Kanibadam, pos. Dusti
Leninabad

45
Phone: 2-22-59, 2-38-32
Products: vegetable oil 18,457 tons

tons

122   KANIBADAM SPINNING and WEAVING

Ownership: state
Industry: Textile industry
Number of Employees: 1,722.00
CEO: Nemat N.Toshmatov
Address: 735900, Republic Tadjikistan,

          Reg., Kanibadam, Dzerzhinsky St.,

Phone: 2-23-03, 2-23-98
Products: yarn of cotton 4,473 tons
          unbleached fabrics of cotton 3,840

          finished fabrics of cotton

123   KANIBADAM TRAINING and PRODUCTION ENTERPRISE

Ownership: joint-stock
Industry: Consumer goods, furniture, household & cultural goods
Number of Employees:

124   KANSAI NON-METALLIFEROUS and FACING MATERIALS PLANT

Ownership: state
Industry: Building materials industry
Number of Employees: 78.00
CEO: Vladimir I.Kondratov

For additional analytical, business and investment opportunities information,
please contact Global Investment & Business Center, USA
at (202) 546-2103. Fax: (202) 546-3275. E-mail: rusric@erols.com

CEO: President
Leninabad
Address: 735900, Republic Tadjikistan, Leninabad
Dairon

Reg., Kanibadam, Leninabadskaya St.,
35

Phone: 2-48-03
Products: floor coverings of cotton 134 ths sq
m   carpets1.2 ths sq m

mattresses

Address: 735744, Republic Tadjikistan,

Reg., Kairakkum, pos. Chorukh-

Phone: 5-42-74
Products: facing tiles 19.5 ths sq m

125   KHODZHENT GINNERY
Ownership: *state*
Industry: *Textile industry*
Number of Employees: *586.00*
CEO: Mirzoakhmad Ismatov
Address: 735690, Republic Tadjikistan, Leninabad
Reg., Khodzhent Dist., Gafurov
Region,

Phone: 3-35-55, 3-24-75
Products: cotton 11,439 tons
seeds 19,391 tons
lint 2,081 tons

126   KHOROG BAKERY
Ownership: *state*
Industry: *Food & food processing*
Number of Employees:
CEO: President
Address: 736000, Republic Tadjikistan,
Gorno-Badakhshan Autonomous

Khorog

Phone: (377910) 23-57
Products: bakers' wares

127   KHOROG CLOTHING FACTORY n3
and
"KHAIET"

Ownership: *state*
Industry: *Clothing industry*
Number of Employees: *545.00*
CEO: Davlater Khumorikov
Address: 736000, Republic Tadjikistan,
Gorno-Badakhshan Autonomous Region,
Region,

Khorog, Lenin St., 90

Phone: (377910) 37-27
Products: articles of apparel and clothing
accessories

128   KHOROG MEAT PROCESSING PLANT
DAIRY

Ownership: *state*
Industry: *Food & food processing*
Number of Employees:
CEO: Kimatys Ilolov
Address: 736001, Republic Tadjikistan,
Gorno-Badakhshan Autonomous

Khorog, Karalishoyev St., 59

Phone: (377910) 23-09
Products: meat
butter
milk and dairy products

129   KHUDZHAND AUTOMOBILE REPAIR
WORKS n4

Ownership: *state*
Industry: *Automobile industry*
Number of Employees: *86.00*
CEO: Kholikdzhon I.Ibragimov
Leninabad
Address: 735712, Republic Tadjikistan, Leninabad
Reg., Khudzhand, Gagarin St., 62

130   KHUDZHAND BAKERY

Ownership: *state*
Industry: *Food & food processing*
Number of Employees: *344.00*
CEO: Mubin A.Kholmatov
Address: 735700, Republic Tadjikistan,

Reg., Khudzhand, Shark St., 84

Phone: (37922) 4-48-75

Phone: (37922) 6-25-11, 4-35-11
Products: repair of motor vehicles

Products: bakers' wares
confectionery
pasta

131 KHUDZHAND CANNERY

Ownership: *state*
Industry: *Food & food processing*
Number of Employees: *824.00*
CEO: **Vasily A.Averin**
Address: 735700, Republic Tadjikistan, Leninabad
Reg., Khudzhand, Lenin St., 252

Leninabad

Phone: (37922) 6-37-55, 6-32-11
Products: **preserved fruit and vegetables
39,085 ths tins**

132 KHUDZHAND CLOTHING PRODUCTION and TRADE COMPANY NAMED AFTER N.K.KRUPSKAYA

Ownership: *state*
Industry: *Clothing industry*
Number of Employees: *2,650.00*
CEO: **Abdukadyr Kamilov**
Address: 735708, Republic Tadjikistan,

Reg., Khudzhand, K.Tsetkin St., 2

Phone: (37922) 6-42-81, 6-78-34
Products: **dresses, bathrobes 638.2 ths pcs**

133 KHUDZHAND CONTAINER REPAIR WORKS

Ownership: *state*
Industry: *Consumer goods, furniture, household & cultural goods*
Number of Employees: *125.00*
Leninabad
CEO: **Dzhumabai Manadzhanov**
Vostochnaya
Address: 735690, Republic Tadjikistan, Leninabad
Reg., Khodzhent Dist., Gafurov, Chekhov St., 54

Phone: 3-16-44, 3-20-37
Products: **repair of containers**

134 KHUDZHAND DAIRY

Ownership: *state*
Industry: *Food & food processing*
Number of Employees: *225.00*
CEO: **Olim Sh.Akhmedov**
Address: 735714, Republic Tadjikistan,

Reg., Khudzhand, Severo-

promzona

Phone: (37922) 5-41-98, 5-42-47
Products: **butter 613 tons**
milk and dairy products
cheese of sheep's milk

135 KHUDZHAND ELECTRIC POWER TRANSMISSION NETWORK ENTERPRISE

Ownership: *state*
Industry: *Power industry*
Number of Employees: *900.00*
CEO: **Akobir K.Umarov**
Address: 735750, Republic Tadjikistan, Leninabad
Leninabad
Reg., Kairakkum, Lenin St., 113
4

Phone: 5-15, 3-14, 2-17-01
Products: **electric power supply 692 mln kWh**

136 KHUDZHAND FURNITURE PLANT

Ownership: *state*
Industry: *Consumer goods, furniture, household & cultural goods*
Number of Employees: *600.00*
CEO: **Takhir A.Radzhabov**
Address: 735700, Republic Tadjikistan,

Reg., Khudzhand, K. Khudzhandi St.,

Phone: (37922) 6-45-71, 6-46-71
Products: **furniture**

137 KHUDZHAND GAS EQUIPMENT ENGINEERING WORKS

Ownership: *state*
Industry: *Machine building industry*
Number of Employees: *367.00*
CEO: **Yevgeny I.Yantsen**
Address: 735700, Republic Tadjikistan, Leninabad Leninabad

Reg., Khudzhand

Phone: **(37922) 2-75-07, 2-76-07**
Products: **consumer goods**
gaseous hydrocarbons
ths

139 KHUDZHAND PLANT "TORGMASH"

Ownership: *state*
Industry: *Metal-working industry*
Number of Employees: *812.00*
CEO: **Gafarkhon N.Mukhitdinov**
Address: 735700, Republic Tadjikistan, Leninabad Leninabad

Reg., Khudzhand, Suleimani Pr., 4
6

Phone: **(37922) 6-42-92, 6-06-17**
Products: **electric cookers 13,459 pcs**
spoons

141 KHUDZHAND SILK MILL PRODUCTION

Ownership: *state*
Industry: *Textile industry*
Number of Employees: *8,960.00*
CEO: **Takhir Babaev**
Address: 735702, Republic Tadjikistan, Leninabad
Reg., Khudzhand, Lenin St., 238

Leninabad

St.,
Phone: **(37922) 4-34-20, 6-31-27,**
Products: **silk yarn 683.1 tons**
twisted articles
fabrics of silk, unbleached
sq

143 KHUDZHAND TRAINING and PRODUCTION WORKS n2

Ownership: *joint-stock*

138 KHUDZHAND LEASING-BASED ENTERPRISE "EMALIROVSHCHIK"

Ownership: *state*
Industry: *Metal-working industry*
Number of Employees: *484.00*
CEO: **Abdusamad Kh.Samadov**
Address: 735700, Republic Tadjikistan,

Reg., Khudzhand, Pravyi bereg, 3-i Microraion

Phone: **(37922) 2-87-10, 2-89-43, 2-87-12**
Products: **steel enamelled tableware 946.3**

pcs

140 KHUDZHAND SHOE FACTORY n2

Ownership: *state*
Industry: *Footwer & tanning industry*
Number of Employees: *1,835.00*
CEO: **Abdukhamid Samadov**
Address: 735708, Republic Tadjikistan,

Reg., Khudzhand, K.Khudzhandi St.,

Phone: **(37922) 6-06-61, 6-83-61, 6-70-63**
Products: **footwear**

142 KHUDZHAND TRAINING and

ENTERPRISE

Ownership: *joint-stock*
Industry: *Consumer goods, furniture, household & cultural goods*
Number of Employees:
CEO: **Boltukhon Rakhimov**
Address: 735700, Republic Tadjikistan,

Reg., Khudzhand, Chernyakhovsky

19

Phone: **(37922) 6-34-10**
Products: **floor coverings of cotton 35.9 ths**

m   lids 13 mln pcs

144 KOFARNIKHON MECHANICAL REPAIR WORKS

Ownership: *state*

For additional analytical, business and investment opportunities information, please contact Global Investment & Business Center, USA at (202) 546-2103. Fax: (202) 546-3275. E-mail: rusric@erols.com

Industry: *Consumer goods, furniture, household & cultural goods*
Number of Employees: *234.00*
CEO: **Saidvali Abasov** Kofarnikhon
Address: 735700, Republic Tadjikistan, Leninabad Reg., Khudzhand, Engels St., 1

Phone: **(37922) 5-67-32, 5-66-51**
Products: **wadding of cotton 1,916 tons** machines

articles of apparel and clothing accessories

Industry: *Machine building industry*
Number of Employees: *870.00*
CEO: **Boris I.Galich**
Address: 735400, Republic Tadjikistan,

Phone: **6-94**
Products: **auxiliary mechanized devices** electric cranes 344 pcs spare parts for road building

---

145 KOFARNIKHON MECHANICAL WORKS "ZARFSOZ"

Ownership: *state*
Industry: *Metal-working industry*
Number of Employees: *390.00*
CEO: **Anvar Kh.Rakhmonov**
Address: 735400, Republic Tadjikistan, Kofarnikhon

Phone: **2-54-45**
Products: **table and kitchen articles of aluminium 620 tons**   trays of aluminium

articles of alloys

146 KOFARNIKHON RICE PLANT

Ownership: *state*
Industry: *Food & food processing*
Number of Employees: *65.00*
CEO: **D.Sh.Erkabaev**
Address: 735400, Republic Tadjikistan, Kofarnikhon, Privokzalnaya St.

Phone: **2-27-00, 2-87-00**
Products: **meal of rice 14 ths tons**

---

147 KOFARNIKHON TRAINING and PRODUCTION ENTERPRISE

Ownership: *joint-stock*
Industry: *Consumer goods, furniture, household & cultural goods*
Number of Employees: *700.00*
CEO: **President**
Address: 735400, Republic Tadjikistan, Kofarnikhon

Phone: **no data**
Products: **floor coverings of cotton 32 ths sq m** carpets 1,051 ths pcs

ropes of cotton

148 KOLKHOZABAD GRAIN PROCESSING PLANT

Ownership: *state*
Industry: *Food & food processing*
Number of Employees:
CEO: **Madzhid Khafizov**
Address: 735200, Repiblic Tadjikistan, Khatlon Reg., pos. Kolkhozabad

Phone: **(37747) 4-34-90, 4-47-08**
Products: **flour, mixed fodder**

---

149 KUIBYSHEVSK FISHING FARM

Ownership: *state*
Industry: *Fishing & fish processing*
Number of Employees: *130.00*
CEO: **Saidbek Sharipov**
Address: 735120, Repiblic Tadjikistan, Khatlon Reg., pos. Kuibyshevsk

Phone: **37-65**

150 KULYAB BRICK YARD

Ownership: *state*
Industry: *Building materials industry*
Number of Employees: *320.00*
CEO: **President**
Address: 735360, Repiblic Tadjikistan, Khatlon Reg., Kulyab, pos. Tuto

Phone: **(37713) 3-23-21**

For additional analytical, business and investment opportunities information, please contact Global Investment & Business Center, USA at (202) 546-2103. Fax: (202) 546-3275. E-mail: rusric@erols.com

Products: live fish 1,116 tons
smoked fish 19 tons

Products: building bricks 7,886 ths pcs

151 KULYAB CREAMERY
Ownership: *state*
Industry: *Food & food processing*
Number of Employees: *100.00*
CEO: **Abdulkazi Sharifov**
Address: 735360, Repiblic Tadjikistan, Khatlon Reg., Kulyab, Frunze St., 122 234

Phone: **(37713) 2-20-06**
Products: **cotton seed oil 2,738 tons**
oil-cake 12,735 tons
hulls

152 KULYAB DAIRY
Ownership: *state*
Industry: *Food & food processing*
Number of Employees: *160.00*
CEO: **Abdurakhim Kholov**
Address: 735360, Repiblic Tadjikistan, Khatlon Reg., Kulyab, Charm-Gorm-Poen St.,

Phone: **(37713) 3-35-61**
Products: **butter 494 tons**
milk and dairy products
fermented milk products

153 KULYAB EXPERIMENTAL MACHINING ATTACHMENTS PLANT
Ownership: *state*
Industry: *Metal-working industry*
Number of Employees: *389.00*
CEO: **Abdukarim Abdurakhimov**
Address: 735360, Repiblic Tadjikistan, Kulyab-4, Krasnykh partizan St.

Phone: **(37713) 2-25-02, 3-15-88**
Products: **metal-working tools**
consumer goods
parts of agricultural machines

154 KULYAB GINNERY
Ownership: *state*
Industry: *Textile industry*
Number of Employees: *558.00*
CEO: **Mirzo Rasulov**
Address: 735360, Repiblic Tadjikistan, Khatlon Reg., Kulyab, Kirov St., 101

Phone: **(37713) 2-26-07, 2-26-13**
Products: **cotton 6,055 tons**
seeds 10,537 tons
lint 889 tons

155 KULYAB GRAIN PROCESSING PLANT
Ownership: *state*
Industry: *Food & food processing*
Number of Employees: *118.00*
CEO: **Manaim K.Kasymov**
Address: 735360, Repiblic Tadjikistan, Khatlon Reg., Kulyab, Lenin St., 1

Phone: **(37713) 2-47-37, 2-25-09, 2-22-84**
Products: **flour 60 ths tons**
bran 13 ths tons
mixed fodder

156 KULYAB MEAT PROCESSING PLANT
Ownership: *joint-stock*
Industry: *Food & food processing*
Number of Employees: *170.00*
CEO: **Khakim Karimov**
Address: 735360, Repiblic Tadjikistan, Khatlon Reg., Kulyab, Khati-rokh St., 324

Phone: **(37713) 2-27-25, 2-27-23**
Products: **meat, incl. edible offal 1,304 tons**
sausages 2,110 ths rbls 70.9 tons
fat

157 KULYAB OIL EXTRACTING ENTERPRISE n2
Ownership: *state*
Industry: *Oil & gas industry*
Number of Employees:
CEO: **D.Negmatova**
Address: 735360, Repiblic Tadjikistan, Khatlon Reg., Kulyab, Kuibyshev St., 398

Phone: **(37713) 2-32-03, 2-20-58**

158 KULYAB TRAINING and PRODUCTION ENTERPRISE
Ownership: *joint-stock*
Industry: *Consumer goods, furniture, household & cultural goods*
Number of Employees: *202.00*
CEO: **President**
Address: 735360, Repiblic Tadjikistan, Khatlon Reg., Kulyab, Lenin St., 111

Products: crude petroleum oils 7 ths tons
gas condensate
sq m

gaseous hydrocarbons

Phone: (37713) 2-33-07
Products: floor coverings of cotton 54 ths

pile carpets

ropes of cotton

159 KURGAN-TYUBE BAKERY

Ownership: *state*
Industry: *Food & food processing*
Number of Employees:
CEO: A. Kayumov
Address: 735140, Repiblic Tadjikistan, Khatlon
Reg., Kurgan-Tyube, Sverdlov St., 10

Phone: (37744) 2-26-24, 2-25-24
Products: bakers' wares
2,566

160 KURGAN-TYUBE CANNERY

Ownership: *state*
Industry: *Food & food processing*
Number of Employees: 290.00
CEO: M I.Mugadov
Address: 735140, Repiblic Tadjikistan, Khatlon
Reg., Kurgan-Tyube, Dzhalilov St., 15

Phone: (37744) 2-27-65
Products: preserved fruit and vegetables

ths tins

161 KURGAN-TYUBE CLOTHING FACTORY

Ownership: *state*
Industry: *Clothing industry*
Number of Employees: 1,100.00
CEO: Subkhon K.Rakhimov
Address: 735140, Repiblic Tadjikistan, Khatlon
Reg., Kurgan-Tyube, Gafurov St., 7/9

Phone: (37744) 2-20-54
Products: trousers
skirts
shorts

162 KURGAN-TYUBE CONFECTIONERY FACTORY "LAZZAT"

Ownership: *state*
Industry: *Food & food processing*
Number of Employees: 40.00
CEO: Abdurakhmon Talbonov
Address: 735147, Repiblic Tadjikistan, Khatlon
Reg., Kurgan-Tyube, Aini St., 22

Phone: (37744) 2-21-43, 2-34-06
Products: confectionery 1,223 tons

163 KURGAN-TYUBE COTTON SPINNING MILL

Ownership: *state*
Industry: *Textile industry*
Number of Employees:
CEO: Akhmad Makhkamov
Address: 735140, Repiblic Tadjikistan, Khatlon
Reg., Kurgan-Tyube, Aini St., 2-a

Phone: (37744) 2-73-64
Products: yarn of cotton

164 KURGAN-TYUBE EXPERIMENTAL FURSKIN FACTORY "MUINNA"

Ownership: *state*
Industry: *Clothing industry*
Number of Employees: 102.00
CEO: President
Address: 735140, Repiblic Tadjikistan, Khatlon
Reg., Kurgan-Tyube

Phone: no data
Products: sheepskins 843 ths sq dm
men's anoraks 2,230 pcs
short coats

165 KURGAN-TYUBE FOLK DECORATIVE HANDICRAFT FACTORY

Ownership: *state*
Industry: *Textile industry*
Number of Employees:
CEO: President
Address: 735140, Repiblic Tadjikistan, Khatlon

166 KURGAN-TYUBE GINNERY

Ownership: *state*
Industry: *Textile industry*
Number of Employees:
CEO: Tavarali Davlyatov
Address: 735140, Repiblic Tadjikistan, Khatlon
Reg., Kurgan-Tyube, Aini St., 39

Reg., Kurgan-Tyube, Abu-Ali ibn Sin St.

Phone: no data
Products: articles of apparel
hosiery 2.4 ths pcs
knitwear articles

Phone: (37744) 2-32-54
Products: cotton

167 KURGAN-TYUBE MEAT PROCESSING PLANT and DAIRY

Ownership: *state*
Industry: *Food & food processing*
Number of Employees: *156.00*
CEO: Vadim S.Tsoi
Address: 735140, Repiblic Tadjikistan, Khatlon Reg., Kurgan-Tyube, Kosmonavtov St., 1

Phone: (37744) 2-30-52
Products: meat, incl. edible offal
building
sausages 90 tons
ferrous metals
semi-prepared products

168 KURGAN-TYUBE MECHANICAL REPAIR WORKS

Ownership: *state*
Industry: *Machine building industry*
Number of Employees: *60.00*
CEO: Yury D.Alimbetov
Address: 735140, Repiblic Tadjikistan, Khatlon Reg., Kurgan-Tyube, Lenin St., 152

Phone: (37744) 2-25-25
Products: metal structures
repair and maintenance of road

machinery and spare parts ucts of

169 KURGAN-TYUBE NON-ALCOHOLIC BEVERAGES and MINERAL WATER PLANT

Ownership: *state*
Industry: *Food & food processing*
Number of Employees: *100.00*
CEO: Nasreddin Ibragimov
Address: 735140, Repiblic Tadjikistan, Khatlon Reg., Kurgan-Tyube, Nekrasov St., 3

Phone: (37744) 2-21-06
Products: mineral waters 19 ths bottles
beer
wine

170 KURGAN-TYUBE OIL EXTRACTING ENTERPRISE n1

Ownership: *state*
Industry: *Oil & gas industry*
Number of Employees:
CEO: R. T.Sharafutdinov
Address: 735147, Repiblic Tadjikistan, Khatlon Reg., Kalininabad

Phone: 2-13-90, 2-40-55
Products: crude petroleum oils 19 ths tons
gaseous hydrocarbons 1 mln cu m

171 KURGAN-TYUBE OILERY

Ownership: *state*
Industry: *Food & food processing*
Number of Employees: *220.00*
CEO: Dzhamildin Tolibov
Address: 735140, Repiblic Tadjikistan, Khatlon Reg., Kurgan-Tyube, Aini St., 37

Phone: (37744) 2-29-57, 2-29-54
Products: cotton oil 10,657 tons

172 KURGAN-TYUBE TRANSFORMER PLANT

Ownership: *state*
Industry: *Electrical engineering*
Number of Employees: *583.00*
CEO: Rakhmatullo Kalandarov
Address: 735140, Repiblic Tadjikistan, Khatlon Reg., Kurgan-Tyube, Gafurov St., 7

Phone: (37744) 2-22-16
Products: high-voltage apparatus 1,705 pcs
electric transformers 45 ths pcs
power transformers 489 ths kWh

For additional analytical, business and investment opportunities information,
please contact Global Investment & Business Center, USA
at (202) 546-2103. Fax: (202) 546-3275. E-mail: rusric@erols.com

173 LEASE-HOLDER COLLECTIVE "VREMYA"

Ownership: *state*
Industry: *Mining industry (building mateirlas)*
Number of Employees: *130.00*
CEO: Amon Eshboyev
Address: 735750, Republic Tadjikistan, Leninabad
Leninabad

Reg., Kairakkum

Phone: no data
Products: crushed stone 186 ths cu m
natural sands 156 ths cu m
blocks of stone

174 LEASING-BASED ENTERPRISE "SHARBAT"

Ownership: *state*
Industry: *Food & food processing*
Number of Employees: *339.00*
CEO: Mavlon Mirzoyev
Address: 735500, Republic Tadjikistan,

Reg., Pendzhikent, Lenin St., 6

Phone: (37775) 2-33-50
Products: jam 6,379 ths rbls 202 ths tins
fruit juices
grape juice

175 LENINABAD RARE METALS PLANT

Ownership: *state*
Industry: *Metallurgy*
Number of Employees: *720.00*
CEO: Makhmudzhon Khalikov
Address: 735744, Republic Tadjikistan, Leninabad
Reg., Kairakkum Dist., pos.
Chorukh-Dairon, Lenin St., 108

Phone: 5-65-91
Products: alloys

176 LENINSKY NON-METALLIFEROUS MATERIALS PLANT

Ownership: *joint-stock*
Industry: *Building materials industry*
Number of Employees: *10.00*
CEO: President
Address: 735100, Republic Tadjikistan, pos.
Leninsky

Phone: no data
Products: crushed stone 80 ths cu m
natural sands 84.6 ths cu m
ferroconcrete articles 868 cu m

177 MATCHINSKY RURAL CONSTRUCTION PLANT

Ownership: *state*
Industry: *Building materials industry*
Number of Employees: *113.00*
CEO: Khadzhi M.Mukhamadiev
Address: 735800, Republic Tadjikistan, Leninabad
Reg., Matchinsky Dist., pos. Buston

Phone: 5-65-25
Products: pre-cast ferroconcrete

equipment

178 MECHANICAL WORKS "KHLOPKOZAPCHAST"

Ownership: *state*
Industry: *Machine building industry*
Number of Employees:
CEO: President
Address: 735400, Republic Tadjikistan,
Kofarnikhon, Shestopalov St., 1

Phone: 2-30-64
Products: wire 991 tons
repair of electric motors
non-standard machinery and

179 MINE "FAN-YAGNOB"

Ownership: *state*
Industry: *Coal mining & peat industry*
Number of Employees:
CEO: Zakhid M.Fazylov
Address: 735520, Republic Tadjikistan, Leninabad
Leninabad

Reg., Aini Dist., pos. Zeravshan

180 MINING ENTERPRISE "TADZHIKSKOYE"

Ownership: *state*
Industry: *Coal mining & peat industry*
Number of Employees: *10.00*
CEO: Azimboi Azizov
Address: 735930, Republic Tadjikistan,

Reg., Isfara Dist., pos. Shurab

Phone: 21-90
Products: coal 29 ths tons

**181   MOSKOVSKY FERROCONCRETE
        STRUCTURES PLANT n1**

Ownership: *state*
Industry: *Building materials industry*
Number of Employees:
CEO: Amrokhon Saidov
Address: 735370, Repiblic Tadjikistan, Khatlon
15
        Reg., Moskovsky Dist., kishlak Rossiya

Phone: 2-21-63, 2-21-60
Products: pre-cast ferroconcrete
          structural components for house
          construction   crushed stone

**183   NAU BUILDING MATERIALS and
        STRUCTURES PLANT**

Ownership: *joint-stock*
Industry: *Building materials industry*
Number of Employees:
CEO: Anvar Kh.Usmanov
Leninabad
    Address: 735830, Republic Tadjikistan, Leninabad
             Reg., pos. Nau, Saidov St., 42

Phone: 2-35-50
Products: pre-cast ferroconcrete
          crushed stone 34.2 ths cu m
          natural sands

185   NAU GRAIN PROCESSING PLANT
Ownership: *state*
Industry: *Food & food processing*
Number of Employees: 498.00
CEO: Makhsud S.Saliev
Address: 735830, Republic Tadjikistan, Leninabad
         Reg., pos. Nau
Leninabad

Phone: 2-24-16
Products: wheat flour 132 ths tons
          bran 35 ths tons
          mixed fodder

187   NEFTEABAD OILFIELD

Ownership: *state*

Phone: 37-49, 41-61
Products: coal 177.7 ths tons

182   MOSKOVSKY GINNERY

Ownership: *state*
Industry: *Textile industry*
Number of Employees: 460.00
CEO: Sikandor Sakhibnazarov
Address: 735370, Repiblic Tadjikistan, Khatlon
         Reg., pos. Moskovsky, K.Marks St.,

Phone: 2-20-12
Products: cotton 4,433 tons
          seeds 8,184 tons
          lint 853 tons

184   NAU GINNERY

Ownership: *state*
Industry: *Textile industry*
Number of Employees: 387.00
CEO: Abdullo F.Ubaidullaev
Address: 735830, Republic Tadjikistan,

         Reg., pos. Nau, Volkov St., 22

Phone: 2-28-38
Products: cotton 10,289 tons
          seeds 18,670 tons
          lint 1,747 tons

186   NAU MECHANIZED QUARRY

Ownership: *state*
Industry: *Mining industry (building
               mateirlas)*
Number of Employees: 92.00
CEO: Abdukhalil A.Abdusattarov
Address: 735830, Republic Tadjikistan,

         Reg., pos. Nau, Volkov St., 52

Phone: 2-24-01
Products: crushed stone 34 ths cu m
          gravel 32.3 ths cu m
          natural sands

**188   NON-ALCOHOLIC BEVERAGES and
        MINERAL WATER PLANT**

Industry: *Oil & gas industry*
Number of Employees: 362.00
CEO: A. A.Kakharov
Address: 735920, Republic Tadjikistan, Leninabad
Reg., Isfara, pos. Nefteabad
Leninabad

Phone: 2-52-42, 2-52-44
Products: crude petroleum oils 38 ths tons
gas condensate
gaseous hydrocarbons

Ownership: *state*
Industry: *Food & food processing*
Number of Employees: 102.00
CEO: Uchkun T.Yusupov
Address: 735690, Republic Tadjikistan,

Reg., Khodzhent Dist., Gafurov,
Vokzalnaya St., 13

Phone: 3-26-48, 3-25-48
Products: beer 120 ths dal
non-alcoholic beverages 46 ths dal
mineral waters

189 NUREK CLOTHING FACTORY

Ownership: *state*
Industry: *Clothing industry*
Number of Employees: 20.00
CEO: Rakhmatullo Asoyev
Address: 735300, Republic Tadjikistan, Nurek, Aini
St., 1

Phone: (37738) 2-28-58, 2-21-81
Products: shirts of cotton 633.3 ths pcs

for use in construction

equipment

190 NUREK EXPERIMENTAL MECHANICAL WORKS

Ownership: *state*
Industry: *Machine building industry*
Number of Employees: 10.00
CEO: Khamrokul Sh.Erov
Address: 735300, Republic Tadjikistan, Nurek,
Promzona

Phone: (37738) 2-28-29, 2-28-39, 2-28-27
Products: spare parts for road building
machines   metal structures

194 tons
non-standard machinery and

191 NUREK HYDROELECTRIC STATION

Ownership: *state*
Industry: *Power industry*
Number of Employees:
CEO: Abdullo E.Erov
Address: 735300, Republic Tadjikistan, Nurek,
Lenin St., 14

Phone: (37738) 2-25-36, 2-14-11
Products: electric power supply 11,541 mln kWh

192 OIL ASPHALT PLANT

Ownership: *state*
Industry: *Oil refining & gas processing*
Number of Employees: 150.00
CEO: President
Address: 735202, Repiblic Tadjikistan, Khatlon
Reg., Kolkhozabad Dist., pos. Isoeva

Phone: 4-30-00, 4-30-03
Products: oil asphalt

193 OKTYABRSKY COTTON PROCESSING MILL

Ownership: *state*
Industry: *Textile industry*
Number of Employees:
CEO: I.K.Safarov
Leninabad
Address: 735162, Repiblic Tadjikistan, Khatlon
Reg., pos. Oktyabrsky

Phone: 2-13-74

194 PENDZHIKENT BRICK YARD

Ownership: *state*
Industry: *Building materials industry*
Number of Employees: 133.00
CEO: K. Shodiev
Address: 735500, Republic Tadjikistan,

Reg., Pendzhikent

Phone: (37775) 2-24-36, 2-39-02
Products: wall materials 7,720 ths pcs

Products: cotton

195   PENDZHIKENT FERMENTED TOBACCO PLANT
PLANT

Ownership: *joint-stock*
Industry: *Tobacco industry*
Number of Employees: *500.00*
CEO: **Akhmat Yarboyev**
Leninabad
   Address: 735500, Republic Tadjikistan, Leninabad
   Reg., Pendzhikent, Khudoiberdyev St., 3

Phone: **(37775) 2-22-90**
Products: **unmanufactured tobacco 6,559 tons**

196   PENDZHIKENT FISH PROCESSING

Ownership: *state*
Industry: *Fishing & fish processing*
Number of Employees: *32.00*
CEO: **Kobir Eshondzhanov**
Address: 735500, Republic Tadjikistan,

   Reg., Pendzhikent

Phone: **(37775) 2-39-58**
Products: **live fish 115.4 tons**
   fish products

197   PENDZHIKENT MEAT PROCESSING PLANT and DAIRY

Ownership: *state*
Industry: *Food & food processing*
Number of Employees: *86.00*
CEO: **Atkhamdzhon Razykov**
Leninabad
   Address: 735500, Republic Tadjikistan, Leninabad
8
   Reg., Pendzhikent, Tereshkova St., 28

Phone: **(37775) 2-34-44, 2-37-73**
Products: **meat, incl. edible offal 184.8 tons**
   sausages 25.7 tons
   fat

198   PLANT "ALMOS"

Ownership: *state*
Industry: *Radio-electronic industry*
Number of Employees: *485.00*
CEO: **Abdulakhat L.Kadyrov**
Address: 735708, Republic Tadjikistan,

   Reg., Khudzhand, K.Khudzhandi St.,

Phone: **(37922) 4-00-74**
Products: **crystal vibrators 1,000 ths pcs**
   quartz filters 19 ths pcs
   television receivers

199   PLANT "ETALON"
Ownership: *state*
Industry: *Medical equipment industry*
Number of Employees: *177.00*
CEO: **Yury V.Gritsaev**
   Address: 735716, Republic Tadjikistan, Leninabad
Leninabad
   Reg., Khudzhand, Syrdarya St., 13-a

Phone: **(37922) 5-67-55, 2-16-74, 2-18-83**
Products: **instruments and apparatus**
   repair of instrumentation

200   PLANT "LENINABADSELMASH"
Ownership: *state*
Industry: *Machine building industry*
Number of Employees: *616.00*
CEO: **Maikham Dodobaev**
Address: 735830, Republic Tadjikistan,

   Reg., pos. Nau, Zavodskaya St., 66

Phone: **2-26-28, 2-26-29, 2-25-28**
Products: **agricultural machines**

201   PLANT "TADZHIKKHIMSELKHOZMASH"
Ownership: *state*
Industry: *Machine building industry*
Number of Employees: *470.00*
CEO: **Rustam M.Khakimov**
   Address: 735830, Republic Tadjikistan, Leninabad
Dushanbe,

202   PRINT-SHOP
Ownership: *joint-stock*
Industry: *Publishing & printing*
Number of Employees: *32.00*
CEO: **Khalik I.Ibragimov**
Address: 734027, Republic Tadjikistan,

Reg., Kanibadam Dist., pos. Makhram,
Leninabadskaya St., 10

Phone: 2-22-64
Products: agricultural equipment

203 PRINTING PRODUCTION COMPANY COMPANY

Ownership: *state*
Industry: *Publishing & printing*
Number of Employees:
CEO: **President**
Address: 735360, Repiblic Tadjikistan, Khatlon
Reg., Kulyab, Dzhumaev St., 26

Dushanbe,
Phone: no data
Products: newspapers 2,400 ths copies
business forms 1,263 ths copies

1,293

205 PRODUCTION COMPANY "KHODZHENTATLAS"

Ownership: *state*
Industry: *Textile industry*
Number of Employees: *1,259.00*
CEO: **Gafar Mukhamedov**
Dushanbe,
Address: 735700, Republic Tadjikistan, Leninabad
Reg., Khudzhand-17, Kosmonavtov St.,
93

Phone: (37922) 6-30-31, 2-65-75
Products: fabrics of silk 838.9 ths m
fabrics of man-made filaments
fabrics of cotton

207 PRODUCTION COMPANY "PAMIRKVARTSSAMOTSVETY"

Ownership: *state*
Industry: *Mining industry (building mateirlas)*
Number of Employees: *679.00*
CEO: **Zurmakhmad Erov**
Dushanbe,
Address: 734013, Republic Tadjikistan, Dushanbe,
Lakhuti St., 16

Phone: (3772) 27-23-69, 27-24-59
Products: consumer goods
semi-precious stones
blocks of marble

Karamov St., 205

Phone: (3772) 36-22-37
Products: printed matter

204 PROCUREMENT PRODUCTION

"TADZHIKVTORTSVETMET"

Ownership: *state*
Industry: *Scrap & waste processing industry*
Number of Employees: *21.00*
CEO: **Akhat Akramov**
Address: 734060, Republic Tadjikistan,

Dzh.Rasulov Ave., 8

Phone: (3772) 31-14-31, 31-14-01
Products: non-ferrous waste and scrap

tons

206 PRODUCTION COMPANY "PAMIR"

Ownership: *state*
Industry: *Machine building industry*
Number of Employees: *822.00*
CEO: **Vladimir G.Lesin**
Address: 734036, Republic Tadjikistan,

40 let Oktyabrya St., 343

Phone: (3772) 31-26-27, 31-22-87, 31-06-23
Products: refrigerators 61 ths pcs
spare parts for refrigerators
refrigerating plants

208 PRODUCTION COMPANY "TADZHIKENERGOLEGPROM"

Ownership: *state*
Industry: *Machine building industry*
Number of Employees: *27.00*
CEO: **Mikhail S.Zubko**
Address: 734013, Republic Tadjikistan,

P.Lumumba St., 41

Phone: (3772) 22-56-72
Products: repair of equipment

**For additional analytical, business and investment opportunities information,
please contact Global Investment & Business Center, USA
at (202) 546-2103. Fax: (202) 546-3275. E-mail: rusric@erols.com**

209 PRODUCTION COMPANY "TADZHIKGIDROAGREGAT"

Ownership: *state*
Industry: *Machine building industry*
Number of Employees: *2,478.00*
CEO: **Akbar M.Fayazov**
Address: 734013, Republic Tadjikistan, Dushanbe, Druzhby narodov Ave., 47

Phone: **(3772) 27-16-23, 23-08-04**
Products: **hydraulic drives and automated devices**
Products:

cast articles of pig iron

211 PRODUCTION COMPANY "TADZHIKNEFT"

Ownership: *state*
Industry: *Oil & gas industry*
Number of Employees: *1,131.00*
CEO: **Nabi Malikov**
Address: 734018, Republic Tadjikistan, Dushanbe, Mushfiki St., 77
Dushanbe,

Phone: **(3772) 33-60-96**
Products: **crude petroleum oils 56.6 ths tons**
gas condensate 4.8 ths tons
gaseous hydrocarbons
conv.

asbestos-cement

213 PRODUCTION COMPANY "TADZHIKZOLOTO"

Ownership: *state*
Industry: *Ore mining industry*
Number of Employees: *1,564.00*
CEO: **Abdunumon A.Abdurazakov**
Address: 734018, Republic Tadjikistan, Dushanbe,
Dushanbe,

Mushfiki St., 77

Phone: **(3772) 33-57-53, 33-44-19, 33-43-56**
Products: **gold**

215 PROLETARSK CENTRAL ELECTROMECHANICAL WORKSHOP

Ownership: *state*
Industry: *Machine building industry*

210 PRODUCTION COMPANY "TADZHIKKHIMPROM"

Ownership: *state*
Industry: *Chemical, pharmaceutical & micribiology industry*
Number of Employees:
CEO: **M.S.Umedov**
Address: 735310, Repiblic Tadjikistan, Khatlon Reg., pos. Yavan, pos. Planernyi

Phone: **(37741) 4-16-71, 2-26-54**
spare parts for hydraulic drives
liquid chlorine 16 ths tons
caustic soda 16 ths tons
calcium chloride

212 PRODUCTION COMPANY "TADZHIKTSEMENT"

Ownership: *state*
Industry: *Building materials industry*
Number of Employees: *845.00*
CEO: **Boris I.Sevastyanov**
Address: 734008, Republic Tadjikistan,

Rudaki Ave., 205

Phone: **(3772) 24-24-58, 24-23-01**
Products: **cement 446.8 ths tons**
pipes of asbestos-cement 1,097.7

km   corrugated sheets of

214 PRODUCTION COOPERATIVE "PISHCHEVIK"

Ownership: *state*
Industry: *Food & food processing*
Number of Employees: *285.00*
CEO: **Orif Raupov**
Address: 734024, Republic Tadjikistan,

Akhmadi Donish St., 55

Phone: **(3772) 23-06-61**
Products: **bakers' wares**
ground rusks 16 tons
corn sticks

216 PROLETARSK GINNERY

Ownership: *state*
Industry: *Textile industry*
Number of Employees: *572.00*

Number of Employees: *249.00*
CEO: **Boris B.Kiyamov**
Leninabad
Address: 735820, Republic Tadjikistan, Leninabad
St., 39

Reg., pos. Proletarsk, Zavodskaya St., 11

Phone: **2-13-54, 2-25-85, 2-13-10**
Products: **cast articles of steel 280 tons**
cast articles of pig iron
spare parts

217 PROLETARSK ORE CONCENTRATING MILL

Ownership: *state*
Industry: *Building materials industry*
Number of Employees: *839.00*
CEO: **Khodzha Khaitov**
Address: 735820, Republic Tadjikistan, Leninabad
Dushanbe,

Reg., pos. Proletarsk, Sovetskaya St., 1

Phone: **2-25-41, 2-19-34**
Products: **concentrated sand 226 ths tons**
ceramic wall tiles 268 sq m
building bricks

219 PUBLISHING HOUSE

Ownership: *state*
Industry: *Publishing & printing*
Number of Employees: *353.00*
CEO: **Vakhid A.Ibragimov**
Address: 734018, Republic Tadjikistan, Dushanbe,
Pravdy Ave., 16
let

Phone: **(3772) 33-32-88, 33-24-16**
Products: **newspapers 78 mln copies**
magazines 18 mln sheets

221 SHAARTUZ CREAMERY

Ownership: *state*
Industry: *Food & food processing*
Number of Employees:
CEO: **Yusuf Abdusamadov**
Address: 735180, Repiblic Tadjikistan, Khatlon
Reg., Shaartuz Dist., pos. Gidrostroitelei

Phone: **2-29-12**
Products: **milk and dairy products**

223 SHAKHRISTAN CREAMERY

CEO: **Khaimamad Yarmatov**
Address: 735820, Republic Tadjikistan,

Reg., pos. Proletarsk, Yubileinaya

Phone: **2-13-47, 2-20-40**
Products: **cotton 15,985 tons**
lint 2,198 tons
seeds

218 PROSTHETIC and ORTHOPAEDIC APPLIANCES PLANT

Ownership: *state*
Industry: *Medical equipment industry*
Number of Employees: *63.00*
CEO: **President**
Address: 734029, Republic Tadjikistan,

Karateginskaya St., 1

Phone: **(3772) 25-04-21**
Products: **orthopaedic footwear**
prosthetic appliances

220 PYANDZH GINNERY

Ownership: *state*
Industry: *Textile industry*
Number of Employees:
CEO: **Zokir Sharipov**
Address: 735330, Repiblic Tadjikistan, Khatlon
Reg., Vose Dist., pos. Pyandzh, 50

Pogranvoisk St., 36

Phone: **25-85, 28-89**
Products: **cotton**

222 SHAARTUZ GINNERY

Ownership: *state*
Industry: *Textile industry*
Number of Employees: *20.00*
CEO: **Abdulmadchid Kakhorov**
Address: 735180, Repiblic Tadjikistan, Khatlon
Reg., pos. Shaartuz, Kirov St., 7

Phone: **2-18-61, 2-28-48**
Products: **cotton**

224 SHURAB MECHANICAL WORKS "FILIZ"

Ownership: *state*
Industry: *Food & food processing*
Number of Employees: *27.00*
CEO: **Karim Gaibullaev**
Address: 735700, Republic Tadjikistan, Leninabad

Khudzhand, pos. Shakhristan St., 5

Phone: **(37922) 2-62-31**
Products: **butter 205.4 tons**
milk and dairy products

Ownership: *state*
Industry: *Metal-working industry*
Number of Employees: *173.00*
CEO: **Subkhon N.Narziev**
Address: 735930, Republic Tadjikistan,

Reg., Isfara Dist., pos. Shurab, Mira

Phone: **2-45-01**
Products: **table and kitchen articles of aluminium 238.2 ths pcs**

225   SMALL ENTERPRISE "BETON"

Ownership: *joint-stock*
Industry: *Building materials industry*
Number of Employees:
CEO: **Khudzhali Khusravov**
Address: 736000, Republic Tadjikistan, Gorno-Badakhshan Autonomous Region, Khorog, Michurin St., 58

Phone: **(377910) 29-03**
Products: **pre-cast ferroconcrete**

226   SOUTHERN ELECTRIC POWER TRANSMISSION NETWORK

Ownership: *state*
Industry: *Power industry*
Number of Employees: *940.00*
CEO: **U. Ubaidulaev**
Address: 735140, Repiblic Tadjikistan, Khatlon Reg., Kurgan-Tyube, Aini St., 80

Phone: **(37744) 2-35-74**
Products: **electric power supply**

227   STATE FARM-PLANT "EFIRONOS"

Ownership: *state*
Industry: *Chemical, pharmaceutical & micribiology industry*
Number of Employees: *20.00*
CEO: **I.Khatamov**
Address: 735000, Republic Tadjikistan, Dushanbe,

Tursunzade, kolkhoz XX parts'ezda

Phone: **4-63**
Products: **geranium oil kWh**

peppermint

228   STATE JOINT-STOCK HOLDING COMPANY "BARKI TOCHIK"

Ownership: *state*
Industry: *Power industry*
Number of Employees:
CEO: **Bakhrom Sirozhev**
Address: 734026, Republic Tadjikistan,

Samoni St., 64

Phone: **(3772) 35-87-38, 24-53-16**
Products: **electric power supply 16,805 mln**

heating 3,648 ths Gcal

229   TADJIK ALUMINIUM WORKS

Ownership: *state*
Industry: *Metallurgy*
Number of Employees: *20.00*
CEO: **Mikhail F.Sinani**
Address: 735014, Republic Tadjikistan, Tursunzade, p/o Seshanbe Leninabad

Phone: **(37730) 2-23-86, 2-23-92**
Products: **primary aluminium 345 ths tons**
anode blocks 240 ths tons

230   TADJIK PRODUCTION COMPANY "SVETOTEKHNIKA"

Ownership: *state*
Industry: *Electrical engineering*
Number of Employees: *1,308.00*
CEO: **Dzhabar Rasulov**
Address: 735926, Republic Tadjikistan,

Reg., Isfara Dist., pos. Kim

Phone: **3-34-28, 2-20-92**
Products: **lighting engineering equipment**

non-standard machinery and equipment
64.5 tons

lighting fixtures 1,185 ths pcs
low-voltage apparatus

231 TAKOB FLUORSPAR WORKS
Ownership: *state*
Industry: *Mining industry (building mateirlas)*
Number of Employees: *414.00*
CEO: Seilkhon M.Barikov
Address: 734046, Republic Tadjikistan, Dushanbe, Dushanbe,

pos. Takob

Phone: 24-96, 1-27
Products: fluorspar

232 TRAINING and PRODUCTION WORKS n1
Ownership: *joint-stock*
Industry: *Consumer goods, furniture, household & cultural goods*
Number of Employees: *273.00*
CEO: President
Address: 734036, Republic Tadjikistan,

40 let Oktyabrya St., 349

Phone: (3772) 31-08-13
Products: bed-linen 82 ths pcs
articles of feather and down

233 TRAINING and PRODUCTION WORKS n3
Ownership: *joint-stock*
Industry: *Consumer goods, furniture, household & cultural goods*
Number of Employees: *148.00*
CEO: President
Address: 734013, Republic Tadjikistan, Dushanbe, Leninabad

Druzhby narodov Ave., 72

Phone: (3772) 27-17-54, 27-17-56
Products: anodized articles
saddlery and harness articles
textile haberdashery

234 TRAINING and PRODUCTION WORKS n4
Ownership: *joint-stock*
Industry: *Consumer goods, furniture, household & cultural goods*
Number of Employees: *624.00*
CEO: Tolib Dodobaev
Address: 735690, Republic Tadjikistan,

Reg., Khodzhent Dist., Gafurov, F.Akhmedov St., 8

Phone: 4-25-32
Products: pile carpets 10,810 sq m
floor coverings of cotton
fabrics of silk

235 TRAINING and PRODUCTION WORKS n5
Ownership: *joint-stock*
Industry: *Consumer goods, furniture, household & cultural goods*
Number of Employees: *115.00*
CEO: President
Address: 734029, Republic Tadjikistan, Dushanbe, Aini Shosse, 5-i km

Phone: (3772) 25-29-67
Products: wadding 2,166 tons
apparel wadding 49 tons

236 TURSUNZADE GINNERY
Ownership: *state*
Industry: *Textile industry*
Number of Employees: *700.00*
CEO: Khasan Manonov
Address: 735000, Republic Tadjikistan, Tursunzade, Khlopkovaya St., 1

Phone: (37730) 2-26-79
Products: cotton 16,011 tons
seeds 29,388 tons
lint 2,833 tons

237 TURSUNZADE PORCELAIN WORKS
Ownership: *state*
Industry: *Building materials industry*
Number of Employees: *30.00*
CEO: Sh. M.Abdusattorov
Address: 735003, Republic Tadjikistan, Tursunzade, Lomonosov St.

Phone: (37730) 2-32-32, 2-21-79, 2-15-34
Products: tableware of porcelain

238 TURSUNZADE PRINT-SHOP
Ownership: *state*
Industry: *Publishing & printing*
Number of Employees: *30.00*
CEO: President
Address: 735000, Republic Tadjikistan, Tursunzade, Lomonosov St., 140

Phone: no data
Products: newspapers
business forms

239 URA-TYUBE BAKERY

Ownership: *state*
Industry: *Food & food processing*
Number of Employees: *189.00*
CEO: Kuli M.Marufov
Address: 735610, Republic Tadjikistan, Leninabad
Leninabad
          Reg., Ura-Tyube, Pushkin St., 13

Phone: 2-19-35
Products: bakers' wares 3,920 tons

240 URA-TYUBE BRICK YARD

Ownership: *state*
Industry: *Building materials industry*
Number of Employees: *170.00*
CEO: Kamil Ayubov
Address: 735610, Republic Tadjikistan,

          Reg., Ura-Tyube

Phone: 2-24-67
Products: building bricks 10,360 ths pcs

241 URA-TYUBE CANNERY

Ownership: *state*
Industry: *Food & food processing*
Number of Employees: *236.00*
CEO: Nabidzhon Naimov
Address: 735610, Republic Tadjikistan, Leninabad
Leninabad
          Reg., Ura-Tyube Dist., pos. Yakkaton, 8

Phone: 2-32-35, 2-51-04
Products: apple puree
          peach puree 69 ths tins
          tomato paste

242 URA-TYUBE CREAMERY

Ownership: *state*
Industry: *Food & food processing*
Number of Employees: *94.00*
CEO: Khabibullo Kh.Abdulloyev
Address: 735610, Republic Tadjikistan,

          Reg., Ura-Tyube, Lenin St., 271

Phone: 2-62-31, 2-15-53, 2-35-00
Products: butter 408 tons
          milk and dairy products
          milk products

243 URA-TYUBE FACTORY "NEKSOZ"

Ownership: *joint-stock*
Industry: *Consumer goods, furniture,
               household & cultural goods*
Number of Employees: *721.00*
CEO: Inom Khatamov
Address: 735610, Republic Tadjikistan, Leninabad
Leninabad
          Reg., Ura-Tyube, Gagarin St., 38

Phone: 2-12-11
Products: articles of plastics
          baby linen
          pile carpets

244 URA-TYUBE KNITTED OUTERWEAR FACTORY

Ownership: *joint-stock*
Industry: *Textile industry*
Number of Employees: *2,558.00*
CEO: Uidzhiboi Obidov
Address: 735610, Republic Tadjikistan,

          Reg., Ura-Tyube, Fabrichnaya St., 1

Phone: 2-22-72, 2-23-22
Products: knitwear

245 URA-TYUBE TRAINING and PRODUCTION ENTERPRISE

Ownership: *joint-stock*
Industry: *Consumer goods, furniture,
               household & cultural goods*
Number of Employees:
Leninabad
CEO: A. M.Kasymov

246 URA-TYUBE WINE PLANT

Ownership: *state*
Industry: *Food & food processing*
Number of Employees: *136.00*
CEO: Abduvakhkhob K.Kayumov
Address: 735610, Republic Tadjikistan,

          Reg., Ura-Tyube, Lenin St., 22

Address: 735610, Republic Tadjikistan, Leninabad Reg., Ura-Tyube

Phone: no data
Products: floor coverings of cotton73.7 ths sq m

lids

Phone: 2-22-82, 2-32-46, 2-10-15
Products: wine 322 ths dal
crude alcohol 1,369.4 dal
carpets grape must

247 UYALP GINNERY

Ownership: *state*
Industry: *Textile industry*
Number of Employees:
CEO: E. A.Gulov
Address: 735130, Repiblic Tadjikistan, Khatlon Reg., Iliychevsky Dist., pos. Uyalp

Phone: 2-12-84, 2-12-87
Products: cotton

248 VAKHSH HYDROELECTRIC STATION CASCADE

Ownership: *state*
Industry: *Power industry*
Number of Employees: 150.00
CEO: T.Sabirov
Address: 735147, Repiblic Tadjikistan, Khatlon Reg., Kalininabad

Phone: (37744) 7-32-50, 2-23-92, 2-23-58
Products: electric power supply

249 VAKHSH NITROGENOUS FERTILIZER PLANT

Ownership: *state*
Industry: *Chemical, pharmaceutical & micribiology industry*
Number of Employees: 1,345.00
CEO: A. Ganiev
Address: 735147, Repiblic Tadjikistan, Khatlon Reg., Kalininabad

Phone: (37744) 2-35-14, 2-35-84
Products: nitrogenous fertilizers 53 ths tons
urea 114 ths tons
ammonia

250 VOSE GINNERY

Ownership: *state*
Industry: *Textile industry*
Number of Employees: 300.00
CEO: Samardin Fazlitdyainov
Address: 735330, Repiblic Tadjikistan, Khatlon Reg., pos. Vose, O.Khaiyam St., 18

Phone: 2-31-47, 2-23-02
Products: cotton 5,304 tons
seeds 9,649 tons
lint 506 tons

251 VOSE SALT WORKS

Ownership: *state*
Industry: *Mining industry (building mateirlas)*
Number of Employees: 100.00
CEO: A. Samadov
Address: 735330, Repiblic Tadjikistan, Khatlon Shakhrinau
Reg., pos. Vose, Amirshoev St., 8

Phone: 2-23-87, 2-20-58
Products: salt 14,916 tons

252 WINE PLANT "SHAKHRINAU" (LEASING-BASED ì

Ownership: *state*
Industry: *Food & food processing*
Number of Employees: 300.00
CEO: P. Karimov
Address: 735020, Republic Tadjikistan,

Dist., ì

Phone: 3-32-18
Products: wine 302 ths dal
vodka 110 ths dal
sparkling wine

253 WOOLEN SHAWL FACTORY "ZARBOF"
Ownership: *state*

254 YAVAN ELECTROCHEMICAL WORKS
Ownership: *state*

Industry: *Textile industry*
Number of Employees: *1,008.00*
CEO: **Abdullodzhon Khoshimov**
Address: 735702, Republic Tadjikistan, Leninabad
         Reg., Khudzhand, Lenin St., 234-a

Phone: **(37922) 4-37-52, 6-47-91, 6-43-85**
Products: **yarn of mixed wool 370 tons**
           fabrics

**255   YAVAN LIME WORKS (JOINT-STOCK
       COMPANY)**

Ownership: *joint-stock*
Industry: *Mining industry (building
              mateirlas)*
Number of Employees:
CEO: **Kh. Tilloev**
Address: 735310, Repiblic Tadjikistan, Khatlon
         Reg., Yavan Dist., kishlak Darash

Phone: **(37741) 2-12-57**
parts
Products: **burnt lime 31 ths tons**
           packed lime
           cement blocks

Industry: *Machine building industry*
Number of Employees:
CEO: **President**
Address: 735310, Repiblic Tadjikistan, Khatlon
         Reg., Yavan Dist., pos. Pionernyi

Phone: **(37741) 4-15-94, 4-16-63**
Products: **cast articles of steel 629 tons**
           electrical-sheet steel 905 tons
           chemical machinery

256   YAVAN MECHANICAL REPAIR WORKS

Ownership: *state*
Industry: *Machine building industry*
Number of Employees:
CEO: **President**
Address: 735310, Repiblic Tadjikistan, Khatlon
         Reg., pos. Yavan

Phone: **(37741) 3-41**
Products: **cast articles of steel 629 tons**
           chemical machinery and spare

           equipment of stainless steel

TAJIKISTAN INDUSTRY: LARGEST COMPANIES BY INDUSTRY

	COMPANY	INDUSTRY	PERSONNEL	
1	KHUDZHAND SILK MILL	Textile industry	8960	141
2	JOINT-STOCK COMPANY "KOLINKHO"	Textile industry	5429	105
3	DUSHANBE JOINT-STOCK LEATHER FOOTWEAR COMPANY "RAFIK"	Footwer & tanning industry	3928	39
4	KHUDZHAND CLOTHING PRODUCTION and TRADE COMPANY NAMED AFTER N.K.KRUPSKAYA	Clothing industry	2650	132
5	URA-TYUBE KNITTED OUTERWEAR FACTORY	Textile industry	2558	244
6	PRODUCTION COMPANY "TADZHIKGIDROAGREGAT"	Machine building Industry	2478	209
7	JOINT-STOCK COMPANY "BOFANDA"	Textile industry	2281	103
8	DUSHANBE SILK MILL	Textile industry	1986	53
9	KHUDZHAND SHOE FACTORY n2	Footwer & tanning industry	1835	140
10	KANIBADAM CLOTHING PRODUCTION COMPANY "KHUSNORO"	Clothing industry	1791	118
11	KANIBADAM SPINNING and WEAVING MILL	Textile industry	1722	122
12	FIRM "NAFISA"	Textile industry	1702	72
13	KANIBADAM BRAKE EQUIPMENT PLANT	Metal-working industry	1682	116
14	CLOTHING FIRM "GULISTAN"	Clothing industry	1668	13
15	ISFARA CHEMICALS PLANT	Chemical, pharmaceutical & micribiology industry	1609	94
16	PRODUCTION COMPANY "TADZHIKZOLOTO"	Ore mining industry	1564	213

For additional analytical, business and investment opportunities information, please contact Global Investment & Business Center, USA at (202) 546-2103. Fax: (202) 546-3275. E-mail: rusric@erols.com

17	DUSHANBE PLANT "TADZHIKTEKSTILMASH"	Machine building industry	1400	49
18	VAKHSH NITROGENOUS FERTILIZER PLANT	Chemical, pharmaceutical & micribiology industry	1345	249
19	DUSHANBE PIPE APPLIANCES PLANT NAMED AFTER ORDZHONIKIDZE	Metal-working industry	1328	47
20	TADJIK PRODUCTION COMPANY "SVETOTEKHNIKA"	Electrical engineering	1308	230
21	PRODUCTION COMPANY "KHODZHENTATLAS"	Textile industry	1259	205
22	CENTRAL ELECTRIC POWER TRANSMISSION NETWORK	Power industry	1237	10
23	DUSHANBE CLOTHING PRODUCTION COMPANY "CHEVAR"	Clothing industry	1196	22
24	DUSHANBE AGRARIAN PRODUCTION COMPANY "NONPAZ"	Food & food processing	1146	17
25	PRODUCTION COMPANY "TADZHIKNEFT"	Oil & gas industry	1131	211
26	KURGAN-TYUBE CLOTHING FACTORY	Clothing industry	1100	161
27	JOINT-STOCK COMPANY "FAIZ"	Textile industry	1055	104
28	WOOLEN SHAWL FACTORY "ZARBOF"	Textile industry	1008	253
29	ANZOBSKY ORE CONCENTRATING MILL	Ore mining industry	985	5
30	DUSHANBE COMPANY "TADZHIKATLAS"	Textile industry	958	24
31	KANIBADAM GINNERY	Textile industry	951	120
32	ISFARA CANNERY	Food & food processing	941	93
33	SOUTHERN ELECTRIC POWER TRANSMISSION NETWORK	Power industry	940	226
34	DUSHANBE FOLK DECORATIVE HANDICRAFT COMPANY "DILOROM"	Textile industry	938	34

35	DUSHANBE OILERY and FAT PLANT	Food & food processing	917	43
36	KHUDZHAND ELECTRIC POWER TRANSMISSION NETWORK ENTERPRISE	Power industry	900	135
37	KOFARNIKHON MECHANICAL REPAIR WORKS	Machine building industry	870	144
38	PRODUCTION COMPANY "TADZHIKTSEMENT"	Building materials industry	845	212
39	PROLETARSK ORE CONCENTRATING MILL	Building materials industry	839	217
40	KHUDZHAND CANNERY	Food & food processing	824	131
41	PRODUCTION COMPANY "PAMIR"	Machine building industry	822	206
42	KHUDZHAND PLANT "TORGMASH"	Metal-working industry	812	139
43	GISSAR COMPANY "GIDROSTROIMATERIALY"	Oil refining & gas processing	800	79
44	DUSHANBE THERMOELECTRIC STATION	Power industry	748	56
45	DUSHANBE KNITTING MILL	Textile industry	743	40
46	KANIBADAM CANNERY	Food & food processing	730	117
47	URA-TYUBE FACTORY "NEKSOZ"	Consumer goods, furniture, household & cultural goods	721	243
48	LENINABAD RARE METALS PLANT	Metallurgy	720	175
49	KOFARNIKHON TRAINING and PRODUCTION ENTERPRISE	Consumer goods, furniture, household & cultural goods	700	147
50	TURSUNZADE GINNERY	Textile industry	700	236
51	PRODUCTION COMPANY "PAMIRKVARTSSAMOTSVETY"	Mining industry (building mateirlas)	679	207
52	AINI GINNERY	Textile industry	650	4
53	CONFECTIONERY FACTORY "SHIRIN"	Food & food processing	644	16
54	TRAINING and PRODUCTION WORKS n4	Consumer goods, furniture, household & cultural goods	624	234
55	PLANT "LENINABADSELMASH"	Machine building industry	616	200

For additional analytical, business and investment opportunities information, please contact Global Investment & Business Center, USA at (202) 546-2103. Fax: (202) 546-3275. E-mail: rusric@erols.com

56	KHUDZHAND FURNITURE PLANT	Consumer goods, furniture, household & cultural goods	600	136
57	KHODZHENT GINNERY	Textile industry	586	125
58	KURGAN-TYUBE TRANSFORMER PLANT	Electrical engineering	583	172
59	PROLETARSK GINNERY	Textile industry	572	216
60	GORNO-BADAKHSHAN ELECTRIC POWER TRANSMISSION NETWORK	Power industry	570	84
61	DUSHANBE MEAT PROCESSING PLANT	Food & food processing	562	42
62	KULYAB GINNERY	Textile industry	558	154
63	CLOTHING FACTORY "FIRUZA"	Clothing industry	550	12
64	KHOROG CLOTHING FACTORY n3 "KHAIET"	Clothing industry	545	127
65	DUSHANBE FURNITURE PLANT	Consumer goods, furniture, household & cultural goods	537	36
66	ADRASMAN LOW-VOLTAGE ELECTRIC EQUIPMENT WORKS	Electrical engineering	529	2
67	GRAIN PROCESSING PLANT	Food & food processing	513	87
68	ISFARA BUILDING MATERIALS PLANT	Building materials industry	508	92
69	PENDZHIKENT FERMENTED TOBACCO PLANT	Tobacco industry	500	195
70	NAU GRAIN PROCESSING PLANT	Food & food processing	498	185
71	JOINT-STOCK ENTERPRISE "LACHP"	Building materials industry	495	106
72	DUSHANBE PLANT "TORGMASH"	Machine building industry	493	50
73	PLANT "ALMOS"	Radio-electronic industry	485	198
74	KHUDZHAND LEASING-BASED ENTERPRISE "EMALIROVSHCHIK"	Metal-working industry	484	138
75	CLOSED JOINT-STOCK COMPANY "BOFANDA"	Textile industry	480	11

76	GANCHI CLOTHING and KNITWEAR FACTORY	Textile industry	471	78
77	PLANT "TADZHIKKHIMSELKHOZMASH"	Machine building industry	470	201
78	DUSHANBE FERROCONCRETE STRUCTURES and PRE-CAST PARTS PLANT	Building materials industry	467	33
79	FACTORY "ZARDUZ"	Textile industry	462	67
80	MOSKOVSKY GINNERY	Textile industry	460	182
81	KAIRAKKUM AGROINDUSTRIAL PRODUCTION COMPANY	Food & food processing	442	107
82	DUSHANBE DAIRY	Food & food processing	439	26
83	DUSHANBE COMPANY "GULDAST"	Clothing industry	426	23
84	TAKOB FLUORSPAR WORKS	Mining industry (building mateirlas)	414	231
85	DUSHANBE JEWELLERY PLANT	Consumer goods, furniture, household & cultural goods	401	38
86	KAIRAKKUM SUBSIDIARY ENTERPRISE	Building materials industry	397	111
87	GAFUROV MEAT PROCESSING PLANT	Food & food processing	390	75
88	KOFARNIKHON MECHANICAL WORKS "ZARFSOZ"	Metal-working industry	390	145
89	KULYAB EXPERIMENTAL MACHINING ATTACHMENTS PLANT	Metal-working industry	389	153
90	NAU GINNERY	Textile industry	387	184
91	BUSTON GINNERY	Textile industry	383	9
92	DUSHANBE PRINTING WORKS	Publishing & printing	382	52
93	DUSHANBE TOWN ELECTRIC POWER TRANSMISSION NETWORK	Power industry	380	58
94	KHUDZHAND GAS EQUIPMENT ENGINEERING WORKS	Machine building industry	367	137

For additional analytical, business and investment opportunities information, please contact Global Investment & Business Center, USA at (202) 546-2103. Fax: (202) 546-3275. E-mail: rusric@erols.com

95	NEFTEABAD OILFIELD	Oil & gas industry	362	187
96	PUBLISHING HOUSE	Publishing & printing	353	219
97	KHUDZHAND BAKERY	Food & food processing	344	130
98	LEASING-BASED ENTERPRISE "SHARBAT"	Food & food processing	339	174
99	KULYAB BRICK YARD	Building materials industry	320	150
100	ISFARA FERROCONCRETE STRUCTURES and BUILDING ARTICLES PLANT n5	Building materials industry	310	97
101	DUSHANBE BRICK YARD PRODUCTION COMPANY	Building materials industry	300	19
102	WINE PLANT "SHAKHRINAU" (LEASING-BASED ì	Food & food processing	300	252
103	VOSE GINNERY	Textile industry	300	250
104	DUSHANBE FOOD PROCESSING ENTERPRISE	Food & food processing	300	35
105	DUSHANBE WOOD-WORKING PLANT	Forestry & timber processing industry	294	61
106	KURGAN-TYUBE CANNERY	Food & food processing	290	160
107	DUSHANBE PAINTS and VARNISHES PLANT "RANGINKAMON"	Chemical, pharmaceutical & micribiology industry	290	44
108	DUSHANBE FERROCONCRETE STRUCTURES and BUILDING ARTICLES PLANT n1	Building materials industry	288	29
109	PRODUCTION COOPERATIVE "PISHCHEVIK"	Food & food processing	285	214
110	DUSHANBE AGROINDUSTRIAL PRODUCTION COMPANY	Food & food processing	275	18
111	TRAINING and PRODUCTION WORKS n1	Consumer goods, furniture, household & cultural goods	273	232
112	DUSHANBE CABLE PLANT "TADZHIKKABEL"	Electrical engineering	271	20
113	ENTERPRISE "TADZHIKENERGOREMONT"	Electrical engineering	268	66
114	INDUSTRIAL and TRADING	Footwer & tanning industry	262	90

FIRM "SIMO"

#	Name	Industry		
115	DUSHANBE WINE PLANT	Food & food processing	260	59
116	PROLETARSK CENTRAL ELECTROMECHANICAL WORKSHOP	Machine building industry	249	215
117	ISFARA MINERAL PAINTS PLANT "NILUFOR"	Chemical, pharmaceutical & micribiology industry	244	102
118	DUSHANBE GRAIN PROCESSING PLANT	Food & food processing	243	37
119	GANCHI BRICK YARD	Building materials industry	240	77
120	URA-TYUBE CANNERY	Food & food processing	236	241
121	DUSHANBE TOBACCO FACTORY	Tobacco industry	235	57
122	KHUDZHAND TRAINING and PRODUCTION WORKS n2	Consumer goods, furniture, household & cultural goods	234	143
123	KHUDZHAND DAIRY	Food & food processing	225	134
124	DUSHANBEPRESSURE PIPES and FERROCONCRETE ARTICLES PLANT	Building materials industry	221	63
125	KURGAN-TYUBE OILERY	Food & food processing	220	171
126	DUSHANBE FERROCONCRETE STRUCTURES and BUILDING ARTICLES PLANT n3	Building materials industry	216	31
127	KULYAB TRAINING and PRODUCTION ENTERPRISE	Consumer goods, furniture, household & cultural goods	202	158
128	KALININABAD FERROCONCRETE STRUCTURES PLANT n1	Building materials industry	202	112
129	ASHTI SALT WORKS n2	Mining industry (building mateirlas)	190	6
130	URA-TYUBE BAKERY	Food & food processing	189	239
131	DUSHANBE FERROCONCRETE STRUCTURES and BUILDING ARTICLES PLANT n6	Building materials industry	178	32
132	BAKERY "NONPAZ"	Food & food processing	178	8
133	PLANT "ETALON"	Medical equipment industry	177	199

134	DUSHANBE SPECIALIZED ENGINEERING DESIGN BUREAU	Machine building industry	174	55
135	SHURAB MECHANICAL WORKS "FILIZ"	Metal-working industry	173	224
136	URA-TYUBE BRICK YARD	Building materials industry	170	240
137	KULYAB MEAT PROCESSING PLANT	Food & food processing	170	156
138	GAFUROV FERROCONCRETE STRUCTURES PLANT n7	Building materials industry	164	74
139	KULYAB DAIRY	Food & food processing	160	152
140	KANIBADAM BAKERY	Food & food processing	159	115
141	KURGAN-TYUBE MEAT PROCESSING PLANT and DAIRY	Food & food processing	156	167
142	VAKHSH HYDROELECTRIC STATION CASCADE	Power industry	150	248
143	OIL ASPHALT PLANT	Oil refining & gas processing	150	192
144	KALININABAD FERROCONCRETE STRUCTURES PLANT n8	Building materials industry	150	113
145	TRAINING and PRODUCTION WORKS n3	Consumer goods, furniture, household & cultural goods	148	233
146	DUSHANBE LEATHER HABERDASHERY FACTORY "CHARMDUZ"	Footwer & tanning industry	143	41
147	DUSHANBE PILOT-PRODUCTION and EXPERIMENTAL PLANT "REMSTROIDORMASH"	Metal-working industry	141	45
148	URA-TYUBE WINE PLANT	Food & food processing	136	246
149	PENDZHIKENT BRICK YARD	Building materials industry	133	194
150	FIRM "BORCHOMA"	Pulp & paper industry	133	70
151	DUSHANBE FERROCONCRETE STRUCTURES and BUILDING ARTICLES PLANT n2	Building materials industry	132	30
152	COMPUTING APPARATUS REPAIR WORKS	High-tech products, PC, research & design services	132	14

153	LEASE-HOLDER COLLECTIVE "VREMYA"	Mining industry (building mateirlas)	130	173
154	KUIBYSHEVSK FISHING FARM	Fishing & fish processing	130	149
155	GRAIN INTAKE PLANT	Food & food processing	126	85
156	KHUDZHAND CONTAINER REPAIR WORKS	Consumer goods, furniture, household & cultural goods	125	133
157	ISFARA BAKERY	Food & food processing	125	91
158	ISFARA MEDICAL PREPARATIONS and FEED PROTEIN PLANT	Chemical, pharmaceutical & micribiology industry	125	101
159	ISFARA MEAT PROCESSING PLANT	Food & food processing	122	100
160	DUSHANBE WOOD-WORKING PLANT	Forestry & timber processing industry	121	60
161	KULYAB GRAIN PROCESSING PLANT	Food & food processing	118	155
162	TRAINING and PRODUCTION WORKS n5	Consumer goods, furniture, household & cultural goods	115	235
163	MATCHINSKY RURAL CONSTRUCTION PLANT	Building materials industry	113	177
164	ISFARA CONFECTIONERY FACTORY	Food & food processing	106	95
165	NON-ALCOHOLIC BEVERAGES and MINERAL WATER PLANT	Food & food processing	102	188
166	KURGAN-TYUBE EXPERIMENTAL FURSKIN FACTORY "MUINNA"	Clothing industry	102	164
167	KANIBADAM FERROCONCRETE STRUCTURES PLANT n2	Building materials industry	100	119
168	KURGAN-TYUBE NON-ALCOHOLIC BEVERAGES and MINERAL WATER PLANT	Food & food processing	100	169
169	KULYAB CREAMERY	Food & food processing	100	151
170	VOSE SALT WORKS	Mining industry (building mateirlas)	100	251
171	DUSHANBE PLANT "STROMMASH"	Machine building industry	98	48

172	FIRM "DOVUD"	Scrap & waste processing industry	96	71
173	DUSHANBE SOUVENIR FACTORY "ARMUGON"	Consumer goods, furniture, household & cultural goods	96	54
174	URA-TYUBE CREAMERY	Food & food processing	94	242
175	DUSHANBE CHEESE PLANT	Food & food processing	93	21
176	NAU MECHANIZED QUARRY	Mining industry (building mateirlas)	92	186
177	DZHILIKUL FISHING FARM	Fishing & fish processing	90	64
178	DZHILIKUL FISHING FARM	Fishing & fish processing	89	65
179	PENDZHIKENT MEAT PROCESSING PLANT and DAIRY	Food & food processing	86	197
180	KHUDZHAND AUTOMOBILE REPAIR WORKS n4	Automobile industry	86	129
181	FERMENTED TOBACCO PLANT	Tobacco industry	85	69
182	DUSHANBE EXCAVATOR REPAIR WORKS	Metal-working industry	82	27
183	CONFECTIONERY FACTORY "MAISHAT"	Food & food processing	80	15
184	FISHING FARM "CHUBEK"	Fishing & fish processing	80	73
185	ISFARA CREAMERY	Food & food processing	79	96
186	KANSAI NON-METALLIFEROUS and FACING MATERIALS PLANT	Building materials industry	78	124
187	DUSHANBE WOOD-WORKING PLANT	Forestry & timber processing industry	74	62
188	DUSHANBE EXPERIMENTAL PLANT "SISTEMAVTOMATIKA"	Medical equipment industry	65	28
189	KOFARNIKHON RICE PLANT	Food & food processing	65	146
190	GISSAR GRAIN INTAKE PLANT	Food & food processing	64	81
191	PROSTHETIC and ORTHOPAEDIC APPLIANCES PLANT	Medical equipment industry	63	218
192	KURGAN-TYUBE MECHANICAL REPAIR WORKS	Machine building industry	60	168
193	KAIRAKKUM MECHANICAL REPAIR WORKSHOP	Metal-working industry	60	109

194	DUSHANBE CONFECTIONERY FACTORY "LAZZAT" (JOINT-STOCK COMPANY)	*Food & food processing*	52	25
195	ISFARA FURNITURE PLANT	*Consumer goods, furniture, household & cultural goods*	52	98
196	KALININABAD GRAVEL SIZING MILL	*Mining industry (building mateirlas)*	50	114
197	KURGAN-TYUBE CONFECTIONERY FACTORY "LAZZAT"	*Food & food processing*	40	162
198	ILIYCHEVSKY FEED MILL	*Food & food processing*	37	88
199	PRINT-SHOP	*Publishing & printing*	32	202
200	PENDZHIKENT FISH PROCESSING PLANT	*Fishing & fish processing*	32	196
201	TURSUNZADE PRINT-SHOP	*Publishing & printing*	30	238
202	TURSUNZADE PORCELAIN WORKS	*Building materials industry*	30	237
203	PRODUCTION COMPANY "TADZHIKENERGOLEGPROM"	*Machine building industry*	27	208
204	SHAKHRISTAN CREAMERY	*Food & food processing*	27	223
205	PROCUREMENT PRODUCTION COMPANY "TADZHIKVTORTSVETMET"	*Scrap & waste processing industry*	21	204
206	SHAARTUZ GINNERY	*Textile industry*	20	222
207	TADJIK ALUMINIUM WORKS	*Metallurgy*	20	229
208	NUREK CLOTHING FACTORY	*Clothing industry*	20	189
209	STATE FARM-PLANT "EFIRONOS"	*Chemical, pharmaceutical & micribiology industry*	20	227
210	GISSAR TEXTILE MILL	*Textile industry*	20	82
211	GRAIN INTAKE YARD	*Food & food processing*	20	86
212	MINING ENTERPRISE "TADZHIKSKOYE"	*Coal mining & peat industry*	10	180
213	GISSAR GINNERY	*Textile industry*	10	80
214	INDUSTRIAL and COMMERCIAL FIRM "ISMAIL"	*Consumer goods, furniture, household & cultural goods*	10	89
215	DUSHANBE PILOT-PRODUCTION and EXPERIMENTAL PLANT	*Machine building industry*	10	46

For additional analytical, business and investment opportunities information, please contact Global Investment & Business Center, USA at (202) 546-2103. Fax: (202) 546-3275. E-mail: rusric@erols.com

"SELEKTSIONNAYA TEKHNIKA"

216	NUREK EXPERIMENTAL MECHANICAL WORKS	*Machine building industry*	10	190
217	BAIRAZA HYDROELECTRIC STATION	*Power industry*	10	7
218	LENINSKY NON-METALLIFEROUS MATERIALS PLANT	*Building materials industry*	10	176
219	ISFARA HYDROMETALLURGICAL PLANT	*Metallurgy*	10	99
220	PRINTING PRODUCTION COMPANY	*Publishing & printing*		203
221	PRODUCTION COMPANY "TADZHIKKHIMPROM"	*Chemical, pharmaceutical & micribiology industry*		210
222	PYANDZH GINNERY	*Textile industry*		220
223	SHAARTUZ CREAMERY	*Food & food processing*		221
224	STATE JOINT-STOCK HOLDING COMPANY "BARKI TOCHIK"	*Power industry*		228
225	URA-TYUBE TRAINING and PRODUCTION ENTERPRISE	*Consumer goods, furniture, household & cultural goods*		245
226	UYALP GINNERY	*Textile industry*		247
227	YAVAN ELECTROCHEMICAL WORKS	*Machine building industry*		254
228	AGROINDUSTRIAL GRAIN PROCESSING PRODUCTION COMPANY	*Food & food processing*		3
229	YAVAN LIME WORKS (JOINT-STOCK COMPANY)	*Mining industry (building mateirlas)*		255
230	SMALL ENTERPRISE "BETON"	*Building materials industry*		225
231	KOLKHOZABAD GRAIN PROCESSING PLANT	*Food & food processing*		148
232	GAFUROV WINE PLANT	*Food & food processing*		76
233	GISSAR TRAINING and PRODUCTION WORKS	*Food & food processing*		83
234	FARKHOR GINNERY	*Textile industry*		68

For additional analytical, business and investment opportunities information, please contact Global Investment & Business Center, USA at (202) 546-2103. Fax: (202) 546-3275. E-mail: rusric@erols.com

For additional analytical, business and investment opportunities information, please contact Global Investment & Business Center, USA at (202) 546-2103. Fax: (202) 546-3275. E-mail: rusric@erols.com

STATION

| 256 | KHUDZHAND TRAINING and PRODUCTION ENTERPRISE | *Consumer goods, furniture, household & cultural goods* | 142 |

For additional analytical, business and investment opportunities information, please contact Global Investment & Business Center, USA at (202) 546-2103. Fax: (202) 546-3275. E-mail: rusric@erols.com

TAJIKISTAN INDUSTRY: BY PRODUCTS

PRODUCTS	COMPANU	Number in Alphabetical Section
1 agricultural equipment	PLANT "TADZHIKKHIMSELKHOZMASH"	201
2 agricultural machines	PLANT "LENINABADSELMASH"	200
3 alloys	LENINABAD RARE METALS PLANT	175
4 anodized articles saddlery and harness articles textile haberdashery	TRAINING and PRODUCTION WORKS n3	233
5 antimony concentrate mercury concentrate	ANZOBSKY ORE CONCENTRATING MILL	5
6 apple puree peach puree 69 ths tins tomato paste	URA-TYUBE CANNERY	241
7 appliances for pipes, boilers, etc gate valves of steel cast articles of pig iron	DUSHANBE PIPE APPLIANCES PLANT NAMED AFTER ORDZHONIKIDZE	47
8 articles of apparel hosiery 2.4 ths pcs knitwear articles	KURGAN-TYUBE FOLK DECORATIVE HANDICRAFT FACTORY	165
9 articles of apparel and clothing accessories trousers for children bed-linen	CLOTHING FACTORY "FIRUZA"	12

For additional analytical, business and investment opportunities information, please contact Global Investment & Business Center, USA at (202) 546-2103. Fax: (202) 546-3275. E-mail: rusric@erols.com

10	articles of apparel and clothing accessories fabrics of cotton fabrics of silk	DUSHANBE FOLK DECORATIVE HANDICRAFT COMPANY "DILOROM"	34
11	articles of apparel and clothing accessories	KHOROG CLOTHING FACTORY n3 "KHAIET"	127
12	articles of jewellery metal haberdashery fittings	DUSHANBE JEWELLERY PLANT	38
13	articles of plastics packing containers of paperboard articles of polyethylene and cellophane	FIRM "BORCHOMA"	70
14	articles of plastics baby linen pile carpets	URA-TYUBE FACTORY "NEKSOZ"	243
15	auxiliary mechanized devices electric cranes 344 pcs spare parts for road building machines	KOFARNIKHON MECHANICAL REPAIR WORKS	144
16	bakers' wares	KURGAN-TYUBE BAKERY	159
17	bakers' wares confectionery pasta	KHUDZHAND BAKERY	130
18	bakers' wares	KHOROG BAKERY	126
19	bakers' wares pasta	DUSHANBE AGRARIAN PRODUCTION COMPANY "NONPAZ"	17
20	bakers' wares ground rusks 16 tons corn sticks	PRODUCTION COOPERATIVE "PISHCHEVIK"	214
21	bakers' wares	ISFARA BAKERY	91

22	bakers' wares	KANIBADAM BAKERY	115
23	bakers' wares 6,415 tons confectionery 362 tons corn sticks	BAKERY "NONPAZ"	8
24	bakers' wares 3,920 tons	URA-TYUBE BAKERY	239
25	bakers' wares 7,038 tons	DUSHANBE AGROINDUSTRIAL PRODUCTION COMPANY	18
26	barium metal 9,812 kg chemical products 6,555 tons precious metals	ISFARA HYDROMETALLURGICAL PLANT	99
27	bathrobes 0.3 ths pcs suits 317.7 ths pcs	CLOTHING FIRM "GULISTAN"	13
28	bed-linen 82 ths pcs articles of feather and down	TRAINING and PRODUCTION WORKS n1	232
29	beer 1,082 ths dal non-alcoholic beverages 216 ths dal mineral waters	DUSHANBE FOOD PROCESSING ENTERPRISE	35
30	beer 120 ths dal non-alcoholic beverages 46 ths dal mineral waters	NON-ALCOHOLIC BEVERAGES and MINERAL WATER PLANT	188

For additional analytical, business and investment opportunities information,
please contact Global Investment & Business Center, USA
at (202) 546-2103. Fax: (202) 546-3275. E-mail: rusric@erols.com

31	building bricks 10,360 ths pcs	URA-TYUBE BRICK YARD	240
32	building bricks 15,844 ths pcs	GANCHI BRICK YARD	77
33	building bricks 17,801 ths pcs	DUSHANBE BRICK YARD PRODUCTION COMPANY	19
34	building bricks 7,886 ths pcs	KULYAB BRICK YARD	150
35	burnt lime 31 ths tons packed lime cement blocks	YAVAN LIME WORKS (JOINT-STOCK COMPANY)	255
36	butter 124 tons cheese 692 tons milk and dairy products	DUSHANBE CHEESE PLANT	21
37	butter 205.4 tons milk and dairy products	SHAKHRISTAN CREAMERY	223
38	butter 226 tons cheese 29 tons milk and dairy products	DUSHANBE DAIRY	26
39	butter 408 tons milk and dairy products milk products	URA-TYUBE CREAMERY	242
40	butter 465.4 tons milk 2,138.6 tons fermented milk products	ISFARA CREAMERY	96
41	butter 494 tons milk and dairy products fermented milk products	KULYAB DAIRY	152

For additional analytical, business and investment opportunities information, please contact Global Investment & Business Center, USA at (202) 546-2103. Fax: (202) 546-3275. E-mail: rusric@erols.com

42	**butter 613 tons** milk and dairy products cheese of sheep's milk	**KHUDZHAND DAIRY** — 134
43	**cables**	**DUSHANBE CABLE PLANT "TADZHIKKABEL"** — 20
44	**cans 100 mln pcs** bottles 8,000 ths pcs paperboard boxes	**JOINT-STOCK ENTERPRISE "LACHP"** — 106
45	**caramel**	**ISFARA CONFECTIONERY FACTORY** — 95
46	**carpets 54 ths sq m** floor coverings vests	**CLOSED JOINT-STOCK COMPANY "BOFANDA"** — 11
47	**carpets and other textile floor coverings 8,297.5 ths sq m** twisted yarn 4,014.5 tons yarn in skeins	**JOINT-STOCK COMPANY "KOLINKHO"** — 105
48	**cast articles of steel 280 tons** cast articles of pig iron spare parts	**PROLETARSK CENTRAL ELECTROMECHANICAL WORKSHOP** — 215
49	**cast articles of steel 629 tons** chemical machinery and spare parts equipment of stainless steel	**YAVAN MECHANICAL REPAIR WORKS** — 256
50	**cast articles of steel 629 tons** electrical-sheet steel 905 tons chemical machinery	**YAVAN ELECTROCHEMICAL WORKS** — 254
51	**cement 446.8 ths tons** pipes of asbestos-cement 1,097.7 conv. km corrugated sheets of asbestos-cement	**PRODUCTION COMPANY "TADZHIKTSEMENT"** — 212

52	cereal meal 4,974 tons rice meal 947 tons	GRAIN INTAKE YARD	86
53	cigarettes 2,607 mln pcs	DUSHANBE TOBACCO FACTORY	57
54	coal 177.7 ths tons	MINING ENTERPRISE "TADZHIKSKOYE"	180
55	coal 29 ths tons	MINE "FAN-YAGNOB"	179
56	concentrated sand 226 ths tons ceramic wall tiles 268 sq m building bricks	PROLETARSK ORE CONCENTRATING MILL	217
57	confectionery 1,223 tons	KURGAN-TYUBE CONFECTIONERY FACTORY "LAZZAT"	162
58	confectionery 1,430 tons preserved fruit 100 ths tins milk and dairy products	CONFECTIONERY FACTORY "MAISHAT"	15
59	consumer goods gaseous hydrocarbons	KHUDZHAND GAS EQUIPMENT ENGINEERING WORKS	137
60	consumer goods semi-precious stones blocks of marble	PRODUCTION COMPANY "PAMIRKVARTSSAMOTSVETY"	207
61	cotton	KURGAN-TYUBE GINNERY	166

62	cotton	SHAARTUZ GINNERY	222
63	cotton	PYANDZH GINNERY	220
64	cotton	UYALP GINNERY	247
65	cotton	OKTYABRSKY COTTON PROCESSING MILL	193
66	cotton 1,035 tons seeds 1,831 tons lint	GISSAR GINNERY	80
67	cotton 10,289 tons seeds 18,670 tons lint 1,747 tons	NAU GINNERY	184
68	cotton 11,439 tons seeds 19,391 tons lint 2,081 tons	KHODZHENT GINNERY	125
69	cotton 15,985 tons lint 2,198 tons seeds	PROLETARSK GINNERY	216
70	cotton 16,011 tons seeds 29,388 tons lint 2,833 tons	TURSUNZADE GINNERY	236
71	cotton 17,499 tons seeds 32,492 tons lint 2,641 tons	KANIBADAM GINNERY	120
72	cotton 4,433 tons seeds 8,184 tons lint 853 tons	MOSKOVSKY GINNERY	182

73	**cotton 5,304 tons** seeds 9,649 tons lint 506 tons	**VOSE GINNERY**	250
74	**cotton 6,048 tons** seeds 10,361 tons lint	**FARKHOR GINNERY**	68
75	**cotton 6,055 tons** seeds 10,537 tons lint 889 tons	**KULYAB GINNERY**	154
76	**cotton 7,320 tons** seeds 13,626 tons lint	**BUSTON GINNERY**	9
77	**cotton 7,514 tons** seeds 14,291 tons lint 1,859 tons	**AINI GINNERY**	4
78	**cotton oil 10,657 tons**	**KURGAN-TYUBE OILERY**	171
79	**cotton seed oil 2,738 tons** oil-cake 12,735 tons hulls	**KULYAB CREAMERY**	151
80	**crude alcohol 286.7 ths dal**	**ISFARA MEDICAL PREPARATIONS and FEED PROTEIN PLANT**	101
81	**crude petroleum oils 19 ths tons** gaseous hydrocarbons 1 mln cu m	**KURGAN-TYUBE OIL EXTRACTING ENTERPRISE n1**	170
82	**crude petroleum oils 38 ths tons** gas condensate gaseous hydrocarbons	**NEFTEABAD OILFIELD**	187
83	**crude petroleum oils 56.6 ths tons** gas condensate 4.8 ths tons gaseous hydrocarbons	**PRODUCTION COMPANY "TADZHIKNEFT"**	211

For additional analytical, business and investment opportunities information, please contact Global Investment & Business Center, USA at (202) 546-2103. Fax: (202) 546-3275. E-mail: rusric@erols.com

84	crude petroleum oils 7 ths tons gas condensate gaseous hydrocarbons	KULYAB OIL EXTRACTING ENTERPRISE n2 — 157
85	crushed stone 22.2 ths cu m natural sands 12.8 ths cu m	KALININABAD GRAVEL SIZING MILL — 114
86	crushed stone 186 ths cu m natural sands 156 ths cu m blocks of stone	LEASE-HOLDER COLLECTIVE "VREMYA" — 173
87	crushed stone 34 ths cu m gravel 32.3 ths cu m natural sands	NAU MECHANIZED QUARRY — 186
88	crushed stone 80 ths cu m natural sands 84.6 ths cu m ferroconcrete articles 868 cu m	LENINSKY NON-METALLIFEROUS MATERIALS PLANT — 176
89	crystal vibrators 1,000 ths pcs quartz filters 19 ths pcs television receivers	PLANT "ALMOS" — 198
90	designing non-standard machinery and equipment	DUSHANBE SPECIALIZED ENGINEERING DESIGN BUREAU — 55
91	dresses 41.1 ths pcs dresses of silk 24.8 ths pcs	DUSHANBE COMPANY "GULDAST" — 23
92	dresses, bathrobes 638.2 ths pcs	KHUDZHAND CLOTHING PRODUCTION and TRADE COMPANY NAMED AFTER N.K.KRUPSKAYA — 132
93	dry ochre 5,980 tons silicate paints paints and varnishes	ISFARA MINERAL PAINTS PLANT "NILUFOR" — 102

94	electric cookers 13,459 pcs spoons	KHUDZHAND PLANT "TORGMASH"	139
95	electric power supply	DUSHANBE TOWN ELECTRIC POWER TRANSMISSION NETWORK	58
96	electric power supply	SOUTHERN ELECTRIC POWER TRANSMISSION NETWORK	226
97	electric power supply	VAKHSH HYDROELECTRIC STATION CASCADE	248
98	electric power supply 680 mln kWh heating 3,245 ths Gcal	DUSHANBE THERMOELECTRIC STATION	56
99	electric power supply 11,541 mln kWh	NUREK HYDROELECTRIC STATION	191
100	electric power supply 16,805 mln kWh heating 3,648 ths Gcal	STATE JOINT-STOCK HOLDING COMPANY "BARKI TOCHIK"	228
101	electric power supply 2,289 mln kWh	BAIRAZA HYDROELECTRIC STATION	7
102	electric power supply 692 mln kWh	KHUDZHAND ELECTRIC POWER TRANSMISSION NETWORK ENTERPRISE	135
103	electric power supply 93,500 ths kwh	GORNO-BADAKHSHAN ELECTRIC POWER TRANSMISSION NETWORK	84
104	electric power supply 96 mln kWh	CENTRAL ELECTRIC POWER TRANSMISSION NETWORK	10

105	fabrics of silk 3,064.8 ths m twisted threads of silk 38.2 ths m folk handicraft articles	DUSHANBE COMPANY "TADZHIKATLAS"	24
106	fabrics of silk 838.9 ths m fabrics of man-made filaments fabrics of cotton	PRODUCTION COMPANY "KHODZHENTATLAS"	205
107	fabrics, unbleached 3,207 ths m	GISSAR TEXTILE MILL	82
108	facing tiles 19.5 ths sq m	KANSAI NON-METALLIFEROUS and FACING MATERIALS PLANT	124
109	fermented tobacco 1,186 tons	FERMENTED TOBACCO PLANT	69
110	fish	DZHILIKUL FISHING FARM	65
111	fish 497 tons live fish 298 tons smoked fish	KAIRAKKUM FISHING INDUSTRY ENTERPRISE	108
112	floor coverings of cotton 134 ths sq m carpets1.2 ths sq m mattresses	KANIBADAM TRAINING and PRODUCTION ENTERPRISE	123
113	floor coverings of cotton 32 ths sq m carpets 1,051 ths pcs ropes of cotton	KOFARNIKHON TRAINING and PRODUCTION ENTERPRISE	147
114	floor coverings of cotton 35.9 ths sq m lids 13 mln pcs	KHUDZHAND TRAINING and PRODUCTION ENTERPRISE	142

115	floor coverings of cotton 54 ths sq m pile carpets ropes of cotton	KULYAB TRAINING and PRODUCTION ENTERPRISE	158
116	floor coverings of cotton73.7 ths sq m carpets lids	URA-TYUBE TRAINING and PRODUCTION ENTERPRISE	245
117	flour 60 ths tons bran 13 ths tons mixed fodder	KULYAB GRAIN PROCESSING PLANT	155
118	flour, mixed fodder	AGROINDUSTRIAL GRAIN PROCESSING PRODUCTION COMPANY	3
119	flour, mixed fodder	KOLKHOZABAD GRAIN PROCESSING PLANT	148
120	fluorspar	TAKOB FLUORSPAR WORKS	231
121	folk handicraft articles	DUSHANBE SOUVENIR FACTORY "ARMUGON"	54
122	footwear	KHUDZHAND SHOE FACTORY n2	140
123	footwear 2,005 ths pairs	DUSHANBE JOINT-STOCK LEATHER FOOTWEAR COMPANY "RAFIK"	39
124	footwear 500 ths pairs	INDUSTRIAL and TRADING FIRM "SIMO"	90

| 125 | furniture | DUSHANBE FURNITURE PLANT | 36 |

| 126 | furniture | KHUDZHAND FURNITURE PLANT | 136 |

127 furniture
tables
beds
ISFARA FURNITURE PLANT 98

128 geranium oil
peppermint
STATE FARM-PLANT "EFIRONOS" 227

129 gold PRODUCTION COMPANY
"TADZHIKZOLOTO" 213

130 gypsum, building bricks ISFARA BUILDING MATERIALS PLANT 92

131 hides
meat 2,657 tons
sausages
GAFUROV MEAT PROCESSING PLANT 75

132 high-voltage apparatus 1,705 pcs KURGAN-TYUBE TRANSFORMER PLANT 172

electric transformers 45 ths pcs
power transformers 489 ths kWh

133 household chemicals
paints and varnishes
mineral fertilizers
ISFARA CHEMICALS PLANT 94

134 hydraulic drives and automated devices PRODUCTION COMPANY
"TADZHIKGIDROAGREGAT" 209

spare parts for hydraulic drives
cast articles of pig iron

135	industrial clothing	DUSHANBE CLOTHING PRODUCTION COMPANY "CHEVAR"	22
	suits 256 ths pcs		
136	industrial clothing	KANIBADAM CLOTHING PRODUCTION COMPANY "KHUSNORO"	118
	dresses, bathrobes 696.7 ths pcs		
137	instruments and apparatus repair of instrumentation	PLANT "ETALON"	199
138	instruments and apparatus	DUSHANBE EXPERIMENTAL PLANT "SISTEMAVTOMATIKA"	28
	maintenance of instruments and automated equipment		
139	jam 6,379 ths rbls 202 ths tins	LEASING-BASED ENTERPRISE "SHARBAT"	174
	fruit juices grape juice		
140	kitchen furniture	INDUSTRIAL and COMMERCIAL FIRM "ISMAIL"	89
	stools 86.6 ths rbls 865 pcs dinner-tables		
141	knitted linen	DUSHANBE KNITTING MILL	40
142	knitted outerwear 687 ths pcs	GANCHI CLOTHING and KNITWEAR FACTORY	78
143	knitwear	URA-TYUBE KNITTED OUTERWEAR FACTORY	244
144	lids for preserves 15,801 ths pcs	GISSAR TRAINING and PRODUCTION WORKS	83
	crown corks 3,724 ths pcs folders		

145	lighting engineering equipment	TADJIK PRODUCTION COMPANY "SVETOTEKHNIKA"	230

lighting fixtures 1,185 ths pcs
low-voltage apparatus

146	linoleum 355.6 ths sq m	GISSAR COMPANY "GIDROSTROIMATERIALY"	79

roll roofing materials 1,811 ths sq m
building bricks

147	liquid chlorine 16 ths tons	PRODUCTION COMPANY "TADZHIKKHIMPROM"	210

caustic soda 16 ths tons
calcium chloride

148	live fish 1,116 tons smoked fish 19 tons	KUIBYSHEVSK FISHING FARM	149

149	live fish 115.4 tons	PENDZHIKENT FISH PROCESSING PLANT	196

fish products

150	live fish 600 tons smoked fish 190 tons	DZHILIKUL FISHING FARM	64

151	live fish 90 tons chilled fish 8 tons	FISHING FARM "CHUBEK"	73

152	low-voltage apparatus	ADRASMAN LOW-VOLTAGE ELECTRIC EQUIPMENT WORKS	2

153	meal of rice 14 ths tons	KOFARNIKHON RICE PLANT	146

154	meat	KHOROG MEAT PROCESSING PLANT and DAIRY	128

butter
milk and dairy products

For additional analytical, business and investment opportunities information, please contact Global Investment & Business Center, USA at (202) 546-2103. Fax: (202) 546-3275. E-mail: rusric@erols.com

155 meat 2,558 tons   DUSHANBE MEAT PROCESSING PLANT   42

156 meat 545.5 tons   ISFARA MEAT PROCESSING PLANT   100

157 meat, incl. edible offal   KURGAN-TYUBE MEAT PROCESSING   167
                                              PLANT and DAIRY
     sausages 90 tons
     semi-prepared products

158 meat, incl. edible offal 1,304 tons   KULYAB MEAT PROCESSING PLANT   156
     sausages 2,110 ths rbls 70.9 tons
     fat

159 meat, incl. edible offal 184.8 tons   PENDZHIKENT MEAT PROCESSING   197
                                              PLANT and DAIRY
     sausages 25.7 tons
     fat

160 metal structures   KURGAN-TYUBE MECHANICAL REPAIR   168
                                              WORKS
     repair and maintenance of road building
     machinery and spare parts
     ucts of ferrous metals

161 metal-working tools   KANIBADAM BRAKE EQUIPMENT PLANT   116

     machining attachments
     consumer goods

162 metal-working tools   KULYAB EXPERIMENTAL MACHINING   153
                                              ATTACHMENTS PLANT
     consumer goods
     parts of agricultural machines

163 milk and dairy products   SHAARTUZ CREAMERY   221

164 mineral waters 19 ths bottles   KURGAN-TYUBE NON-ALCOHOLIC   169
                                              BEVERAGES and MINERAL WATER
                                              PLANT
     beer
     wine

For additional analytical, business and investment opportunities information,
please contact Global Investment & Business Center, USA
at (202) 546-2103. Fax: (202) 546-3275. E-mail: rusric@erols.com

165	mixed fodder	ILIYCHEVSKY FEED MILL	88
166	mixed fodder 31 ths tons	GRAIN INTAKE PLANT	85
167	newspapers business forms	TURSUNZADE PRINT-SHOP	238
168	newspapers 2,400 ths copies business forms 1,263 ths copies	PRINTING PRODUCTION COMPANY	203
169	newspapers 78 mln copies magazines 18 mln sheets	PUBLISHING HOUSE	219
170	nitrogenous fertilizers 53 ths tons urea 114 ths tons ammonia	VAKHSH NITROGENOUS FERTILIZER PLANT	249
171	non-ferrous waste and scrap 1,293 tons	PROCUREMENT PRODUCTION COMPANY "TADZHIKVTORTSVETMET"	204
172	oil asphalt	OIL ASPHALT PLANT	192
173	orthopaedic footwear prosthetic appliances	PROSTHETIC and ORTHOPAEDIC APPLIANCES PLANT	218
174	oxygen 61 ths cu m non-standard machinery and equipment 343.7 tons	DUSHANBE PLANT "STROMMASH"	48

175	paints and varnishes 996 tons	DUSHANBE PAINTS and VARNISHES PLANT "RANGINKAMON"	44
	floor oil paints pottery articles		
176	pile carpets 10,810 sq m floor coverings of cotton fabrics of silk	TRAINING and PRODUCTION WORKS n4	234
177	pre-cast ferroconcrete articles of concrete, not reinforced concrete	DUSHANBE FERROCONCRETE STRUCTURES and BUILDING ARTICLES PLANT n2	30
178	pre-cast ferroconcrete	MATCHINSKY RURAL CONSTRUCTION PLANT	177
179	pre-cast ferroconcrete structural components for house construction crushed stone	MOSKOVSKY FERROCONCRETE STRUCTURES PLANT n1	181
180	pre-cast ferroconcrete chutes power transmission line supports	DUSHANBEPRESSURE PIPES and FERROCONCRETE ARTICLES PLANT	63
181	pre-cast ferroconcrete structural components for house construction 3.3 ths sq m supports for power transmission lines	ISFARA FERROCONCRETE STRUCTURES and BUILDING ARTICLES PLANT n5	97
182	pre-cast ferroconcrete	KAIRAKKUM SUBSIDIARY ENTERPRISE	111
183	pre-cast ferroconcrete crushed stone 34.2 ths cu m natural sands	NAU BUILDING MATERIALS and STRUCTURES PLANT	183

For additional analytical, business and investment opportunities information,
please contact Global Investment & Business Center, USA
at (202) 546-2103. Fax: (202) 546-3275. E-mail: rusric@erols.com

| 184 | pre-cast ferroconcrete | KALININABAD FERROCONCRETE STRUCTURES PLANT n1 | 112 |

185 pre-cast ferroconcrete — DUSHANBE FERROCONCRETE STRUCTURES and BUILDING ARTICLES PLANT n3 — 31

wall panels

186 pre-cast ferroconcrete — SMALL ENTERPRISE "BETON" — 225

187 pre-cast ferroconcrete 26,763 cu m — GAFUROV FERROCONCRETE STRUCTURES PLANT n7 — 74

concrete 1,331 cu m

188 pre-cast ferroconcrete 7.7 ths cu m — KALININABAD FERROCONCRETE STRUCTURES PLANT n8 — 113

welded metal structures 639 tons
bars and rods for use in construction

189 pre-cast ferroconcrete 16.8 ths cu m — DUSHANBE FERROCONCRETE STRUCTURES and PRE-CAST PARTS PLANT — 33

articles of concrete, not reinforced
concrete

190 pre-cast ferroconcrete 25.2 ths cu m — DUSHANBE FERROCONCRETE STRUCTURES and BUILDING ARTICLES PLANT n1 — 29

pipes
concrete

191 pre-cast ferroconcrete 4.3 ths cu m — KANIBADAM FERROCONCRETE STRUCTURES PLANT n2 — 119

ferroconcrete articles
concrete

192 pre-cast ferroconcrete 6.2 ths cu m — DUSHANBE FERROCONCRETE STRUCTURES and BUILDING ARTICLES PLANT n6 — 32

193 precious metals — KAIRAKKUM MINE — 110

194	preserved fruit and vegetables 2,566 ths tins	KURGAN-TYUBE CANNERY	160
195	preserved fruit and vegetables 39,085 ths tins	KHUDZHAND CANNERY	131
196	preserved vegetables 6,657 ths tins	ISFARA CANNERY	93
197	preserved vegetables 4,232 ths tins preserved fruit 13,501 ths tins	KANIBADAM CANNERY	117
198	primary aluminium 345 ths tons anode blocks 240 ths tons non-standard machinery and equipment 64.5 tons	TADJIK ALUMINIUM WORKS	229
199	printed matter	PRINT-SHOP	202
200	printed matter	DUSHANBE PRINTING WORKS	52
201	printed matter	DUSHANBE PRINT-SHOP n18	51
202	processing of metal scrap 40,234 tons	FIRM "DOVUD"	71
203	refrigerators 61 ths pcs spare parts for refrigerators refrigerating plants	PRODUCTION COMPANY "PAMIR"	206
204	repair of automatic data processing machines	COMPUTING APPARATUS REPAIR WORKS	14

205 repair of containers	KHUDZHAND CONTAINER REPAIR WORKS	133
206 repair of equipment	PRODUCTION COMPANY "TADZHIKENERGOLEGPROM"	208
207 repair of motor vehicles	KHUDZHAND AUTOMOBILE REPAIR WORKS n4	129
208 repair of power equipment spare parts for power machinery	ENTERPRISE "TADZHIKENERGOREMONT"	66
209 salt 14,916 tons	VOSE SALT WORKS	251
210 salt 28,454 tons	ASHTI SALT WORKS n2	6
211 sheepskins 843 ths sq dm men's anoraks 2,230 pcs short coats	KURGAN-TYUBE EXPERIMENTAL FURSKIN FACTORY "MUINNA"	164
212 shirts of cotton 633.3 ths pcs	NUREK CLOTHING FACTORY	189
213 silk yarn 683.1 tons twisted articles fabrics of silk, unbleached	KHUDZHAND SILK MILL	141
214 socks for men 7 ths pairs socks for children panty hoses for children	JOINT-STOCK COMPANY "FAIZ"	104

215	spare parts for road building machines	NUREK EXPERIMENTAL MECHANICAL WORKS	190

metal structures for use in construction 194 tons
non-standard machinery and equipment

216	steel enamelled tableware 946.3 ths pcs	KHUDZHAND LEASING-BASED ENTERPRISE "EMALIROVSHCHIK"	138

217	stockings 4,260 ths pairs	FIRM "NAFISA"	72

panty hoses
socks

218	structural aluminium 172 tons	DUSHANBE PILOT-PRODUCTION and EXPERIMENTAL PLANT "REMSTROIDORMASH"	45

welded metal structures 6.7 tons

219	sugar confectionery	CONFECTIONERY FACTORY "SHIRIN"	16

220	sugar confectionery 112.7 tons	DUSHANBE CONFECTIONERY FACTORY "LAZZAT" (JOINT-STOCK COMPANY)	25

221	suitcases 7.5 ths pcs	DUSHANBE LEATHER HABERDASHERY FACTORY "CHARMDUZ"	41

satchels 18.9 ths pcs
bags 118.6 ths pcs

222	table and kitchen articles of aluminium 238.2 ths pcs	SHURAB MECHANICAL WORKS "FILIZ"	224

223	table and kitchen articles of aluminium 620 tons	KOFARNIKHON MECHANICAL WORKS "ZARFSOZ"	145

trays of aluminium
articles of alloys

224	tableware of porcelain	TURSUNZADE PORCELAIN WORKS	237

For additional analytical, business and investment opportunities information, please contact Global Investment & Business Center, USA at (202) 546-2103. Fax: (202) 546-3275. E-mail: rusric@erols.com

225	**textile haberdashery 240 mln pcs** articles of apparel and clothing accessories 100 mln pcs	**FACTORY "ZARDUZ"**	67
226	**threads of silk, unbleached 70 tons** fabrics of silk twisted threads of silk	**DUSHANBE SILK MILL**	53
227	**trade equipment and spare parts** electric ovens 23,911 pcs electric cabinets	**DUSHANBE PLANT "TORGMASH"**	50
228	**trousers** skirts shorts	**KURGAN-TYUBE CLOTHING FACTORY**	161
229	**unmanufactured tobacco 6,559 tons**	**PENDZHIKENT FERMENTED TOBACCO PLANT**	195
230	**unwrought lead 3,800 tons** silver 27.2 tons	**ADRASMAN LEAD and ZINC WORKS**	1
231	**vegetable oil 11.2 ths tons** hydrogenated fat 3.5 ths tons household soap 5 ths tons	**DUSHANBE OILERY and FAT PLANT**	43
232	**vegetable oil 18,457 tons**	**KANIBADAM OILERY and FAT PLANT**	121
233	**vodka 258 ths dal** wine 110 ths dal brandy	**DUSHANBE WINE PLANT**	59
234	**wadding 2,166 tons** apparel wadding 49 tons	**TRAINING and PRODUCTION WORKS n5**	235
235	**wadding of cotton 1,916 tons** articles of apparel and clothing accessories	**KHUDZHAND TRAINING and PRODUCTION WORKS n2**	143

| 236 | wall materials 7,720 ths pcs | PENDZHIKENT BRICK YARD | 194 |

237 warehousing equipment — DUSHANBE PILOT-PRODUCTION and EXPERIMENTAL PLANT "SELEKTSIONNAYA TEKHNIKA" — 46

238 welded metal structures 447 tons

repair of building machinery — KAIRAKKUM MECHANICAL REPAIR WORKSHOP — 109

239 welded metal structures 898 tons

repair of motor vehicles — DUSHANBE EXCAVATOR REPAIR WORKS 27

240 wheat flour 93,206 tons

pasta 7,701 tons
bran — KAIRAKKUM AGROINDUSTRIAL PRODUCTION COMPANY — 107

241 wheat flour 110,390 tons — DUSHANBE GRAIN PROCESSING PLANT 37

242 wheat flour 132 ths tons
bran 35 ths tons
mixed fodder — NAU GRAIN PROCESSING PLANT — 185

243 wheat flour 142 ths tons
bran 40 ths tons
semolina — GRAIN PROCESSING PLANT — 87

244 wheat flour 44 ths tons
bran 11 ths tons — GISSAR GRAIN INTAKE PLANT — 81

245 winding machinery and spare parts 200 pcs
textile spinning machines 152 pcs
trade equipment — DUSHANBE PLANT "TADZHIKTEKSTILMASH" — 49

For additional analytical, business and investment opportunities information,
please contact Global Investment & Business Center, USA
at (202) 546-2103. Fax: (202) 546-3275. E-mail: rusric@erols.com

246	**window assemblies 25.5 ths sq m** door assemblies 14.7 ths sq m wood sawn lengthwise	**DUSHANBE WOOD-WORKING PLANT**	61
247	**window assemblies 4.9 ths sq m** door assemblies 1.9 ths sq m PVC pipes	**DUSHANBE WOOD-WORKING PLANT**	62
248	**window assemblies 9.4 ths sq m** door assemblies 3.5 ths sq m floor panels	**DUSHANBE WOOD-WORKING PLANT**	60
249	**wine 302 ths dal** vodka 110 ths dal sparkling wine	**WINE PLANT "SHAKHRINAU" (LEASING-BASED ì**	252
250	**wine 322 ths dal** crude alcohol 1,369.4 dal grape must	**URA-TYUBE WINE PLANT**	246
251	**wine of fresh grapes 368.1 ths dal** vodka	**GAFUROV WINE PLANT**	76
252	**wire 991 tons** repair of electric motors non-standard machinery and equipment	**MECHANICAL WORKS "KHLOPKOZAPCHAST"**	178
253	**yarn of cotton**	**KURGAN-TYUBE COTTON SPINNING MILL**	163
254	**yarn of cotton 4,473 tons** unbleached fabrics of cotton 3,840 tons finished fabrics of cotton	**KANIBADAM SPINNING and WEAVING MILL**	122
255	**yarn of cotton 6,371 tons**	**JOINT-STOCK COMPANY "BOFANDA"**	103
256	**yarn of mixed wool 370 tons** fabrics	**WOOLEN SHAWL FACTORY "ZARBOF"**	253

For additional analytical, business and investment opportunities information,
please contact Global Investment & Business Center, USA
at (202) 546-2103. Fax: (202) 546-3275. E-mail: rusric@erols.com

SELECTED EXPORTERS AND IMPORTERS

THE FOREIGN ECONOMIC ACTIVITY.

With the export and import operation in the Republic of Tajikistan are engaged 749 entities of the foreign economic activity officially registered in the Ministry of economy and the foreign economic relations including 515 collective farms and state farms. According to the information of the state statistical agency at the Government of the Republic of Tajikistan, the trade economic partners of Tajikistan are 71 countries of the world , from them 10 countries of CIS. In January-August of 2000, the foreign trade turnover of the Republic of Tajikistan including electrical energy and natural gas made 265,9 million dollars of USA, and has exceeded the level of the last year to 11% or to 92,0 million dollars. There are exported goods for January - August of 2000 on the amount of 522,9million dollars that in 19% is more than in January - August of 1999. There are imported goods to the Republic on the amount 443,0 million dollars that in 2% is more than the last year. For the countries of the CIS in the foreign trade turnover is 66% or 636,8 million dollars and for remote countries is 34%. The deficit of the balance of trade with the countries of the CIS turned out negative and made 94,4 million dollars. In export a little advantage belongs to the countries of the CIS and makes 52% or 271,2 million dollars. In import a considerable share are occupied by the countries of CIS-83% or 365,6 million dollars.

The share of the electrical energy in the foreign trade turnover made 16%. For January-August of 2000 its export made 2855,3 million kilowatt / hours on 85,0 million dollars. The import of the natural gas made 474,9 million cubic metre on the amount of 23,0 million dollars. In the export of the republic 54,5% takes aluminum. For January - August of 2000 it has been sent outside the country 179,7 thousand tones on the amount 285,2 million dollars , from them a considerable part on the amount of 160,0 million dollars are sent to the remote countries. An average cost for one tone in comparison with the last year has increased up to 22% and made 1587 dollars. The export of cotton-fibre has made 36,9 thousand tones on the amount 41,4 million dollars and has decreased with the comparison of the last year on 17,5% or 8,7 mill. dollars. The deliveries to the remote countries has decreased on 27% and to the countries of the CIS has increased up to 86%.

FOOD AND LIGHT INDUSTRY

Company or firm	Information
Production corporation "TAJIKTEXTILE" Adress: 6 Sherozi ave., Dushanbe, Tajikistan, 735042 phone: 21-36-73 fax: 21-33-55	• Established: in 1942. • Pattern of ownership: collective. • Number of the workers: 4490 persons. • The industrial areas: 6000 sq. m. • The join makes deep processing cotton of a fiber. • Subject of the basic activity: production of a cotton yarn. Rough and ready cotton fabrics. • Volume of demand: 90 millions meters annually. • The name of the project: " Modernisation of the basic production ".

For additional analytical, business and investment opportunities information, please contact Global Investment & Business Center, USA at (202) 546-2103. Fax: (202) 546-3275. E-mail: rusric@erols.com

	• The purpose of the project: modernizing of operating productive capacities of join on the basis of modern foreign equipment and issue of competitive products • Direction of usage of the investments: purchase of the equipment and enforcement of circulating assets. • Cost of the project: 178,7 millions USD. • Necessary volume of the investments: 155,85 millions USD. • Payback time: 5 years. • Realization of production: a home market 45 %, export to countries of CIS 30 % in other countries 25 %. • The warranty of realization of production: the agreements, and also designed measures on the extension of a seller's market. • Beginning of return of the investments in 24 months. • Final payment in 60 months. • Security of return of the investments: the state warranty. • The solutions on support of state organs is present. • Enterprise manager Anvar Kurbanov
Joint venture "ASIA LTD" Address: 1, Krasnoarmeiskay str., Leninabad area, Chkalovsk, 735737 phone.: (37771) 5-46-35 fax 6-53-51	• Patterns of ownership: joint ventures. • Established: in 1997. The founders: republics a Tajikistan and Switzerland. • The basic activity: production of cooling drinks and mineral water. • Productive capacities: a line on issue of water and drinks (Italy), productivity 2500 litres / hours per polyethylene capacities in volume 1,5 l.; a line on a blowing of capacities (Francium) of volume 1,5, productivity 5 thousand units/hour. They have completely automized the production. • Number of the workers: 90 persons. • Realization of production: On territory of a Tajikistan (up to 80%), is exported to countries of CIS, Central Asia (15 - 20%). • The charter capital: 2,5 million's USD. • The investment projects: "Factory on issue of oil ". • The purpose of the project: construction of a factory on issue of oil in polyethylene capacities in volume 1,0 l. • Now construction is completed, but investments for the investments for the investments for the investments for investments • Total cost of the project: 900 thousand $. • Necessary volume of the investments: 500 thousand $. • Payback time of the project: 3 years. • Beginning of return of the investments in 24 months. • The warranty of return of the investments the lien of own assets.

	• Enterprise manager Rahim Ismoilov
Joint Stock company "ABRESHIM" Address: 238, Lenin St., Khudjand city,Republic of Tajikistan 725702 phone: 6-34-20	• Established: in 1992 on the base of Leninabad's silk factory. S.C. Abreshim is one of the largest enterprises in its branches in the North of Tajikistan. • Type of property: - Stock 51.2 percent, states 48.8 % • Main activities: production & realization of heat network, cotton & silk fabrics as well as sewing items. • Number of Workers: 3280 people • Facilities/Assets: good communications including auto & railway access as well as great production premises. • Name of Project: "Spinning factory". • Project's purpose: construct cotton-spinning factory. • Overall value of the project: USD 6.7 million. • Required volume of investments: USD 6.7 million. • Use of investments: to buy equipment. • Payback period: 2.5 years. • Beginning of return on investments: in 30 months. • Final payment: in 60 months. • On the base of marketing, sales market the volume of demand for realization defined. • Product realization planned to be carried out on the territory of Tajikistan 2,5 percent, âxport to CIS countries - 75 %. Warranties to products sale are presence of agreements on delivery. • Guarantee: At present, S.C. Abreshim prepared pilot model to ensure returns on investments (i. e. defined by state warranties as well as guarantee of S.C. Assets). • There is a decision of state & regional bodies to support the investment project. • Project Manager Tohir Babaev
Joint venture "JAVONI" Address: 1, Javoni Str., Khujand, 735400 phone: 4-02-95 fax 4-08-61	• Established: 1993. • Number of the workers: more than 1000 persons. • Own assets: about 39 million's USD. • The basic activity: deep processing cotton of a fiber from modern technique, production and sale of a cotton yarn, fabrics, sewing articles of a broad assortment (ready man's, female and children's clothes) consumer goods. • Operating productions: spinning, weavers', sewing and plot on furnish velvet of a fabric. The civil works on shops of furnish and they carry on colour of production that will allow the enterprise to begin export of finish products and will increase volumes in money terms. • The name of the project: "Extension of a finishing shop of spinning production ". • Total cost of the project: 5 millions USD.

	- Necessary volume: 3 million's USD. - The warranty of return of the investments - liens of own assets. - Enterprise manager Sharif Kalandarov
Joint venture "KABOOL TAJIK TEXTILE" Address: 238, Lenin Str., Khujand city, 735702 phone: (37922) 4-32-28, 6-68-77 fax: (3772) 51-00-80	- Established: 1994. - The basic activity: production of a yarn, cotton, severe fabrics and finished products. - The charter capital: 10 million's USD, Korean side - 56 %, Tajik sides - 44%. - Number of the workers: more than 2000 persons. Annual design volume of sale of production 30 million's USD. - Annual productive capacity: 12 thousand tons of a clap - fiber and issue of a cotton yarn of 10 500 tons, cotton fabric 22 million's m, jeans' fabric 6 million's m., ready sewing articles 158000 thousand pieces annually. - Based on more deep processing of a clap - fiber, issue of fabrics and sewing articles, increases of production and realization of production, they ensure the seizure working and receipt in a republic of convertible currency. - The joint venture is ready for mutually advantageous cooperation to the foreign investors in matter of overgrowth issue of competitive production. - Enterprise manager Keun Woo Lim
Joint Stock company of close type "KOLOS LTD" Address: 69 Chehova Str., Leninabad region phone: 3-28-79, 3-29-45	- Established: 1930. - In they transform 1997 in a JSCCT. - The basic activity: processing of a grain wheat and its processing. - Number of the workers: 45 persons - Productivity: 70 tons / day. - The basic production assets: 104 thousand USD. - The common area: 130 hectares. - The industrial areas 1,90 hectares; under the sowing area 94 hectares. - Names project: "Modernisation of a mill". The purpose of the project: increase of volume of processing of a grain about 100 tons / day. - Total cost of the project: 350 thousand USD. - Necessities in the investments 250 thousand USD. - Period of return: 2 years, beginning of return in 6 months. - The warranty of return of the investments: the lien of own assets, insurance. - Enterprise manager Nazar Kasimov

For additional analytical, business and investment opportunities information, please contact Global Investment & Business Center, USA at (202) 546-2103. Fax: (202) 546-3275. E-mail: rusric@erols.com

| Production corporation "KULOB" Address:36, Lenin St. , Kulob, Khatlon area, 35360 phone: 2-32-30, 2-55-38 | <ul><li>Established: 1993.</li><li>Type of prorety: collective</li><li>Main activities: remaking of cotton and production of competitive products: production and sale of sewn wares.</li><li>Facilities/ Assets: The construction of sewing and looms, for paper production, sock/stocking and carpet production, and juice production. The corporation has a comfortable hotel in the city of Kulob.</li><li>Authorized capital stock USD 200,000.</li><li>Value of immovable assets: USD 3200 thousand. Established: 1993.</li><li>Type of property: Collective.</li><li>Main activities: remaking of cotton and production of competitive products: production and sale of sewn wares.</li><li>Number of workers: 60 people.</li><li>Facilities/Assets: The construction of sewing factory on the project of American specialists was begun by the approval of Government of the Republic of Tajikistan in 1993. At present the construction of complex of buildings realized on 80%. The power substation (4000 kWh/h) and 5 km of electro-transmission line built and delivered into complex. Has a sewing workshop, which has Japanese machinery (30). Yet to be constructed: Total area of 6240 sq.m: Production area (4320 sq.m.); Storage (880 sq.m.), Offices: (1200 sq.m.).</li><li>Available power: electric: 4000 kW/h, water consumption: 24 liters/sec. Output can be used to operate different equipment:</li><li>Total area of production premises 6240 sq. m.</li><li>Name of project: "Sewing-knitted fabric".</li><li>Project's purpose: complete construction of sewing factory, issue and sale of products.</li><li>Total value of project: USD 8000 thousand.</li><li>Necessary volume of investments: USD 6000 thousand.</li><li>Payback period: 3 years.</li><li>Main use of investments: buying of equipment.</li><li>The realization of commodity output: 10%, export to CIS countries: 90%.</li><li>Guarantee: state warranties.</li><li>There is decision from state and local bodies supporting the enterprise.</li><li>Enterprise manager: Zafar Mirzoev</li></ul> |
| Joint Stock company of openning type "NONPAZ" | <ul><li>Established: in 1938.</li><li>Type of property: State</li><li>Main activity: production of bread and lacer's articles.</li></ul> |

For additional analytical, business and investment opportunities information, please contact Global Investment & Business Center, USA at (202) 546-2103. Fax: (202) 546-3275. E-mail: rusric@erols.com

Address: 28, T.Pulodi St., Dushanbe, Republic of Tajikistan, 743013 phone: 21-87-66	Formally the enterprise produced bread, macaroni, spaghetti, confectionery articles, and caramel. Enterprise productivity - 120 tons of bread a day. Number of workers: 182 people • Facilities/Assets: Authorized capital: USD 187,000. Cost of fixed and turnover means: USD 193,000. Immovable property (as assessed in 1998): USD 540,000. Production areas: more than 8,000 sq.m. • Name of project: "Re-equiping and stockholding of corporation Nonpaz." • Project's purpose: technical modernization and reequiping of production to increase quantity and improve quality of products. The project passed through complex examination. Business plan is elaborated. Use of investments: purchase of complecting articles and materials, issue of shares for joint stock corporation. • Overall value of the project: USD 300,000. Necessary volume of investments: USD 200,000. Payback period: 2 years. • Guarantee: bank guarantees and insurance. Beginning of return on investments: in 12 months Final payment: in 24 months. • There is a decision of state and local bodies supporting the enterprise. • Enterprise manager Abdurasul Mukhidov
Joint Stock company "POIAFZOL" Address: 14 Rudaki str., Dushanbe, 734012 phone: 23-24-23	• Established: in 1999. • They created the factory in 1938. • Subject of the basic activity is having sewed children's and school footwear. • Medial-list numbers working - 50 persons. A production area of the plant - 8450 sq. m. • Investment's project "Reconstruction of a shop on production of footwear". • Purpose - modernisation and retrofit of acting productive capacities, for a quality improvement of commodities. • A direction of investments usage - acquisition of knowledge, purchasing of machinery and furnishing articles, replenishment of current assets. • Overall value of the project: 1,5 million. USD. • Necessary volume of investments: 1 million. USD. • Payback time: 3 years. • Beginning of returning: in 12 months. • Final repayment: 36 months. • Guarantee: liens of own assets. • Enterprise manager Rahmatjon Davlatov

Company or firm	Information
State enterprise "RESMON" Adress: 45, Hoji Sodik St., Kanibadam 735900 phone/fax: 2-23-03	• Established: in 1962. • Form of property: state. Main activities: production of cotton yarn and fabric. Number of workers: 1,330. Facilities/Assets: 23,873 sq. m. Regulations capital of the enterprise: 1,401,000 $ US. • Cost of the major and turnover facilities: 7,884,000 $ US. • Name of Project: "Technical re-equipment of enterprise or creation of joint venture". • Project's purpose: installing new technological lines for processing fiber. Increasing production of cotton yarn and fabric, meeting international standards. • Use of investments: purchase of equipment and materials, plenishement of the turnover facilities. Total value of project: USD 35,000.Demand volume: 6,000 tons of cotton yarn fabric, 910 mln. of ready-made fabric. Payback period: 5 years. • There is adecision of the regional bodies on supporting of the project. • Enterprise manager Abdumadjid Kahharov
Stock company of opened type "SAMAR" Address: 13 Omar Khayam str., Khatlon area, Voge region, The Republic of Tajikistan	• SCOT "Samar" was founded on 01/01/96 on the bas of Vose cotton enterprise. • Which was created in 1982 on the bas of Vose storing cotton. • After the SCOT "Samar" was formed, much energy and means were spent on it's reconstruction, expansion and creation of the modern technological lines. • The main for today form of the activity of SCOT "Samar" processing of raw cotton, commodity output of consumer goods and productive-technological goods. • The assortment of SCOT "Samar" includes 88 names. • The cost of main funds 2146 thousand $ • The cost of equipment 1062, 3 thousand $ • The total area of production premises 13604 sq. m. • The cost of the project of enterprise (three shifts work) 1466511 thousands rubles. • The capital of SCOT "Samar" is 500,4 $

	• Besides the processing of raw cotton SCOT "Samar" has:
	○ oil factory output of oil
	○ textile factory (spinning yarn, weaving mill)
	○ factory for the output of socks
	○ production of Knitting articles
	○ mini tinned factory (tomato-paste, compotes and etc.)
	○ assembling telephone set uses
	○ sewing factory and etc.
	• Enterprise manager Samaridin Phazliddinov
Stock company of opened type "SUMAN" Address: 78, International str., Dushanbe city, 734001. phone: 24 86 81.	• Established: in 1992. • Main activity production of sewing manufactured articles consumer & artistic handicraft goods. At Present schedule number of employees 142 people. • Production area of enterprise 5372 sq. m. more than 100 sewing makers work there. • They produce national quilted blankets "Kuurpa" & "kurpachi", pillows, mattresses & lots of other items. • Name of project "Expansion & reconst-ruction of sewing produc-tion & products of consu-mer and artistic handicraft goods". • Project's purpose is increasing of volume & assortment of sewing production & creation of a shop on production of people's artistic handicraft items. It allows to revive & save ancient people's handicrafts, as well as organizing of skilled workmen from talented youth number. • Direction of using investments buying equipment, construction of a shop, raw material purchase overall value of investments 3,5 mln USD. • Necessary volume of investments 3 mln USD. • Pay-back period 6 years. Beginning of returning investments in 36 months. • At present series of products production is carrying on. • Ensuring investments returning is a transmission of rights on property, insurance. • There is a Decision of regional bodies on supporting. • The project allows enlarging a volume & assortment of

	sewing production & people artistic handicraft trade will attract workman in order to use their talent largely. • Enterprise manager Fajizimo Ibragimova
State enterprise "SHIRIN" Address: 10, Djabar Rasulov str., Dushanbe city, 734049 phone/fax: 35-82-83.	• The form of property - collective. • They formed the factory in 1964 and considered being the first large confectioner's factories in Tajikistan, fully satisfying population demand in confectionery. Production capacities allowed to produce broad assortments of articles (caramel, biscuits, zephyrs, sweets, etc.) right now demand for products compose 10 thousands tons per annum. • Production areas of premises 3442 sq. m., including shops, refrigerator chambers, etc. • Right now schedule number of employees 489 persons. • Project's name is "Reconstruction and introduction of modern techniques". • Project's aim is acquisition of new techniques and world standard technology. • Overall value of project and necessary volume of investments compose 6000 thousands USD investments are to be used on equipment acquisition and supplement of turnover means. Taking into consideration own production there is an idea of the project, and scientific technological documentation is elaborated, as well as prepared active models, collaborate technico-economic ground. • Principal sale market domestic market (100%). • Ensuring investments returning are assets pledge. There is a decision of local bodies on supporting. • Beginning of investments returning in 2003 year ultimate payment in 2000 year. • Enterprise manager Mustafo Davlatov

INDUSTRY

Enterprises or facility	Information
Stock Company of opening type "CHEMICAL PLANT" Address: Navobod Str..	• Established: in 1965. • In 1997 is transformed in joint-stock company. The basic activity: production of industrial explosives. Number of the workers 1100 persons. The issue of complex fertilizers for needs of an agriculture is

Isfara, 735920 phone:2-21-90 fax: 2-29-46	organized on the basis of usage of local raw resources in volume 50 thousand MTA. • The basic activity: production of explosives granulits an AC - 4, AC - 8, AC - 4B, AC - 8B, C - 6M gramonits 30/70, 79/21, 82/18, intended for open and underground operations, except for operations dangerous on gas and dust. There is sorting railway a station. Cost of a fixed capital 2.380 millions rublov. The charter capital 1.108 millions rublov. Names project [1] 1: " Construction of a line of a factory on production of ammoniacal niter ". Productivity 50 thousand ton / year on the basis of local raw material. Total cost of the project 10,2 million. USD. • The required investments 6 million. USD. • The project [1] 2: "Architecture of production of automobile storage batteries ", productivity 300 thousand pieces /year. A total cost 3,1 million. USD. • The required investments 1,5 million. USD. The purpose of engaging of the investments: acquisition of the process equipment. • There is a warranty of Government. • Enterprise manager Ilias Aslamov
State enterprise "TRANSFORMER PLANT" Address: #1 Gafurov str., Kurgan-Tube, Republic of Tajikistan phone: 2-37-53.	• Established: in 1937. • Emitted production was exported to many foreign countries. • Number of the workers: 140 persons. • The charter capital: 545 million's rublov. • Own assets: 464 million's rublov. • Names project: "Completion of construction of 2 queues of Kurgan - Tyube of a transformer factory ". • Projects purpose: issue of power transformers TM-63 Kwa and TM-10000 Kwa. Modernisation and modernizing of operating productive capacities. Usage of the investments: purchase of furnishing articles and materials; construction; enforcement of circulating assets. • Realization of production: republics a Tajikistan - 80%, country of CIS - 20% from total amounts. • Cost of the project: 26 million. USD. • Payback time: 5 years. • Attractiveness of the project: absence of a similar factory and productions of transformers in Central Asia, vast sellers' market. • Security of return of the investments: the lien of assets, cession of rights on permanent assets. • Enterprise manager Nurali Kukiev

For additional analytical, business and investment opportunities information,
please contact Global Investment & Business Center, USA
at (202) 546-2103. Fax: (202) 546-3275. E-mail: rusric@erols.com

State enterprise "PORCELAIN PLANT" Address: # 28 Lomonosova str., Tursun-zade, Republic of Tajikistan.	• Established: in 1980. • Number of the workers: 1255 persons. • Productive capacities: 5750 thousand pieces of articles annually. • The basic activity: production of ware. • Assortments of emitted production: porcelain ware, piala, teapots, the trays, are oblique, dishes and other. • Production of a factory is in demand not only in republics, but also abroad. • Names project: " Mastering of new aspects of production ". • The basic purposes: production of new aspects of production and improvement of the quality manufactured production. • Total cost: 700 thousand USD. • Indispensable volume of the investments 500 thousand USD. • Use of investments: purchase of materials, equipment, dye markers. • Payback time: 1,5 years. • Beginning of return of the investments in 12 months. • Security of return of the investments the state warranties. • There is a solution on support of state organs.
State enterprise "TAJIK ALUMINIUM PLANT" Address: Tursun-zade, 735014, Republic of Tajikistan phone: 2-23-86,2-32-87 fax: 2-23-86.	• Established: in 1975. • Number of the workers: 15000 persons. • The basic activity: production of aluminum and articles from him. • Productive capacity: 340 thousand tons of aluminum annually. • Names project: "Reconstruction of production calcination of anodes, overhauls of electrolytic baths ". • Projects purpose: restoring of productive capacities, reconstruction of production Calcination of anodes, overhauls of electrolytic baths, modernisation and modernizing of operating productive capacities. • Total cost of the project: 150 million. USD. • Indispensable volume of the investments: 120 million. USD. • Payback time: 5 years. • Usage of the investments: purchase of the equipment and materials. • Security of return of the investments - state warranties and granting of the rights on acquisition up to 49 % of the shares of the enterprise. • Beginning of return of the investments - in 3 years. • The solution on support of state organs - is present.

	• Enterprise manager Abdukadyr Ermatov
Production corporation "TAJIKTEXTILEMACH" Address: #7, Nazarhoev str., Dushanbe, 734042, Republic of Tajikistan phone: 23 27 - 88 fax: 21-65 - 83.	• Established: in 1944. • Main activity production of textile & equipment, spare parts for cotton purify industry, consumption goods. • Schedule number of employees 810 persons . • Production area of undertaking 190000 m2. • Authorized capital 720 thousands USD. • Cost of main circulating assets 1427 thousands USD. • Project's name "Gas counter of consumer mark CGB 6". • Project's purpose arrangement of production of consumer instruments ensuring Supervision & account of consumption of natural gas. • Realization of project allows significantly shorten consumption of natural gas. • Direction of using investments buying completing products. • Overall value of project 4 years. • Beginning of returning investments in 12 months; Ultimate payments in 36 months. • Ensuring of returning investments a guarantee of assets, insurance. • There is a decision on supporting of state bodies. Volume of supply & demand 200 thousands pieces of CGB-6. • Enterprise manager Hamid Abdulloev
Srock company Dushanbe refrigerator plant "PAMIR" Adress: # 343, R.Nabiev str., Dushnbe, Republicof Tajikistan, 734036 phone: 31-05-47 fax: 31-07-97	• They formed SCDRP "Pamir" in 1964. • The plant exported its production to 15 countries of the world. • Main activities mass production of a powerful being engine (refrigerators). • Schedule number of employees 578 persons. • Authorized capital of the enterprise 254,1 thousands USD. • The cost of fixed and turnover means 615,9 thousands USD. • Immovable property 460,6 thousands USD.(1.01.1998) • Production premises 17044 sq. m. • The plant possesses auto and railway excess ways. They arrange stable contacts with the plants of CIS countries. • Accountings above mentioned material SCDRP "Pamir" elaborated business-plan and investment project "Mastering production of new models of refrigerators".

For additional analytical, business and investment opportunities information, please contact Global Investment & Business Center, USA at (202) 546-2103. Fax: (202) 546-3275. E-mail: rusric@erols.com

	<ul><li>Projects' aim is to produce two-chambered refrigerators at the level of world standards at the expense of foreign investments and at the expense of own production, (purchase of completing articles, materials).</li><li>Market investments determine demand which form 92 thousands refrigerators per annum.</li><li>Sale markets: domestic 20 percent, export to CIS countries 60 percent, export to the other countries 20 percent.</li><li>Guarantee of realization presence of agreements, determination of a sale market. Now SCDRP "Pamir" is ready to transfers into production two-chambered refrigerators. Investment projects supported either local and sated bodies. Overall cost of the project 1000 thousands USD. Necessary volume of investments 500 thousands USD. Payback period three years.</li><li>Beginning of investments returning 12 months.</li><li>Enterprise manager Ibodullo Mirov</li></ul>
State enterprise "SANGTUDINSK Hudroelectric Station" Address: # 64, I.Somoni str., Dushanbe, Republic of Tajikistan, 734026 phone: 35-06-82 fax: 35-86-92.	<ul><li>Established: in 1957.</li><li>Type of property: state, joint-stock, including percentage of the state - 1 %.</li><li>Main activity: production and distribution of electrical power.</li><li>Number of workers: 11 thousand people.</li><li>The exploitation of existing hydro-electric stations permits cheap electrical power to keep factories operating and to provide the population with electric power.</li><li>Name of project: "Sangtudin HES", elaborated by "Tajikhydroenergyproject".</li><li>Project's purpose: construction of a complex irrigation-power hydronode; production of electrical power as well as regulation of the drainage of Vakhsh river. Bulk of supply and demands - 2,7 milliards Kw/hour; electrical power realized: in Tajikistan 50%; in CIS countries - 25%; in other countries 25%.</li><li>Total cost of project: USD 360,9 million.</li><li>Necessary volume of investments: 265,9 million USD.</li><li>Payback period: 4 years.</li><li>Guarantee: state warranties.</li><li>There is a decision of state and regional bodies supporting the project.</li><li>Enterprise Manager Bahrom Sirojev</li></ul>
Joint-stock company	<ul><li>Rogun the hydro power node is largest on p. Vakhsh.</li></ul>

"ROGUNGESSTROI" Address: 734026 Dushanbe, I. Somony str., 64. Tel.: 35-06-82, 35-86-92.	With lead it in maintenance, probably, practically completely to run in a water-energy potential of all rivers, and for to regulate a drain of Amu Darya. Alongside with it, the common development of the electric power on will be increased Vakhsh on 0,7 milliards. kw. Hour. Not the smaller value has and water-economic effect of reservoir Rogun HYDROELECTRIC POWER STATION, in a part of regulation of a drain and water of distribution. • The charter capital - 150 million. USD. • The name of the project "Rogun HYDROELECTRIC POWER STATION ". The purpose of the given project: construction of a complex irrigation-power hydro node. • Usage of the investments: construction, purchase of the equipment. Manufactured production - electric power, at volume of demand - 10 milliards. kw. Hour. • Realization of production: republics a Tajikistan - 50%; export to countries of CIS - 25%; export to other countries - 25%. A total cost: 1250 million. USD. • Payback time of the project - 6 years. Attractiveness of the project: economically net production of the cheap electric power for all locales. • Security of return of the investments: the state warranty. • Enterprise manager S. Siyamardov
Joint-stock company "ISFARA FBM" Address: village Honobod, Isfara, Leninabad area, Republic of Tajikistan, 735920 phone: 2- 32 04 fax 2-31-03	• Established: in 1973, they share the Isfara Combine of building materials " in 1998 in joint-stock company". • The basic activity: production of building materials based on local raw material. The annual power of the enterprise is issue in volume 102 thousand ò. Gypsum, 26 thousand tons' Inform, 750 thousand ò. Fossil rock and 42 million. Pieces of bricks. Number of the workers: 550 persons. The charter capital: 200 thousand USD. • Fixed capital: 1,25 million. USD. Cumulative assets: 2,8 million. USD. Names project "Architecture and construction a small of a cemented factory". • Projects purpose: mastering issue of cement with annual volume 60 thousand tons. Overgrowth of power of industry of building materials based on local raw material. Total cost of the project: 3,5 millions USD • Necessities in the investments: 2,1 millions USD • Period of return of the investments: 3 years • Beginning of return in 12 months • Enterprise manager Nematullo Muhamadov

Enterprises or facility	Information
StocStock enterprise of closed type "LAHL" Address: #262, Lenin str., Khujand, Leninabad oblast, 735702 phone: 6-45-94 telex: 275235 "Soda"	• JSCOT "Lahl" is founded in 1999 on the basis glass of a tare factory grounded in 1943. • The majors revalue of a factory, and nowadays joint-stock company "Lahl" was and there is a production of a glass container for needs of an industry. • The Leninabad area is rich by gardens, grapes, plantations of vegetables etc. On territory of area many of canning and other refining factories. The normal operation of these factories wholly depends on availability of empties. Therefore a main role of a JSCOT "Lahl" - solution of a problem, bound with empties not only for needs of area, but also other locales of a Tajikistan. • The basic line of business of a JSCOT is: production and delivery of empties for an industry making a wine, canning and lactic factories. • The manufacturing floor spaces of a JSCOT "Lahl" compound 3,16 hectares. 350 persons here work. • The charter capital of the plant - 15 million. USD. The installed power of the plant compounds 182 million. The conditional jars annually. • Now on a JSCOT "Lahl" the investment design is prepared "Modernisation flown down productions". The given design is designed TASIS and favoured by Worldwide Bank. • Overall costs of the design - 6 million. USD (Installment financing). • The own facilities, put in this design, compound 2,0 million. USD.Payback time of the design - 3 years. A beginning of returning of the investments - in 18 months. • Warranties of returning of the investments own assets. • Enterprise manager Mirzohalim Mirzokarimov
State enterprise "ADRASMAN ORE-MINING AND PROCESSING ENTERPRISE " Address: #72, Ganchbakhsh str., Adrasman, Kairakkum, 735780 phone: 2-23-13, ext. 2-12	• Established: 1943. • The basic activity: production of leaden silver ores and leaden concentrate. • Number of staff: 1128 persons. • The industrial areas of 8820 sq. m. • The charter capital: 980 thousand USD. • Own assets: 1047 thousand USD. • Names project: " Architecture of an ore mining, production of a leaden - silvered concentrate ". • The purpose of the project: increase of productive capacity of an ore mine up to 600 thousand ò of ore annually on the basis Adrasman enterprise, extension of development of a field Eastern Kanimansur at the

	expense of padding commissioning of three refining blocks, implicating(involving) in handling stores of a part Large Kanimansur. Construction of a complex of buildings and buildings for a service of an ore mine. Usage of the investments: purchase of the equipment, acquisition of gears of materials, construction. Indispensable volume: 7,2 million. USD. Payback time: till 5 years, after a termination of construction. Security of return of the investments: the state guarantees. There is a solution on support of state and regional organs. • Enterprise manager Rahimdjan Nurmatov

State enterprise "ANZOB AND PROCESSING ENTERPRISE" Address: Zeravshan, Aini district, Sogd oblast, 735522 phone: 24-21	• Established: in 1954.
	• Source of raw materials: a field "Djijikrud", (90 % of known reserves). The field is rich by different minerals (antimony, quicksilver, gold, argentum, taxes etc.).
	• Number workers: 920 persons.
	• Industrial plants: a underground ore mine, dressing-works, central, repair-mechanical, transport shop and etc.
	• Names project "Reconstruction of productive capacities of combine ",
	• Projects purpose:
	  o increase of power on production and processing of ore up to 700 thousand ò. Annually;
	  o commissioning of padding powers on dressing-works;
	  o construction of a mercury factory on demercury of a concentrate on furnaces of a boiling bed ;
	  o construction surma of a factory for deriving finish products.
	• Indispensable volume: 102 million. USD.
	• Payback time of the project 8, 6 years.
	• After a realization of the first stage - creation of metallurgical powers and engaging to processing ores containing precious metals, the sum of effect from the investments will be significant and, accordingly, payback time will make 3-4 years.
	• The creation of joint ventures or other forms of co-operation on mutually advantageous conditions is possible.
	• Enterprise manager Holnazar Halikov

Joint-stock company "BODOM" Address: #257, Lenin str., Khudgand, region Kanibadam. Republic of	• Established: in 1939. • Since 1992. Joint-stock company of "Bodom". • The enterprise emits: automobiles spare, back bridges, boxes of a change of transmissions, cylinders of the principles brake. forward and back brakes. rudder

Tajikistan phone:(37968)2-77-90 fax:(37967)2-42-07	control, differentials, brake drums and other details, for automobiles of the mark "GAS". They run in the issue: bicycles, bicycle shops and bicycle trailers. • Divisions: a bicycle factory, power 6000 articles annually; mechanical assembly shop [1] 1 and other. • Cost of annual production: 2 milliards. 380 million. Rbl. • Names project: "Modernizing bicycles of production". Projects purpose: improvement of the quality and competitive strengths of bicycles, overgrowth of production. • Total cost of the project: 14 million. US dollars. • Indispensable volume of the investments: 9 million. US dollars. Period of return: 5 years. A beginning of return in 12 months. • The warranty of return: government of a RT - 15% and lien of own assets - 85%. • Enterprise manager Yusuf Ahmedov
State enterprise "VOSTOKREDMET" Address: #10, A.Oplanchuk str., Leninabad region, Chkalovsk, 735730 teletype:27-51-35, 27-51-89 "Seagulls". fax:5-09-45. phone:(37771)5-24-51, 5-53-70	• Established: 1945. The Tajikistan is in immediate subparameter of Government of Republic. • In composition of join consist: a metal works; Chkalovsk machine works; joint venture a Khudjand - ÇÈË (Tajikistan - Russia); research-and-production Center "Know-how"; research-and-production Center "ELTA"; the manufacturing - collective plant " an ore Mine of opened mining operations "; control of a central heating and delivery of energy; control of a motor-vehicle transport; Center of economical studies; pioneer camp - Preventive sanatorium "Orlenok"; the house of rest "Kairakkum"; state farm "Palass". • The main commodity and aspects of services: the monoxide - Protoxide of uranium, efinirovan of gold and silver, jeweller and souvenired articles(workpieces), signs of the state awards, dressing tungsten of inclusive concentrates, buses "Tajikistan", parts and clusters to minihydroelectric power station, sprinkling systems, mining equipment and other machine-building commodity, facing tile from a natural rock, assembly of electronic package, agricultural commodity, service in the field of programming, link, is warm energy of procurement, motor transportation carriages, technological minings, civil and erection works etc. • The design #1. The indispensable investments: the uranium design - "Creation of joint venture on a mining of ores" - 15 million. US dollars. Period of returning of the investments - 5 years. • The design #2. "Assembly both implementation computer and consumer electronics" - 500 thousand

	USD. A beginning of returning of the investments - during 2 years (there are manufacturing floor spaces and trained staff); • The design #3. "Fabrication of a facing tile" - 200 thousand USD. A beginning of returning of the investments - in 2 years (there are 2 open casts of pink marble and gabbro, rock cut shop, grinding lines. The carved machinery is necessary a modern rock. Warranty of returning - lien of own assets. • Enterprise manager Zafar Razykov

TELECOMMUNICATION

Company or firm	Information
Internet service provider "TELECOMM TECHNOLOGY" Adress: 734001, Republic of Tajikistan, Dushanbe city, Bokhtar street 35/1 phone/fax: 21-14-22, 51-01-44	• Established: in 1994. • Type of property: private. • Main activity: telecommunications services and computer technology. Number of workers: 25 people. • Facilities/Assets: Premises with total area 40 sq.m. • Name of project: "Integrated satellite communication". Project's purpose: creation of developed telecommunications satellite network on the basis of VSAT technology and presentation telecommunication services to Bank Stock exchanges and population. Guarantee of the project's realization is considered to be the presence of agreements as well as determination of demand channels realization and services. Company has elaborated scientific-technological and constructive documentation, and prepared experimental sample. Realization of its services and technology: in Tajikistan 75-85%; rest to be exported to other countries. Business plan prepared by company. • ATK "Telecomm Technology Ltd." is first Internet service provider in Tajikistan. Since January 1999 the company has begun submission of services on network access to Internet to users in Tajikistan. The company plans by 2000 to supply access of all regions of Tajikistan to services of the world web Internet. Total cost of the project: USD 5,500,000. • Necessary volume of investments: USD 2,800,000. • Use of investments: acquisition of technology and equipment purchase. Payback period: 2-3 years. • Beginning of return on investments: in 24 months • Final payment: in 48 months. • Guarantee: insurance, ownership part of the share of enterprises. There is a decision of the state bodies

	supporting this enterprise.
	• Enterprise Manager Shavkat Khalilov

COMMERCIAL STRUCTURES

Company or firm	Information
Private firm "RASULIEN" Address: 735718, Leninabad area, Khudjand, 18 microregions. phone.: (37922) 2-62-09; 2-84-93; 2-56-37. fax: 6-06-30.	• Established: in 1998. • Main activity: processing of agricultural production, drying of vegetables and fruit. • The corporation is arranged with unique drying aggregates. The soft process drying high density finites infrared, allows completely (about 90%) to save vitamins, flavouring qualities, erasing thus, parasitic micro flora. For drying the ecological net vegetables and fruit are used. • Manufactured production: 900 tons / years. • The industrial areas: 1,5 thousand's sq.m. • Productive capacity: 800 MTA. • The charter capital 240 million. USD. • Number of the workers: 350 persons. • Names project: "Project of a line of sorting and prepacking of production in small-sized packaging ". • Return of investments: in 7 years. • Beginning of return: in 12 months. • The warranty of return: own assets. • Enterprise manager Abdugaffor Rasulov
State enterprise "TAJIK RAILWAY" Address: 734012, Dushanbe 35, Academician Nazarshoev St. phone.: 23-35-29 fax: 21-57-91	• Established: in 1994 on the basis of Tajik section of the Middle Asian railway, which they built in 1929. • Facilities/Assets: Authorized capital stock USD 1,335,814,000; principles sum and turnover means USD 2,139,933,000 (as of 1996) • Project #1: "Electrification Tajik railway road in Leninabad regions". • Project's purpose: The creation of an electrification railway road the northern parts of Tajik railways. The construction began, but because of the lack of the means is frozen. • Total cost of the project: USD 10,700,000 • Necessary volume of investments: USD 35,000,000 • Payback period: 5 years. • Beginning of the return on investments: in 24 months. • Final payment: in 96 months. • Guarantee: state and banking warrants. • There is a decision of state bodies supporting this project.

	• Project #2: "The construction of new railway line Kurgan-Tjube Yavan". • Project's purpose: Construction of an iron line for improvement of a transport service of a southeast part of a Tajikistan. An expansion: 116 km. The realization of services: in Tajikistan - 12%; in CIS - 88%. Total cost of the project: USD 270,000,000 Necessary volume of investment: USD 112,000,000. • Payback period: 5 years. • Beginning of return on investments: in 24 months. • Final payment: in 96 months. • Guarantee: state and banking warrants. • There is a decision of state bodies supporting this project. • Project #3: "Construction of new railway Vakhsh-Yavan". • Project's purpose: The reestablishment of the section rail road Termez-Yavan by the clay torrents Termez - Yavan. • Project period: 5 years. The realization of services: in Tajikistan: 15%; in CIS: 85%. • Total cost of the project: USD 200,000,000. • Necessary volume of investments: USD 195,000,000. • Payback period: 8 years. • Beginning of the return on investments: in 24 months. • Final payment: in 96 months. • Guarantee: state and banking warrants. • There is a decision of state bodies supporting this project. • Chief of the Enterprise Muhamad Habibov
Jointstock company of opened type "LADA - HULBUK" Address: Khatlon area, Vose region collective farm M. Mahmadaliev, Site "Aral" phone: 2-28-56 (switchboards) 3-42 phone in in Dushanbe: 31-73-73, 31-88-89	• Established: in 1994 • Patterns of ownership mixed. • The basic activity: rendering of services to the citizens, enterprises, architectures in maintenance service and repair of cars, them before selling preparation and realization; leasing, and also buying up, restoring both realization of the supported automobiles and renewals; manufacture of new renewals both other own production and their realization. • Number of the workers: 25 persons. • Own assets: 120 thousand US dollars. • Cost of the real estate: 240 thousand US dollars. • Industrial locations: more than 1000 sq. ì. • The common area: 1,2 hectares. The building HUNDRED is included by a one-storeyed industrial location. and also double stored administrative body.

	The building HUNDRED modular - block, production of the "engineering Design" corporation (Poland, Warsaw) also is in good condition. • Throughput: 1500 automobiles. • Cost a HUNDRED as of 1986 about 1 million. roubles. • A HUNDRED is supplied with automobiles electrical engineering supply. • Names project "Car-service centres". • Project purposes: reconstruction of powers for rendering all aspects of services, including services in the foreign marks. • Total cost: 300 thousand US $. Own means (location, equipment and etc.) constitute 100 thousand US $. • Indispensable volume of the investments 200 thousand US $. • Beginning of return of the investments in 18 months, termination in 36 months. • Security of return of the investments a property as security, insurance. • The solution of local organs on support is present. • Enterprise manager Shodi Musoev
Joint-stock company "NURI-NAV" Address: 734044, Dushanbe, Chorteppa, 44 phone: 35-75-01	• The fruit of vegetable facilities of a republic is established on March 3, 1989 on the basis of abandoned Ministry. • Number of the workers: 2800 persons. • Circulating assets: 15% of the budgets of republics, 70% of the agricultural enterprises - had the agreement with the corporation "Nuri Nav". Assist 8 children's houses (1500 children). • In 1997 is constructed: a polyethylene factory, productivity 700 MTA (film for lemons, hothouses); 2 canning plants, productivity 10 million. The conditional jars; a factory on issue of cooling drinks (stage of surrender in maintenance). • In 1990 the joint venture "Indium - Tajikistan - Germanium " is created. • In 1997 the joint venture " Railway a RT " on construction of petroleum refineries, productivity 400 thousand tons of processed oil annually are created. • The basic activity: preform, storage, processing of agricultural production (more than 100 names), production of cooling drinks. • The industrial areas: 12 hectares. • Cost of the equipment: 5 million. USD. • Own assets: 1,6 million. USD. • Names project: " Issue of cooling drinks ".

	<ul><li>Total cost: 18 million. USD.</li><li>The own means put in the project constitute 7 million. $.</li><li>Indispensable volume of the investments: 11 million. $.</li><li>Sellers' market: Russia, Arabian countries, Europe, Central Asia, Tajikistan.</li><li>Payback time: 2 years.</li><li>Enterprise manager R. Abdurahmanov</li></ul>
Stock company "INTOURIST - TAJIKISTAN" Address: 734001, Republic of Tajikistan, Dushanbe city, Shotemur str.22 phone: 21-62-62 fax: 21-52-37 e-mail: ashurov@intoun.td.silk.org	<ul><li>The form of property collective (70 % preliminary payment, 30 % sate).</li><li>SC Intourist Tajikistan was formed in 1991 on the base of Tajik corporation on foreign tourism Tajik intourist founded in 1956.</li><li>Main activity organization of reception and provision of cultural and living facilities of foreign tourists and other visitors of the country, renderings informational, mediators, advertisement and other services.</li><li>SC Intourist Tajikistan organized material-technical supply of hotel complex by means of resources acquisition at domestic and foreign market and services directly from producers in wholesale trade, including fairs and auctions. All above mentioned activity is carrying out on the base of market conjuncture publishing and possibilities of potential partners.</li><li>Schedule number of employees 268 persons.</li><li>Authorized capital 119,8 thousands USD.</li><li>The cost of fixed and turnover means 722,7 thousands USD. The cost of immovable property 438,6 thousands USD (24.03.1996).</li><li>In order to perfect services SC Intourist Tajikistan elaborated business-plan and prepared investment project "Reconstruction and modernization of hotel complex".</li><li>Project's aim is Reconstruction accounting requiThe form of property collective (70 percent preliminary payment, 30 percent sate).</li><li>SC Intourist Tajikistan was formed in 1991 on the base of Tajik corporation on foreign tourism Tajik intourist founded in 1956.</li><li>Main activity organization of reception and provision of cultural and living facilities of foreign tourists and other visitors of the country, rendering informational, mediator, advertisement and other services.</li><li>SC Intourist Tajikistan organizes material-technical supply of hotel rements of hotels 3 stars.</li></ul>

For additional analytical, business and investment opportunities information, please contact Global Investment & Business Center, USA at (202) 546-2103. Fax: (202) 546-3275. E-mail: rusric@erols.com

	• Overall value of the project - 10100 thousands USD.
	• Necessary volume of investments construction,
	• Purchase of uncompleted articles, materials and equipment.
	• Payback period 6 years.
	• Sale market:
	    ○ - republic of Tajikistan, Dushanbe 95 percent
	    ○ - export 5 percent
	• Guarantee of project realization to determine sale markets of their services.
	• Ensuring investments returning assets pledge.
	• Beginning of investments returning 12 months.
	• Enterprise manager Inoajtullo Ashurov

BANKING SYSTEM AND BANKS IN TAJIKISTAN

The reform of the banking system in Tajikistan started in 1994 with the financial assistance of the World Bank, IMF, EBRD and technical assistance of companies such as "Arthur Andersen" (U.S.) and "IDP" (Italy.) The new Law "On Banks and Banking Activities" became a logical step in reforming Tajikistan's banking system. Reforms of the system will improve after the promulgation of the following normative acts:

- On the Qualification Committee of the National Bank;
- On Forming Procedures of the Statutory Capital;
- Procedures for Starting and Terminating Commercial Banks'Activities;
- Procedure for Issuing and Recalling Licenses for Banking Activities' Auditing;
- Procedures for Establishing Non-Banking Financial Organizations;
- On Banks' Bankruptcy.

These legislative acts are aimed at regulating both banks' and non-banking financial organizations activities. Non-banking financial organizations are legal entities which may execute some banking operations and provide some financial services for individuals and companies after they get a license of the National Bank. According to Mr Valiev, such financial organizations in the future will be reorganized into loan companies, clearing houses, etc. Right now the experiences of other NIS countries are being examined to develop appropriate laws for Tajikistan.

At the beginning of 1998, 27 commercial and private banks were officially registered in the country. Before January 1, 1998, $300,000 was sufficient to establish a bank. According to Tajikistan's National bank decision, since January 1, 1998 the statutory minimum capital requirement of already existing and newly established joint-stock, commercial, and private banks is to be $1,000,000. After all those restrictions were introduced, only 19 banks with their branches have survived. Three banks such as Bahtovar, Toribank, and Ziroat failed
to reach the required capital requirement and were closed down. Two other banks, Ilhom and Rishta, which also failed to meet the necessary capital requirement, were

For additional analytical, business and investment opportunities information,
please contact Global Investment & Business Center, USA
at (202) 546-2103. Fax: (202) 546-3275. E-mail: rusric@erols.com

transformed into branches of Agroinvestbank. As the Deputy National Bank Navruz Valiev said, after the National Bank raised the minimum capital requirement, they have received no application for getting licenses for banking activities and opening any new banks.

The National Bank also introduced a minimal working capital amounting to $500,000 by January 1, 1998. By July, 1, 1999 it will have to be $750,000 and by January 1, 2000 $1,000,000. The increase of the minimum capital requirement and of the working capital level is supposed to help settle the problem with banks' liquidity.

For registering a bank and issuing a license for banking activities the National Bank charges 0.5% of the announced capital requirement. A license provides a right for banking operations for the entire period of its activity.

In implementation of the Memorandum on Restructuring the Banking System in Tajikistan signed between the National Bank and the World Bank, the National Bank signed agreements with the four biggest commercial banks Agroinvestbank, Tajikbankbusiness, Sberbank, and Vnesheconombank on their reorganization. According to this document, by November 30, 1998 these four banks are to increase their statutory capital, reduce expenditures, try harder to collect earlier issued loans and to reimburse overdue loans, and liquidate unprofitable branches. Another important requirement of the agreement is the implementation of International Accounting Standards by local banks.

Mr Valiev is of the opinion that the future of the banking system in Tajikistan will depend on strict observance of the adopted laws and regulations.

BANKS IN DUSHANBE

1. National Bank of the Republic of Tajikistan

Murodali Alimardonov
Chairman
23/2, Rudaqi Ave.
734025 Dushanbe, Tajikistan
Tel: 7(3772) 21 26 28
Fax: 7(3772) 21 25 02
Telex: 201 129

2. Joint Stock Commercial Agroindustrial Investment Bank Agroinvestbank (Agroinvestbank)

Maqsud Kodirov
Chairman
31, Sherozi Ave.
734018 Dushanbe, Tajikistan
Tel: 7(3772) 33 31 04, 36 79 89

Fax: 7(3772) 901 50 16
Telex: 201 221

3. Joint Stock Commercial Industrial
and Construction Bank Orionbank (Orionbank)

Gaffor Idiev
Chairman
95/1, Rudaqi Ave.
734025 Dushanbe, Tajikistan
Tel: 7(3772) 21 09 20
Fax: 7(3772) 21 16 62
Telex: 201 136

4. Tajik Joint Stock Commercial Bank of Social and Economic
Development Tajikbankbusiness (Tajikbankbusiness)

Kayum Kavmiddinov
Chairman
29, Shotemur Street
734025 Dushanbe, Tajikistan
Tel: 7(3772) 21 05 03, 21 06 34
Fax: 7(3772) 23 44 17, 21 06 21, 21 08 46
Telex: 201 113

5. State-Commercial Bank for Foreign Economic Affairs of the
Republic of Tajikistan Vnesheconombank (Vnesheconombank)

Izatullo Lalbekov
Chairman
4, Husrav Dehlavi Street
734012 Dushanbe, Tajikistan
Tel: 7(3772) 23 35 61
Fax: 7(3772) 21 47 38
Telex: 201 121

SAVINGS BANK OF THE REPUBLIC OF TAJIKISTAN (TAJIKSBERBANK)

Kurbonali Juraev, Chairman
67, Rudaqi Ave.
734025 Dushanbe, Tajikistan
Tel: 7(3772) 21 70 81
Fax: 7(3772) 23 14 53

7. Joint-Stock Commercial Industrial Bank of Reconstruction and Development
Tajprombank (Tajprombank)

For additional analytical, business and investment opportunities information,
please contact Global Investment & Business Center, USA
at (202) 546-2103. Fax: (202) 546-3275. E-mail: rusric@erols.com

Jamshed Zeyeyev
Chairman
12/3, Dehlavi (Ostrovskogo) Str
734025 Dushanbe, Tajikistan
Tel: 7(3772) 21 27 20, 21 26 42
Fax: 7(3772) 21 27 96
Telex: 201 197

8. Joint-Stock Investment Commercial Bank Tajbank
59/1, Somoni Ave.
Dushanbe, Tajikistan
Tel: 7(3772) 24 53 15

9. Commercial Bank Somonbank

N Kalandarov, Chairman
3, 1y Proezd Tursun-Zadeh Str
734003 Dushanbe, Tajikistan
Tel: 7(3772) 21 78 13
Fax: 7(3772) 21 78 13, 21 86 02

10. Commercial Bank Fonon

Tatyana Dedurova, Chairman
113/1, Lomonosov Str
734025 Dushanbe, Tajikistan
Tel: 7(3772) 35 27 03, 35 28 83
Fax: 7(3772) 35 27 13

11. Commercial Bank Texinvestbank

Atobullo Babaev
Acting Chairman
35/1, Bohtar Str
Tel: 7(3772) 21 79 52
Tel/fax: 7(3772) 21 80 00
734011 Dushanbe, Tajikistan

12. Commercial Bank Dushanbe

Goib Davlaytov
Chairman
24, Aini Str
Dushanbe, Tajikistan
Tel: 7(3772) 23 46 76
Tel/fax: 7(3772) 21 36 24

13. Commercial Bank Kafolat

For additional analytical, business and investment opportunities information,
please contact Global Investment & Business Center, USA
at (202) 546-2103. Fax: (202) 546-3275. E-mail: rusric@erols.com

Davlatahmad Gadoev
Chairman
4/1, Kuibishev Str.
Tel: 7(3772) 21 59 13, 21 76 22
Fax: 7(3772) 21 88 61

BANKS IN KHOJAND AND LENINABAD REGION

14. Commercial Joint-Stock Bank Akbarbank

Shahodat Mahmajonova, Chairman
1B, Pushkin Str
735730 Chkalovsk
Leninobod Region, Tajikistan
Tel: 7(271)5 39 41
Fax: 7(271)5 44 24

15. Commercial Joint-Stock Bank Ganjina

Valentina Zdunyuk
Chairman
Chief Post Office, Post Box 26
735700 Khojand, Tajikistan
Tel: 7(37922) 2 54 41
Tlx: 201 150

16. Commercial Bank Khojand

Ahmajon Shukurov, Chairman
5, Kvartal 120
Gafurov, Khojand District
Leninabad Region, Tajikistan
Tel: 7(37942) 3 15 33, 3 19 09
Fax: 7(37942) 3 25 52

17. Commercial Bank Eskhata

Khurshed Nosirov, Chairman
40, Lenin Str
735700 Khojand, Tajikistan
Tel: 7(37922) 4 39 45
Fax: 7(37922) 6 74 10

18. Joint-Stock Commercial Bank Ayem in Kanghurt, Sovetsky District, Khatlon Region

Contact information is not available.

19. State Bank on Rehabilitation and Development of Executive Committee of Khatlon Regional Council of People's Deputies
Khatlonbank

FOREIGN BANKS

1. Central Asian Bank (Tajik-Cyprus Joint Venture)

Alisher Tajiev
Chairman
42, Negmat Karabaev Str
734018 Dushanbe, Tajikistan
Tel: 7(3772) 33 36 15, 33 59 79
Fax: 7(3772) 33-33-33, 33-33-57
Tlx: 201 164

2. Joint-Stock Commercial Bank "East Credit Bank" (Tajik-Luxemburg Joint Venture), (East Credit Bank)

Serj Chernousan
Chairman
91, Rudaki Ave.
734001 Dushanbe, Tajikistan
Tel: 7(3772) 21 74 84, 21 81 86
Fax: 7(3772) 24 14 24

3. Branch of Commercial Bank "Tijorat" (Iran), (Tijorat)

Hushang Razmhoh
Chairman
70, Rudaki Ave.
734001 Dushanbe, Tajikistan
Tel: 7(3772) 21 14 76

IMPORTANT LAWS AND REGULATIONS AFFECTING BUSINESS

LAW ON PROPERTY IN THE REPUBLIC OF TAJIKISTAN

DIVISION I COMMON REGULATIONS

Article 1. The right of ownership

1.1 The right of ownership in the Republic of Tajikistan is recognized and protected by law.

1.2 An owner possesses, enjoys and disposes of his property. An owner has the right to take any allowable actions relating to his property provided the rights of co-owners are not violated. The owner may use his property for any economic activity or other activities not prohibited by law.

1.3 An owner is responsible to preserve his property from deterioration or accidental damage in case it is not already provided for by law or contract.

1.4 In certain cases, under the terms of the law, an owner may be obliged to allow a limited use of his property by other persons.

1.5 An owner may alienate his property, and also give it into the possession of other persons for their enjoyment and disposition without alienation.

1.6 An owner has the right under the terms of the law of the Republic of Tajikistan to conclude contracts with physical persons in order to use their labor while exercising his rights.

Article 2. Enforcement of the right of ownership

2.1 Enforcement of the right of ownership must not harm the environment and the health of citizens nor must it breach the rights and lawful interests of citizens, enterprises, organizations and the State.

2.2 Enforcement of the right of ownership on historical and cultural artifacts is regulated by the legislation of the Republic of Tajikistan.

Article 3. Legislation of the Republic of Tajikistan on property

3.1 Legislation of the Republic of Tajikistan on property is based on the Constitution of the Republic of Tajikistan and comprises the present law, other legislative documents adopted in accordance with the constitution and the present law, international legal documents recognized by Tajikistan as well as international agreements and interstate treaties signed and accepted by the Republic of Tajikistan.

3.2 The state guarantees and protects property rights and non-property author rights on discoveries, inventions, and scientific achievements. Property rights connected with the creation and enjoyment of achievements of science, literature and art, discoveries, inventions of manufacture models, electronic programming devices and other objects of intellectual property are regulated by copyrights and other legislation of the Republic of Tajikistan as well as international agreements and interstate treaties signed and approved by the Republic of Tajikistan.

Article 4. Objects falling under ownership rights

4.1 Objects falling under the right of ownership may be enterprises, the ground and its resources, water, flora, fauna, tracts of mountains, buildings, constructions, equipment, raw materials, food products, money, securities, industrial consumer goods, social and cultural articles and the produce, income and profits on economic and other intellectual and creative activities of the owner.

4.2 Objects of intellectual property include scientific achievements, works of literature, artistic creations and other activities involving discoveries, inventions, production models, electronic programming devices, sources of education, testing systems, know-how, commercial secrets, consumer indexes, company trademarks, and service indexes.

Article 5. Those entitled to the right of ownership

5.1 Those entitled to the right of ownership in the Republic of Tajikistan are physical and legal persons, public and religious organizations, other unions of citizens and collectives,

local state authorities and the self governing authorities of towns and villages, the State, foreign States, foreign citizens, persons without citizenship and foreign legal persons.
5.2 The Republic of Tajikistan guarantees the inviolability of property and the possibility of exercising the right of ownership for every owner.

Article 6. Forms of property
6.1 The state guarantees equal rights and protects the rights of all forms of ownership including private ownership.
6.2 Ownership in the Republic of Tajikistan can be either private, collective or public.
6.3 Ownership by other states, international organizations, foreign citizens, persons without citizenship and foreign legal persons is allowed in the Republic of Tajikistan.
6.4 Joint property of citizens, legal persons and the State may be established under mixed forms of ownership including ownership of joint enterprises with the participation of foreign citizens, persons without citizenship and foreign legal persons.
6.5 Property, regardless of the form of ownership, may be simultaneously owned by several owners by having each owner's share defined (joint stock ownership) or not defined (joint ownership).
6.6 Ownership, use, and disposal of joint property is carried out with the permission of all the owners; in case of absence of an agreement, the case is settled by a court according to the actions of each owner.
6.7 The state prohibits the establishment of limitations or preferences in the enforcement of property rights related with the form of ownership.

Article 7. Ownership of land and other natural resources
7.1 Land and all it contains, water, air, fauna, flora and other natural resources are the inherent property of the State which also guarantees their productive usage in peoples favor. Tracts of land according to the land code and other legislation of the Republic of Tajikistan may be granted for possession and exploitation to physical and legal persons according to the law of the Republic of Tajikistan.
7.3 Tracts of mountains for the exploitation and extraction of minerals are owned by the State and may be granted for possession and exploitation to physical and legal persons according to the law of the Republic of Tajikistan.
7.4 Alienation and unification of tracts of land and mountains is provided for by the law of the Republic of Tajikistan.

Article 8. Acquisition and loss of ownership rights
8.1 If not otherwise specified by law or contract, a citizen or other person has the right of ownership on legally acquired property, on raw materials created or fully reproduced by him or her, on his or her output, its profit and other income earned through the exploitation of his or her property, natural resources or other property under his or her responsibility for the latter purposes even if it doesn't belong to him.
8.2 If not otherwise specified by law or contract, a buyer of property acquires ownership rights on the object of the purchase as soon as the payment is settled and the object of the purchase is remitted.
8.3 Breaking ownership rights without the owner's will is prohibited except for cases when the owner is forfeited for debt in accordance with the law of the Republic of Tajikistan and in cases when property is legally confiscated.
8.4 In cases of natural disasters, accidents, epidemics, loss of cattle and other circumstances of extra-ordinary nature, property may be confiscated in the interest of

society according to the law of the Republic of Tajikistan with compensation for the value (according to current market prices) of the property.

8.5 In cases determined for by the law of the Republic of Tajikistan, property may be confiscated by a decision of court or other authorities as a sanction for committing a crime or for having violated the law.

8.6 If private property, property of associations, and public property, involves property that according to the law cannot belong to the owner, it must be alienated from the owner for a period of one year should another duration fixed by law not specify otherwise. In case the owner has not been alienated from the property within the fixed period, the property must be alienated by a court's decision with a compensation for the cost of the property and a deduction including alienating expenses.

Article 9. Exaction of forfeiture from the owner's property

9.1 An owner is not responsible for the obligations of legal persons created by him and these legal persons are not responsible for the owner's obligations, barring cases defined by law, legislative documents, or documents establishing the status of legal persons.

9.2 According to the obligations of a legal person, forfeiture is exacted from every property owned by him or her, or under his or her full right of disposal.

9.3 Legal persons are responsible for their financial obligations and in case these obligations can not be met, the owner concerned takes the responsibility for the financial obligations on himself.

9.4 Compulsory forfeiture by the state for debts related to the owner including sums due to the State, is allowed according to the law of the Republic of Tajikistan. In case of disagreement with forfeiture, the owner has the right to appeal to court.

Article 10. The responsibilities of an owner

10.1 Should other terms not be specified by law or contract, the owner is responsible for the obligations concerning his or her property.

10.2 A list of the property of a physical person which is not forfeit to the claims of creditors is fixed by the laws of the Republic of Tajikistan.

DIVISION II PRIVATE PROPERTY

Article 11. Common regulations on private property

11.1 The amount and value of the property of a citizen is created and increased by virtue of his or her income from participation in production and other realizations related to his or her hard working capabilities, from entrepreneurial activity, from profits on credit, shares and other securities, from inheriting property, and from other sources not prohibited by the law of the Republic of Tajikistan.

11.2 A citizen with the owner's permission has the right to make pecuniary or other investments in property of enterprises, other economic organizations, farms or other businesses, functioning according to their contract, and may take part in the distribution of the income of the enterprise in proportion to his investment or as defined by an agreement.

11.3 The right of inheritance of a citizen's property is recognized, accepted and protected by the Constitution of the Republic of Tajikistan, the Civil Code, other laws of the Republic, and international legislation approved by Tajikistan.

Article 12. Objects of private property covered by law

12.1 The followings objects of private property are covered by law:

a) Dwelling premises including houses, flats and datchas, garages, housekeeping and personal material;

b) Pecuniary investments, shares, loans and other securities;

c) Mass media equipment;

d) Enterprises, complexes producing consumer goods and providing living facilities, complexes involved in trade and other spheres of entrepreneurial activity, buildings, constructions, equipment, transport vehicles, and other means of production.

e) Any sort of property meant for industrial, consumer, social, cultural, and other purposes except for specific types of property that cannot belong to citizens for state security and social motives as well as international obligations, defined by legislation of the Republic of Tajikistan.

12.2 The structure, quantity and value of property acquired by a citizen according to law or contract is unlimited.

12.3 The terms and conditions of privatization of enterprises or means of production belonging to the State are fixed by the law of the Republic of Tajikistan.

Article 13 Joint ownership

13.1 Private property jointly owned for the benefit of a business may include several families, members of families and other persons, workshops, enterprises producing consumer goods or providing living facilities, dealing in trade, public nutrition and other spheres of economic activity, dwelling premises, office buildings, machinery, equipment, transport means, raw material and other property necessary for the business.

13.2 The property of business including its produced output and income is jointly owned by the members of the family and other persons participating in the business unless an agreement between themselves provides for other conditions.

Article 14 Property of farms and personal farming entities

14.1 The ownership of farms consists of dwelling premises, farm buildings, plantations, cattle, poultry farms, agricultural implements, vehicles- and other property necessary for independent farming, production and realization of output.

14.2 Produced output and the earned income belongs to the farm and may be disposed of as the owner wishes as long as the Law does not specify otherwise.

14.3 The property of the farm belongs to its members jointly if the Law and other legislation of the Republic of Tajikistan does not specify otherwise.

14.4 The rules of this article also apply to personal farming entities.

Article 15 Property rights of citizens conducting entrepreneurial activity

15.1 A citizen may use his private property for commercial activity.

15.2 Property of members of family and other citizens, which is jointly used for entrepreneurial activity and its output and income belong to them under the status of joint ownership unless a contract among themselves provides for other terms.

15.3 A citizen may use his property as a form of company share or contribution to the associations, cooperatives, collective and other enterprises, other unions of citizens and legal persons, necessary for his entrepreneurial activity.

Article 16. The right of disposal and exploitation of land plots

16.1 In order to encourage agricultural production, promote construction of dwelling premises, and develop kitchen gardening, a citizen may be granted a right of exploitation and inheritance on land plots.

16.2 Products and income of these land plots are property of the citizen and can be disposed of as he wishes.

Article 17 The citizen's property right

17.1 A citizen owning private property, may dispose of the property as he or she wishes.

DIVISION III COLLECTIVE PROPERTY

Article 18. Common regulations on collective property

18.1 Collective property consists of property of leased enterprises, collective enterprises, cooperatives, collective farms, joint-stock companies, profit societies and associations, public and religious organizations, ownership of the mahalla (neighborhood) and other associations possessing a legal identity.

18.2 The creation and increase of the amount and value of collective property is ensured by the leasing of state enterprises, by providing working collectives the possibility of using earned income for purchase of state property, by the transformation of state enterprises into joint companies, and by voluntary unification of the property of citizens and legal persons for the creation of cooperatives, joint-stock companies, and other productive societies and associations.

18.3 The list of enterprises and production facilities which may not be transferred into collective ownership is defined by the law of the Republic of Tajikistan.

Article 19 Property of a collective enterprise

19.1 Property of a collective enterprise is created by transferring all the property of state enterprises to the ownership of a working collective, by purchase of leased property, or by other legal means of property acquisition.

19.2 The collective enterprise's property, including the output and income earned from the property is for the common benefit of the collective.

19.3 The property share of the workers of a collective enterprise should be defined. This share includes the sum of each worker's contribution to the state or leased property on which the collective enterprise has been created as well as each worker's contribution to increase the amount and value of property in question after creation of the enterprise.

19.4 The measuring of a worker's contribution to increasing the amount and value of the property is defined according to his participation in the enterprise's activities. Workers contributions to the collective enterprise are mandatory and paid according to a percentage reflecting the results of the economic activities of the enterprise and rules defined by the working collective. A worker who is no longer employed by an enterprise or an inheritor of a dead worker must be paid the value of the worker's contribution.

19.5 In case of liquidation of the collective enterprise, the value of each worker's contribution is paid to the worker or his inheritor from the remaining properties after settling due payments to the state budget, banks and other creditors of the enterprise.

Article 20. Property of a leased enterprises

20.1 Leasing property does not give ownership right on the property. The output and income from the activities on the leased property belongs to the lessee. Material values excluded from the leased property and legally acquired by a lessee, belong to the lessee.

For additional analytical, business and investment opportunities information, please contact Global Investment & Business Center, USA at (202) 546-2103. Fax: (202) 546-3275. E-mail: rusric@erols.com

20.2 The terms of participation of the members of the working collective of the leased enterprise in the management of its activities and distribution of its income is regulated by the law of the Republic of Tajikistan on "Leasing in the Republic of Tajikistan".

Article 21. Property of a cooperative

21.1 The property of a cooperative is formed by money and property contributions of its members, the output of the cooperative, its income, sale proceeds and activities provided for in the charter of the cooperative and by the law of the Republic of Tajikistan.

21.2 In case of liquidation of a cooperative, remaining property, after settling due payments to the State Budget, banks and other creditors, is distributed among the members of the cooperative.

Article 22. Property of companies and the property of businesses

22.1 Property of companies and the property of businesses which is constituted into a legal identity, is formed by participant's contributions and property acquired as a result of economic activity and other legal means.

22.2 Share contributions of participants into business or public funds may include ordinary circulating funds, capital, securities and the right of enjoyment of property.

22.3 Participants in a business or company may be enterprises, institutions, organizations, the Government and citizens unless their participation is prohibited by the laws of the Republic of Tajikistan.

Article 23. Property of joint-stock companies

23.1 A joint-stock company owns property created by the sale of shares related to its economic activities, and other legal means.

23.2 Legal and physical persons may be shareholders unless otherwise prescribed by Law or the company's charter.

23.3 Upon joint decision of the working collective and the state authority, a state enterprise may be reorganized into a joint-stock company by distributing shares reflecting the value of the enterprise. Revenue obtained from the sale of shares, after settling the debts of the state enterprise, is deposited in the company's new budget.

Article 24. Property of business associations

24.1 A business association of enterprises or organizations has the right to own property that has been acquired as a result of its economic activities.

24.2 A business association does not have the right to own the property of its constituent enterprises and organizations.

24.3 Property remaining after the disbanding of a business association is distributed among its constituent enterprises and organizations.

Article 25. Property of public associations and funds

25.1 Public associations and funds, including charities, may own buildings construction, housing funds, the means of production, equipment, stock, property for cultural, educational and health purposes, money, shares, and other securities and properties, required for their activities which are defined by their own charter. Enterprises serving economic, industrial or social purposes, created by investments of public funds or associations according to the charter of the enterprise, may be property of public funds or associations.

25.2 Property of public associations or public funds is formed by initial contributions, should this be required by their charter, by voluntary contributions, income earned from lotteries and other activities, by income from production, income from publications and other legal activities. Legislation of the Republic of Tajikistan may determine types of property that may not be owned by public associations.

25.3 In cases where a member of a public association leaves the association, he does not have the right to have his contributions, whether in payments or property, be returned to him unless provided for otherwise by the law of the Republic of Tajikistan.-

25.4 Property remaining after liquidation of a public association after settling due payments to the State Budget, banks and other creditors is invested according to the charter of the association.

Article 26. Property of the mahalla (neighborhood)

26.1 A mahalla may own buildings; construction; equipment; warehouses; plantations;- property serving cultural, educational and public health purposes; money; and other property necessary for the well-being of the mahalla provided the property does not belong to other public associations.

26.2 The property of the mahalla is formed by the voluntary payments and contributions of it's inhabitants as long as the donations are legal.

Article 27. Property of religious organizations

27.1 The following may be owned by religious organizations: buildings, objects of worship serving industrial, social and charitable purposes, money and other property that is necessary for the functioning of religious organizations.

27.2 Religious organizations have the right to own to property acquired or created by contributions of its members- or ac-quired by- other means fixed by law.

27.3 Problems related to the use of a religious organization's property after quitting its religious activities, are solved by the administrative staff of the association or the higher authority of the religious organization in coordination with State Religious Authorities.

27.4 After ending its religious activities, property of a religious organization that had been granted to it by state organizations, public associations and/or citizens must be returned to its former owner.

27.5 Forfeit on a religious organization may be exacted in cash or from its property. Forfeit or demands of creditors may however not be exacted from property related to objects of worship.

STATE PROPERTY

Article 28. Common regulations on state property

28.1 The State of Republic of Tajikistan enjoys exclusive ownership rights on its property, and can dispose of it according to its discretion.

28.2 State property in the Republic of Tajikistan includes: property of the Republic of Tajikistan (Republican Property), property of the Autonomous Mountainous Region of Badakhshan, and property of Local Assemblies of People's Representatives (Communal Property).

28.3 Disposal and administration of state property are carried out by:

a) A Representative for the administration of state property, appointed by a State Authority in the name of the State to deal with Republic Property.

b) A Representative appointed by a Local Assembly to deal with Communal Property.

28.4 Property created or acquired at the expense of public funds from the State Budget or other means of the Republic of Tajikistan, the Autonomous Mountainous Region of Badakhshan, Local Assemblies of People's Representatives, or State owned enterprises, organizations, and institutions, belongs to either the Republic of Tajikistan, the Autonomous Mountainous Region of Badakhshan or Local Assemblies of People's Representatives.

28.5 The Republic of Tajikistan, the Autonomous Mountainous Region of Badakhshan, Local Assemblies of People's Representatives, Town and Village Authorities and other entities entitled to the right of ownership, are not responsible for mutual obligations arising from the exploitation and disposal of their property, except for cases stipulated by the law of the Republic of Tajikistan.

Article 29. Property of the Republic of Tajikistan

29.1 The Republic of Tajikistan owns the land within its borders, its resources, water, air, flora, fauna, and other natural resources, the State Budget, the banks of the Republic, including currency reserves and state property granted to joint stock companies, enterprises and compounds serving the needs of the national economy, insurance and welfare funds, state schools of higher education, property of State Administrative Authorities, cultural and historical heritage of the Republic of Tajikistan, objects of social and -cultural value, and other property acquired by the Republic of Tajikistan or gifted to it by foreign countries, legal entities or citizens including persons without citizenship in order to ensure- the sovereignty and economic independence and development of the Republic of Tajikistan.

Article 30. Property of the Autonomous Mountainous Region of Badakhshan

30.1 The Autonomous Mountainous Region of Badakhshan owns the property of its Local Assemblies of People's Representatives (entities of Republican Property and Communal Property), the Regional State Budget, other state funds, state engineering infrastructure, and other entities, enterprises, association, institutes of public education, public health and welfare insurance, cultural and scientific organizations, acquired through the Regional State Budget or other means of the Autonomous Mountainous Region of Badakhshan including contributions or other sources like securities and financial assets gifted to Local Assemblies of People's Representatives.

Article 31 Property of Local Assemblies of People's Representatives

31.1 Regions, towns and districts own Local State Budgets, housing funds, the Municipal Housing Fund of Local Assemblies of People's Representatives, industrial enterprises specialized in the production of raw materials for the benefit of the region, town or district, constructions-, trans-portation vehicles, commercial goods, agricultural enterprises, daily services, educational institutes, public health and cultural institutes and other necessary property for the social and economic development of regions, towns or districts, including securities and financial assets.

Article 32. Property of Local Self-Managed State Authorities

32.1 Objects serving public and social purposes including objects constructed or purchased by Local Self-Managed State Authorities or objects legally granted to them; transportation vehicles, commercial goods, including money and other material means allotted by Municipal and District Assemblies of People's Representatives to Local Self-Managed State Authorities, voluntary donations of citizens and working collectives, and contributions from charitable funds and other legal sources are all property of Local Self-Managed State Authorities.

Article 33. Property of state enterprises

33.1 State property granted for the use of a state institution operating on the account of the State Budget is directly controlled by the institution. State enterprises have the right to fully dispose and enjoy property owned by the state and granted for use to state enterprises.

33.2 A state enterprise enjoys full property rights while implementing its right of disposal and enjoyment on state property granted to it within the limits of the law of the Republic of Tajikistan and the enterprise's objectives. Regulations concerning ownership rights and related to the right of full property disposal are applied only if legislation of the Republic of Tajikistan has not provided for any other terms.

33.3 State Authorities having the right to manage state property, may decide matters related to the creation of state enterprises, the definition of its aims, and the reorganization or liquidation of state enterprises, they may also control the effective use and preservation of state property entrusted to state enterprises and accomplish obligations stipulated by the law of the Republic of Tajikistan.

33.3 In case a state authority entrusted with the administration of state property decides to reorganize or liquidate a state enterprise for reasons excluding bankruptcy, the working collective may legally request to lease the enterprise or have the enterprise be reorganized on a basis of collective ownership. Disputes between the State and the employees of a state enterprise are arbitrated in court.

Article 34. Property of state institutions

34.1 State property granted for use to a state institution operating on the account of the State Budget is under the direct control of the state institution.

34.2 State institutions functioning at the expense of the State Budget, and being able to legally undertake entrepreneurial activities, obtain the right to freely dispose of incomes related to these activities and the property acquired at the expense of the latter income.

34.3 State institutions must meet their pecuniary obligations. In case such obligations can not fully be met by the state institution, they should be met by the owner of the property of the state institution.

DIVISION V PROPERTY OF JOINT VENTURES, FOREIGN STATES, ORGANIZATIONS AND CITIZENS

Article 35. Property of joint ventures

35.1 Joint ventures with the participation of legal persons of the Republic of Tajikistan and foreign legal persons and citizens created within the Republic of Tajikistan or abroad in the form of joint-stock companies and associations, and other legal forms, may own any property necessary for the activities listed in the company's charter.

Article 36. Property of foreign states and international organizations

36.1 Foreign states and international organizations have the right to own property necessary for diplomatic, consular, social, cultural and other activities within the Republic of Tajikistan according to the terms of international legal treaties approved by the Republic of Tajikistan.

Article 37. Property of foreign legal entities

37.1 Foreign legal entities may own industrial enterprises and other companies, buildings, constructions, and other property necessary for their economic activities in accordance with the legislation of the Republic of Tajikistan.

Article 38 Property of foreign citizens and persons without citizenship

38.1 Regulations of this law valid for Tajik citizens except for cases stipulated by the law of the Republic of Tajikistan, may also be applied for foreign citizens and persons without citizenship.

DIVISION VI GUARANTEES AND PROTECTION OF PROPERTY RIGHTS

Article 39. Guarantees of property rights
39.1 The Republic of Tajikistan guarantees the order of ownership relations fixed by this law.
39.2 Nobody has the right to confiscate the owner's property, except for cases defined by the law of the Republic of Tajikistan.
39.3 Nobody has the right to deprive or limit any citizen of his property rights.
39.4 The State fosters conditions for the free development of different forms of property and the increase of their value and ensures their protection equally.
39.5 In case the Republic of Tajikistan approves legislation depriving owners of their rights, resulting damages are compensate for by the State upon approval of a court.

Article 40. Protection of property rights
40.1 The Republic of Tajikistan ensures equal protection of property rights for all owners. Nobody has the right to deprive or limit the rights of an owner.
40.2 In accordance with the Civil Code of the Republic of Tajikistan, an owner has the right to demand his property from a person illegally exploiting it.
40.3 An owner has the right to demand the settling of all kinds of feuds involving the breaching of his rights even if these violations are not connected with the deprivation of his property rights.
40.4 Property rights are protected by State Courts.
40.5 Rights provided for by this article also apply for persons who are not owners but have been granted full disposal rights, the right of disposal for a lifetime, or other disposal rights provided for by law or contract. Such persons have the right to defend their property rights even from the actual owner.

Article 41. Protection of an owner's interests upon legal expiry of his rights
41.1 The right of ownership may terminate upon decision to expropriate a plot of land where a house, building, construction, or plantations belonging to the owner is situated; or upon approval of the decision of another State Authority that is not directly in charge with the expropriation of the owner's property. Such an expropriation may only take place under circumstances determined by the law of the Republic of Tajikistan and in cases where resulting damages are fully compensated for.
41.2 When an owner disagrees, the resolution to expropriate his or her property may not be implemented until the issue is not settled by a State Court or the High Economic Court. During the settling of this dispute, the matter of paying compensation for damages to the owner has to be solved.

Article 42. Invalidation of acts which infract on the right of ownership
42.1 In case the Government or a Local State Authority approves an Act which contradicts the law and the rights of an owner and other persons having full right of disposal of the property, the Act should be challenged as invalid on request of the owner or the person who's rights have been violated.
42.3 Resulting damages are compensated to concerned citizens, organizations, and other persons at the expense of the corresponding Local State Authority.
42.4 Material and moral damages caused to a person as a result of the illegal action of a State Authority are compensated for at the State Authority's expense according to the law.

For additional analytical, business and investment opportunities information,
please contact Global Investment & Business Center, USA
at (202) 546-2103. Fax: (202) 546-3275. E-mail: rusric@erols.com

The President of
The Republic of Tajikistan, Mr. I. Rahmonov
Dushanbe, December 14, 1996

LAW ON CONCESSIONS

THE PRESENT LAW DEFINES THE MAIN PRINCIPLES OF AN CONCESSION ACTIVITY ON THE TERRITORY OF THE REPUBLIC OF TAJIKISTAN AND DETERMINES LEGAL, ECONOMIC, AND OTHER PROPERTY RELATIONS CONNECTED WITH THIS ACTIVITY.

I. COMMON REGULATIONS

ARTICLE 1. CONCEPTS OF TERMS USED IN THIS LAW

CONCESSION (YIELDING) - AN AGREEMENT ON PASSING TO A FOREIGN INVESTOR FOR TEMPORARY EXPLOITATION ON CERTAIN CONDITIONS OF ENTERPRISES (ASSOCIATIONS) BELONGING TO STATE, LAND WITH THE RIGHT TO EXTRACT MINERALS, CONSTRUCTION SITES, WATER RESOURCES, WATER AND AIR SPACE, FLORA AND FAUNA, AND OTHER NATURAL RESOURCES NOT PROHIBITED BY LEGISLATION OF THE REPUBLIC OF TAJIKISTAN.

CONCESSION AGREEMENT - AN AGREEMENT ON PASSING BY AN AUTHORIZED STATE BODY OR A LOCAL STATE BODY WITHIN THEIR COMMISSION TO A FOREIGN INVESTOR FOR A TEMPORARY USE OF LAND, OTHER NATURAL RESOURCES, ENTERPRISES (ASSOCIATIONS), AND OTHER STATE PROPERTY, NOT PROHIBITED BY LEGISLATION OF THE REPUBLIC OF TAJIKISTAN.
FOREIGN INVESTOR - A LEGAL ENTITY OR AN INDIVIDUAL PERFORMING LONG-TERM INVESTMENT INTO ECONOMY OF ANOTHER COUNTRY.
CONCESSIONAIRE - A FOREIGN INVESTOR WITH WHOM A CONCESSION AGREEMENT IS CONCLUDED.

OBJECTS OF CONCESSION - TYPES OF ECONOMIC ACTIVITIES CONNECTED WITH TEMPORARY YIELDING TO A FOREIGN INVESTOR OF PROPERTY, LAND, AND OTHER NATURAL RESOURCES ALLOWED BY LEGISLATION OF THE REPUBLIC OF TAJIKISTAN.

SUBJECTS OF CONCESSION - SIDES PARTICIPATING IN CONCESSION RELATIONS.

CONCESSION BODIES ARE BODIES AUTHORIZED BY THE GOVERNMENT OF THE REPUBLIC OF TAJIKISTAN OR LOCAL GOVERNMENT BODIES WHICH ARE AUTHORIZED TO BE ENGAGED IN THE ESTABLISHED ORDER IN THE CONCESSIONS ISSUES.

ARTICLE 2. LEGAL REGULATING OF CONCESSION ACTIVITY

LEGAL RELATIONS IN THE PROCESS OF THE CONCESSION ACTIVITY ARE REGULATED BY THIS LAW AND OTHER LEGISLATIVE ACTS OF THE REPUBLIC OF TAJIKISTAN.

ARTICLE 3. BASIS OF CONCESSION ACTIVITY

THE CONCESSION ACTIVITY IN THE REPUBLIC OF TAJIKISTAN IS IMPLEMENTED ON THE BASIS OF:

- MUTUAL BENEFIT;
- CHOOSING A CONCESSIONAIRE IS TO BE COMPETITIVE AND THROUGH AUCTIONS;
- NON-INTERFERENCE INTO THE CONCESSIONAIRE'S ECONOMIC ACTIVITY PERFORMED IN ACCORDANCE WITH LEGISLATION OF THE REPUBLIC OF TAJIKISTAN;
- OBSERVING LEGISLATION OF THE REPUBLIC OF TAJIKISTAN ON PROTECTION OF LAND AND MINERAL WEALTH, LABOR SAFETY, NATURE AND WATER RESOURCES USE, ENVIRONMENTAL PROTECTION, ECOLOGICAL AND SANITARY-HYGIENIC SAFETY, SOCIAL INSURANCE AND PROVISION;
- MANUFACTURING PRODUCTS WHICH ARE ECOLOGICALLY SAFE AND WHICH MEET STANDARDS AND NORMATIVE DOCUMENTS OF THE REPUBLIC OF TAJIKISTAN, IF OTHERWISE NOT STIPULATED BY INTERNATIONAL AGREEMENTS OR AGREEMENTS WITH PARTICIPATION OF THE REPUBLIC OF TAJIKISTAN.

ARTICLE 4. PROPERTY RELATIONS IN CONCESSION ACTIVITY

PASSING OBJECTS IN CONCESSION DOES NOT MEAN TRANSFER OF THE RIGHT FOR THESE OBJECTS TO THE CONCESSIONAIRE OR GRANTING HIM THE UNLIMITED RIGHT TO PERFORM SOME SPECIFIC RIGHTS OF STATE. PRODUCTS AND PROFITS, OBTAINED BY THE CONCESSIONAIRE IN THE RESULT OF THE CONCESSION ACTIVITY, ARE HIS PROPERTY IN THE LIMITS STIPULATED BY THE CONCESSION AGREEMENT.

THE REPUBLIC OF TAJIKISTAN HAS A PRIMARY RIGHT FOR PURCHASE OF PRODUCTS FROM THE CONCESSIONAIRE.

COMPETENCE OF STATE BODIES IN REGULATING CONCESSION RELATIONS

ARTICLE 5. STATE REGULATING OF CONCESSION RELATIONS
THE STATE REGULATING OF CONCESSION RELATIONS IS IMPLEMENTED BY THE GOVERNMENT OF THE REPUBLIC OF TAJIKISTAN OR BY AN AUTHORIZED STATE MANAGEMENT BODY, AND ALSO BY LOCAL STATE MANAGEMENT BODIES.

ARTICLE 6. COMPETENCE OF GOVERNMENT OF TAJIKISTAN
THE GOVERNMENT OF THE REPUBLIC OF TAJIKISTAN IS ENTITLED:

For additional analytical, business and investment opportunities information,
please contact Global Investment & Business Center, USA
at (202) 546-2103. Fax: (202) 546-3275. E-mail: rusric@erols.com

- TO DEVELOP THE PROGRAM OF PRIORITIES IN THE CONCESSION ACTIVITY;
- TO ESTABLISH THE STATE EXPERTISE PROCEDURE OF CONCESSION PROJECTS AND PROGRAMS;
- TO ESTABLISH THE REGISTRATION PROCEDURE OF CONCESSION AGREEMENTS AND TO CONTROL THEIR OBSERVANCE;
- TO PROVIDE THE LIST OF OBJECTS WHICH ARE NOT SUBJECT TO CONCESSION OR LIMITED TRANSFER;
- TO CONCLUDE CONCESSION AGREEMENTS FOR USING MINERAL RESOURCES;
- TO SETTLE OTHER ISSUES RELATED TO CONCESSION RELATIONS IN ACCORDING WITH LEGISLATION.

ARTICLE 7. COMPETENCE OF AUTHORIZED STATE MANAGEMENT BODY
THE AUTHORIZED STATE MANAGEMENT BODY IS ENTITLED:
- TO CONDUCT CONTESTS AND AUCTIONS;
- TO CONCLUDE CONCESSION AGREEMENTS WITHIN GRANTED AUTHORITIES;
- TO CONTROL CONDITIONS' OBSERVANCE OF CONCESSION AGREEMENTS;
- TO SETTLE OTHER ISSUES IN ACCORDANCE WITH LEGISLATION OF THE REPUBLIC OF TAJIKISTAN.

ARTICLE 8. COMPETENCE OF LOCAL STATE BODIES
LOCAL STATE BODIES ARE ENTITLED:
- TO CHARACTERIZE OBJECTS CONTROLLED BY LOCAL STATE BODIES WHICH MAY BE CONCLUDED IN CONCESSION AGREEMENTS;
- TO CONDUCT CONTESTS AND AUCTIONS ON OBJECTS BELONGING TO THEM;
- TO CONCLUDE CONCESSION AGREEMENTS WITHIN THEIR AUTHORITY AND TO CONFORM CONDITIONS OF OTHER CONCESSION AGREEMENTS ON OBJECTS LOCATED ON THEIR TERRITORY;
- TO SETTLE OTHER ISSUES IN ACCORDANCE WITH LEGISLATION OF THE REPUBLIC OF TAJIKISTAN.

III. PROCEDURE AND CONDITIONS FOR GRANTING CONCESSIONS

ARTICLE 9. PREPARATION OF CONCESSION OFFERS
PREPARATION OF CONCESSION OFFERS IS IMPLEMENTED BY CONCESSION BODIES TAKING INTO CONSIDERATION THEIR PRIORITY AND ECONOMIC EXPEDIENCY FOR THE REPUBLIC OF TAJIKISTAN AND IT INCLUDES DEFINING THE TYPE OF ACTIVITY AND THE LIST OF PROPERTY PASSED IN CONCESSION.

ARTICLE 10. PROCEDURE OF GRANTING CONCESSIONS
GRANTING CONCESSIONS IS IMPLEMENTED THROUGH TENDERS. IN EXCEPTIONAL CASES, IN ACCORDANCE WITH DISCRETION OF THE GOVERNMENT OF THE REPUBLIC OF TAJIKISTAN, GRANTING CONCESSIONS IS PERFORMED THROUGH DIRECT NEGOTIATIONS BETWEEN CONCESSION BODIES AND POTENTIAL INVESTORS.

CHOOSING THE WAY OF GRANTING CONCESSIONS THROUGH CONTESTS OR AUCTIONS IS MADE BY THE CONCESSION BODY.

PROCEDURES AND CONDITIONS FOR CONDUCTING CONTESTS AND AUCTIONS ARE DETERMINED BY THE GOVERNMENT OF THE REPUBLIC OF TAJIKISTAN.

BIDS FOR PARTICIPATING IN CONTESTS AND AUCTIONS ARE FORWARDED BY POTENTIAL CONCESSIONAIRES TO THE CONCESSION BODY.
THE BID SHOULD INCLUDE:

A) DATA OF THE CONCESSIONAIRE, INCLUDING HIS MAIN JOB AND HIS RELATIONS WITH FINANCIAL AND BUSINESS PARTNERS;
B) DATA OF FINANCIAL POSITION OF THE CONCESSIONAIRE WHICH DEMONSTRATE HIS ABILITY TO FULFILL PLANNED WORKS;
C) DATA OF TECHNICAL AND TECHNOLOGY POTENTIAL OF THE CONCESSIONAIRE AND OTHER COMPANIES ACTING AS CONTRACTORS;
D) INFORMATION ON FORTHCOMING PROJECTS OF THE BIDDER-CONCESSIONAIRE, INCLUDING THE LIST OF COUNTRIES OF HIS BUSINESS IN THE LAST FIVE YEARS;
E) THE BIDDER'S PLANS ON USING CONCESSIONS, INCLUDING THE WORK PLAN AND ESTIMATE OF EXPENSES;
F) THE PERIOD OF CONCESSION;
THE CONCESSION BID FOR EXTRACTING MINERAL RESOURCES SHOULD ALSO INCLUDE:
G) CONCESSION DATA ON PROSPECTING AND THE CONCESSION RESULTS IF ANY;
H) THE PLANNED CAPACITY AND STARTING DATE OF EXTRACTING MINERAL RESOURCES;

INFORMATION ON CONCESSION CONTESTS AND AUCTIONS IS PUBLISHED IN MASS MEDIA IN FIXED PERIODS WITH INDICATION OF THEIR TERMS, PLACE, AND DEADLINE.
T
HE CONTEST OR AUCTION BID MAY BE REFUSED IN THE FOLLOWING CASES:
- THE BID HAS BEEN SUBMITTED BEYOND FIXED PERIODS;
- THE BIDDER HAS SUBMITTED FALSE INFORMATION ON HIS FINANCIAL AND TECHNICAL CAPABILITY.

ARTICLE 11. CONCLUDING CONCESSION AGREEMENT AND ITS CONTENT
THE CONCESSION AGREEMENT IS CONCLUDED BETWEEN THE FOREIGN INVESTOR AND THE GOVERNMENT OF THE REPUBLIC OF TAJIKISTAN OR BY APPROPRIATE CONCESSION BODY. THE AGREEMENT BECOMES EFFECTIVE FROM MOMENT OF ITS REGISTRATION.
THE CONCESSION AGREEMENT SHOULD INCLUDE:
- SUBJECT OF THE AGREEMENT, NAMES AND COST OF PROPERTY PASSED IN CONCESSION;
- SPACE BORDERS OF LAND, MINERAL WEALTH, WATER, AND AIR;
- TERMS OF THE CONCESSION AGREEMENT AND THE STARTING DATE OF WORKS;
- RIGHTS AND RESPONSIBILITIES OF SIDES;

- AMOUNTS, PROCEDURES, AND TERMS OF TAX AND OTHER PAYMENTS ACCORDING TO LEGISLATION OF THE REPUBLIC OF TAJIKISTAN;
- PRODUCTION SHARES AND NET PROFITS OF THE CONCESSIONAIRE AND THE CONCESSION BODY;
- FIXED AMOUNTS AND TERMS OF YEARLY INVESTMENT AND THE PRODUCTION VOLUME STIPULATED IN THE BUSINESS PLAN;
- REQUIREMENTS ON ENVIRONMENTAL PROTECTION, PROTECTION OF MINERAL RESOURCES, AND WORKS SAFETY;
- RESUME OF STATE ECOLOGICAL EXPERTISE;
- RIGHT OF SIDES FOR INFORMATION RECEIVED IN THE PROCESS OF THE CONCESSION ACTIVITY;
- CONDITIONS OF HIRING, TRAINING, INSURING, AND SOCIAL PROTECTION OF EMPLOYEES NOT CONTRADICTING TO LEGISLATION OF THE REPUBLIC OF TAJIKISTAN;
- PROCEDURES, CONDITIONS, AND TERMS OF BY-STEP RETURN OF THE AGREEMENT SUBJECT, LAND, AND MINERAL WEALTH FOR THEIR REHABILITATION OR RE-CULTIVATION;
- LEGAL, ECONOMIC, AND ORGANIZATIONAL CONSEQUENCES UNDER FORCE MAJEURE;
- PROCEDURES FOR SETTLING DISPUTES AND RESPONSIBILITIES OF SIDES WHEN BREACHING AGREEMENT CONDITIONS;
- FINANCIAL GUARANTEES OF SIDES, JURIDICAL ADDRESSES, AND BANKS' DATA;
- AMENDMENTS AND CANCELLATION CONDITIONS OF THE CONCESSION AGREEMENT.
THE CONCESSION AGREEMENT MAY INCLUDE OTHER CONDITIONS WHICH DO NOT CONTRADICT TO THE CURRENT LEGISLATION OF THE REPUBLIC OF TAJIKISTAN.

ARTICLE 12. CONCESSIONAIRE'S PAYMENTS
THE CONCESSIONAIRE IS COMMISSIONED TO PAY:
- FEE FOR STATE REGISTRATION OF THE CONCESSION AGREEMENT;
- FEE FOR CONCESSION IN THE ORDER ESTABLISHED BY THE AGREEMENT;
- TAXES AND OTHER PAYMENTS STIPULATED BY LEGISLATION OF THE REPUBLIC OF TAJIKISTAN.

ARTICLE 13. PERIOD OF CONCESSION PERIOD
THE CONCESSION AGREEMENT MAY BE CONCLUDED FOR A PERIOD NOR EXCEEDING 50 YEARS, DEPENDING ON TECHNICAL-ECONOMIC CHARACTERISTICS OF CONCESSION OBJECTS. EXCEPTIONAL ARE DEPOSITS OF MINERAL RESOURCES DEMANDING MAJOR INVESTMENT AND KNOWN FOR A LONG-TERM REPAY PERIOD. DURATION OF THE CONCESSION AGREEMENT MAY LAST AS LONG AS IT IS NECESSARY TO FULLY EXPLOIT THE DEPOSIT BUT NOT LONGER THAN 99 YEARS:

- WHEN THE CONCESSION AGREEMENT EXPIRES, THE CONCESSIONAIRE WHO HAS CONSCIENTIOUSLY FULFILLED THE AGREEMENT CONDITIONS, HAS A PRINCIPAL RIGHT TO PROLONG A SHORT AND MEDIUM-TERM AGREEMENT.

ARTICLE 14. AMENDING AND CANCELING CONCESSION AGREEMENTS

CONDITIONS OF CONCESSION AGREEMENTS MAY BE AMENDED IN THE ORDER STIPULATED BY THE AGREEMENT OR BY SIDES' CONSENT.

IF ONE OF THE SIDES BREAKS THE AGREEMENT CONDITIONS, THE CONCESSION AGREEMENT MAY BE CANCELED AT MUTUAL CONSENT OF SIDES, BY COURT'S DECISION, OR BY THE CONCESSION BODY IF THE CONCESSIONAIRE HAS PROVIDED FALSE INFORMATION WHEN CONCLUDING THE CONTRACT.

THE CONCESSION AGREEMENT IS CANCELED FROM THE MOMENT OF ITS EXCLUDING FROM THE STATE REGISTER.

ARTICLE 15. TRANSFER OF RIGHTS AND RESPONSIBILITIES ON CONCESSION AGREEMENTS

IN CASE OF REORGANIZATION OF ONE OF THE SIDES OF THE CONCESSION AGREEMENT, HIS RIGHTS AND RESPONSIBILITIES GO TO THEIR LEGAL LEGATEES, IF OTHERWISE NOT STIPULATED BY LEGISLATION OF THE REPUBLIC OF TAJIKISTAN.
FULL OR PARTIAL YIELDING OF THE CONCESSIONAIRE'S RIGHTS ON THE CONCESSION OBJECT TO THIRD PERSONS IS NOT ALLOWED.

ARTICLE 16. INSURANCE

THE CONCESSIONAIRE INDEPENDENTLY INSURES RISKS OF CONCESSION AGREEMENTS, THE CONCESSION ACTIVITY, AND EMPLOYEES.

IV. CONCESSIONAIRE'S RIGHTS AND RESPONSIBILITIES

ARTICLE 17. CONCESSIONAIRE'S RIGHTS

THE CONCESSIONAIRE IS ENTITLED:
- IN ACCORDANCE WITH LEGISLATION OF THE REPUBLIC OF TAJIKISTAN AND THE CONCESSION AGREEMENT, TO USE THE AGREEMENT SUBJECT, TO BUILD ON USED TERRITORY
PREMISES, ACCESS ROADS, HIGHWAYS, AND COMMUNICATIONS INFRASTRUCTURE;
- IN ACCORDANCE WITH THE CONCESSION BODY AND, IF THE POSITIVE ECOLOGICAL EXPERTISE IS AVAILABLE, TO AMEND THE PROPERTY STOCK, TO RENOVATE, TO EXPAND, AND TO TECHNICALLY MODERNIZE IT RESULTING IN PROPERTY COST INCREASE;
- TO BRING IN HIS OWN PROPERTY AND NECESSARY MATERIALS FOR OWN PRODUCTION NEEDS AND PERSONAL NEEDS OF EMPLOYEES;
- TO BRING OUT HIS PROPERTY AND PRODUCED PRODUCTS;
- TO APPEAL IN COURT ILLEGAL ACTIONS OF STATE BODIES, THEIR OFFICIALS, COOPERATIVE, PUBLIC ORGANIZATIONS, AND INDIVIDUALS OF THE REPUBLIC OF TAJIKISTAN.

ARTICLE 18. CONCESSIONAIRE'S RESPONSIBILITIES

For additional analytical, business and investment opportunities information,
please contact Global Investment & Business Center, USA
at (202) 546-2103. Fax: (202) 546-3275. E-mail: rusric@erols.com

THE CONCESSIONAIRE IS RESPONSIBLE:
- TO OBSERVE THE CONCESSION AGREEMENT CONDITIONS;
- TO PERFORM AN ECONOMIC ACTIVITY IN STRICT ACCORDANCE WITH
LEGISLATION OF THE REPUBLIC OF TAJIKISTAN AND THE CONCESSION
AGREEMENT;
- TO KEEP RECORDS IN THE ORDER ESTABLISHED BY LEGISLATION OF THE
REPUBLIC OF TAJIKISTAN;
- TO RETURN TO CONCESSION BODIES THE PROPERTY AND OBJECTS PASSED
TO HIM IN ACCORDANCE WITH THE AGREEMENT, AND ALSO TO TAKE CARE OF
HIS OWN PROPERTY IN A TWO-MONTH PERIOD FROM THE DAY OF THE
CONCESSION AGREEMENT'S EXPIRATION OR CANCELLATION;
- TO FULFILL OTHER RESPONSIBILITIES STIPULATED BY LEGISLATION OF THE
REPUBLIC OF TAJIKISTAN.

ARTICLE 19. CONCESSIONAIRE'S PROFITS

THE CONCESSIONAIRE'S PROFITS LEFT AFTER PAYMENT OF TAXES AND
OTHER FEES, REMAINS AT HIS FULL DISPOSAL.

V. FINAL REGULATIONS

ARTICLE 20. PROCEDURE FOR CONSIDERING DISPUTES

DISPUTES BETWEEN THE CONCESSIONAIRE AND CONCESSIONAIRE BODY ARE
SUBJECT TO CONSIDERATION IN ECONOMIC COURTS OF THE REPUBLIC OF
TAJIKISTAN, IF OTHERWISE NOT STIPULATED BY INTERNATIONAL
AGREEMENTS AND TREATIES OF THE REPUBLIC OF TAJIKISTAN.
DISPUTES OF CONCESSIONAIRES WITH STATE ENTERPRISES, PUBLIC
ASSOCIATIONS, OTHER LEGAL ENTITIES, AND INDIVIDUALS OF THE REPUBLIC
OF TAJIKISTAN, AS WELL AS DISPUTES AMONG CONCESSIONAIRES ON ISSUES
CONNECTED WITH THEIR ACTIVITY, ARE SUBJECT TO CONSIDERATION IN
COURTS OF THE REPUBLIC OF TAJIKISTAN AND, IF AGREED WITH SIDES, IN
ECONOMIC COURT OR ARBITRATION ABROAD.

ARTICLE 21. RESPONSIBILITIES OF CONCESSION RELATIONS SUBJECTS

THE SIDES WHICH HAVE CONCLUDED THE CONCESSION AGREEMENT ARE
RESPONSIBLE FOR ITS NON-FULFILLMENT OR IMPROPER FULFILLMENT IN THE
ORDER ESTABLISHED BY LEGISLATION OF THE REPUBLIC OF TAJIKISTAN.

NOTE: THIS LAW IS THE MAIN DOCUMENT FOR U.S. MINING COMPANIES WHICH
WOULD LIKE TO ENTER TAJIKISTAN'S MINERAL WEALTH MARKET. MINING,
EQUALLY WITH HYDRO POWER ENERGY AND COTTON GINNING ARE PRIORITY
SECTORS IN THE COUNTRY'S ECONOMIC REFORM PROGRAM TILL 2000.
TAJIKISTAN HAS CONSIDERABLE MINERAL RESERVES WITH MORE THAT 400 OF
DIFFERENT DEPOSITS, INCLUDING THOSE OF PRECIOUS AND NON-PRECIOUS
METALS. HOWEVER, DUE TO THE WEAK COUNTRY'S CAPACITY TO DEVELOP
THESE DEPOSITS, THE MINING SEGMENT IN TAJIKISTAN'S TOTAL INDUSTRIAL
OUTPUT IS LOW (LESS THAN FIVE PERCENT.)

THE FLOW OF FOREIGN INVESTMENT TO THE MINING INDUSTRY STARTED
AFTER 1992. IT IS KNOWN THAT DEPOSITS' DEVELOPMENT REQUIRES THE
CONCESSION OF A CERTAIN TERRITORY FOR A LONG PERIOD OF TIME WITH

For additional analytical, business and investment opportunities information,
please contact Global Investment & Business Center, USA
at (202) 546-2103. Fax: (202) 546-3275. E-mail: rusric@erols.com

THE RIGHT TO EXTRACT MINERALS. HOWEVER, THE PAST LEGISLATION AND LEGAL LEXICON IN THE COUNTRY DID NOT PROVIDE EVEN THE CONCEPT CHARACTERIZING THESE LEGAL RELATIONS. THE CONCEPT OF "CONCESSION" IN THE LOCAL LEGISLATURE DID NOT EXIST AND THE PUBLIC'S ATTITUDE TO IT WAS RELATIVELY NEGATIVE. IN ORDER TO REMOVE THE LEGAL SHORTAGES AFFECTING THE FLOW OF FOREIGN INVESTMENT TO MINING AS WELL AS OTHER INDUSTRIES AND GIVE MORE GUARANTEES TO INVESTORS, THE PARLIAMENT OF TAJIKISTAN (MAJLISI OLI) AT ITS MAY SESSION IN 1997 ADOPTED THIS LAW ON CONCESSIONS.

ACCORDING TO THE LAW, CONCESSION IS AN AGREEMENT PROVIDING FOREIGN INVESTORS WITH A PASS FOR A TEMPORARY EXPLOITATION OF LAND, WATER, AND AIR SPACE WITH THE RIGHT TO EXTRACT MINERALS, EXPLOIT FLORA AND FAUNA, AND OTHER NATURAL RESOURCES NOT PROHIBITED BY THE LEGISLATION OF TAJIKISTAN. THE TERM OF CONCESSION AGREEMENT IS 50 YEARS. IN CASE OF LONG COMPENSATED DEPOSITS REQUIRING CONSIDERABLE INVESTMENT, THE TERM OF THE AGREEMENT MAY BE PROLONGED UP TO 99 YEARS. PRODUCTS AND PROFITS RECEIVED BY THE CONCESSIONAIRE BELONG TO HIM IN THE AMOUNT DETERMINED BY THE CONCESSION AGREEMENT. THE STATE MANAGEMENT OF CONCESSIONS IS EXECUTED BY THE GOVERNMENT OF TAJIKISTAN OR OTHER AUTHORIZED AUTHORITY, OR BY LOCAL STATE ENTITIES.

CONCESSIONS ARE GRANTED ON A TENDER OR AUCTION BASIS. IN SOME CASES, IN ACCORDANCE WITH THE GOTI DECISION, CONCESSION MAY BE GRANTED ON THE BASIS OF DIRECT NEGOTIATION BETWEEN THE CONCESSION BODIES AND THE INVESTOR. LOCAL AUTHORITIES MAY INITIATE TENDERS AND AUCTIONS ON THE SITES WHICH BELONG TO THEM. BIDS FOR ACTIONS AND TENDERS SHOULD BE SENT BY THE INVESTOR TO THE CONCESSION ORGAN. THE TENDER OR AUCTION WINNER SIGNS THE CONCESSION AGREEMENT WITH THE GOTI OR OTHER AUTHORIZED CONCESSION ENTITY. THE CONCESSIONAIRE MUST PAY A FEE FOR REGISTRATION OF THE AGREEMENT, A CONCESSION FEE, AND TAXES PROVIDED BY LOCAL LEGISLATION. PROFITS LEFT AFTER PAYMENT OF TAXES AND OTHER PAYMENTS ARE AT FULL DISPOSAL OF THE CONCESSIONAIRE. DISPUTES BETWEEN THE CONCESSIONAIRE AND THE CONCESSION ENTITY ARE SUBJECT TO CONSIDERATION OF ECONOMIC COURTS OF TAJIKISTAN, IF OTHER NOT PROVIDED BY INTERNATIONAL AGREEMENTS SIGHED BY TAJIKISTAN.

REGISTRATION OF FOREIGN LEGAL ENTITIES BY NOTARIES IN TAJIKISTAN

In accordance with the 15 May 1997 Law of the Republic of Tajikistan "On State Notary", all enterprises, regardless of forms of property (including private, collective, state, joint ventures, branches, and filials) are acknowledged as a legal entity from the moment's of

state registration at
state notaries on the territory where the legal entity is located. The state registration procedure is determined by the above mentioned law.

The enterprise is registered by the state notary in the period of not later than five days from the moment when the registration application with all necessary documents attached is presented.

The registration certificate is issued to the registered enterprise afterwards.
Applying to the state notary, the enterprise founders (legal entities and individuals) are to submit the following documents:

-- registration application - one copy
-- constituent documents (charter) - two copies
-- resolution of constituent documents issued by the Justice Ministry of the Republic of Tajikistan
-- statistical classification code
-- certificate stating the enterprise's location
-- receipt on state fees payment
-- for joint ventures - feasibility study and financial resolution issued by Finance Ministry
The Charter of the enterprise should meet the following requirements:
-- name of enterprise and its organizational-legal form
-- enterprise's location
-- activity's subject and aims
-- bodies of management and control and their competence
-- established order to form property and distribute profits
-- conditions of re-organization and cancellation of activity.
The legislation stipulates the cases when the legal entity is refused in registration:
-- violation of the established order of setting up the enterprise (for instance, lack of the necessary
number of enterprise founders)
-- non-conformity of constituent documents to legislation requirements.

The enterprise location may be confirmed by several ways:
   a) rental of premises. The charter should be attached by a letter of guarantee issued by the enterprise-landlord to the new enterprise-tenant confirming a lease of premises and its address.

   b) any enterprise is entitled to provide the new enterprise with its legal address so that the new enterprise could use it as its own legal address. In this case, the copy of the agreement granting the legal address or an appropriate letter from the legal entity are provided to the notary.

The new Housing Code adopted on December 12, 1997 prohibited using houses, apartments, and residences for non-housing residences. Using of private apartments and houses of citizens for establish various enterprises is allowed only if district governments permit this.

For additional analytical, business and investment opportunities information,
please contact Global Investment & Business Center, USA
at (202) 546-2103. Fax: (202) 546-3275. E-mail: rusric@erols.com

The state fee for enterprise registration excluding joint ventures is 100,000 Tajik rubles (USD 125). For registration of joint ventures is 500,000 Tajik rubles (USD 620). To register amendments to constituent documents and to re-register enterprises, regardless of their forms of property, is charged 50% of the previuosly imposed sum for registration.

LAW OF THE REPUBLIC OF TAJIKISTAN ON PRIVATIZATION OF STATE PROPERTY IN THE REPUBLIC OF TAJIKISTAN

ARTICLE 1. GENERAL PROVISIONS

The present Law regulates relations between the State and its authorized bodies and legal and natural persons in the process of privatization of state property.

ARTICLE 2. DEFINITION OF PRIVATIZATION

Privatization shall be defined as actions of the state to transfer the rights in state property to natural and legal persons in the manner prescribed by laws and other legal and regulatory acts.

ARTICLE 3. LAWS OF THE REPUBLIC OF TAJIKISTAN ON PRIVATIZATION

The laws of the Republic of Tajikistan on privatization shall consist of the Constitution and laws of the Republic of Tajikistan, this Law, legal acts of the President and the Government of the Republic of Tajikistan, and legal acts of local governments.
The privatization of property of the Republic of Tajikistan located outside its borders shall be regulated by this Law, unless otherwise provided by international legal acts recognized by the Republic of Tajikistan.

ARTICLE 4. BASIC PRINCIPLES OF PRIVATIZATION

Privatization shall be conducted according to the following basic principles:

- legality;
- transparency;
- equal rights of citizens;
- competition;
- succession.

ARTICLE 5. AUTHORIZED BODIES IN PRIVATIZATION

Decisions on the privatization of objects of Republican property shall be made by the Government of the Republic of Tajikistan.
Decisions on the privatization of communal property of Gorno-Badakhshan Autonomous Oblast, oblasts, cities and districts shall be made by the corresponding Majlisi of People's Deputies of GBAO, oblasts, cities and districts, and, within the limits of their authority, chairmen of GBAO, oblasts, cities and regions.

ARTICLE 6. POWERS OF GOVERNMENT AGENCIES IN THE AREA OF PRIVATIZATION

The Government of the Republic of Tajikistan, within the limits of its competence, shall:

For additional analytical, business and investment opportunities information, please contact Global Investment & Business Center, USA at (202) 546-2103. Fax: (202) 546-3275. E-mail: rusric@erols.com

- manage the process of privatization of state property in the Republic of Tajikistan;
- approve programs for the privatization of state property;
- establish the order and methods of valuation for objects, subject to privatization
- make other decisions on privatization issues.

The Government of the Republic of Tajikistan may, in the manner established by law, delegate a portion of its powers to the agency for the management of state property in the Republic of Tajikistan.

ARTICLE 7. AUTHORITY OF LOCAL BODIES IN PRIVATIZATION

The authority of the local Majlisi' Oli of people's deputies, GBAO, oblasts, cities and regional chairmen in privatization arising from Article 5 of this Law shall be regulated by the Constitution and other laws of the Republic of Tajikistan.

ARTICLE 8. OBJECTS OF PRIVATIZATION

Objects of privatization shall be:

- property of state enterprises which is used in executing their activity, the land tenure rights of the property on which the enterprise rests, state enterprises as property complexes, which shall consist of all types of property used for its activity, including buildings, facilities, equipment, inventory, raw materials, goods produced, rights of use in the parcels of land on which they are located, receivable, debts, and all exclusive rights belonging to the enterprise as a legal entity;
- production and non-production subdivisions and structural units of a state enterprise as a property complex, the privatization of which will not violate the closed technological cycle;
- the property of state enterprises;
- shares in enterprises and organizations belonging to the state.

State property became the object for privatization when decision on privatization is made by the authorized body in the Article 5 of this Law.

ARTICLE 9. OBJECTS EXCLUDED FROM PRIVATIZATION

Property belonging to the state shall be subject to privatization, with the exception of objects that are the exclusive property of the state under Article 13 of the Constitution of the Republic of Tajikistan, objects of historical value and national heritage, defense enterprises, enterprises engaged in the disposal of radioactive wastes, and administrative buildings and facilities.

Privatization of objects providing the support for the infrastructure of the cities and regions : electrical energy, water supplying buildings, railway and auto way communications, communications, objects of health protection and education is implemented after the decision of the government.

The list of objects not subject to privatization shall be approved by the Government of the Republic of Tajikistan.

ARTICLE 10. PARTICIPANTS IN PRIVATIZATION

Subjects of privatization shall be natural and legal persons.
Legal persons in which the state owns greater than a 25% share shall not be participants in privatization.
Foreign natural and legal persons shall participate in the privatization of state property on terms determined by the laws of the Republic of Tajikistan.

ARTICLE 11. FORMS OF PRIVATIZATION

Privatization is conducted through the following mechanisms:

 a. Sale
 b. Case by case privatization on tender basis

The forms and conditions of privatization, order of organizing the sale or case by case privatization shall be determined by the Government of the Republic of Tajikistan.

ARTICLE 12. SALE OF OBJECTS OF PRIVATIZATION

Sales are conducted as tenders or auctions.
Prior to sale, the seller is to prepare complete information on the object of privatization.

ARTICLE 13. CASE BY CASE PRIVATIZATION

Large and unique objects, the list of which is approved by the Government of the Republic of Tajikistan, are subject to case by case privatization.
Case by case privatization consists of:

 a. Analysis of the activity and competitiveness of the object;
 b. Valuation of the property complex
 c. Decision on the percentage of the shares to be sold ;
 d. Decision on the technological and organizational changes which may be proposed;
 e. Decision on the form of privatization.

Execution of case by case privatization shall be executed by the body approved by the Government of the Republic of Tajikistan.

ARTICLE 14. PRIVATIZATION SECURITIES

In order to create equal starting conditions for participation in privatization, to attract broad participation by the population in the acquisition of state property, and to guarantee social justice, privatization securities may by used in the privatization of state property, which shall give their owners the right to a share in freely distributed state property.
The terms of the issuance and the manner of circulation and use of privatization securities shall be established by the Government of the Republic of Tajikistan.

ARTICLE 15. TRANSFER OF PROPERTY RIGHTS IN OBJECTS OF PRIVATIZATION

The right of property in objects of privatization shall arise from the moment of state registration of the right of acquisition of property in the manner established by law.

ARTICLE 16. FUNDS RECEIVED FROM PRIVATIZATION

Funds received from privatization shall be deposited in the state budget of the Republic of Tajikistan.

ARTICLE 17. PROTECTION OF LEGAL RIGHTS IN PRIVATIZATION

The legal rights of subjects of privatization shall be protected in the manner established by the laws of the Republic of Tajikistan.

REGULATION ON PROCEDURE FOR THE SALE OF OBJECTS OF PRIVATIZATION AT AUCTIONS AND TENDERS

I. GENERAL PROVIZION

The Regulation is developed in accordance with the law of the Republic of Tajikistan of May 16, 1997 "On privatization of state property", and it established the general procedure and terms for sale of objects of privatization of the republican and communal property at auctions and tenders.

1. Words and expressions of the Regulation, as they are further defined, will have the following meaning unless otherwise foreseen by the context:

   a. "Auction" - advertised bidding for sale of objects of privatization when fulfillment of any terms in relation to the object being privatized is not required;
   b. "Tender" - closed bidding for sale of objects of privatization when fulfillment of some definite terms is required;
   c. "Object of privatization" - a state owned enterprise or organization as a property complex; segmented production and non-production subdivisions and structural units of the enterprise which do not infringe technological cycle; separate property of a state owned enterprise; the state shares of enterprises and organizations;
   d. "Object for sale" - an object of privatization on which the decision of selling it at auction or tender is taken by an authorized body;
   e. "Seller" - a body authorized by the Government of the Republic of Tajikistan to implement privatization process in relation to the objects of the republican property, and appropriate Majlisis Oli of people's deputies in relation to the property of GBAO, oblasts, cities and regions;
   f. "Organizer" - a seller or any other legal person selected by the seller on the competitive basis who organizes and holds an auction to sell objects of privatization;
   g. "Bidder" - a legal or natural person being registered in the established order to bid in the auction or tender;

For additional analytical, business and investment opportunities information, please contact Global Investment & Business Center, USA at (202) 546-2103. Fax: (202) 546-3275. E-mail: rusric@erols.com

h. "Commercial tender" - bidding between the bidders who agreed to fulfill the terms of the tender when the highest bidder is considers to be the winner by the tender commission;

i. "Investment tender" - bidding when the tender commission considers the bidder offering the best program which meets the tender requirements to be the winner;

j. "Lot" - an object of privatization offered for tender. In case shares are sold, lot is a whole number of shares of a concrete joint stock company offered for bidding

k. "Bidding" - sale of lots at auction or tenders;

l. "Lot bidder" - a bidder who agrees to the announced price of the lot by rising his number;

m. "English method" - an auction method when the starting price is increased by previously announced step up to the moment when there is one highest bidder;

n. "Dutch method" - an auction method when the starting price is reduced by announced step up to the moment when one of the bidders agrees to buy the lot at the announced price;

o. "Starting price of the lot" - the price with which auction on every lot begins;

p. "Minimum price of the lot" - the price below which the lot cannot be sold;

q. "Price of sale" - the final price of the lot ascertained in the result of auction;

r. "Winner" - a highest bidder at auction or commercial tender, or a bidder presenting the most effective business plan;

s. "Purchaser" - the winner who made the purchase and sale contract on the object of privatization with the seller;

t. "Auctioneer" - a natural person appointed or hired by the Organizer to auction objects of privatizatin.

2. Specifically important and significant objects of privatization affecting environment and infringing upon economic interests of the Republic of Tajikistan, and objects of unfinished construction being of great importance for the economy of the republic are subject to sale at tender. The list of objects of privatization subject to sale at tender is approved by the Government of the Republic of Tajikistan.

Seller makes a decision on the term of putting the object of privatization for tender. Sale of the object at first three auctions is executed by English method. If the object is not sold at the English auction, the seller has the right in agreement with the Government of the Republic of Tajikistan as for the republican property, and with the Madjlisis Oli of people's deputies and in the limits of competence of the chairmen of GBAO, oblasts, the city of Dushanbe, cities and towns, and regions as for the republican property to continue English auction or use the Dutch auctions.

3. If the object of privatization is a state shareholding of a joint stock company, the seller takes a decision to put it up for auction or tender as a whole, or divides the shareholding into lots, the number of shares in each lot must be whole.

4. The state shareholdings in the joint stock companies which have already registered their prospectus in the order established by the Ministry of Finance of the Republic of Tajikistan are put up for auctions and tenders .

5. Seller sells the state shareholdings in the procedure prescribed by the present Regulation.

6. Functions of the Seller are:

a. distribution of objects of privatization to be sold at specific auctions and tenders, setting their term and location;
b. division the shares into lots;
c. definition of the starting price of the lot;
d. creation of the auction and tender commission;
e. receipt of guaranteed fees;
f. making contracts with the Organizers to organize and conduct auctions;
g. carrying out control over the course of organization and conducting auctions and tenders;
h. making purchase and sale contracts with the Winner and control over their implementation;
i. effecting settlements with the Bidders, Purchasers and Organizers.

7. The Seller organizes and conducts the auction by himself, or in exclusive cases with the Republic of Tajikistan Government's consent he can make a contract with the Organizer on organization and conducting one or several auctions on sale the objects of privatization.
8. Contract on organization and conducting one auction for sale of objects of privatization is made in writing between the Seller and the Organizer and is to contain:
    o list of objects for sale;
    o deadline for conducting auctions;
    o number of shares put up for auction; number of lots, number of shares in each lot, face value of shares;
    o auction method for sale of each lot;
    o starting and minimum prices of each lot;
    o powers the Seller gives to the Organizer to organize and conduct the auction;
    o size of the guaranteed fees and procedure of its payment;
    o list of documents on each object for sale to be transferred to the Organizer;
    o periodicity and the Organizer's form of reporting on preparation and conducting the auction;
    o size and remuneration for the Organizer and procedure of mutual settlements with the Seller;
    o mutual obligations and property liabilities;
    o term of the contract and provisions for cancellation of the contract.

Contract on organization and conducting several auctions for sale of objects of privatization is made in writing between the Seller and the Organizer and it is to contain:

- powers the Seller gives to the Organizer to organize and conduct the auction;
- periodicity and the Seller's form of information about the coming auction is to contain: list of objects for sale put up for the auction; deadline for conducting auctions; number of shares put up for auction; number of lots, number of shares in each lot, face value of shares; the auction method for sale of each lot; starting and minimum prices of each lot; size of the guaranteed fees and procedure of its payment;

For additional analytical, business and investment opportunities information, please contact Global Investment & Business Center, USA at (202) 546-2103. Fax: (202) 546-3275. E-mail: rusric@erols.com

- periodicity and the Organizer's form of reporting on the process of preparation and conducting the auction;
- size and remuneration for the Organizer and procedure of mutual settlements with the Seller;
- mutual obligations and property liabilities;
- term of the contract and provisions for cancellation of the contract.

The seller does not have the right to transfer to the Organizer the contractual functions prescribed Paragraph 6 of the present Regulation except sub-points a, b, c, d, f, and g.

9. Natural and legal persons including foreigners, who have been registered in the procedure defined by Paragraph 32 of the present Regulation, with the exception of those persons indicated in Paragraph 10, are admitted to take part in auction.

Participation of foreign natural and legal persons in auctions and tenders is regulated by a specific Law of the Republic of Tajikistan.

10. Bidders at auction and tenders cannot be:
    - Legal entities of the republic of Tajikistan whose state share in the charter fund exceeds 25 %;
    - The Organizer of the auction and members of the auction commission;
    - The Organizer of the tender and members of the tender commission;
    - The Winners of the previous auctions who did not fulfill obligations prescribed by the present Regulation are deprived the right to participate in the subsequent auctions and tenders within 6 months.

II. CREPARATION FOR AUCTION AND TENDER

11. The Seller of the auction creates an auction commission to execute control over the organization and conducting the auction. Staff, competence and organization of the auction commission activity is defined by the 'Regulation on auction commission' to be approved by the Seller.
12. To prepare and conduct the tender, the Seller creates a tender commission which consists of representatives of the Seller, the Ministry of finance of the Republic of Tajikistan, the Ministry of economy and external economic relations of the Republic of Tajikistan, the Ministry of justice of the Republic of Tajikistan, the higher ministry or department of the republican object being privatized, and the representatives of financial, economic, banking bodies, the Khukumat, other bodies of local government, the higher body of the communal object being privatized. The commission should consist of not less than 5 persons, the number of the members of the commission should be odd. The chairman of the commission is the representative of the Seller.

The tender commission is to:

- independently develop and approve the rules of the work;

For additional analytical, business and investment opportunities information, please contact Global Investment & Business Center, USA at (202) 546-2103. Fax: (202) 546-3275. E-mail: rusric@erols.com

- define and approve the terms and conditions of the tender;
- make a decision on the publication of official announcement;
- conduct the tender;
- announce the winner of the tender.

13. Decisions of the auction or tender commission is taken by a simple majority of votes of the total number of the members of the commission. In case of equality of votes, the chairman's vote is decisive.
14. Preparation for auction or tender is cried out in the following procedure:
    o lots are formed;
    o lots are distributed for specific auctions or tenders;
    o term for conducting auctions is set;
    o starting prices of the lots are determined;
    o procedure of the guaranteed fee payment is defined;
    o in case of need a tender for the right of making contract to organize and conduct auction for sale of objects of privatization is held;
    o sale prospectus, auction cards and schedules for visiting objects are made;
    o official announcement of auction or tender is published and other advertisement is carried out;
    o guaranteed fees received;
    o participants are registered.

15. With the purpose of complex study of the structure of expenses for financing the object, state of the object, valuation of the object of privatization, studying of the tender terms, the Seller has the right to involve independent consulting firms or an auditor during the period of preparation for tender.
16. The tender commission determines the terms of tender. The terms of tender can be:
    o determination of a certain level of volumes of production, nomenclature of the manufacture produced or the services rendered in the term set by the tender commission;
    o delivery of production to the certain consumers within the term set by the tender commission;
    o preserving, cutting down of not more than on the size established by the tender commission or creating of working spaces in term set by the tender commission;
    o obligations on the indicated volume, type and term of investments into the objects of privatization;
    o redemption of wage arrears in the term set by the tender commission;
    o redemption of the accounts payable in the term set by the tender commission;
    o restriction on fulfillment of the bargains (resale, pledge, transfer to management, lease out) in the term set by the tender commission;
    o ecological requirements.

17. The starting price of the object of privatization put up for auction or tender is calculated in accordance with Instruction on valuation of objects of privatization approved by the Government Resolution of May 4, 1997, # 181.

18. When selling the object by Dutch method, the starting (primary) price is defined by multiplying the starting price by increasing coefficient. The coefficient is established by the Seller, but it cannot be lower then 5.
19. While putting up the object for the Dutch auction, the floor price of the lot is established in the identical size for all objects at the level of minimal wages multiplied by 100.
20. Guaranteed fee is to ensure the fulfillment of the following obligations of the participant:
    o signing the record of the auction results in case he becomes a winner;
    o making a purchase and sale contract in accordance with the record of auction results.

21. The guaranteed fee to participate in the auction or tender is established in the identical size for all lots being out up for auction or tender, and is equal to the size which is equivalent to US$ 200 and is entered in the national currency of the Republic of Tajikistan.
22. The participant has the right to pay any of guaranteed fees, but one guaranteed fee gives the right to purchase one lot.
23. The guaranteed fee is paid in the procedure established in the official announcement. The recipient of the guaranteed fee is the Seller.
24. The Guaranteed fee of the Winner who made a purchase and sale contract is included due to the payments on the purchase and sale contract.
25. The guaranteed fee is not returned to the participant in case of:
    o refusal to participate in the auction or tender less than three days before they are conducted;
    o refusal of the Winner to sign the record of the auction results, or to make purchase and sale contract;
    o non-performance or improper performance of the purchase and sale contractual obligations;
    o participant's violation of the present Regulation.

In all other cases the guaranteed fees are returned within 10 banking days after the auction or tender is closed; if the money is entered into the Seller's account after the auction or tender is closed then - within ten banking days after the money is entered.

26. Official announcement to sell the objects of the republican property by auction or tender should be published in the state and Russian languages in the republican mass media and the objects of the communal property - in local newspapers not less than 30 days before auction .
27. Official announcement should contain:
    o date, place and time of the auction or tender;
    o name, location and major characteristics (type of activity, square of the site and the characteristic of the buildings located on the site, square of the object /general and industrial/, average number of employees) of the object for sale;
    o size of the accounts payable;
    o size of lots put up for sale (in percentage of the charter fund) from each joint stock company;
    o starting prices of the lots put up for sale;

For additional analytical, business and investment opportunities information,
please contact Global Investment & Business Center, USA
at (202) 546-2103. Fax: (202) 546-3275. E-mail: rusric@erols.com

- o size of the commission collected by the Seller;
- o size of the guaranteed fee defined by Paragraph 21 of this Regulation, procedure of its payment, recipient's settlement account in case of - the fee transfer;
- o place and term of submitting applications;
- o telephone numbers and addresses where at the indicated time one can get prospectus of sale, auction and tender regulations;
- o terms and conditions of tender;
- o criterion to define the Winner;
- o other additional information on the Seller's decision.

28. Before the publication of the official announcement there must be prepared:

a) the prospectus on every object for sale containing the data on the object and consisting of:

- o at selling state owned enterprises as a property complex, production and non-production subdivisions and structural units:
  - copies of the legal persons' founder documents;
  - copies of the balance sheet (separate balance sheet) with attachments for the recent accounting period before the decision to put up an object of privatization for auction or tender is taken by the Seller;
  - acts of valuation;

- - at selling shares of joint stock companies:
  - o copies of prospectus of emission and certificate of registration;
  - o acts of valuation of the object of privatization;
- - at selling a property unit of the enterprise:
  - o technical certificate of a property unit to be the object for sale, or any other document characterizing technical condition of the object;
  - o acts of valuation.

The prospectus can also contain other additional data (staff of the bodies of management of the object of privatization, analysis of investment risk, data on possible variants of technical re-equipment, settlements of the enterprise's profits after the re-equipment, estimation of necessary investments for production, valuation of perspective of the production manufactured at the world and domestic markets);

a. Auction card contains the list of lots, indicated in the official announcement, put up for auction which is given to every BIdder at the moment of registration.
b. Objects' visiting schedule

29. After publication of the official announcement, the Seller must ensure free access to study the objects for sale for all interested parties, including visiting and examination of the object, and regulations of the auction and tender.
30. Other kinds of advertisement may be done in any form to attract as many participants as possible.

31. Registration of the of the Bidders is started on the day of the official announcement publication in the republican press and is over one hour before the auction or tender begins.
32. For registration as the Bidder it is necessary to submit:
    - two copies of application form for participation in auction or tender without the indication in it the object of sale which the Bidder is going to purchase (Attachment # 1-4). One copy of the application with the indication of the date it is received, certified and stamped by the Organizer is at once returned to the Bidder as the document certifying the application is received and the guaranteed fee is paid;
    - passport or any other identification card;
    - original and a copy of the payment agreement confirming that the guaranteed fee is paid in the size equivalent to US$ 200;
    - notarized document certifying the representative's authority of the legal and natural person.

Legal persons additionally submit:

- - notarized copies of the charter and legal person's registration certificates.

Joint stock companies additionally submit the extract from the stockholders' list with the information of the state share in the charter fund of the company to be signed and stamped by the first chairman.
In case of conducting a commercial tender, the Bidder additionally submits five copies of his agreement to fulfill the condition (conditions) of the tender in the stamped envelope where should be indicated:

- the name of the object of sale;
- agreement to fulfill the condition (conditions) of the tender with the indication of the condition (conditions) published in the official announcement on auction;
- suggestion on the purchasing price of the object of sale;
- information about the Bidder;
- signature of the Bidder.

The Investment bidder additionally submits a business plan (Attachment # 5) on the above mentioned object of sale.

33. The Seller and Organizer have no right:

- to demand that the Bidder should provide them with the information of his intentions to purchase this or that lot from those put up for auction or tender;
- to divulge the information dealing with the Bidders or interfering the course of bidding during the whole period of preparation for auction or tender and the time of their conducting. A person bears responsibility for divulging the above mentioned information in accordance with law of the Republic of Tajikistan;
- to demand that additional documents should be submitted for the Bidder's registration besides those enumerated in Paragraph 32 of the present Regulation.

34. The Organizer or tender commission carries out registration of Bidders separately for each auction or tender in a special paginated register in the order the documents are received.

In case the auction is held, the Bidder's number of registration should coincide with the number of registration in the register.

35. The documents of the registered Bidders are kept in a separate safe until the day of auction or tender.
36. The person, who has got registration, gets an auction number on the day of auction when he shows the second copy of the application. Use of the auction number by other person is forbidden.
37. On the day of auction, the envelopes are transferred to the tender commission in accordance with the attached Record (Attachment #5) on receiving Bidders' applications, signed by the person responsible for receiving the applications.

III. CONDUCTING AUCTIONS

38. Auctioneer conducts Auction. Auction is started with the explanations of the auction regulations.

Decision of sequence to put out lots to tender is taken by the Auctioneer. This procedure may differ from the procedure established in the auction card.
The process of auction is watched by the auction commission, representatives of the Organizer (provided his participation in organization of auction). Representatives of mass media and international organizations have the right to attend the auction.
The Bidders and the persons present who try to influence the course of auction or breaking its regulations, are removed from the hall.
Auctioneer begins the auction on every lot with the announcement of the object of sale, its brief characteristics, auction method starting price and the step of changing the price. Auctioneer has the right to change the step in the course of auction, announcing it. The step of changing is established in the limits between 5 - 10 % of the current price of the lot.

39. Auction is held by one of the two methods described below:
    o English method:

The Auctioneer announces a starting price of the lot and the step of increasing the price. By rising their numbers, the lot bidders increase the starting price for the step announced. The Auctioneer announces auction numbers of the bidders on the lot, fixes the price and suggests to increase it. Auctions of the lot continue until the maximum price is proposed. The lot bidder who has offered the highest price for the lot is announced by the Auctioneer. The Auctioneer repeats the last price of the lot three times, and if there are not any other numbers raised, he declares by banging the gavel that the lot is sold.

Auction of the lot is considered to have gone through if there are not less than two lot bidders.

Dutch method:

1. The Auctioneer announces a starting price of the lot and reduces it with the step declared, announcing a new price. The Auctioneer calls the number of the lot bidder who is the first to raise the auction number when the price is announced, and he declares the bidder to be the winner of the given lot. If not a single bidder desires to purchase the given lot when the Auctioneer announces the minimum price, the lot is removed from auction.
2. If two or more numbers are raised simultaneously, it is up to the Auction Commission to take decision who is the first, and the bidders have no right to dispute the decision. In some exclusive cases the Auction Commission has the right to decide by random drawing.

40. The result of auction on every lot are recorded and the record is signed by the Organizer, the Auction Commission and the Winner at the end of auction on every lot (Attachment # 6). The Auctioneer has the right to declare a break to sign the record. The record is made in three copies, one copy for each - for the Seller, the Purchaser and the Auction Commission. The Auction Commission must hand a copy of the record on the auction results to the Seller on the day not later than the next day after the auction if conducted.
41. The record on the auction results is a document which fixes the auction results and obligations of the Winner and the Seller to make a purchase and sale contract on the object of privatization at the price of sale. The Winner has the right to make a purchase and sale contract within not more than 5 banking days after signing the record, at the expiration of the term this right is lost.
42. If the lot is not sold by Dutch method after having been put up for auction several times, the Seller takes the decision to use the procedures on restructurization and liquidation in relation to the object of privatization.

IV. CONDUCTING TENDERS

43. The sittings of the tender commission are closed and are conducted if one or more envelope with the offer of the price have been received.
44. The envelopes are opened by the commission during the tender. All the members of the commission have to study and compare the Bidders' suggestions.
45. During the commercial tender, the tender commission announces the Bidder, who bids up and if his bid meets the requirements of the tender, to be the Winner of the tender.
46. During the investment tender, the bidders' business plans are considered by the tender commission. The Winner of the investment tender is defined by the tender commission proceed from the criteria established by the commission.

For additional analytical, business and investment opportunities information,
please contact Global Investment & Business Center, USA
at (202) 546-2103. Fax: (202) 546-3275. E-mail: rusric@erols.com

The tender commission announces the Bidder of the investment tender, whose business plan is more effective and meets the requirements of the tender, to be the Winner of the tender.

47. If the bids of two or more Bidders at the commercial tender contain one and the same price, or business plans of two or more Bidders at the investment tender contain adequate proposals on the investments and other factors, the person who has registered first is considered the Winner.

48. In case of registration of one Bidder of the tender on sale of an object of privatization, the tender commission announces him the Winner under condition he offers the price higher than the starting one.

49. The record is drawn up on the results of every lot (Attachment # 7) with the indication of:
    o   the staff of the commission;
    o   terms and conditions of the tender;
    o   number of the Bidders and their registration numbers in accordance with those indicated in the envelopes;
    o   the list of prices offered in accordance with the Bidders' registration numbers;
    o   the Winner, his registration number, his offered price;
    o   the selling price of the object of privatization.

In case of adequate prices, the date of receiving the application is additionally indicated in the record.

In case of the investment tender, the number of Bidder's balls gained is indicated the record, and also the best proposal in accordance with the business plan submitted.

50. The record is signed by all the tender commission members. Any member of the commission has the right express his own point of view in writing and attach it to the record.

51. The record is made in three copies, one copy for each - for the Seller, the Winner and the tender commission. Two copies of the record are handed to the Seller who must inform the Bidders of the tender results not later than the next day after the tender.

52. The record on the tender results is a document which fixes the tender results and obligations of the Winner and the Seller to make a purchase and sale contract within not more than 10 banking days after signing the record, at the expiration of the term this right is lost.

53. In case of non-conclusion the Winner does not make a purchase and sale contract, the Seller suggests that the other Bidders conclude the purchase and sale contract on the base of the tender commission's record with taking into account the price offered by them.

54. The rest of the Bidders are informed of the number of Bidders on the object declared by them and the list of prices offered by them not later than the next day after the tender. In case of adequate prices, the date of applications is indicated.

55. In case the applications for the commercial and investment tenders on sale of the object of privatization are not submitted, on the day of conducting the tender the commission has to take the decision:

- o either to conduct the second tender on sale of the above mentioned object of privatization changing the conditions of tender in the term of not later than one month after the first tender. Commercial tenders cannot be but two;
- o or to transfer the Seller the above mentioned object of privatization to be put up for the next auction in the term not later than one month after the tender.

V. PROCEDURE OF EFFECTING ETTLEMENTS WITH PURCHASERE AND REGISTERING OWNERSHIP

56. The Winner enters the commission to the Seller's account, the size of which should not exceed 2 % of the selling price of each lot, which after entering into the budget of the Republic of Tajikistan is spent for organization and realization of auctions and tenders.
57. The purchase and sale contract of the object of privatization between the Seller and the Purchaser is made in the written form and it should have reference to the record on auction or tender results (Attachments # 8 and #9).
58. Settlements on the purchase and sale contract are executed between the Seller and the Purchaser, for all this the Seller executes settlement in the following procedure:

   a. advance payment is made in the size of not less than 15 % of 10 banking days after the purchase and sale contract is signed. The guaranteed fee is included into the advance payment.
   b. the remained sum should be made not later than 30 banking days after the purchase and sale contract is signed.

59. Privatization securities can be used to pay for the object of privatization (privatization checks until their expiration term). The terms and procedure to use privatization securities are defined by the Government of the Republic of Tajikistan.
60. In case the final payment is delayed for more than 10 banking days, the Seller has the right to cancel the contract in the unilateral manner and claim to indemnify for real losses not covered by the guaranteed fee.
61. After full payment of the object of privatization, the Seller and the Purchaser should sign the act of transfer the object within three days (Attachment # 10).
62. The Purchaser has got ownership of the object of privatization after the state registration in the order prescribed by the law and full payment of the price indicated in the purchase and sale contract.
63. The ownership certificate is the document certifying ownership being given by the state notary offices at the place of the sold object's location.
64. Auction or tender results can be protested within 30 calendar days after the auction or tender.
65. In case the terms and obligation of the tender prescribed by the purchase and sale contract are not fulfilled , legal consequences prescribed by the purchase and sale contract come into force.

For additional analytical, business and investment opportunities information, please contact Global Investment & Business Center, USA at (202) 546-2103. Fax: (202) 546-3275. E-mail: rusric@erols.com

VI. MONEY RECEIVED FROM SALE OF OBJECTS OF PRIVATIZATION

66. Money received from sale of objects of privatization is entered to the state budget.
67. The remuneration due to the Organizer is included in the charges of the Seller on preparation and conducting the auction.

SUPPLEMENTS

REPRESENTATIVES OF THE REPUBLIC OF TAJIKISTAN ABROAD

Country	Ambassador's name	Telephone	Fax	Mailing address
Austria e-mail: tajikembassy@telering.at g.at	Zaripov Khamrohon	(43-1) 409 826 611 650 505 55 00	(43-1) 409 826 614	1090 Vienna Universitats Strasse
Islamic Republic of Iran ??? e-mail: tajiribem@apanda.com	Nazirov Toshmad Radzhabovich	(98-21) 2299584	(98-21) 229 16 07 229 70 39	Майдю Ниёваон Хиеб Шахид Зинали кю3,б10
China	Karimov Dzhamsheдeд Khilolovich	(86-10) 6532 30 39 6532 25 98	(86-10) 6532 30 39 6416 82 12	100 600, Pekin Ta Uan, д,4 / office1 Кв, 31
Pakistan	Khodzhiev Bobodzhon	(92-51) 229 46 75	(92-51) 229 97 10	Islamabad
	Bobokalonov Yusyf T.	(92-021) 583 82 45	(92-021) 583 74 22	Karachi
USA	Alimov Rashid Kutbudinovich	(1-212) 744 21 96	(1-212) 472 76 45	136 East 67th Str.NY USA
Turkey	Dododzhonov Rustam Nachmiddin I.	(90-312) 446 16 02 0535-232 18 02	(90-312) 446 36 21	M. Gandhi Str. 06700 Ankara, Turkey
Germany	Mirzoev Akbar	(49-30) 347 93 00 05364 7289-1576	(49-30) 3479 30 29 3479 30 18	Otto-Suhr-Allee 84 10585 Berlin

REPRESENTATIVES OF THE REPUBLIC OF TAJIKISTAN IN CIS COUNTRIES

Country	Ambassador's name	Telephone	Fax	Mailing address
Republic of Byelorussia	Rakhimov Olim Sabirovich	8-10 (37517) 226 19 44	8-10 (37517) 227 76 13	Minsk, Kirova Str.17
Republic of Kazakhstan	Iskandarov Akbarsho	8-10 (7-3272) 54 28 69	8-10 (7-3272) 54 28 69	Almaty Dzhandosova Str. 58
Russian Federation	Mirzoev Rhamazan Zariphovich	8-10 (7-095) 290 41 86 290 38 46 290 57 36	8-10 (7-095) 291 89 98	Moscow Granatniy pereulok 13
	Mirzoev Komil	8-10 (7-095)	290 57 36	
Republic of Turkmenistan	Mardonov Tadzhiddin Nuriddinovich	8-10 (998-712) 35 56 96 39 34 31	8-10 (993-12) 39 31 74	Ashgabat Turkmenbashy Str. 13
Republic of Uzbekistan	Amirzaev Kulyamzhan Amirzaevich	8-10 (998-712) 54 99 66 185 75 16 (сот.)	8-10 (998-712) 54 89 69	Tashkent M. Torobi Square 19
CIS Secretariat Minsk			(37517) 227 23 39	Minsk Kirova Str.17
Central Asia Association on Economics Bishkek	Sobirov Makhmud Nosirovich	(996-312) 22 12 36 66 13 51	(996-312) 22 74 57	Bishkek
Integration Committee			62 48 97	Almaty
ЭКО ???	Mirshakarov Mirafzad		283 17 32	Teheran
Mardonov T.N.		43 47 46		Tashkent
Spinerov D.N.	23 61 15	26 96 18 (home)		Almaty

INTERNATIONAL ORGANIZATIONS

AAN (Action Against Hunger) (8 Firdausi St.)
Head of Mission Philippe Mougin 24-14-09
Administrator Mahina Safarmamadova 21-51-73
Assistant Firuz tel/fax: 901-50-43

ABA (American Bar Association)/CEELI (Central East European Law Initiative) (72 Tolstoy St.)
Liaison to Tajikistan 24-15-05
Legislative Specialist/Rule of Law Liaison Bernard Ryan 21-15-02
Office Manager Zarona Ismailova 24-68-62
Translator Larisa Petrosyan fax: 24-26-80

ACCELS /American Center (American Council for Collaboration in Education and Language Study)
(105 Rudaki Ave. Apart. 13-14)
Deputy Director Matluba Mamadjanova tel/fax: 21-17-95
Program Assistant Yelena Lodde tel/fax: 21-21-03
Program Assistamt Zarrina Muhiddinova

oseas@amc.tajik.net
ACTED (Agency for Technical Cooperation and Development) (15 Academicians Rajabovs Ave.)
Regional Coordinator Frederic Roussel 21-92-89
Country Director Stephan Nicolas 24-65-83
Administrative Assistant Mavluda Kamalova fax: 51-01-12
Secretary Anna

ADB (Asian Development Bank)
(3 Academicians Rajabovs St., Bldg. of the Ministry of Finance, 3rd fl., Room 30)
Liasion Officer Oxana Nazmiyeva 27-24-97
Office Manager Muhabbat Salimova fax: 901-50-51 mobile: 901-05-15

ADRA (Adventist Development and Relief Agency) (43 Schors St.)
Country Director Vladimir Kononkov 21-47-05 Office Manager Svetlana Babanina 34-69-95
fax: 21-47-06

AED /Global Project (Academy for Educational Development) (40 Rudaki Ave., Rooms 300-303)
Director Shamsiddin Karimov 21-06-00
Senior Training Specialist Savriniso Rasulova 21-08-44
Admin. & Finance Manager Mahmadsodiq Tolibov 21-82-49

American Business Resource Center
Manager Faridun Kamoliddinov 21-05-22
Assistant Savriniso Qurbonbekova 21-05-26
tel/fax: 21-05-18
fax: 51-01-02

AKDN (Aga Khan Development Network) (6 Hamza Hakimzoda St.)
Resident Representative Hakim Feerasta 24-65-00 *(Secretary Latofat)* 21-71-94
Assistant Finance Manager Firuz Vatanshoyev tel/fax: 21-70-87
AKFED Project Manager Mathew Scanlon 24-65-65
Executive Aid Mahina tel/fax: 51-00-66
Assistant Amina 21-56-63
21-87-48

AKF (Aga Khan Foundation) (10 Hamza Hakimzoda St.)
Chief Executive Officer Mirzo Jahani 21-84-06 Executive Assistant Yevgeniya
Mordenskaya 21-84-06 *Receptionist Nargis* 24-34-42

AKHPCA (The Aga Khan Humanities Program for Central Asia) (75 Tolstoi St.)
Director Rafique Keshavjee 24-58-23
Deputy Firuza Tursunzade 24-07-02
Secretary Dilorom 24-52-97

ARD/CHECCHI/USAID (Commercial Law Project) (4 Govorov St.)
Director Garland Boyette 21-17-79
Deputy Akbar Muratov 24-22-84
Attorney/Office Manager Suhrob Jabborov 24-03-52
tel/fax: 21-26-50

CAAEF (Central Asian-American Enterprise Fund) (31 Kirov St., Apart. 1)
Vice President Benjamin Ryan 21-50-14 Office Manager Nazar Nabiyev 21-60-13
Secretary Gulchin 21-56-01
tel/fax: 51-00-88
Khujand Office (1 Lenin St.)
Office Manager 4-35-32; 6-53-48
fax: 6-00-73

CAD (Children's Aid Direct)
(9 Samad Gani St.)
Country Representative Dr. Julian Paul Edward 21-66-05
Administrator Zuhra Irgasheva tel/fax: 24-83-27

CADA (Central Asian Development Agency)
(40 Rudaki Ave., Room 307)
Director David Lovett 21-22-10
(Secretary Shukufa) res: 24-62-64
Deputy Tim Austin 21-21-75
Nigina 21-71-59
fax: 51-00-52

CARANA Corporation (44 Rudaki Ave., Room 159)
Project Manager Julian Simidjiyski 21-75-50
Office Manager Tatiana Khairova fax: 21-88-87

For additional analytical, business and investment opportunities information,
please contact Global Investment & Business Center, USA
at (202) 546-2103. Fax: (202) 546-3275. E-mail: rusric@erols.com

CARE International (Coordination for American Relief Everywhere) (25 Behzod St. 1st & 2nd fl.)
Country Director Jenevieve Abel 21-17-83
res: 24-06-46
Food Program Coordinator Benoy B. Saha 21-00-91
Health Sector Advisor Paula Boogart 21-75-42 21-78-71
Admin. Assistant Gulchin 24-43-06
fax: 21-17-78 fax: 51-00-36

Counterpart Consortium (20 Huseinzoda *(Kirov)* St.)
Country Director tel/fax: 21-75-59
Deputy Farhod Boqiyev tel/fax: 21-65-14
tel/fax: 21-82-65
Office Manager Adiba Ansori
Secretary Shoira tel/fax: 51-01-31
jbarbee@counterpart-tj.org

DEXTER Construction Corporation
President Yakov Krivoruk tel/fax: 34-88-96
Vice-President Vitaly Basteyev

EBRD (European Bank for Reconstruction and Development) (38 Shotemur St., Rooms ## 36, 38) **Assistant/Mission Coordinator** Nasiba Ahrorova tel/fax: 21-07-63
Mission Advisor Muzaffar Usmanov mobile: 901-00-78

ECHO (European Community Humanitarian Office)
(25 M. Tursunzoda St., 3rd fl.)

ECHO Correspondent Peter Burgess tel/fax: 21-60-83
Administrator Sitora Ahrori tel/fax: 23-16-15 Operations Officer Zafar Teshayev
Information Officer Azamat Khasanov

EF (Eurasia Foundation) (18 Rudaki Ave. 2nd fl.)
Regional Director Elizabeth Coll (Tashkent)
Country Representative Tatyana Falko tel/fax: 21-69-86
res: 21-52-98

FOCUS USA (Disaster Preparedness and Mitigation Project) - affiliate of AKDN
(15 Mamadali Qurbonov St.)
Program Director Goulsara Pulatova tel/fax: 21-98-30
Program Assistant Vladimir Kuimov tel/fax: 21-96-11
tel/fax: 23-02-20

GAA (German Agro - Action) (20/1 Behzod St.,)
Project Coordinator Beate Schoreit 21-54-79
21-33-68
fax: 21-21-68

Global Partners (184 Zainabbibi St.)

Country Director Greg Gamble 21-07-95
fax: 51-00-37

GTZ (German Technical Assistance Agency)
(21 Rudaki Ave.)
Head of Office Karlfried Metzler 21-71-26
Assistant Lyuba Frolova tel/fax: 51-00-37

ICRC (International Committee of Red Cross) (14/3 Aini St.)
Head of Delegation Elizabeth Knecht 21-68-23
21-73-37
Assistant Madina 21-86-60
fax: 51-00-53

IFES (International Foundation for Election Systems) (25 Behzod St., 3rd fl.)
Project Manager Philip Griffin (*Zumrad*) 21-80-52
Assistant Mouqim Mallayev 21-70-98
Finance Coordinator Farangis fax: 21-25-80

IFRC (International Federation of the Red Cross) (120 Omar Khayam St., 3rd fl.)
Head of Delegation Charlotta Relander 24-59-81
Secretary Shahlo Rajabova 24-42-96
24-00-33
tel/fax: 24-85-20

IMF (International Monetary Fund) (23/2 Rudaki Ave. #34, National Bank)
Resident Representative Henri Lorie 21-24-80
Assistant/Interpreter Munira Soliyeva tel/fax: 51-01-21
"Internews" (92 Rudaki Ave., 4th fl., Apart. 24)
Country Director Roshan Khadiri tel/fax: 21-43-12
mobile: 901-50-32
Director Bahodur Qosymov tel/fax: 24-54-83
Administrator *Roziya Jalilova*

IOM (International Organization of Migration) (5 Zakariyoi Rozi St.)
Chief of Mission Igor Bosc tel/fax: 24-71-96
Administrator Natalia Karpova tel/fax: 21-03-02
Assistant/Interpreter Mavsuma Valiyeva sat.fax: 51-00-62
MCI (Mercy Corps International) (1 Firdausi St., behind "Saodat" tea-house)
Country Director Kurt Gibson 24-00-16
24-06-89
Admin/Finance/Food Aid Shah Jalal Bhyian 21-08-60/64/79
Assistant Janat 21-36-21
tel/fax: 51-01-33

MERLIN (Medical Emergency Relief International) (8 Karamov St.)
Program Coordinator Paul Handley 24-45-89
Administrator Parvina Sadiyeva 21-47-64 tel/fax: 51-01-20

MSDSP (Mountain Societies Development Support Program) (2nd Proyezd,14 Azizbekov St.)
General Manager Mahmadamin Mahmadaminov 21-87-48
Secretary Nisso 21-56-63
fax: 21-38-93

MSF (Medecins Sans Frontiers/Holland) (21 Guliston St.)
Country Manager Ton Koene 21-44-25
Medical Coordinator Marie Skinnider 24-34-49
Admin. & Financial Coordinator Ms. Jose Hulsenbek 24-52-34
24-75-40
tel/fax: 51-00-71

ORA (Orphans, Refugees & Aid/Germany) International (17 Academicians Rajabovs St, Apart. 11)
Director Jeffrey Paulsen 27-46-10
Assistant Mamlakat res: 24-40-77
tel/fax: 21-64-42
OSCE (Organization for Security & Cooperation in Europe) (12 Zikrullo Khojayev/Mendeleyev/ St.)
Ambassador/Head of Mission Marc Gilbert 21-40-63
Deputy Head of Mission Jan Malekzade 24-58-79
Finance/Admin. Officer Mathieu Goodstein
Mission Assistant Dilorom (901-05-98) tel/fax: 24-91-59

OSI (Open Society Institute/ Soros Foundation) (65 Tolstoy St.)
Executive Director Zuhra Halimova tel/fax: 21-19-58
Grants Manager Sirojiddin Nasriddinov 21-32-60
Assistant 24-22-41
tel/fax: 51-01-42

English Language Center (Bldg. of the Firdausi Library, 2nd fl.)
Director Valentina Sobko 21-48-73
PSF CI(Pharmaciens Sans Frontiers Comite International) (122 Proletarsky St.)
General Coordinator Bruno Clary 24-64-33
Administrator Nicolas Molle 24-34-40
tel/fax: 51-01-32

Swiss Cooperation Office (20 Pavlov St.)
Coordinator Luigy De Martino 24-38-97
National Program Officer Sayora Dodikhudoyeva 24-73-16
tel/fax: 901-50-40

SCF/UK (Save the Children Fund/UK) (1st Proyezd, 14 Shota Rustaveli St.)
Program Manager Mandal Urtnasan 21-81-57
Information/Admin. Assistant 21-40-23
21-70-84
27-54-47
fax: 51-00-75

For additional analytical, business and investment opportunities information, please contact Global Investment & Business Center, USA at (202) 546-2103. Fax: (202) 546-3275. E-mail: rusric@erols.com

SC/US (Save the Children Fund/US) (53 Ibn Sino St.)
Field Office Director A. K. M. Jamaluddin 21-07-71
Deputy Director/Admin. & Finance Rashid Massaud 24-02-06
Secretary Tahmina 24-33-88
Victoria (Telephone Directory) tel/fax: 51-00-79
SNI (Shelter Now International) (5 Lutfi St.)
Country Director Randall B. Olson 21-48-35
Secretary Malika res: 24-57-97
Deputy Mark Baltzer 21-51-98
mobile: 901-06-08

Swedish Committee for Afghanistan (9 Lutfi St.)
24-65-62
UMCOR (United Methodist Committee on Relief) (108 Lohuti St. 2nd floor)
Head of Mission Eileen Ihrig 21-42-39
Office Manager Rasul Sharipov 21-70-48
fax: 51-01-60

UNDP (United Nations Development Program) (39 Aini St.)
Resident Representative/UN Resident 901-01-83
Coordinator Matthew Kahane *(Dilbar)* 21-06-79
res: 24-53-24
Deputy Akbar Usmani *(Nargis)* 21-06-85 *Receptionist Aishe Muratova* 21-06-70/80
21-06-86/94

UNHCR (United Nations High Commissioner for Refugees) (106 Druzhba Narodov St.)
Program Officer Taslimur Rahman *(Secretary Galiya)* 901-02-39
res: 24-10-86
NGO Coordinator/NRG Mahmoud Naderi 21-74-24
Radio Operator Malika 21-83-78
21-44-06
24-62-65
24-61-84
tel/fax: 51-00-39

UNICEF (14/1 H. Hakimzoda St.)
Assistant Representative Branislav Jekic 21-82-61
Assistant Project Officer Sobir Qurbonov 24-72-61
Secretary/Translator Marina Zhukova 24-91-08
fax: 24-19-05

UNIFEM (UN Development Fund for Women) (25 Behzod St., Room 7)
Program Coordinator Nushin Yovari D'Hellencourt 21-70-31
Program Officer Shuhrat Rajabov 23-09-61 Program Assistant Jahongir Munzim
Training Center (270 Huvaidulloyev St., former bldg. of the Ministry of Social Welfare)
Manager Khiromon 35-36-86
35-05-38

UNOCHA (OCHA Office in Tajikistan) (39 Aini St.)
Head of Office Valentin Gatzinski 21-78-27
Program Assistant Marziya Nazarova 21-06-08
21-06-86

UN ODCCP (UN Office for Drug Control and Crime Prevention) (25 Said Nosyrov St.)
Acting Program Coordinator Timur Aziz Ahmad tel/fax: 21-33-67
Senior Technical Advisor Sergei Ratushnyy tel/fax: 24-00-96
24-66-08
24-86-60

UNOPS (UN Office for Project Services) (25 Behzod St.)
Acting Program Manager Jan Harfst 21-06-82
21-08-96
Senior Admin. Assistant Natalia Azizova 21-03-89
Admin. Assistant Viktoriya 23-09-16
21-09-34
Social Sector Rehabilitation Project (SSRP) (2nd Proyezd, 28 Telman St.)
International Team Leader Janny Bosscher 24-55-94
res: 21-09-79
National Director Mahmadsharif Nozimov mobile: 901-06-62
Assistant Rukhshona

UNTOP (UN Tajikistan Office of Peace-Building) (7 Tehron St.)
Head of Mission/RSG Ivo Petrov 21-01-25
(Personal Secretary Marlene Keffer) res: 24-31-31
Assistant Saifiddin
Deputy Head of Mission Hiroshi Takahashi
Political Affairs Officer Waldemar Rokoszewski
Political Affairs Officer Ms. Gisela Nauk
Human Rights Officer Lilia Zaharieva
Administrative Officer Fermino Balangtaa
Communications Officer David Padi
Switch-board operator 21-01-10/27/47

USAID (US Agency for International Development) (10 Pavlov St.)
Country Program Officer Michael Harvey 7(3272) 50-76-12/17
7(3272) 63-28-80
fax: 7(3272) 69-64-90
fax: 7(3272) 50-76-36
Project Management Specialist Abdurahim Muhidov 21-03-48/50/52/54
Admin. Assistant Sayora Halimova

VI (Vision International Healthcare) (15 Lutfi St.)
Project Director Dorothy Finlay 24-64-47
Deputy Dr. Zarina Musayeva

For additional analytical, business and investment opportunities information,
please contact Global Investment & Business Center, USA
at (202) 546-2103. Fax: (202) 546-3275. E-mail: rusric@erols.com

World Bank/IBRD (International Bank for Reconstruction and Development) (105 Rudaki Ave.)
Country Manager Mustafa Rouis 21-07-56
Assistant Saodat Ibragimova 21-67-43
Receptionist Dilshod 21-03-81
21-15-18
fax: 51-00-42

WFP (UN World Food Program) (13 Pushkin St.)
Representative/Country Director Bouchan Hadj-Chikh 21-09-07
Emergency Officer Romein Sirois 21-09-19 21-57-15
Receptionist Malika 24-39-50
23-38-75

tel/fax: 51-00-87
WHO (UN World Health Organization) (106 Druzhba Narodov St.)
Head of Office Prof. Lyubomir Ivanov 21-01-08 Liaison Officer Nazira Artykova 21-48-71 *Secretary/Accountant Dilafruz Tursunova* tel/fax: 21-48-71

BUSINESS AND GOVERNMENT CONTACTS FOR TAJIKISTAN

U.S. Embassy Dushanbe c/o U.S. Embassy Almaty
Ambassador - The Honorable Robert Finn
Political/Economic Officer - Arlene Ferrill
Furmanova Street 99/97
Almaty 480091
Tel: +7-(3272)-63-39-21
Fax: +7-(3272)-63-38-83

Agency for International Development
Richard Fraenkel
105 Rudaki, Apt 3
734025 Dushanbe
Tel: 7-3772-21-00-77; Fax: 21-01-71
E-mail: dushanbe@usaid.gov

Tajikistan Embassy in the U.S.
[Tajikistan does not yet have an embassy in Washington]

Tajikistan Mission to the United Nations
Ambassador Rashid Alimov
136 East 67th Street
New York, NY 10021
Tel: (212) 744-2196; Fax: (212) 472-7645

United States - Tajikistan Chamber of Commerce
Sadriddin Akramov, Executive Director

1250 24th Street, NW, Suite 350
Washington, D.C. 20037-1124
Tel.: (202) 776-7779; Fax: 9202) 776-7765
Email: ustajcc@aol.com

Central Asian-American Enterprise Fund
Dushanbe
Daniel R. Dougherty, Vice President
14 Pushkin Street
Dushanbe, Tajikistan
Tel: 7 (3772) 21-56-01, 21-60-13
Fax: 7 (3772) 51-00-88
E-mail: daniel@aclc.khj.td.silk.org

Washington
Brian Mercer, Chief Financial Officer and Senior Vice President
Frederic B. Francke, Chief Investment Officer
1634 Eye Street, NW Suite 200
Washington, DC 20006
Tel: (202) 737-7000
Fax: (202) 737-7077
E-mail: us@caeef.com
Web: http://www.caaef.com

European Bank for Reconstruction and Development (EBRD)

Kazuya Murakami, Director
Central Asia Team
Banking department
EBRD
One Exchange Square
London EC2A 2JN
United Kingdom
Tel.: (44-171) 338-6617
Fax: (44-171) 338-7590

Ken Tanimura
Senior Banker
Central Asia Team
Tel.: (44-171) 338-6658
Fax: (44-171) 338-7590

Muzaffar Usmanov
Mission Adviser
Naciba Ahrorova
Mission Assistant
EBRD Dushanbe Office
Room 38, 29 Shotemur Street

For additional analytical, business and investment opportunities information,
please contact Global Investment & Business Center, USA
at (202) 546-2103. Fax: (202) 546-3275. E-mail: rusric@erols.com

734025 Dushanbe
Tajikistan
Tel./Fax: (7-3772) 21-07-63
E-mail: naciba@ebrd.td.silk.org

SELECTED TAJIKISTAN GOVERNMENT CONTACTS

President
Emomali Rakhmonov
80 Rudaki Street
Dushanbe 734023
Tel: 7-3772-21-29-14

Chairman, National Assembly (Majlisi Oli)
Safarali Rajabov

Prime Minister
Yakhyo Azimov
80 Rudaki Street
Dushanbe 734023
Tel: 7-3772-21-19-47

Ministry of Agriculture
1 Rudaki Prospekt
Dushanbe
Tel: 7-3772-21-10-94 or 21-71-18

Ministry of Economy and External Economic Affairs
42 Rudaki Street
Dushanbe 734025
Tel: 7-3772-21-64-00 or 21-30-24
Fax: 7-3772-21-69-14 or 21-38-54

Ministry of Finance
3 Academic Rajabov Street
Dushanbe
Tel: 7-3772-27-39-41 or 21-6-37 or 21-38-04
Fax: 7-3772-21-33-29

Ministry of Foreign Affairs
40 Rudaki Prospekt
734025 Dushanbe
Tel: 7-3772-21-19-87 or 21-18-08 or 21-39-21
Fax: 7-3772-21-02-59
E-mail: dushanbe@mfaumo.td.silk.org

Chairman, National Bank
Murodali Alimardonov

For additional analytical, business and investment opportunities information,
please contact Global Investment & Business Center, USA
at (202) 546-2103. Fax: (202) 546-3275. E-mail: rusric@erols.com

23/2 Rudaki Prospekt
734025 Dushanbe
Tel.: (7-3772) 21-26-19 or 21-54-51
Fax: (7-3772) 21-25-02 or 21-77-92
E-mail: root@natban.tajikistan.su

State Customs Committee
49 Negmat Karabaev Street
Dushanbe 734018
Tel: 7-3772-33-01-33 or 33-92-08; Fax: 7-3772-34-87-19

State Statistical Agency
17 Bokhtar Street
Dushanbe 734025
Tel: 7-3772-27-63-31
Fax: 7-3772-27-54-08

KEY PHONE NUMBERS IN TAJIKISTAN

OFFICE OF THE PRESIDENT (80 RUDAKI)

President
Emomali Rahmonov   21-29-11

President's Administration
Chief Mamadnazar Salihov   1-22   21-68-00
1st Deputy Chief Hasan Khudoyorov   3-45   21-06-25

President's Secretariat
Chief Saimurod Fattoev   3-14   21-04-18

Security Council (80 Rudaki)
Secretary Amirqul Azimov   5-87   21-46-33
Consultant Murod Shoimov   4-02   21-31-24

State Advisors to the President

State Advisor on International Affairs
Karim Yuldoshev   4-29 fax: 21-69-71

State Advisor on Defense
Mizrob Kabirov   9-67   21-39-13
Senior Advisor Zafar Ikromov   1-85   21-76-82

State Advisor on National Economy
Gulom Babaev   9-49   21-34-46

State Advisor on Parliamentary and Legislative Affairs
Khalifabobo Homidov   3-86   21-04-19

State Advisor on Personnel Policy
Amirsho Miraliev   2-81   21-70-26

**State Advisor on Contacts with Public Organizations
and Interethnic Relations**
Davlatali Davlatov   4-82   21-25-22

State Advisor on Science, Culture and Social Affairs
Niyoz Safarov   3-27   21-65-00

Press-Secretary
Zafar Saidov   5-00   21-25-20
Turanboy Tuychiev   21-26-69

PRESIDIUM OF THE GOVERNMENT RT

(80 Rudaki)

Prime Minister
Yahyo Azimov   3-77 21-18-71
Reception   4-89 21-26-36
                21-06-24
             fax 21-51-10
First Deputy Prime Minister
           3-22 21-59-56
           21-26-36
Deputy Prime Minister
Abdurahmon Raupovich Azimov 6-36 23-32-43
Asst Uktam Ergashevich Toshmatov 8-84 23-35-84
Deputy Prime Minister
           4-00 21-30-83
Deputy Prime Minister
Bozgul Dodkhudoeva   6-44 21-37-74
Deputy Prime Minister
Jamoliddin Mansurov   1-55 21-43-34
Deputy Prime Minister
           6-65 21-66-81
Deputy Prime Minister
Ismat Eshmirzoev   6-48 21-86-01

Prime Minister's Secretariat
Chief Valijon Musaev   1-11 21-40-42
          res 23-22-75

Foreign Economic Relations Department

Chief Faizali Musovirov	4-60	21-41-49
Deputy Ikrom Burkhan Rahimov		21-47-36
Chief Specialist Mansur Oripov	3-20	21-70-66

Strategic Research Center at the President RT

Director Nuriddin Kayumov	1-98	21-16-90
		21-17-47
Deputy Mirmahmad Nurmahmadov		21-08-26

President's Guards Office

General Ghaffor Rahmonovich Mirzoev	1-92	31-16-97
	res 34-46-21	
Deputy Col Ubaid Narzulloev	0-57	31-12-07
Chief of Unit Davlat Karimov	31-09-93	

CNR (Commission on National Reconciliation) (Hotel Vakhsh)

Chairman Said Abdullo Nuri	21-07-32
Deputy Abdumajid Dostiev (Majlisi Oli)	21-59-12
Ibrohim Usmonov	21-06-40
Otakhon Latifi	21-01-98
Shukurjon Zukhurov	21-05-10
Habib Sanginov	21-02-89
pocket telephone	21-00-96

MAJLISI OLI (PARLIAMENT) OF THE REPUBLIC OF TAJIKISTAN

(42 Rudaki)

Chairman

Safarali Rajabov	1-61	21-22-53
Assistant Abdufatoh Sharipov	21-62-51	

First Deputy Chairman

Abdumajid Dostiev	7-35	21-59-12
	21-32-97	
Through: Usmon Sabzov, Chief of Dept	3-83	21-33-44
	21-14-54	

Deputy Chairman

Qozidavlat Qoimdodov	5-63	21-22-54

Deputy Chairman

Gulafzo Savriddinova	6-22	21-53-42

Majlisi Oli Committees

For additional analytical, business and investment opportunities information, please contact Global Investment & Business Center, USA at (202) 546-2103. Fax: (202) 546-3275. E-mail: rusric@erols.com

Economics and Budget Cmt
Chairman Safar Safarov   6-37   21-11-10

Legislation and Human Rights Cmt
Chairman Safarali Kenjaev   0-69   21-78-93

Law, Order, Defense and Security Cmt
Chairman Muzaffar Ashurov   6-19   21-63-44

State Construction Cmt
Chairman Rafika Musoeva   4-44   21-11-22

Int'l Affairs, Interethnic Relations and Culture Cmt
Chairman Ibrohim Usmonov   0-73   21-11-21
                                 fax 21-18-16

Agricultural Policy, Foodstuffs and Employment Cmt
Chairman Karimjon Faqirov   2-23   21-76-21

Science, Education and Youth Policy Cmt
Chairman Mahmadsho Ilolov   6-80   21-24-65

Women's Affairs, Health, Social Protection and Ecology Cmt
Chairman Khujiahmad Khidiraliev   1-09   21-79-95

Deputy's Ethics and Privileges Cmt
Chairman Mehmon Bakhti   24-57-71

Central Elections and Referendums Commission
Mirzoali Boltaev   9-91   21-13-75

Inter-Parliamentary Relations Dept
Chief Saadi Aminov   0-78   21-01-41
CONSTITUTIONAL COURT /42 Rudaki
Chairman Faizullo Abdulloev   0-49   21-60-96
Deputy Chairman Zarif Aliev   3-43   21-39-08

SUPREME COURT /17 Karabaev St.
Chairman Ubaidullo Davlatov   4-53   33-48-21
1st Dep. Ch. Shuhrat Mustafakulov   7-30   33-49-72
Deputy Chairman Sabzali Rahmonov   1-39   33-52-62

SUPREME ECONOMIC COURT /37 Foteh Niyazi St.
Chairman Bakhtiyor Khudoyorov   5-56   23-28-52

For additional analytical, business and investment opportunities information,
please contact Global Investment & Business Center, USA
at (202) 546-2103. Fax: (202) 546-3275. E-mail: rusric@erols.com

REPUBLICAN PROSECUTOR'S OFFICE /12 Profsoyuz St.

Prosecutor General Salomiddin Sharopov	5-45	36-77-53
1st Deputy Bobojon Bobokhonov	0-29	36-04-45
Deputy	9-83	36-99-97
Deputy Sharif Rajabov	4-01	36-27-23
Department Chief Mamadjon Khairullaev		36-96-79

MINISTRIES

Ministry of Security /8 Gorky St./

Minister Saidamir Zuhurov	0-11	21-23-12
1st Dep. Minister Anatoly Kouptsov	7-23	21-32-38
Deputy Minister Davlat Mamadruzibekov	2-87	21-39-54
Department Chief COL Ahtam Pirov		21-05-97
Duty Officer	5-52	21-37-37
Drug Enforcement Section		
Nazirkhon Zoirov	21-11-59	
Press Center		
Zafar Zakirov	1-46	27-86-53
Educational Center Farhod Sharipov		21-13-93

Ministry of Internal Affairs /29 Gorky St.

Minister Humdin Sharipov	4-66	21-10-71
Advisor LTC Emomali Azimov	8-12	21-83-44
		27-83-34
First Deputy Minister Nikolay Majar	6-31	21-10-60
	21-06-52	
Deputy Minister Abdusattor Rajabov	9-57	
Deputy Minister Abdumannon Gaziev	9-42	21-09-94
Deputy Minister Davlat Bulbulshoev	8-46	21-25-50
Duty Officer	0-92	21-08-30
Antinarcotics Department		
Chief Turaboy Komilov		21-04-87
Department to combat organized crime		
Col Tohir Nurmatov		21-32-64

State Commission on Drug Control (3 Parvina St.)

Chairman Rustam Nazarov	8-01	24-92-27
Office	24-79-84, 24-91-10	
	fax 24-68-79	

Ministry of Health /69 Shevchenko St.

Minister Alamkhon Ahmadov	8-44	21-30-64
First Deputy Minister Ismoil Usmonov	0-17	21-12-48
Deputy Minister Nasrullo Abdujabborov	1-26	21-04-63
Deputy Minister Zuhra Mirzoeva	1-04	21-10-74

Deputy Minister Muzaffar Mamadnazarov   5-29   21-17-03
Diagnostic Center Chief Nurullo Shukurov   34-92-00

Ministry of Foreign Affairs /42 Rudaki St.
Minister Talbak Nazarov   4-61   21-18-08
1st Dep. Minister Erkin Rahmatullaev   4-80   21-19-87
Asst to 1st Dep. Minister Hisrav Goibov   21-15-03
Deputy Minister   2-54   21-39-21
Deputy Minister Gulomjon Mirzoev   6-49   21-15-34
Personnel and special information Dept
Davlamad Gulmadov, Chief   7-58   21-01-17
Bilateral and Multilateral links Dept
Abdullo Yuldoshev, Chief   6-42   21-15-46
Analysis and Strategic Researches Dept
Alijon Salibaev, Chief   4-49   21-10-93
Information Dept (Press-Center)
Chief Igor Sattarov (Olga)   8-87   21-43-53
Deputy Chief Davlatali Nazriev   21-01-26
Sulaimon Rashidov   fax 21-43-69
International Organizations Dept (Room 28)
Chief Erkin Kasimov   4-13   21-15-08
State Protocol Dept
Chief Zubaidullo Zubaidov (Nigora)   0-12   21-15-62
Deputy Chief Mirafzal Mirshakar   4-25   21-61-05
Muhamad Surkhov   21-61-05
Rahimjon Nosyrov   4-25   21-09-14
Yatimshoh Musofirov   21-09-14
Komil Mirzoev   21-09-14
Consular Dept
Chief Garibsho Shabozov   1-24   21-15-60
Deputy Nurullo Sharipov (visa for foreigners)   21-04-70
Deputy Chief Sharifa Azamovna Yakubova   21-04-70
Deputy Lyubov Kulikova (visa for Tajik citizens)   21-10-51
Deputy Chief Isamatov   21-10-51
Administrative Dept
Chief Saidjafar Safarov   1-06   21-10-40
Dep. Chief, Head of Dip. Corp Services Section
Masaid Komilov   21-17-37
Financial Dept
Chief Zebinisso Vasiyeva   4-52   21-08-41

Ministry of Agriculture (44 Rudaki)
Minister Muso Barotov   1-88   21-15-96
                                        21-64-61
Deputy Minister Aziz Sharipov   9-69   21-10-94

For additional analytical, business and investment opportunities information,
please contact Global Investment & Business Center, USA
at (202) 546-2103. Fax: (202) 546-3275. E-mail: rusric@erols.com

Deputy Minister Ikhtiyor Ashurov	4-69	21-71-18

Ministry of Culture (34 Rudaki St.)

Minister Bobokhon Mahmadov	0-33	21-03-05
		23-43-77
First Deputy Minister Akbar Juraev	8-77	21-34-01
Deputy Minister Jamshed Ismoilov	3-73	21-36-30
Deputy Minister Olimjon Salimzoda	1-93	21-53-34
Dep. Minister(Econ/Fin) Guljon Mirzoeva	3-21	21-04-06
Cultural & International Ties Department		
Chief Buston Shukurov		21-53-07

Ministry of Melioration and Water Management (78 Rudaki)

Minister Davlatbek Makhsudov	9-52	21-10-12
First Deputy Minister Nurullo Ashurov	5-08	27-39-96

Ministry of Defense (59 Bokhtar St.)

Minister Sherali Khairullaev	3-09	21-18-09
Aide Major Tagaimurod Menglibaev		21-69-83
1st Dep. Min. Abdullo Habibov	2-00	21-22-78
Dep.Min./Chief of Staff Sodiq Bobojonov	8-15	21-23-69
Deputy Min. COL Latif Faiziev		
Deputy Min. COL A. Abulasanov		
Aide to Bobojonov Ltnt Avaz Timurov		
Asst to the Minister Ltnt-Capt Abdullaev		21-32-47
Asst on Special Orders Capt Andrey Kovalenko		23-17-83
Chief of Admin Dept LtntCol Qodyr Teshaev		23-16-57
Int'l Dept Major Maaruf Hasanov	0-94	23-43-02
extension		1-86
Duty Officer	9-11	21-18-53
Telephone operator		21-50-18
Military College		32-18-10
Khairullo Khaidarov		32-18-06

Ministry of Education (13 Chekhov St.)

Minister Munira Inoyatova	6-33	23-33-92
1st Dep. Minister Abdulbashir Rashidov	8-59	27-43-74
Dep. Ismoil Davlatov		
Dep. Minister Kurbonmamad Goibnazarov	8-29	23-37-66
Foreign Relations Department		
Kadir Berdiev		23-23-73

Printing House (7 Kuibyshev St.)

Director Nabi Rabievich Tohirov		21-73-58

For additional analytical, business and investment opportunities information, please contact Global Investment & Business Center, USA at (202) 546-2103. Fax: (202) 546-3275. E-mail: rusric@erols.com

Ministry of Environmental Protection (12 Bokhtar St.)

Minister	2-66	23-28-78
1st Dep. Minister Negmatullo Safarov	6-81	21-42-71
Science Department		
Chief Sirojiddin Aslov		22-30-39

Ministry of Communications (57 Rudaki)

Minister Nuriddin Muhiddinov	4-32	21-22-84
First Deputy Ibrohim Usmonov	5-88	21-23-84
Deputy Minister Tukhtaboy Kayumov	4-55	23-28-63
Administration Chief Mavluda Rustamova		21-60-18

Republican Center for International Accounts

Director Saodat Niyazova		
Deputy Director Yelena Zenkova		21-49-86
Specialist Maruf Muhamedov		21-71-79
		fax: 21-47-39

State Department "Pochtai Tojik" (Tajik Post Office)(42/2 Ibn-Sino St.)

Director General Shukurullo Komilov	2-64	35-07-41

Joint-stock Company "Tojiktelecom" (Mezhgorsvyaz) (53 Rudaki)

Director General Farhat Shukurov	6-24	23-44-44

Ministry of Social Welfare (61 Borbad St.)

Minister Abdusattor Jabborov	7-00	31-37-57
First Deputy Minister Navruz Afzalov	3-02	31-56-56

Ministry of Transport and Roads (14 Aini St.)

Minister Faridun Muhiddinov	2-11	21-17-13
First Deputy Minister Narzullo Dustov 2	-94	21-25-93

Ministry of Labor and Employment (5/2 A. Navoi St.)

Minister Khudoiberdy Kholiqnazarov	1-65	36-18-37
1st Dep. Minister Beg Kurbonov	8-22	36-24-15
Deputy Minister Alisher Yarbabaev	9-19	36-25-21

Ministry of Finance (3 Academicians Rajabovs St.)

Minister Anvarsho Muzafarov	5-66	27-39-41
First Deputy Sharif Mulloev	6-27	21-62-37
	21-57-06	
"Tajikinvest" (1 Proyezd Lohuti #6)	27-08-98	
	6-33	27-09-00

Ministry of Economics and Foreign Economic Relations/44 Rudaki

Minister Davlat Usmon	2-45	21-69-14
		21-64-00
1st Dep. Minister Isroil Makhmudov	3-88	21-30-24
Deputy Minister	1-33	21-62-09
Deputy Minister Victor Boltov	3-16 fax	21-37-54
Deputy Amonullo Ashurov		21-30-26

Ministry of Justice (25 Rudaki)

Minister Shavkat Ismailov	6-11	21-44-05
		23-22-50
1st Dep. Minister Shermahmad Shoev	7-07	21-87-97
Deputy Minister Larisa Smeyanova	7-08	21-36-96
		21-87-97

STATE COMMITTEES OF THE REPUBLIC OF TAJIKISTAN

State Committee for Administration of State Property (44 Rudaki)

Matlubkhon Davlatov	3-91	21-86-59
First Deputy Chairman Asror Rashidov	5-49	21-81-50

State Committee for Industry (22 Rudaki)

Chairman Rajabali Kadyrov	3-49	21-69-97
First Deputy Chairman	1-34	21-88-89

State Committee for Contracts and Trade (37 Bokhtar St.)

Chairman Hakim Soliev	0-22	27-34-34
First Deputy Chairman Akbar Akhmedov	1-50	27-12-51

GOVERNMENT COMMITTEES AND DEPARTMENTS

State Statistical Agency /Gosstatagentstvo/ (17 Bokhtar St.)

Director Habib Gaibullaev	2-88	27-63-31
First Deputy Director Shamsidin Saifov	2-37	27-34-29
Deputy Director Barot Turaev	8-27	27-56-28

Committee for Precious Metals (Tajikdragmetsamotsvety) (77 Mushfiki)

Chairman Saidullo Khairulloev	7-51	33-44-19
		33-43-56
First Deputy Azim Jangiev		33-41-41

Committee for Precious Stones and Semi-precious Raw Materials

(6 Rudaki)

Chairman Jahongir Ruziev	7-17	21-44-24
Asst Avaz Kurbonov		21-84-19

Customs Committee /Tajiktamozhnya/ (40? Bukhoro St.)

Chairman Rahim Karimov	6-07	21-16-92
First Deputy Chairman Kenja Hasanov		5-91
Deputy Chief Abdujalilov		1-84
Foreign Department Chief Tohir Oripov		7-72
Telephone operator		23-27-26

Tax Committee (155 Kirov St.)

Chief Sulton Quvvatov	4-11	21-31-74
First Deputy Chief Hairullo Alimadov	9-05	27-12-82
Deputy Aslidin Sohibnazarov	6-02	21-35-88
Tax Police: Chief Sanginmurod Abdullaev		21-63-47
		21-34-54

Committee for Extraordinary Situations and Civil Defense
(59 Bokhtar)
Chairman

Husanboy Achilov	2-77	23-17-78
1st Dep. Chairman Ziyoratsho Ashurov	5-17	21-13-31

Committee for Meat and Milk Industry /Tajikmyasomolprom
(35 Kaharov)

Chairman Habibullo Tabarov	5-84	21-77-46
First Deputy Chairman Bahtiyor Gadoev	7-56	21-78-22

Committee for Physical Culture and Sports (31 Shotemur St.)

Chairman Saimumin Rahimov	5-85	23-16-24
1st Dep. Chairman Sulaimon Abdulvahidov	0-47	23-39-16

Committee for Women and Family Affairs (44 Rudaki)

Chairman Latofat Nasriddinova	6-57	21-34-71
Deputy Mukarramhon Buzurukova		21-86-97

Committee for Religious Affairs (80 Rudaki)

Chairman Said Akhmedov	2-61	23-33-66
		21-60-05
Deputy Ikromiddin Nematov	1-68	21-40-65

Committee for Architecrure and Construction (11/6 Valamatzoda)

Chairman Bahovadin Zuhurdinov	1-44	23-18-82
First Deputy Chairman Yuri Potekhin	8-05	23-26-57

Committee for Oil and Gas /Tajikneftegas/ (77 Mushfiki St.)
Chairman   9-61   33-36-51
1st Deputy Chairman Saidjon Saidrahmonov   33-41-82

Committee for Food and Processing Industry /Tajikpishcheprom
("Tojikmatlubot", 5 Floor)
Chairman Faizullo Quvvatov   7-77   21-15-91
First Deputy Chairman Ismonkul Bilolov   2-33   21-17-80

Industry and Mining Security State Control Cmt /Gosgortekhnadzor
(63 Karabaeva)
Chairman Ayub Aliev   7-47   34-87-30
1st Dep. Chairman Vyacheslav Kuznetsov   3-30   34-87-10

Special Property Providing Committee
Chairman Hukmat Odinaev   4-77

Committee for Land Resources (Giprozem)
Chairman Bakhtiyor Kabilov   31-16-83

Tajik State Center for Standartization and Metrology
(42/2 Karabaev)
Director Amir Kataev   4-20   33-68-69

Chief Department for Cotton-Cleaning Industry /"Pakhtai Tojik"
(44 Rudaki)
Chief Gulom Boyakov   1-66   21-32-22
First Deputy Chief Bayon Davlatov   21-77-66

Chief Department for Archives /Glavarkhiv/ (38/1 Karabaev St.)
Chief Zafar Dustmuhamedov   3-41   33-95-71
Deputy Chief Dilovar Komilov   33-63-52

Defense Industry Committee
Chairman Ghafforkhon Muhitdinov

Border Guarding Committee
COL Rustam Akramov   0-14
Duty officer   21-81-21

Chief Dept for Geology /Tajikglavgeologiya/ (27 Tursunzade St.)
Chief Ayubjon Orifov   8-00   27-27-29
Deputy Chief Alexander Akhmedov   1-05   27-27-49

TV and Radio Committee (Dom Radio)
Chief Saif Rahimov   3-69

Chief Department for Geodezy and Cartography /Tajikglavgeodeziya/
(4/1 Abai St.)
Chief Muzaffar Ishanov   31-24-23
Deputy Chief Gul Oimahmadov   31-35-41

Tajik Information Agency "Hovar" ((37 Rudaki)
Director Nabijon Karimov   3-19   21-33-13

UNION OF CONSUMERS SOCIETY (Tajikmatlubot)(137 Rudaki)
Chairman Yatim Mirzoev   4-83   21-00-35
First Deputy Chairman Sharif Saidov   0-59   24-87-04

GBAO Representation at the Government of RT (40 Rudaki)
Representative Plenipotentiary
Shodavlat Shodavlatov   27-85-97

HUKUMAT (DUSHANBE CITY COUNCIL)

Mayor Mahmadsaid Ubaidullaev   7-33   21-27-04
                                                                21-27-39
First Deputy Akbar Mirzoevich Fayazov   3-82   21-02-85
  Deputy Mayor Muslima Valieva   4-65   21-20-60
  Deputy Mayor Husnoro Mirzoeva   7-28   21-46-67
International Department
  Chief   6-52   21-45-14
                                                                21-27-43
  Secretary Tamara Alekseevna   21-45-14
  Interpreter Ibragim Murodov   23-18-31
Inquiry office   21-26-95

EDUCATIONAL INSTITUTIONS

Tajik State University
  Rector Habib Safarov   21-62-25
  Pro-Rector for Foreign Relations Nazir Jumaev   21-76-71

Tajik State Medical University
  Rector Hamdam Rofiev   24-45-83
  Pro-Rector Karim Gafarov   24-89-65

Dushanbe State Pedagogical University

For additional analytical, business and investment opportunities information,
please contact Global Investment & Business Center, USA
at (202) 546-2103. Fax: (202) 546-3275. E-mail: rusric@erols.com

Rector Kurbon Rasulov 24-78-09
24-83-13
Pro-Rector for Foreign Relations Mavjuda Abdulloeva 24-16-82

Tajik Agricultural University
Rector Yusuf Nasirov 24-72-07

Tajik Technical University (in Dushanbe)
Rector Khisrav Sadikov 23-43-42
Deputy Ikram Negmatov 22-36-87
Foreign Students Dept Dean Sharofiddin Nuriddinov 27-37-81

(In Khojand: Rector 7(37922)6-04-54/6-18-42)

Tajik Institute of Physical Culture/Natinal Olympic Cmt
Rector Burikhon Jobirov 24-14-61

Tajik Technological University (63/3 Karabaev Str.)
Rector Pulat Pulatov 5-19 34-79-87
fax 34-79-88
res 37-05-43
Personnel Office 34-59-10
e-mail: pulatov@tecnol.td.silk.glas.apc.org.

Tajik Institute of Languages
Rector Mavluda Abdullaeva 32-95-15
Head of Foreign Languages Chair Holida Astanova 35-87-01
32-95-17

Tajik Institute of Services and Enterpreneuship
Rector Khabibullo Umarov 34-88-30
Head of Foreign Languages Chair Normat Khaibatov 34-88-26

Tajik Commercial Institute
Rector Olim Boboev 34-86-22
Head of Foreign Languages Chair Ganijon Rahmonov 34-85-80

Tajik Institute of Fine Arts
Rector Rajabahmad Amirov 31-18-27
Deputy Said Shamsov 31-45-45
Deputy Abdurahim Rahimov 31-13-51

Slavic University (34 Tursunzade St.)
Rector Abdujabbor Sattorov 27-99-93
Pro-Rector Svetlana Balkhova 27-42-27
Dean of Humanities Dept Khusrav Shambezoda 27-78-93

For additional analytical, business and investment opportunities information, please contact Global Investment & Business Center, USA at (202) 546-2103. Fax: (202) 546-3275. E-mail: rusric@erols.com

CENTRAL INSTITUTIONS AND ORGANIZATIONS

ACADEMY OF SCIENCES (33 Rudaki)
President Ulmas Mirsaidov	8-55	21-50-85
Vice-President Muso Dinorshoev	6-01	21-37-63
Institute of Philosophy and Law		21-77-96

Central Scientific Library of the Academy of Sciences
Director   off 27-55-46

Institute of Chemistry
Director Ulmas Mirsaidov   25-26-04

Institute of Gastroenterology
Director Hamid Mansurov   23-36-09
                                                                            21-72-40
                                                                            24-81-47

Institute of Seismology
Director Sobit Negmatullaev   25-06-69
                                                                            25-11-93

Institute of World Economics & International Relations
Director Rashid Rahimov   23-27-32

ACADEMY OF AGRICULTURAL SCIENCES (25 Rudaki)
President Bobo Sanginov	4-78	23-18-32
Vice-President Abdurahim Khojibaev	1-70	21-70-04

Botanical Garden
Director Abdullo Asrakulovich Madaminov	24-71-88
Dep. Dir. Muhabbat Mirzotash. Sharipova	24-43-57

Firdavsi State Library
Director Sohib Goibnazarov	27-47-26
Law and Democracy Center: Elena Degtyareva	21-44-07
	21-49-64

BANKS

Tajik National Bank (23/2 Rudaki)
Chairman Murodali Alimardonov	4-91	21-26-28
		21-26-79
First Deputy Chairman Sharif Rahimov	7-25	21-54-51
Foreign Economic Relations Department	21-78-50	

Tajikagroprombank "Sharq" (97 Rudaki)
   Chairman Maqsud Kadyrov   2-08   21-10-14
   1st Deputy Chairman Mirzo Sharipov   1-95   21-10-77

Tajikvnesheconombank (4 Khisrav Dehlavi St.)
   Chairman Izatullo Lalbekov   8-14   23-35-61

Orionbank (95/1 Rudaki)
   President Abdumutalib Abdusattorov   4-36   21-09-20
                                                          21-19-69
Foreign Econ. Relations Dept Chief Alisher Babajanov   21-16-62
                                                          21-16-42

Tajikbankbusiness (29 Shotemur St.)
   President Kayum Kavmiddinov   9-07   21-05-03
   1st Vice-President Murodjon Vafaev   9-56   21-06-34

Savings Bank /Tajiksberbank/ (67 Rudaki)
   Chairman Kurbonali Juraev   0-13   21-70-81

Tajbank (59/1 Somoni St.) President   1-42   24-53-15

Fononbank Chairman Tatyana Dedurova   35-27-13
                                                            35-27-03

Interbank Currency Exchange
   Director Negmatullo Rahimov   21-11-89

CONCERNS, COMPANIES, ASSOCIATIONS

State Concern "Tajikcommunservice" (31 Shotemur St.)
   Chairman Aziz Inoyatov   3-66   27-99-10

Tajik State-Cooperative Concern "TAJIKSELSTROY"(Village building)
                    (50 Dehoti St.)
   President Rahimjon Gafurov   0-50   34-79-77

Tajik State Concern "MADAD" on Technical Service and Support of
Agricultural Complexes
(27 Rudaki)
   President Abdujalol Salimov   8-81   21-81-07

Tajik Republican Concern "KHIZMAT" /Service/ (14 Lohuti St.)
   President Abdulahat Normatov   4-88   21-43-98

For additional analytical, business and investment opportunities information,
please contact Global Investment & Business Center, USA
at (202) 546-2103. Fax: (202) 546-3275. E-mail: rusric@erols.com

Tajik State Concern "Furuzon" (734060, PB 889)
   President Tukhtasin Teshabaev   5-98   35-85-76

State Building Company "TAJIKSTROY" (36 Khuseinzoda St.)
   Chairman Abdumalik Azimov   6-29   21-61-43

State Joint-Stock Holding Company "Barqi Tojik" (Tajik Power)
(64 Ismoili Somoni St.)
   President Bahrom Sirojev   7-11   35-87-66
                                            29-56-50

State Company "Tajiknefteproduct" (Tajik Oil Product)
(14 Khuseinzoda St.)
   Chairman Amonullo Hukumov   5-64   21-59-37

State Company for Building Power Units "Tajikhydroenergostroy"
(39a Kakharov St.)
   President Vladimir Shichkin   7-22   23-38-87

Joint-Stock Company "Intourist-Tojikiston" (22 Shotemur St.)
   President Murtazo Ostanaev   1-28   21-62-62

National Tourism Company "Tajiktourism" (14 Pushkin St.)
   President Qosym Abdusalomovich Gafarov   off 23-14-01
                                      res 24-14-06

Tajik State Aviation Company "TOJIKISTON" (32/1 Titov St.)
   General Director Mirzo Mastangulov   0-77   21-21-45
   Reception   29-82-01
                                            21-32-83
                     51-01-10
                     fax 21-86-85
                   fax 51-00-41
   First Deputy Vilsuor Avidzba   5-58   27-85-76
   Airport Director Rustam Rustamov   9-33   21-09-52
                                            21-03-48
   Chief Dispatcher Alisher Rustamov   21-09-62
   Dispatcher/Inquiry Desk   23-26-31
                                            29-85-31
   Airport Tower   29-86-10
   Aeroflot Intourist Cashier   21-79-19
   VIP Waiting Room   29-82-39
   Intourist Waiting Room   29-87-51
   Intn'l Dpt, Firuz Ishankulov   5-66   21-22-47
                                            29-85-45
                   fax 21-22-47

For additional analytical, business and investment opportunities information,
please contact Global Investment & Business Center, USA
at (202) 546-2103. Fax: (202) 546-3275. E-mail: rusric@erols.com

Telephone operator		21-32-28
Commercial Warehouse		29-82-71
Airport Garage		29-82-09

Aeroflot Agency

Galina Gonchar		29-83-30
		27-74-02
Inquiry desk		21-65-89
Airtickets dispatcher Komil / Natasha		21-70-78

Tajik Republican Commercial-Industrial Company "Tajikles"
(Tajik Wood)(31 Shotemur St.)

Director General Gaibullo Fazylov	9-25	27-68-88
		27-98-79

State Joint-Stock Company "Umron" (build. materials industry)
(3-a Rudaki)

President Kim Nazirov	1-77	21-88-13

State Corporation "Tajikmontazhspetsstroy" (3 Tursunzade St.)

President Sirojiddin Saidov	5-03	21-87-65

Tajik State Insurance Company "Tajikgosstrakh"
(3 Academikov Rajabovykh St.)

Director General Mansur Ochildiev	7-01	27-58-49

Forestry Industrial Association "Tajikles" (22 Sh. Rustaveli St.)

Director General Gaibullo Avzalov	7-55	23-19-92

Republican Industrial Association "Mohiparvar"(Fishing industry)
(44 Rudaki St.)

Director General Nazir Mullojanov	5-24	21-40-49

Tajik Railway (35 Shapkin St.)

Chief Muhammad Khabibov	5-96	21-88-54
		27-37-90

Republican Industrial Association "Tajikselkhozkhimiya"
(Tajik Agricultural Chemistry) (21-a Rudaki)

Chairman Vahob Vahidov	8-10	27-98-40

Joint-Stock Industrial-Investment Corporation "Somoniyon"
(48 Rudaki)

President Abdurahmon Mukhtashov	5-05	23-29-03

For additional analytical, business and investment opportunities information,
please contact Global Investment & Business Center, USA
at (202) 546-2103. Fax: (202) 546-3275. E-mail: rusric@erols.com

Republican Association "Tojikboghbunyod"(Tajik Gardens)(126 Aini)
Chief Aslan Anvarov   6-40   25-16-59

Republican Association "Tajikvneshtrans"(3 Yuzhno-Obkhodnaya St.)
President Alamhon Kurbanov   31-56-17

Joint-Stock Industrial Commercial Firm "Pamir-Lada"(125 Karabaev)
President Yusufali Khudoikulov   31-94-63

Tajik Republican Association "Automotoservice"(1 October 40 let)
Director General Farhod Ashurov   31-09-36

State Holding Company "Ghalla" (5/1 Shamsi St.)
Chairman Bekmurod Uroqov   2-55   32-14-36
First Deputy Chairman Manaim Kasimov   3-65   32-15-22
Deputy Chairman Urunboy Isakov   4-30   32-19-69
Deputy Chairman Inom Turaboev   5-36   32-16-14
                                32-18-65
Asst to Chairman Bahodur Mahmudov   32-18-28

COMMERCIAL STRUCTURES
Foreign Economic Company "IMPEX"
General Director Ahad Abdulkholov   27-58-11

Chamber of Commerce
President Kamol Sufiev   9-41   27-95-19

Tajik-American Joint Venture "Interfur"(40 Let Tajikistana, N141)
General Director Raf Yadgarov   34-92-92
                                                                     34-92-78
Tajik-Lebanese Joint Venture "Tolib"
General Director Mamadnazar Karimov   33-97-75

"Guliston": Commercial Manager Bakhtiyor Makhkamov   27-15-93

"Russia-Tojikiston"
President Mahbuba Kosimi   24-89-38
                                                                     24-18-92
"Shukur" President Kakhor Mahkamov   27-71-93

RT Corporation "Hima" (21 Pavlova Str.)
President Ismatullo Izzatulloevich Khayoev   24-81-36

UNIONS
Union of Architects (1 Behzod St.)

For additional analytical, business and investment opportunities information,
please contact Global Investment & Business Center, USA
at (202) 546-2103. Fax: (202) 546-3275. E-mail: rusric@erols.com

Chairman Rustam Karimov	6-10	27-18-71
Union of Artists (89 Rudaki)		
Chairman Suhrob Kurbonov	0-15	24-15-71
Union of Cinematographers (43 Bukhoro St.)		
Chairman Anvar Turaev	1-90	21-75-09
Union of Composers (1 Tehron St.)		
Chairman Damir Dustmuhamedov	7-15	27-62-33
Creative Union		
General Director Abdugaffor Abdujaborov		27-33-87
Union of Cooperators and Businessmen		
Chairman S. Komilov		27-63-58
Union of Designers		
Chairman Anatoly Zanevsky		34-47-19
	Res	33-80-19
Union of Journalists (31 Bukhoro St.)		
Chairman Khayot Davlatov	8-09	21-75-23
Union of Photo Journalists (18 Rudaki)		
Chairman Gennady Ratushenko		27-75-37
	res	32-94-48
Commercial Creative Union "Romish"		
Chairman Botur Karimov		22-79-51
Scientific Industrial Union of Tajikistan (6 Rudaki)		
Chairman Abdurahmon Dadabaev	4-76	27-23-29
Union of Theater Workers (107 Rudaki)		
Chairman Ato Muhamadjonov	24-29-68	
Deputy Nurullo Abdulloev	24-50-07	
Deputy Abdugaffor Abdujaborov	24-89-38	
Union of War and Labor Veterans (3 Tehron St.)		
Chairman Rauf Dadabaev	7-92	27-13-42
Union of Afghan War Veterans		
Chairman Suhrob Alimov		21-06-91
Union of Writers (8 Somoni St.)		
Chairman Askar Hakim	8-98	24-57-37

For additional analytical, business and investment opportunities information,
please contact Global Investment & Business Center, USA
at (202) 546-2103. Fax: (202) 546-3275. E-mail: rusric@erols.com

Deputy Chairman Abdurahmon Abdumanonov 7-97 24-57-67
Deputy Chairman Abdulhomid Samadov 24-57-46

Trade-Unions Federation (20 Rudaki)
Chairman Murodali Salikhov 8-66 23-35-16
Deputy Chairman Shakir Kashaev 8-22 21-88-63

Central Soviet of the Youth Union (42 Rudaki)
Chairman Ibod Rahimov 3-42 21-63-14
23-05-41
Association of University Women RT
President Guljahon Bobosadykova 21-17-50
fax 21-05-55

SOCIETIES
Tajik Society of Friendship and Cultural Relations with Foreign Countries (7 Gorky St.)
Chairman Maisara Kalonova 9-01 27-74-94
Reception 21-01-84

Tajik Center of Civic Education (NGO)
Director Gulchehra Nosirova 27-73-69
fax 21-70-33
res 33-98-66
"Paivand" (17 Bokhtar St.)
Chairman Kamol Aini 8-36 27-77-39
1st Deputy Chairman Uktam Kholikov 27-77-39
Deputy Chairman Nuriddin Kurbanov 27-04-23

Red Crescent Society (120 Omar Khayam)
President Jura Inomzoda 5-46 24-03-74
Vice-President Davron Muhamadiev 24-44-86

Society of the Deaf (270 Khuvaidulloev St.)
Chairman Galina Malisheva 36-71-21

Society of the Invalids (4 Telman St.)
Chairman Hakim Khaknazarov 21-15-74

Society of the Blind (205 Karamov St.)
Chairman Turabek Davlatov 37-32-31

"Znaniye": 23-26-73
27-84-70

HOTELS

"Oktyabrskaya"
Director Marhamat Akramova	21-12-70
Reception	21-12-80
Chief Accountant	21-12-86
Chief Engineer	21-12-16
Restaurant Director Rizvon Rahmonov	21-12-29

"Tajikistan"
Director General Samijon Sadyev	21-70-00
Reception	21-82-28
	21-62-62
	21-33-56
Restaurant Manager Rustam Muradov	21-70-77

MUSEUMS

Ethnographic Museum
Director Zebo Kavrakova	res 21-07-64

Republican Museum
Director Sangin Khafizov	23-15-44
	23-08-72

Shahidi Museum of Musical Culture (108 K. Marx/Shahidi St.)
Director Munira Shahidi	24-23-42
	Res 27-08-66

Museum of National Musical Instruments
Director Gurminj Zavkibekov	res 23-42-29
Deputy Director Tamara Pavlovna	

THEATERSOpera & Ballet Theater
Director Nariman Karimov	0-90	21-80-47
		21-62-91

Russian Drama Theatre
Director Suhrob Mirzoev	21-36-22
Chief Conductor Anatoly Mamaev	21-73-73

Lohuti Tajik Drama Theater
Director Iso Abdurashidov	21-78-43
	21-43-76

Vohidov Youth Theater
Manager Mahamdnazar Kholov	23-08-74
Deputy Manager Makhkam Hojikulov	33-34-36

Experimental Miniature Theater "Oina"

Chief Director Ubaidullo Rajabov   25-04-97

Puppet Theater
  Manager Rustam Ahmadov   23-15-83
                                                  23-15-93
State Dance Ensemble "Lola"
  Manager Radif Yafaev   21-12-13

State Dance Ensemble "Zebo"
  Art Director Zarrina Yadgarova   34-56-44

Theater-Studio "Akhorun"
  Chief Director Farrukh Kosimov   27-09-68

MASS MEDIA

"Biznes i Politika"
  Editor-in-Chief Nina Pak   3-46   33-32-26
  Correspondent Ilhom   33-43-96
"Golos Tajikistana"
  Editor-in-Chief Inom Musaev   33-76-27

"Khalq Ovozi" (Uzbek) (16 Sherozi St.)
  Editor-in-Chief Ismoil Mukhsinov   6-21   33-12-27

"Jumhuriyat" (16 Sherozi St.)
  Editor-in-Chief   4-93   33-08-11
                                         33-05-64
"Narodnaya Gazeta" (16 Sherozi St.)
  Editor-in-Chief Vladimir Vorobyev 8-24   33-08-25
  Deputy Editor-in-Chief Tatyana Karatygina

"Navruzi Vatan"
  Editor-in-Chief Muhammadjon Mirzoshoyev   33-57-05

"Sadoi Mardum"
  Editor-in-Chief Mirzomahmud Mirbobev 2-43 33-10-77

"Vecherny Kuryer"
  Editor-in-Chief Javohir Kabilov   33-55-59
                                      33-13-16, 33-24-13
"Payomi Dushanbe"
  Editor-in-Chief Ibod Fayzullaev   6-14

"Asia Plus", "Komsomolskaya Pravda"
  Editor Umed Babakhanov   off 21-78-63

res 21-21-93

"Naqsuz"
Habibullo Boturov   21-38-33

"Stolichnaya Gazeta" (36 Karabaev)
Victor Kim   33-44-17

CORRESPONDENT POINTS

"Ostankino" (ORT) (72/1 Somoni St.)   2-24   36-43-21
Correspondent Tatiana Lagunova   1-29   36-42-21

"Vesti" (26 Tehron): Zarina Baranova   21-62-11
                                               21-50-48
"ITAR-TASS" (55 Rudaki)
Galina Gridneva   8-21   21-30-97

RIA "Novosti" (18 Rudaki)
Najmiddin Azizov   5-72   23-49-06
Yevgeny Ratushenko   27-75-37

"Interfax": Surayo Sobirova   9-46 fax 21-42-96

TV Company "MIR" (55 Rudaki)
Negmat Mirsaidov   9-35   21-16-53
Tolib Shahidi   21-15-67
                                               fax 27-23-22
BBC Monica Witlock   21-00-81
Mardoni Muhammad   24-16-73

INTERNATIONAL ORGANIZATIONS AND COMPANIES

ACCELS/ACTR (American Center) /Freedom Support Act/
(Firdavsi Library, 1st floor)
Laura Meenk   off 21-17-95
                                               res 24-73-09
Matluba Mamadjanova   27-45-41
Lena Logge, Zarrina Muhiddinova
Ilhom Kadyrov   27-45-41

ACTED (Agency for Technical Cooperation and Development)
(66 Tolstoy Str.)
Technical Director Dean Harvey   24-70-58

ADRA (Adventist Development and Relief Agency) (43 Schorsa Str.)
  Tajikistan Director Conrad Vine   33-15-70

AED/Globe Project (Academy for Educational Development)
              (40 Rudaki, Room 301)
  Country Repres. Tamara Lashbrook   off 21-06-00
  Program Specialist Niso Rasulova   21-08-44
  Gulru Azamova   21-82-49
                                           fax 21-05-18
American Business Center
  Manager Faridun Kamoliddinov   21-05-22
  Asst to Manager Savriniso Kurbonbekova   21-05-26
                Turkish line: 51-01-02

AKF (Aga Khan Foundation)/AKDN (Aga Khan Development Network)
              (6 Hamza Hakimzade)
  Chief Executive Officer Hakim Feerasta   21-51-18
  Asst Natasha Avakova   24-65-00
  Firuz Vatanshoev   fax 21-70-87
  Admin. Asst   24-19-42
              Turkish line: 51-00-66
                        mob tlx: 583-492-282-520
      E-mail for internet users: akftjk@atge.automail.com

  Pamir Relief and Development Program/Khorog Office
        tel: 27-19, 26-99, 67-99, 60-37, 65-99
        AKDN/ Khorog   tel: 25-99, 43-45

Project Office
  Project Director Rafique Keshavjie   off 24-58-23
                                             res 23-09-44
                                                  27-69-35
ABA (American Bar Association) (44 Shevchenko St., Apt. 37)
  Chief Jack Martin   off 21-18-67
              fax 21-17-86
BASICS/PROJECT USAID/CCCID (20/1 Behzod Str., 7)
  Chief Ibod Sharifi   res 24-34-43
                                             off 21-83-12
                                                  21-46-91
CAAEF (Central Asian-American Enterprise Fund) (35 Kirov Str.)
  Vice-President Dan Dougherty (in Khojand)   21-50-14
  Consultant Bakhtiyor Umarov   21-56-01

CADA (Central Asian Development Agency)(40 Rudaki Av., Room 307)

For additional analytical, business and investment opportunities information,
please contact Global Investment & Business Center, USA
at (202) 546-2103. Fax: (202) 546-3275. E-mail: rusric@erols.com

Chief David Lovett   off 21-21-75
                                                        res 24-62-64, 24-51-77
  Acting Director Teh Seng Chuan (till March 22)
  Susan Layman   off 21-08-80
                                                                 res 24-51-11
  Doctor Beverley Ankerman   res 24-58-93
   office address: 64 Rudaki, Apt 37

  Administration (Sitora)   fax 21-22-10
  Administrator/Interpreter   21-11-27
  E-mail: cada@cada.silk.glas.asc.org   21-01-56

CARANA (44 Rudaki, Room 159)
  Project Manager Mathew Scanlon   21-88-87
  Joseph Sean Morris   21-75-50

CARE (4 Mendeleyev St.)
  Country Representative Peter Goossens   off 21-17-83
                                                                 res 24-06-46
  Food Project Advisor Golam Azam   21-00-91
  Project Manager (agriculture) Anthony Johnson   24-04-89
  Admin. Manager Gulchin Sarkorova (Munira, adiba) 24-70-39
                                                                 fax 21-17-78
        Turkish line   51-00-36

CARITAS Switzerland (20/2 Ahmadi Donish Str., Apt.13-14)

Chief Lutz Leichtfuss   23-05-44
  Prof. Abdumumin Sharifov (TTU)   21-62-27

Counterpart Consortium (20 Kirova St., Apt. 7)
  Country Director John Barbee   21-82-65
                                                                  21-65-14
EBRD (29 Shotemur Str., Apt. 19)
  Mission Asst Nasiba Ahrorova   21-07-63

ECHO (European Community Humanitarian Office) (European Union)
(25 Tursunzade St., 3rd Floor)
  Representative Janny Bosscher   23-24-86

EF (Eurasia Foundation) (18 Rudaki)
  Regional Director Daniel Bliss (Tashkent)
  Coordinator Alla Kuvvatova   off 21-69-86

GAA (German Agro Action) (Sharq Str., 3rd proyezd, h. 14)

Project Coordinator 24-74-11
21-23-48
GTZ (German Agency for Technical Development) (14 Aini)
Project Manager Karlfried Metzler 21-71-26
21-74-51
fax 51-00-37
ICRC (International Committee of the Red Cross) (14/3 Aini St.)
Head of Mission Mark Hofstetter 21-68-23
Deputy Denis Berthoud 21-82-14
Admin. Coordinator Irene Zuend 21-73-37
Fax 21-86-60
IFRC (International Federation of the Red Cross)
(120 Omar Khayam St., 3rd Floor)
Head of Delegation George Heron 24-59-81
Admin. Asst Aishe Muratova 24-42-96
Operator Victoriya fax 24-85-20

IMF (International Monetary Fund) (23/2 Rudaki)
Chief 9-95 21-24-80

"Internews" (92 Rudaki, Apt. 24)
Jennifer Minor off 24-54-83
fax 21-43-12
res 24-16-32
IOM (International Organization for Migration)(30 Sino St.)
HOM Raynald Blouin 24-71-96
Program Asst Jamilla Babaeva fax 21-03-02
fax 51-00-62

MCI (Mercy Corps International) (12 Tehron St.)
Head of Mission 21-08-60
Michael Allen 27-61-13
Koryun Alaverdian fax 21-08-64

MERLIN (Medical Emergency Relief Int'l)
(1 Proyezd Shota Rustaveli Str., h. 16)
Head of Mission Ms. Taz Khaliq 21-47-64
Medical Coordinator 51-01-20

MSF (Holland) (166 Zainab-bibi Str.)
Kurian Bos off 24-67-93
Paul McPhun

ORA International (Orphans, Refugees and Aid (Germany)
(17 Kuibishev Av., Apt. 11)

Chief Jeffrey Paulsen   27-46-10
                                             21-64-42
                                             res 24-40-77
Rich Berghan   res 24-08-78
Vince Simmonds   res 24-63-68

OSCE (Organization for Security & Cooperation in Europe)(53 Sino)
    Head of Mission Dimitri Manjavidze   off 24-42-01
    DCM William Ferrell
    Lara Griffith
    Oinihol Bobonazarova   24-91-59
Vladimir Nickolaevich Chernyakov
    Thomas Bolinger (Shaartuz)

OSI (Open Society Institute) Soros Foundation (Presidium of
               Academy of Sciences, 3rd Floor)
    Resident Represent.   off 21-19-58
                                             23-22-05

PSF (Pharmaciens sans Frontieres) (35/1 Bokhtar St., Room 703)
    Chief Geoffroy de Vaulgrenant   21-09-67
    Technical Administrator Andre Olivier   fax: 27-70-69

RI (Relief International) (70 Rudaki, 4th Fl., Apt 76)
    Acting Country Director   fax: 21-86-53
                                             21-07-17

Save the Children Fund (UK) (2 Proyezd Ozodi Zanon, House 17)
    Bronwen Lewis (Program Manager)   24-03-39
    Consultant Joanna Raikes
    Nicole Hurtubise (Khatlon)
                      Turkish line: 51-00-75
            e-mail:office@scfuk.td.silk.glas.apc.org

Save the Children (US) (18 Turdiyev St.)
    Director Bharat Devkota   off 21-07-71
    Program Manager Rob Kaufman   res 24-75-40
                                             21-18-86
                      Turkish line: 51-00-79
                e-mail: scdush@glas.apc.org
                    satphone: (873) 153-6374/5

Shelter Now International (54 Zainab-Bibi Str.)
    Country Director Kumar Periasamy   21-51-98
                res 24-01-55

Deputy Director Brad Rust   24-70-29
Regional Program Director Harry J.R. Van Burik
Liaison Officer Glen Taylor
Craig Simonian
Joachim Jackle

TACIS (Ministry of Agriculture, 46 Rudaki, 2nd floor)

Coordination Unit (room 104)
Acting Director Rahmat Yusupov. Haqqulov   21-26-09
(comes to the office periodically)   21-02-26
                                                            21-82-94

UNDP (United Nations Development Program)(25 Bekhzod St.)
Res. Repres. Paolo Lembo   21-06-70
Dep. Res. Repr. Blanche de Bonneval   21-06-85
Program Adviser Pamela Khussein   23-08-51
Junior Professional Officer Shoko Noda   21-06-79
OPS Program Manager Basil Comnas (Gulya)   21-06-82
                res 24-03-73
Secretary Gulnora Burkhanova   23-05-96
Senior Program Asst Tatiana Falco   23-06-12
Community Development Coordinator Sukumar Mishra   23-07-71
Peace Building Project Coordinator Prosper Bani   23-07-71
ACU Director Bahrom Alizade   fax 21-41-81
Janna Yusupjanova   fax 21-50-25
                                                        fax 51-00-43
DHA Chief Jamie McGoldrick   fax 21-03-89
NGO Liasion Officer Guissou Jahangiri-Jeannot
FAO (Food and Agriculture Org-n) Pavel Chernogorsky 23-05-53
Junior Professional Officer Luigi de Marfino   23-07-81
Emergency Specialist Greg Sanchez   21-06-79
Program Officer Abdukahor Nurov   21-06-80
Administrator Matlyuba Turayeva   21-06-88
Finance Assistant   21-06-86
Muna Khamidova   21-06-94
Secretary Dilbar Jalolova   21-06-79

UNESCO (MFA building)
Guljahon Bobosadykova   21-17-50
Munzifa Bobojanova   fax 23-29-64
                                         tlx 201137 PAMIR SU

UNICEF (14/1 H. Hakimzade St.)
Head of Mission Johan Fagerskiold   off 21-82-61

John Conteh	24-72-61
	fax 24-19-05

UNHCR (United Nations High Commissioner for Refugees)
              (25 Said Nosirov St.)

Res. Coordinator for CA John McCallin	21-74-24
Head of Office Gang Li (Asst. Dilrabo)	
Regional Workshop Manager Silas Itiveh	
Program Officer George Labor	
Sudang Kaentrakool	
Senior Legal Officer Annika Linden	
Gulnora Ibragimova	24-61-84
Aziza, Muhabbat	24-62-65
Radio Operators Turkish line:	51-00-40

UNMOT (United Nations Mission of Observers to Tajikistan)
(7 Gorky St.)

Head of Mission, SGSR Gerd Dietrich Merrem	21-01-25
Chief Military Observer Gen Boleslav Izydorczyk	21-02-51
Deputy Chief Military Observer COL Jan Andersen	21-01-27
Head of Civil Affairs Yogesh Saksena	21-01-03
Senior Civil Affairs Officer Wlodek Cibor	21-01-05
Civil Affairs Officer Hasmik Egian	21-33-80
Security Officer Kenrick Cato	21-01-29
Chief Admin. Officer Marcellin Savard (Zarina)	21-01-10
Chief General Services/Procurement Officer	21-34-43
24-Hour Duty Officer	21-01-47

USAID (Agency for International Development)(US Embassy)

Christine Sheckler	ext 102	off 21-03-56
		res 24-74-63
Turkish line/fax		51-00-49
Admin. Asst. Olga Krylova	ext 126	fax 21-01-71
Progr. Asst Abdurahim Muhidov	ext 126	fax 21-04-29

VI (Vision International-U.K.)	24-64-47

WFP (World Food Program) (51 Turdiyev Str.)

Country Director Gerard Viguie	21-09-07
Abu Sayod Saifuzzaman	21-09-07
Duty Officer	24-39-50
Turkish line/fax	51-00-87

WHO (World Health Organization) (8 Chapaev Str.)	21-48-71

World Bank (95/1 Rudaki, "Orion Bank", 7th Floor)
    Field Office Repres. Mustafa Rouis   21-15-18
    Operations Officer Muzaffar Usmonov   21-14-03
    Secretary Saodat   21-27-10
    Tohir Mirzoev   21-16-00

INTERNATIONAL BUSINESS ORGANIZATIONS

Commonwealth & British Minerals (CBM)(27 Tursunzade, 3rd Floor)
Craig Brown   21-29-64
                            23-17-84
                         fax 21-30-25

DHL Dushanbe (8 Somoni St.)
    Mahbuba Jumankulova   24-62-79
    Parviz   21-02-80

Arthur Andersen Company of Lawyers (National Bank building)
    Chief Wilfredo Alvarez   off 21-25-81

INTERNATIONAL SCHOOLS

Dushanbe International School (2 Bofanda Str.)
Eric Prost   off 21-77-91
                         23-85-04

Quality School International (8 Sharq Str.)   24-53-49

THE NATIONAL ASSOCIATION OF SMALL BUSINESSES OF TAJIKISTAN

The National Association of Small and Medium Sized-Businesses of Tajikistan (NASMB) is a non-governmental organization set to assist small and medium-sized firms in Tajikistan. It was established in September 1993 after the Government issued the regulation "On Support of Enterpreneurial Structures within the General Strategy Developing the Private Sector of Tajikistan's Economy." The main goal of the Association is to assist the development of small and medium-sized businesses, of the market infrastructures, and to coordinate the activities of Tajik entrepreneurs.

The NASMB Board members are businessmen, bankers, business associations, business consulting centers, etc. The Government of Tajikistan granted the NASMB with a legislative initiative right.

Due to objective reasons, the NASMB activities were temporarily stopped in 1994-1996. After April, 1996 the NASMB resumed its operations:
-- at present the NASMB has more than 500 members;
-- the NASMB has regional offices in Khojand, Kulyab, the Khatlon Region, and Gorny Badakhshan. Businessmen from districts of the republican subordination, such as Leninsky, Hissar, Garm, Faizabad also expressed an interest to join the NASMB;
-- the NASMB conducts regular educational seminars for its members at the Dushanbe American Business Center;
-- more than ten NASMB members improved their qualification abroad through the U.S. NET Program funded by the Academy through Educational Development (AED);
-- since 1994 the NASMB started cooperation with the EBRD on opening the EBRD credit lines for small and medium businesses in Tajikistan;
-- in August, 1996 the NASMB jointly with the EBRD conducted research on lending possibilities for the private sector in Tajikistan and opening of Business Consulting Centers in Dushanbe and Khojand;
-- since April, 1996 the NASMB established a close cooperation with Dushanbe TACIS office and participated in the TACIS program "Europartenariat" (5 NASMB members took part in the Partenariat session in Italy, 16 companies - in the Partenariat session in CIS, 3 companies - in Partenariat Greece, 6 companies - in Partenariat France) and the TACIS Project on Spread of Technical Assistance;
-- the MASMB established cooperation with various entrepreneurial associations in CIS and all around the world;
-- since 1995 the NASMB members participated in the SABIT Experts Program funded by USDOC;
-- the NASMB represents its members' interests in Dushanbe-cited international and financial organizations as Mercy Corp., the Central Asia America Enterprise Fund, Carana Corporation, Counterpart Consortium, etc.
-- the NASMB actively participated in conducting the 1st Economic Forum in Dushanbe in November, 1996 under the aegis of the UNDP, OSCE, and the Government of Tajikistan;
-- the NASMB jointly with the German Society of Technical Assistance GZT arranged training workshops for local entrepreneurs;
-- the NASMB established close contacts with local NGOs, such as the Tajik Center for Entrepreneurship and Management in Khojand, Women in Development, etc.

Note: For U.S. companies looking for business partners in Tajikistan the NASMB can be the right entity to contact.

Contact: Matljuba Uljabaeva
Chairman
9, Bofanda Str. Dushanbe Tajikistan
Tel: 7(3772)27 79 78

RESTAURANTS IN DUSHANBE

EUROPEAN/TAJIK CUISINE

Restaurant Elite

Varied selection of European and Tajik dishes with Elite specials. Any dish by preliminary order. Full desert table and wide bar selection. Soft music and nice Western interior. No credit cards accepted. The most expensive restaurant in Dushanbe. Cash only.
$25-40 per person.
Location: Chapaev Street (opposite Radio House)
Tel: {7}(3772) 21-25-12
Hours: 11 a.m.-11 p.m.

Bar-Restaurant Polonaise

Exquisite European and Tajik cuisine (red and black caviar, sturgeon, trout, mushrooms, beef, lamb, smoked meat, and chicken.) Any course by preliminary order. Natural juices. Wide bar collection. Exclusively nice design. Cash only.
$5-20 per person.
Location: 2nd floor, 35/1 Bohtar Street (in building of Avtotranstechnika)
Tel: {7}(3772)21-25-26
Hours: 9 a.m.-11 a.m.

Restaurant Continent

Mostly European cuisine with Continent specials. Delicious desert. Wide range of Moldovan, Bulgarian, licensed French and Italian wines. Any dish on preliminary order. Nice indoor and outdoor seating. Cash only.
$5-20 per person
Location: 32, Buhoro Street
Tel: [7](3772)21-44-98
Hours: 12 p.m.-till last client

Bar/Restaurant Intourist-Tojikiston

Two bars, four indoor (purely Tajik, European, and mixed design) and outdoor seating. European and Tajik dishes with restaurant's specials. Any dish by preliminary morning order. Wide bar selection including Tajik, Georgian, and Moldovan wines. Cash only.
Breakfast - $4-5 per person
Lunch - $5-6 per person
Dinner - $7-10 per person
Location: 22, Shotemur Street
Tel: [7](3772)21-70-77, 21-33-52
Fax: [7](3772)21-64-26

Cafe Shahrom

European cuisine only (meat and vegetable salads, mushrooms, shrimps, clear and cabbage soups, fish, chicken, fried meat, and natural juices. Alcohol beverages are temporarily not available. Cash only.
Location: 16, Kirov (Husein-Zoda) Street
Hours: 12 p.m.-23 p.m. daily except Sunday.

Bar Manhattan

Excellent selection of poultry: chicken, duck, turkey, partridge. Rabbit, fish, and meat courses are also available. Anything by preliminary order. Private rooms available. Wide bar selection. Cash only.
$7-15 per person.
Location: 32, Shotemur Street, Dushanbe
Hours: 9 a.m.-9 p.m.daily except Sunday

Bar Vostochny

Tajik food mostly and some European. Nice indoor and outdoor seating. Private cabins for 8/6/4/2 persons are available. Various alcoholic beverages. Ice-cream. Cash only.
$5 per person without alcohol, $6-7 with strong beverages.
Location: 56, Rudaki Avenue (along the main street of Dushanbe)
Hours: 11 a.m.-till last client daily except Sunday

Cafe Romashka

Snack and beer. Oudoor ground. No credit cards. Cash only.
$5-10 per person
Location: 33, Rudaki Avenue (along the main street of Dushanbe)
Hours: daily except Sunday

Restaurant Kapris

Standard European (salads, chicken, beefsteak, sausages) and Tajik food. Wide selection of Georgian wines, champagne, and liqueurs. No vodka. Indoor and outdoor seating. Western interior and private cabins available.
$10-12.5 per person.
Location: 32, Ghafurov Street, 82-y mikrorayon
Tel: [7](3772)37-94-50
Hours: 9 a.m.-9 p.m. daily

U.S. TAJIKISTAN EXPORT AND IMPORT STATISTICS

U.S. Exports to Tajikistan

CALENDAR YEAR

For additional analytical, business and investment opportunities information, please contact Global Investment & Business Center, USA at (202) 546-2103. Fax: (202) 546-3275. E-mail: rusric@erols.com

HS Description	Millions of U.S. Dollars			% Share			% Change
	1996	1997	1998	1996	1997	1998	98/97
Tajikistan	17	19	12	0.00	0.00	0.00	-34.59
10 CEREALS	6.529	5.004	4.939	37.92	26.93	40.64	-1.28
11 MILLING;MALT;STARCH	2.850	6.709	2.967	16.56	36.11	24.42	-55.77
98 SPECIAL OTHER	0.785	0.266	1.215	4.56	1.43	10.00	356.82
04 DAIRY,EGGS, HONEY,ETC	0.000	0.426	1.165	0.00	2.29	9.59	173.40
15 FATS AND OILS	1.469	2.905	0.648	8.53	15.63	5.33	-77.69
84 MACHINERY	2.098	0.837	0.409	12.18	4.51	3.36	-51.19
49 BOOK+NEWSPAPR; MANUSCRPT	0.000	0.228	0.220	0.00	1.22	1.81	-3.30
85 ELECTRICAL MACHINERY	0.799	0.045	0.125	4.64	0.24	1.03	176.47
20 PRESERVED FOOD	0.000	0.000	0.058	0.00	0.00	0.47	###.##
88 AIRCRAFT, SPACECRAFT	0.000	0.000	0.054	0.00	0.00	0.44	###.##
28 INORG CHEM;RARE ERTH MT	0.266	0.406	0.051	1.54	2.19	0.42	-87.32
69 CERAMIC PRODUCTS	0.000	0.000	0.050	0.00	0.00	0.41	###.##
70 GLASS AND GLASSWARE	0.000	0.113	0.046	0.00	0.61	0.38	-58.81
29 ORGANIC CHEMICALS	0.000	0.000	0.039	0.00	0.00	0.32	###.##
39 PLASTIC	0.723	0.309	0.033	4.20	1.66	0.27	-89.17
22 BEVERAGES	0.575	0.300	0.033	3.34	1.62	0.27	-89.03
71 PRECIOUS STONES, METALS	0.000	0.000	0.031	0.00	0.00	0.25	###.##
82 TOOL,CUTLRY, OF BASE MTL	0.000	0.000	0.024	0.00	0.00	0.20	###.##
21 MISCELLANEOUS FOOD	0.024	0.088	0.019	0.14	0.47	0.16	-77.89
63 MISC TEXTILE ARTICLES	0.000	0.000	0.010	0.00	0.00	0.08	
35 ALBUMINS;MOD STRCH;GLUE	0.000	0.010	0.006	0.00	0.05	0.05	-43.03
30 PHARMACEUTICAL PRODUCTS	0.000	0.000	0.005	0.00	0.00	0.04	
48 PAPER,PAPERBOARD	0.004	0.000	0.005	0.02	0.00	0.04	
61 KNIT APPAREL	0.003	0.000	0.000	0.02	0.00	0.00	0.00
68 STONE,PLASTR, CEMENT,ETC	0.000	0.000	0.000	0.00	0.00	0.00	0.00
87 VEHICLES, NOT RAILWAY	0.224	0.497	0.000	1.30	2.68	0.00	0.00
90 OPTIC,NT 8544;MED INSTR	0.000	0.008	0.000	0.00	0.04	0.00	0.00

For additional analytical, business and investment opportunities information, please contact Global Investment & Business Center, USA at (202) 546-2103. Fax: (202) 546-3275. E-mail: rusric@erols.com

94 FURNITURE AND BEDDING	0.000	0.000	0.000	0.00	0.00	0.00	0.00
32 TANNING,DYE,PAINT,PUTTY	0.042	0.000	0.000	0.24	0.00	0.00	0.00
37 PHOTOGRAPHIC/ CINEMATOGR	0.012	0.000	0.000	0.07	0.00	0.00	0.00
41 HIDES AND SKINS	0.134	0.000	0.000	0.78	0.00	0.00	0.00
07 VEGETABLES	0.680	0.423	0.000	3.95	2.28	0.00	0.00
12 MISC GRAIN,SEED,FRUIT	0.000	0.006	0.000	0.00	0.03	0.00	0.00

Source of Data: U.S. Dept of Commerce, Bureau of the Census

U.S. IMPORTS FROM TAJIKISTAN

CALENDAR YEAR

	Millions of U.S. Dollars			% Share			% Change
HS Description	1996	1997	1998	1996	1997	1998	98/97
Tajikistan	33	9	33	0.00	0.00	0.00	281.69
76 ALUMINUM	27.386	5.544	29.912	83.48	64.89	91.73	439.56
52 COTTON FABRIC	3.311	2.840	2.034	10.09	33.24	6.24	-28.38
62 WOVEN APPAREL	0.000	0.000	0.225	0.00	0.00	0.69	###.##
84 MACHINERY	0.002	0.000	0.215	0.01	0.00	0.66	###.##
10 CEREALS	0.000	0.000	0.113	0.00	0.00	0.35	###.##
99 O SPECL IMPR	0.095	0.018	0.096	0.29	0.21	0.30	437.49
98 SPECIAL OTHER	0.113	0.000	0.010	0.34	0.00	0.03	
49 BOOK+NEWSPAPR; MANUSCRPT	0.002	0.000	0.002	0.01	0.00	0.01	###.##
61 KNIT APPAREL	0.015	0.000	0.000	0.04	0.00	0.00	0.00
64 FOOTWEAR	0.012	0.000	0.000	0.04	0.00	0.00	0.00
03 FISH AND SEAFOOD	0.020	0.000	0.000	0.06	0.00	0.00	0.00
21 MISCELLANEOUS FOOD	0.017	0.000	0.000	0.05	0.00	0.00	0.00
28 INORG CHEM;R.ERTH MT	1.117	0.000	0.000	3.41	0.00	0.00	0.00
39 PLASTIC	0.001	0.000	0.000	0.00	0.00	0.00	0.00
43 FURSKIN+ARTIFICIAL FUR	0.001	0.000	0.000	0.00	0.00	0.00	0.00
85 ELECTRICAL MACHINERY	0.041	0.000	0.000	0.12	0.00	0.00	0.00
87 VEHICLES, NOT RAILWAY	0.022	0.000	0.000	0.07	0.00	0.00	0.00
97 ART AND ANTIQUES	0.000	0.103	0.000	0.00	1.20	0.00	0.00
71 PRECIOUS STONES,METALS	0.026	0.014	0.000	0.08	0.17	0.00	0.00
72 IRON AND STEEL	0.626	0.000	0.000	1.91	0.00	0.00	0.00
73 IRON/STEEL PRODUCTS	0.000	0.025	0.000	0.00	0.29	0.00	0.00

Source of Data: U.S. Dept of Commerce, Bureau of the Census

LAWYERS IN DUSHANBE

Office of judicial consultation of the **Tsentralny district,**

#46A N. Karabayev Pr.; phone: 33-96-01:

1. Odinayev, Saidalimsho   10 yrs, criminal
   Khukumatovich

   2. Burkhanova, Svetlana Pavlovna24 yrs, civil and   criminal

3. Komilov, Saidakram Saidovich   19 yrs, criminal
home phone: 36-24-38

4. Yunusova, Alexandra Pavlovna19 yrs, civil
home phone: 33-22-69

5. Yatimov, K.   criminal and civil

6. Sharipova, B.   civil and criminal
Office of judicial consultation of the **Zheleznodorozhny (Railway) district**, phone: 27-85-04

1. Kurbanov, Saidkomil11 yrs, criminal
2. Khushvakhtova, Gulniso8 yrs, criminal
Abdullayevna
phone: 27-01-39

3. Urinbayev, Gani Odilovich9 yrs, criminal
4. Kurbonov, M.   civil and criminal
5. Ms. Nusratova   civil and criminal
6. Ms. Rasulova   criminal
7. Mr. Yorov   civil and criminal
Office of judicial consultation of the **Frunzensky district**,
#57 Ismoili Somoni Pr., phone: 36-18-30

1. Khametova Nailya11 yrs, criminal
Ismoilovna
2. Ubaydov, Nodirsho Saydulloevich11 yrs, civil and   criminal
3. Beknazarov, S.
4. Mr. Anandiyev
Office of judicial consultation of **the October district**,
#91 Rudaki Pr., phone 21-76-51, 24-12-97:
1. Boboyeva, Zebo14 yrs, civil and   criminal
2. Boturov, Bakhtiyor Mirzomuradovih9 yrs, civil and
                                   criminal
4. Faiziyev, Akbar20 yrs, civil and   criminal
5. Ms. Soliyeva civil and   criminal
6. Mr. Badriddinov   criminal
7. Karimov, N.   civil and
                                           criminal
Chairman of the Presidium of Collegiate of Lawyers of the Republic of

Tajikistan - Amirbekov, Naim Amirbekovich, phone: 21-24-03; 27-84-77, address: #12 Parhar St., Dushanbe
Vice chairman of the Presidium of Collegiate of Lawyers of the Republic of Tajikistan
– Abduzoda, Mirzo, phone:
27-84-77
Commercial Law Project, Dushanbe, Akbar Muratov, some knowledge of English, phone: 21-26-50, 21-17-79, e-mail: Akbar79@hotmail.com
"Contract" judicial company - #54 Ostrovsky St., Dushanbe,
phones: 21-14-10, 21-27-38, 23-09-20

NEAR-BY REGIONS
Office of judicial consultation of **Leninskiy District:**
Ms. Umarova   civil and criminal
Office of judicial consultation of **Kofarnihon district**,
phone: 2-44-81, 2-41-05
Mr. Asatullayev   civil and criminal
Office of judicial consultation of **Ghissar district**
Mr. Rajabov   civil and criminal
Office of judicial consultation of **the City of Tursunzade**
Mr. Khojankulov   civil and criminal
Office of judicial consultation of **the City of Kughan-Tyube, Khatlon Region**
1. Ms. Amonova   civil and criminal
2. Mr. Nuritdinov   civil and criminal

OFFICIAL MATERIALS

CHALLENGES FACING THE TRANSITION ECONOMIES OF CENTRAL ASIA[2]

Thank you, President Akayev, Chairman Sultanov, ladies and gentlemen.

It is a great pleasure to join you at this conference marking the fifth anniversary of the introduction of the som. I say this for two reasons. First, you have given me a most welcome opportunity to visit the Kyrgyz Republic, a country which, under the leadership of President Akayev, has been at the forefront of reform within the countries of the former Soviet Union. The introduction of the som, which we are commemorating today, was one of many courageous and forward-looking decisions that have contributed to your country's economic progress.

Allow me to elaborate somewhat on that. The Kyrgyz Republic is now at a promising stage of its history. After several years of an extremely difficult transition, your country starts experiencing the benefits of its orientation toward a market economy. Not only has the dramatic decline in output been reversed, but for two years in a row growth of output has been around 7 percent, while the introduction of the som has been key in bringing inflation down from the destructive hyperinflation level of 1,259 percent, where it was in 1992, to the single digit level where it stands now, and you know that further progress is

[2] Address by Michel Camdessus Managing Director of the International Monetary Fund at a conference on "Challenges to Economies in Transition" Bishkek, Kyrgyz Republic - May 27, 1998

at hand. These achievements are still fragile and, in the framework of the new program on which we have just agreed, your government, Mr. President, wants to consolidate them, to make sure that the trends toward increased poverty are also reversed, and that the poorest in the country benefit particularly from the economic expansion of the years to come.

This is an ambitious but realistic program and, in visiting Bishkek today, I wanted to tell you and the people of this country our full determination to make a maximum effort to support this program and to convince the international community to join us in this endeavor. This is also a unique occasion to pay tribute, Mr. President, to your vision and leadership in conducting this transition, which not only has laid the grounds for a promising future, but has also been a source of inspiration for other countries in similar situations.

Second, your invitation also provides an excellent occasion to reflect upon the critical issues facing Central Asia. From the earliest days of the transition, the IMF has been providing policy advice, technical assistance, and financial support to help your countries develop efficient market economies and integrate themselves into the global economy. Thus, we have in some sense accompanied you during your "transition," sharing your pride in your achievements and your determination to overcome the problems you still face.

At the same time, however, the IMF is also in a continuous policy dialogue with its other member countries. So, our views on the issues facing Central Asia are colored not simply by our experience with your countries, or even by our involvement with transition economies in general, but by our experience in 182 countries at every stage of economic development, in every conceivable economic situation, and in every region of the world. It is from this broader perspective that I would like to discuss the issues facing your countries. Let me begin with a few words on the opportunities and challenges in the global economy and how various of our member countries have responded to them. Then I will turn to the implications for Central Asia.

Challenges in the global economy

It is frequently said that the world has entered the age of "globalization" or that we now live in a "global economy." But what does that really mean? For over fifty years, the world economy has been growing more closely integrated in terms of trade and capital flows. To a great extent, globalization is simply the continuation of that trend. But with greater freedom of trade and investment and new breakthroughs in telecommunication and information technology, markets have become much larger, more complex, and more closely linked than ever before. Moreover, capital now moves at a speed and in volumes that would have been inconceivable just a few years ago.

Asia, in particular, has been the showcase of the benefits of globalization. In 1996, private capital flows to developing and transition economies reached an all time high of $235 billion, of which nearly half went to Asia. Subsequent events have shown that some of those funds were not invested wisely. Nevertheless, over the last several decades, the forces of globalization have allowed many countries in Asia to accelerate investment and growth, create more jobs, reduce poverty, and attain other important human development goals. In Malaysia, for example, the share of the population living below the poverty line declined from almost 50 percent in 1970 to less than 10 percent in

1995. In Korea, the literacy rate increased from around 30 percent in the mid–1950s to over 95 percent today. Globalization has helped make such human progress possible.

But if globalization offers many opportunities, it also holds two major risks. The first can be seen in the recent experience of Thailand, Korea, and Indonesia, all of which have suffered major financial crises during the last year, when investors lost confidence in their economies and large capital inflows turned into massive capital outflows. Countries that attract large volumes of private capital are more vulnerable to sudden shifts in investor confidence, which can be very destabilizing to their own economies and have negative effects on other countries, as well. Indeed, some of your countries have felt a chill breeze from East Asia, as commodity prices weakened, conditions in international capital markets became less favorable, and some East Asian investors scaled back planned investments.

The second risk can be seen in the experience of many African countries. Countries that are unable to participate in the expansion of world trade or attract significant amounts of foreign capital risk becoming marginalized from the global economy and falling farther and farther behind the rest of the world in terms of growth and human development. This marginalization, in turn, poses the very real threat of economic stagnation and increasing poverty.

The challenge for all countries is how to make the most of the opportunities that globalization has to offer, while minimizing these risks. This is not an easy task. However, among the members of the IMF, there is a tremendous wealth of experience as to how countries can best meet this challenge. One purpose of the IMF is to help disseminate this experience as broadly as possible, so that countries can learn from each other's successes and failures. In this spirit, let me turn now to the lessons of our members' experience.

* * * * *

Ingredients of economic success

Experience shows that in order to be successful in the global economy, countries must first have properly functioning domestic economies. What does this involve? Let me mention three key requirements.

The first is to allow market forces to set prices and allocate resources so that the economy can operate efficiently. Progress in this area has been uneven in Central Asia, particularly in the agricultural sector, and private investment, labor productivity, output, and rural incomes have suffered. Countries that hesitate to liberalize agriculture, or indeed, other sectors of their economies, should consider the dramatic example of Vietnam, which went from being a net importer of about half a million tons of food annually in 1986–88 to being the world's third largest rice exporter in 1989, following sweeping reforms in the agricultural sector.[1] Today, Vietnam is still one of the world's leading rice exporters.

Of course, one key aspect of improving resource allocation—as well as taking advantage of the opportunities in global markets—is to open the economy up to foreign trade and hence to international price signals and competition. However, these benefits of trade liberalization will only materialize in the context of a unified exchange rate and the removal of restrictions on current transactions.

The second requirement for domestic economies to perform well is a stable macroeconomic environment, beginning with a relatively stable price level. There is now nearly universal consensus that low single-digit inflation is a necessary condition for sustained and equitable economic growth.

There is also wide agreement on the policies needed to achieve this objective—notably a disciplined fiscal policy that keeps government expenditure in line with government revenues, while providing for a satisfactory level of public investment in basic infrastructure and human capital and a well-targeted social safety net. In this regard, there is considerable scope for strengthening fiscal management in most transition economies—from improving tax systems and tax administration, establishing effective treasury systems, prioritizing public expenditure, and putting pension systems on a sustainable footing.

Such reforms are essential, among other reasons to ensure that the fiscal position is consistent with a non-inflationary monetary policy and a sustainable level of external debt. Yes, countries must also manage their external debt wisely. One needs only think about the debt crisis in Latin America during the 1980s and the so-called "lost decade" of economic stagnation that accompanied it, or the problems of heavily indebted poor countries in Africa today, to see how excessive external borrowing—or borrowing on inappropriate terms—can compromise a country's financial stability and economic growth for years to come.

Finally, for the private sector to fulfill its intended role as the main engine of growth and job creation, there is a third requirement, which for the most part is still missing here in Central Asia, and that is a suitable institutional framework that will give domestic and foreign entrepreneurs the confidence to invest. In particular, I would point to the need for:

- simple and transparent regulatory systems—so that businesses won't waste precious time and resources trying to find out what the rules are and how to comply with them; so that new firms can enter the market without complication or being driven underground; and so that foreign investors are encouraged to bring in their capital, technology, and skills;

- effective legal and judiciary systems that protect property rights, enforce contracts, and help create an atmosphere of law, order, and personal security—so that domestic and foreign investors will expand their businesses and create new ones; and

- tax systems that are simple and broad-based, with limited exemptions and reasonable and uniform rates—so that companies and individuals will not be discouraged from trying to fulfill their tax obligations; so that taxes can be more easily enforced; and so that governments receive the revenues they need to carry out their basic responsibilities in such areas as health and education.

Experience also shows that in order to make a decisive difference in the domestic economic climate, policies must be reasonably consistent and achieve a critical mass of reform, thereby convincing investors that reform is irreversible, and that the country is truly integrating into the international economy. Partial reform may not elicit much response if substantial impediments to economic activity remain in place.

As you may have surmised, meeting these three requirements implies a redefinition of the role of the State in the economy. In successful market economies, the State disengages from activities that markets and the private sector can perform more effectively, such as setting prices, allocating credit and other domestic resources and running commercial activities. Instead, it concentrates on carrying out a few core responsibilities well, such as upholding the rule of law, providing reliable public services, maintaining prudent macroeconomic policies, and establishing a fair and transparent regulatory framework for private sector activity. Of course, governments must also give their full attention to stamping out corruption in every form. These are all aspects of "good governance," which is an essential condition for saving, investment and sustained growth.

Lessons from East Asia

If these are the lessons of experience from developing and transition economies, what does the experience of the misfortunes of the "Asian tigers" imply for Central Asia?

First, it is worth noting that the reason why countries such as Thailand, Korea, and Indonesia were so successful economically for so many years is that they instituted many of the requirements I just mentioned—including macroeconomic stability, outward looking economic policies, and a high priority on human development—at a relatively early stage. So what went wrong? Put simply, domestic institutions were not strong enough, and domestic policies were not flexible enough, to meet the increasing demands of economic success. These institutional and policy shortcomings manifested themselves in various ways, including:

- in the failure to address the overheating pressures and the lack of sufficient exchange rate flexibility, which, along with implicit guarantees of support to banks and corporations, led to excessive external borrowing and exchange rate exposure, often at short maturities;

- in the high degree of inappropriate government intervention the economy, including lending based on personal connections and government directive, which led to inefficient investment and a deterioration in the quality of bank balance sheets, while prudential rules were lax and banking supervision was weak;

- in the lack of data and transparency, which concealed the extent of these countries' problems—and not just to the rest of the world, but also to their own eyes. This led to complacency on the part of the authorities, a false sense of security on the part of foreign investors, and later when the facts became known, to market panic.

From this experience, I would highlight three points that are particularly relevant for countries in Central Asia and, indeed, for every other country that hopes to tap international capital markets.

The first point concerns the need to maintain sound macroeconomic policies, correct macroeconomic imbalances promptly when they arise, and continue with the structural changes needed to sustain macroeconomic stability and high quality growth. Even countries that appear to have reasonably sound policies must be vigilant.

The second point concerns the importance of sound domestic financial systems. In Thailand, Korea, Indonesia, and many other countries, we have seen the tremendous human cost of allowing delaying key structural reforms, especially steps to strengthen the domestic financial system. Overcoming a domestic banking crisis is a very costly undertaking. We don't know yet what the price tag will be in East Asia, but I can tell you that the cost of the banking crisis in Chile, with all its indirect costs, exceeded 30 percent of GDP; the one in Venezuela, certainly more than 20 percent of GDP. Can you imagine the cost of this in terms of schools, health care centers, and basic infrastructure? The countries in Central Asia are in the process of reforming and restructuring their banking sectors; they should make sure that the systems they are creating are built on solid rock—not on sand—by establishing strong market incentives for prudent bank management and a framework of domestic regulation and supervision consistent with international standards.

The third point concerns the need for transparency. When governments are in the habit of providing the public with full information about their policies and the country's economic performance, policymakers have more incentive to pursue responsible policies, and costly policy mistakes and disruptive financial crises are less likely to occur. Moreover, when the financial markets have reliable economic and financial data, they are better able to distinguish between countries that have sound policies and those that do not, and the risk that a crisis will spill over from one country to another is reduced. Transparency also contributes to a more responsible use of public resources for the public good and reduces opportunities for corruption.

In this regard, and let me be very candid here again, one cannot help but observe the similarities between the relationships that existed among enterprises, banks, and government in some East Asian countries under the system of "crony capitalism" and the tendencies one can observe—which still survive or start developing again—in a number of transition economies. As we have seen in East Asia, when the structure of ownership is not transparent, when regulation is inadequate and unevenly applied, when too many ad hoc decisions are taken, and when market forces are prevented from playing their normal disciplining role, serious imbalances and deadly inefficiencies can build up. And, once exposed, these problems can provoke an abrupt market correction.

* * * * *

So these are some of the lessons of experience from other IMF members that face, or have faced, many of the same challenges confronting your countries. These lessons are particularly worthy of consideration today, as we commemorate the introduction of the som. A good currency can only be beneficial insofar as it is strong and stable. And, of course, all of that depends on the quality of the macroeconomic and structural policies that underpin it. In this regard, my remarks today have mostly concerned what the transition economies of Central Asia can learn from the experience of other IMF member countries. But when I come back for the tenth anniversary of the som, I hope to bring a different message—not what your countries can learn from, say, the East Asian "tigers," but what other countries can learn from the success of the "snow leopards" of Central Asia.

---

[1]These reforms included liberalizing agricultural prices, introducing competition among agricultural trading companies, granting families and individuals long-term rights to land use, and

removing internal barriers to trade. See: *Vietnam: Transition to a Market Economy*, IMF Occasional Paper no.135 (Washington: International Monetary Fund, March 1996).

PRIVATIZATION IN TADJIKISTAN

RESOLUTION ON THE STATE PROPERTY COMMITTEE OF THE REPUBLIC OF TAJIKISTAN

State Property Committee (SPC) is the privatization agency of the Republic of Tajikistan.
The SPC is headed by Mr. Davlatov, the Chairman.

I. GENERAL PROVISION

1. The State Property Committee of the Republic of Tajikistan, hereinafter referred as the Committee, is a republican entity of State management which within the limits of its rights delegated by the Government of the Republic of Tajikistan, manages the process of privatization of State property in the Republic of Tajikistan, statues on the order of possession, use, and disposal of State property.
2. The Committee's activity is regulated by the Constitution of the Republic of Tajikistan, the laws of the Republic of Tajikistan, resolutions of Majlisi Oli of the Republic of Tajikistan, Decrees of the President of the Republic of Tajikistan, resolutions and regulations of the Government of the Republic of Tajikistan, international-legal acts recognized by the Republic of Tajikistan, and the present Regulation.
3. The Committee's activity is subordinate to decisions of the Government of the Republic of Tajikistan.

II. BASIC TASKS

4. The basic tasks of the Committee are to:

   Organize and implement the privatization of state property in order to diversify the State's economy and the transformation of State property into other forms of property;

   Manage State property matters of State entities throughout the territory of the Republic of Tajikistan;

   Coordinate the activity of ministries, State Departments, and State Executive Authorities at the local basis on privatization of state property, including the development and realization of the programs of privatization of republican and communal property;
   Participate in creation of stock exchanges and other structures associated with the process of privatization and realization of state policy in the attraction of investments;

Take under control the safety and effective use of State property and accordingly enforce legislation;

5. To fulfill its tasks, the Committee:

Develops programs of privatization of republican and communal property objects together with local Majlisis of People's Deputies, Ministries and State

Departments of the Republic of Tajikistan;

Organizes the implementation of the privatization programs, reports on the privatization process to the Government of the Republic of Tajikistan, and if necessary develops proposals to introduce changes and modifications in the programs;

Generalizes the implementation of the legislation related to its sphere, develops proposals to promote legislative and standard acts of the Republic of Tajikistan on privatization of objects of state property, bankruptcy of enterprises, issues within the limits of its competence as well as standards and other acts regulating the process of privatization and management of state property, and also carries out the control for their performance;

Provides protection of the property rights and interests of the State in the Republic of Tajikistan and abroad;

Carries out control for the proper use and safety of property by legal and physical persons and in case of infringement of the established rules and order on the use the property, the Committee takes necessary measures to enforce the law according to the legislation of the Republic of Tajikistan;

Participates within the limits of its competence in the development and realization of investment programs, elaboration of conditions for concession agreements, and also represents the interests of the proprietor in accordance to the legislation of the Republic of Tajikistan;

Acts on behalf of the Government of the Republic of Tajikistan as an authorized representative for matters related to the property of the former USSR; Participates in the elaboration and fulfillment of measures to support privatized enterprises at the expense of the State Budget in accordance to programs related to post privatization support;

Participates in the elaboration and fulfillment of state policy on prevention of bankruptcy of State enterprises;

Officially approves State property status (whether republican or communal) of economic entities and State Management Authorities, agrees for the sale or lease of real estate property of economic entities, keeps track in a register book of lease contracts of objects of republican property;

Examines and carries out valuations of State property;

Manages Local State Property Committees and issues related to privatization of State Property of Local State Executive Authorities (hukumats);
Concludes agreements and contracts in the name of the Government of the Republic of Tajikistan, on interaction and cooperation in the management of property of the Republic of Tajikistan with foreign state entities and legal persons;
Carries out in accordance with its mandate, necessary actions to eliminate infringement of legislation of the Republic of Tajikistan related to the privatization of State property;

Supervises the privatization of state property carried out by Local Executive Authorities (hukumats). In cases of non abidance to the policy of privatization of state property, the Committee elaborates reasonable proposals to the Government;
Diffuses civic information on legislation of the Republic of Tajikistan on privatization of State property, organizes the training of the staff of the Committee in the headquarters and its local representations;
Determines main measures on privatization of state property and carries out the transformation of state property into other forms of property in accordance with other resolutions of the Government of Tajikistan;

May be the founder of joint-stock company, or other market structures transformed from state owned enterprises, or disposing state property;
Take decisions on the lease of state enterprises and other state property of republican property, organizes their sale to economic entities and individuals;
Organizes and conducts tenders and auctions on sale of state property;

Requests provision of proof and information on the fulfillment of privatization programs as well as information on the safe use of state property, from State Authorities and Local State Executive Entities (hukumats) and economic entities;
Requests provision of documents and information proving infringement of legislation of the Republic of Tajikistan on privatization issues, regulations and management of objects of Republican Property from Ministries, State Departments, and state enterprises, and undertakes appropriate corrective measures;

Stops the sale of property and actions related to the use of state property in case they do not conform to current legislation;

Contests in court decisions on privatization of state property violating the law;
Cancels decisions of Local Property Committees infringing legislation or of exceeding their powers;Publishes periodic printed editions on questions related to its field.

III. ORGANIZATION OF WORK

6. The Chairman of the Committee directs the Committee and is appointed and relieved of his post by the President of the Republic of Tajikistan in accordance

For additional analytical, business and investment opportunities information,
please contact Global Investment & Business Center, USA
at (202) 546-2103. Fax: (202) 546-3275. E-mail: rusric@erols.com

with the Constitution of the Republic of Tajikistan and Decrees of the Majlisi Oli of the Republic of Tajikistan.

7. Deputy Chairmen are appointed and relieved of their posts by the Government of the Republic of Tajikistan upon request by the Chairman of the Committee. The distribution of duties between the Deputy Chairmen is carried out by the Chairman.

8. The chairman of the Committee bears personal responsibility for the fulfillment of the tasks and duties assigned to the Committee, the realization of its powers, and establishes the degree of the Deputy Chairmen's and Chiefs' of Departments' responsibility in the headquarters of the Committee for the organization and management of its respective spheres activity and the performance of duties assigned to them.

9. A Management Board is established within the Committee consisting of the Committee's Chairman, his deputies, chiefs of Departments in the headquarters, as well as other persons.

10. Members of the Management Board are approved and relieved of duty by the Government of the Republic of Tajikistan.

11. Major organizational issues on the development and improvement of the process of privatization of state property, selection and placing of Managerial Committee Staff and issues on the practical management of the activity of different departments and local representations are considered by the Management Board, provided that necessary accounts are given by Local Executive Authorities (hukumats), Ministries, State Departments, enterprises, organizations and other economic entities related to the field.

12. Resolutions of the Management Board are enforced as a rule by order of the Chairman of the Committee. In case of disagreements between the Chairman of the Committee and the Management Board, the Chairman enacts his decision, reporting disagreements to the Government of the Republic of Tajikistan; the members of Management Board may however, in their turn, inform the Government of the Republic of Tajikistan about their opinion.

13. In order to consider professional recommendations and proposals concerning the basic activity of the Committee, its improvement, methods and techniques of privatization of state property and important programs of privatization of state property, councils and commissions are created within the Committee by leading specialists and highly skilled experts without being additionally financed and with the consent of the chiefs of the bodies of state governing of industrial structures, and trade-union bodies.

14. The structure, number and payment fund for the central apparatus employees of the Committee are approved by the Government of Republic of Tajikistan. The Chairman of the Committee has the right to introduce changes and modifications in the structure of the Committee in the limits of established number and payment fund.

15. Manning table and estimate of the expenses of the central apparatus of the Committee and also regulations on structural divisions of the territorial bodies of the Committee are approved by the chairman of the Committee.

16. Running costs for the central apparatus of the Committee are made at the expense of the republican budget.

17. The Committee is a legal entity, has its own balance, accounts in the savings bank departments, a seal with the State Emblem of the Republic of Tajikistan and its name in the Tajik and Russian languages.

PRIVATIZATION PROCESS

While political and criminal violence are what generally place Tajikistan in the news, almost unnoticed is the dramatic progress the country has made in stabilizing the economy, promoting growth, and particularly in accelerating privatization. On the one hand, the Government is dealing with a myriad of factions and military groups, settling its own prolonged civil war, and working to maintain civil stability. Impressively, at the same time the Government, backed by the IMF and World Bank, is pushing through an aggressive and far reaching privatization program.

Small scale privatization is over 60% complete in the country, and will be complete in 1999, if the current pace is sustained. More small scale businesses have been privatized in the first 7 months of 1998 than in any other year, and the country currently plans to sell 1000 small scale businesses before the end of the year, about half of all those remaining.

The degree of medium and large scale enterprise privatization is not as high, but in the first 8 months of 1998, 4 auctions were held for shares, and the Government's target is to reach 50 enterprises sold by end September. In 1998 147 state enterprises registered as corporations and prepared the necessary documents for sale, while in the previous 7 years of the privatization program, only 23 did so.

Much of the pressure for this acceleration of privatization comes from privatization conditions established by the World Bank and International Monetary Fund, which have transformed the privatization process over the last year and a half. In 1997, a new Privatization Law was passed, which changed the process from a bottom up, negotiated sale to collectives on an enterprise by enterprise basis to an open, competitive and top down program with more rapid wholesale transfer of assets into the private sector. Additional legal measures were adopted through 1997 and 1998 to support this new process, and the World Bank and IMF have kept up constant monitoring to ensure that the momentum continued.

Changing a privatization system that developed over 7 years into a corrupt, closed sales process cannot be achieved overnight. Privatization is always and everywhere a highly politically charged undertaking without a strong base of support, since the benefits (lower prices, lower taxes, better products or services) are widespread, while the costs (lost jobs, lost power) are concentrated. In Tajikistan these problems are further compounded by the presence of paramilitary groups and armed criminals, who are not afraid of using their muscle to take whatever they can.

While the auction process has accelerated, and has proven successful particularly in the more developed and commercial northern part of the country, in other areas auctions have not always been easy to implement. In the capital, an auction held in May featured soldiers shouting and waving their guns around, arguing that they had already paid for the object (in bribes). Further east, auctions have been canceled completely due to the fighting which still flares up occasionally. In one shares auction in Dushanbe, a single bidder was given two numbers, and proceeded to bid against himself (the law requires at least two bidders). When asked what he was doing, he replied candidly "My friend couldn't come."

Even when the small scale privatization process is declared "complete" in 1999, in fact there will remain many small scale enterprises which should be sold or whose ownership will have to change. The state property committee database contains 6974 small scale enterprises, of which 3178 are privatized, and 1694 not subject to automatic privatization. This database seems like a large number of small businesses until two other factors are considered: Tajikpotrebsoyuz, the nominally private consumer cooperative, and enterprises on farms, which are subject to privatization as the farm privatizes. The former controls about 12,000 enterprises all over the countryside, while the latter compromises about 2000 small enterprises. Until these issues are dealt with, the retail sector in the countryside will not develop fully.

In medium and large scale businesses, share sales are really just beginning, and the State Property Committee is still working out the kinks. Thus far, shares have been offered for sale in 125 enterprises. Of these, 47 have been privatized through auctions, with the criteria for privatization set at 75% sold. In September, the State Property Committee will be conducting at least two more auctions, in order to reach the Government's target of 50 medium and large enterprises sold by the end of September.

Share sales equally are not without their own specific problems. Many buyers of shares do not truly understand the nature of corporations, and there are continuing legal issues to be resolved within the securities market framework. The World Bank is providing technical assistance to assist the Government in this, and over the last year the laws on corporations and securities and stock exchanges have both been amended and improved. The basic framework for the securities market is therefore in place, while smaller technical questions will be solved in the coming months.

Privatization is a difficult undertaking in any environment. In Tajikistan, with continuing political and rule of law problems, provides even more challenges than usual. Prices received for enterprises are lower than could be expected, depriving a strapped budget of badly needed revenues, and increasing criticism of the process. Corruption and violence still affect the privatization process, though decreasingly. In spite of this, the process moves forward, creating a base of new entrepreneurs and owners who have a greater stake in peace and stability, which could, over the long run, contribute to solving the larger problems.

CURRENT SITUATION IN PRIVATIZATION

PROBLEMS AND RECOMMENDATIONS

I. OVERALL SITUATION

The current pace of privatization is very slow. Small scale privatization has made hardly any progress since September, and there are few objects scheduled until the end of the year. Incorporation of medium and large enterprises is going too slowly as well, and the target of 200 registered shares emissions will most likely not be met soon. Share auctions are taking place, but in many cases enterprises are being offered repeatedly and not sold, and in other cases enterprises are sold, but buyers refuse to pay in the end. Privatization of truck transport is very slow, and more trucks are becoming completely unusable each month than are being sold. Unfinished construction is not being sold at a reasonable pace. Cotton ginneries, the most important aspect of the privatization program, are not even registering as joint stock companies and a huge amount of work remains to be done in this sphere.

II. SMALL SCALE PRIVATIZATION - CURRENT SITUATION

Since September, when an IMF deadline caused a sharp increase in sales, only 42 small scale enterprises have been sold. At this time, if we do not count Dushanbe, only 4 auctions are being prepared, for 29 objects. At a time when not fewer than 100 objects per month should be sold, only 21 objects are being sold per month. The World Bank has set an overall target of 2000 small scale objects to be sold before the second tranche is given. Currently, 979 small scale objects have been sold in 1998. If the current pace continues, the second tranche, small scale privatization condition will be met in April 2004. The IMF and the Government's medium term economic program require that small scale privatization be completed by March 1999, which would require 250 small scale enterprises to be sold per month.

III. SMALL SCALE PRIVATIZATION - PROBLEMS

There are many problems with the small scale privatization process at this time. First among these is the fact that there is no consistent force requiring small scale privatization to move forward. Whenever an IMF target comes up, pressure is applied through telegrams from the Government. These telegrams have less effect each time, and more raions do not meet their targets. As soon as the deadline passes, privatization is forgotten until the next panic.

Related to this problem is that in spite of a clear legal framework giving the Government authority to delegate privatization authority to the SPC, no object is privatized without the approval and assent of some committee, ministry, torg or association. All these approvals and cooperations require additional time, and frequently petty officials refuse to cooperate, which means more objects are lost to the process.

Another problem is that for many, the primary focus of the privatization process is to raise revenues immediately. Thus, when an object is sold for a low price, officials begin to cry foul and create a scandal over it. In fact, many small scale objects still in state hands are completely closed and being robbed of their glass, window frames and anything else that can be removed. This emphasis on raising revenue means that small scale enterprises are not sold because the state authorities demand too much money for them. The recently approved inflation coefficients, which increase starting prices about 3 times over what they were before. Already, sales rates at auctions in the south are dropping (we are now selling about 30% of offered objects, compared to 50% before), and in some cases the local authorities simply don't bother organizing auctions because they know the prices will be too high.

Related to this is the fear of organizing Dutch auctions. Dutch auctions are a useful mechanism for selling a large number of objects quickly. As long as there is a focus on receiving high prices for objects, Dutch auctions cannot be used.

The focus of privatization is not to raise revenue, but to change ownership, encourage investment and maximize use of assets. Privatization builds a tax base and generates employment and these messages need to be emphasized over the revenue from sales. Ironically, the at the same time as officials complain about low prices received for objects, they also complain that the population does not have money to purchase enterprises. Basic economics teaches that low prices are precisely the result of this low purchasing power. Privatization gives the citizens the chance to make themselves rich, which is the point of the policy.

IV. SMALL SCALE PRIVATIZATION - RECOMMENDATIONS

The recommendations for the privatization process are simple, but not easy to implement. They are mostly political in nature.

    a. Punish raions which do not meet their privatization target. Thus far, there has been no punishment for local officials who refuse to sell small scale objects. Unless they feel this is an important government policy, they will not bother to implement it.

    b. Punish ministries or committee heads who refuse to cooperate with the privatization process. Again, many low level bureaucrats are simply stalling the privatization process, and nothing is done.

    c. Insist on sale of Republican objects. Over 500 objects of Republican property exist which can be sold. The Chairman of the SPC has moved too slowly on selling these objects, and has increased prices to such an extent that there are no interested buyers. These objects must be sold if the Government is to meet its target.

    d. Approve the sale of pharmacies and gas stations. Two draft decrees are in process to include pharmacies and gas stations in the privatization process. There are approximately 400 pharmacies which can be sold, and over 100 gas stations. The gas stations are technically already subject to privatization, and legally this decree is not necessary, but Tajiknefteprodukt is one example of the kind of organization which has stopped privatization of "its" enterprises so far.

V. INCORPORATION OF MEDIUM AND LARGE ENTERPRISES - CURRENT SITUATION

The World Bank requires that 600 medium and large enterprises be incorporated (register shares emissions) by end March 1999 (second tranche)

For additional analytical, business and investment opportunities information, please contact Global Investment & Business Center, USA at (202) 546-2103. Fax: (202) 546-3275. E-mail: rusric@erols.com

At this time, only 182 enterprises have registered their shares emissions since January 1998, and the pace of incorporation has slowed tremendously in recent months. Since September, only 32 emissions have been registered, and the process is slowing down. Ministries, enterprise directors, the Center for Valuation and the State Property Committee are all slowing the process down. Many enterprise directors are refusing to cooperate in registering their shares emissions, and others are refusing to register their enterprises as joint stock companies.

VI. INCORPORATION OF MEDIUM AND LARGE ENTERPRISES - PROBLEMS

The problems in incorporation of medium and large enterprises are similar to those with small scale privatization, and are related to pricing and political issues.

Enterprise directors are not interested in cooperating in the incorporation and shares emission process. In many cases they fear that someone else will buy their enterprise and they will lose their jobs. Because starting prices are set so high, the enterprise directors and collectives cannot purchase the enterprises, and so the process stops. In fact, 32 enterprises have documentation prepared for registering their shares emission (although in many cases this will have to be re-done, because of the new coefficients) and simply refused to submit their documentation.

Fees for enterprises registering as joint stock companies and registering their shares emission also prevent the process from moving forward. The Republican Center for Valuation charges for its services in many cases, and has a monopoly on the valuation process. Some enterprise directors insist that they cannot pay for these services, and the process stops.

VII. INCORPORATION OF MEDIUM AND LARGE ENTERPRISES - RECOMMENDATIONS

The problems with incorporation need to be solved at a high level, and line ministries and enterprise directors need to be forced to participate in the program. If problems with share sales can be solved (see below) then the process will likely move forward on its own.

  a. First, line ministries must be given clear orders to require their enterprises to complete incorporation and registration of shares emission. This has recently been done, with letters signed by the Prime Minister. Close control needs to be maintained over these orders, and if there are non compliances, some form of punishment must be given out. Unless there is some punishment for failure, there will be no success.
  b. Second, enterprise managers must be made to understand that they are required to complete this process, regardless of whether they will buy the enterprise or not.
  c. Third, those organizations participating in the process (notaries, Center for Valuation, local authorities) must also be made to understand that this process is

of the highest priority and that they must not slow it down. The incorporation process involves many approvals and authorizations, and each step along the way is slowing the process.

VIII. PRIVATIZATION OF MEDIUM AND LARGE ENTERPRISES - CURRENT SITUATION

The requirement of the World Bank for second tranche, and of the IMF for the next ESAF, is that 70 enterprises be sold by end 1998 and 120 by end March 1999. At this time, only 30 medium and large enterprises have been privatized since January, according to the World Bank and IMF definition (75% shares sold and paid for). This means that in December, 40 companies must be sold, and in the first three months of 1999, another 30 companies must be sold.

There are currently 144 companies which are ready to sell, with prepared shares emissions registered. In fact, 150 of these companies have been offered at auction already once, 42 have been offered twice, 24 have been offered three times, and 13 have been offered four or more times. 10 auctions have been organized in 1998, and another auction is to be organized soon.

IX. PRIVATIZATION OF MEDIUM AND LARGE ENTERPRISES - PROBLEMS

There is only one main problem in the sale of shares in medium and large enterprises, and that is price. Price continues to be the most important issue in selling medium and large enterprises, and because the SPC is so concerned about selling enterprises for a high price, the Government risks losing the IMF and World bank supports.

The problem of too high prices also affects incorporation. Because the prices are too high, the enterprise directors refuse to participate in the incorporation process. They know they cannot afford to buy the enterprise, so they refuse to cooperate at all. If we can solve the problem of high prices, then the process will move forward.

X. PRIVATIZATION OF MEDIUM AND LARGE ENTERPRISES - RECOMMENDATIONS

The only way to increase sales of medium and large enterprises is to lower the prices of the enterprises. Until prices fall, the enterprises will remain unsold. There is not enough money in the population to buy the shares at the current prices. It is ironic that the SPC is trying to take more money from locals, and in the process losing money that could be gotten from the international organizations. The SPC is choking Tajiks for a few pennies while the foreigners are willing to give money.

XI. COTTON GINNERIES PRIVATIZATION - CURRENT STATUS

The privatization of cotton ginneries is the most important aspect of the privatization program at this time. The World Bank and the IMF require that the international tender for cotton ginneries begin in mid December, and the World Bank requires that the ginneries be privatized by end March 1999. At this time, only 7 ginneries have registered shares emissions. An additional 6 are incorporated but without registered shares emissions, an additional 4 are in the process of incorporation and 6 are not being prepared for incorporation at all. the status of the various ginneries is given in Attachment 1. A great deal of work remains to be done on these ginneries, but the directors of the ginneries refuse to cooperate, and Pakhtai Tojik has so far not ordered them to do so.

In addition, no progress is being made on the procedure for the international tender itself. The advertisement draft, which was left by the World Bank, contains quite specific information about the tender procedure. Before the advertisement is placed, these procedures must be agreed upon and established. Attachment 2 gives some ideas about what needs to be done.

XII. COTTON GINNERIES PRIVATIZATION - PROBLEMS

There are three fundamental problems with cotton ginnery privatization.

a. First, the ginneries are not cooperating with the incorporation process. Glavhlopkaprom has for a long time slowed the process, and other organizations are also slowing down the process as well.
b. Second, the Regulation on Case by Case Privatization is not passed. The sale cannot take place without this regulation approved by the Government.
c. Third, the advertisement for the international tender is not yet prepared, and the main policy decisions regarding this are not made. There are many important issues that must be decided, regarding the cotton ginnery privatization.

XIII. COTTON GINNERIES PRIVATIZATION - RECOMMENDATIONS

The problems with the privatization of cotton ginneries are not complicated to resolve, but it will take consistent attention from the highest levels of government.

First, the Government must order the immediate incorporation of all ginneries, and registration of their shares emissions. All intermediate organizations, such as Pakhtai Tojik, the Ministry of Agriculture, the Republican Center for Valuation, the notaries and others must be aware that nothing should delay this process.

Second, the Government must review and approve the Regulation on Case by Case Privatization. Without this, international investors will have no idea how the tender is to proceed.

Third, the Government must establish the Commission for the tender, which must immediately work out the exact procedures for the tender. Some sample questions are given in Attachment 2.

XIV. LIQUIDATION OF RCPT

The World Bank requires, as a second tranche condition, the sale of the RCPT, sale of its assets, and transfer of its non commercial functions to the Ministry of Agriculture by 1 January 1999.

No progress is being made on this issue, as far as we are aware.

XV. TRUCK TRANSPORT PRIVATIZATION - CURRENT SITUATION

The World Bank requirement for truck transport privatization is that 30,000 state owned trucks be either written off or sold by the time of the second tranche, which the World Bank and IMF envision as end March. Virtually no progress has been made on this issue at all, and the process has continued very slowly. Exact data is not known, since there is no centralized mechanism for monitoring privatization of truck transport. The only statistics available are from the GAI, and those will be known only in January. However, it is safe to say that it will require a massive national effort to meet this goal by end March.

At this time, an estimated 71 vehicles are falling out of use every day from the national truck fleet, and the state owned trucking enterprises cannot replace them for lack of funds. 51 transport enterprises, meanwhile, were amalgamated into 4 joint stock companies, and none of these could be privatized, because the charter fund was too high. The enterprises themselves cannot operate, because the new structure of the joint stock companies is exactly the same as that of the old ministry, and the enterprise managers have no freedom to restructure. This mistake seems to be slowly being corrected.

Recently, a decree on writing off and sale of trucks and means of transport was adopted, which will help accelerate the process. This will require a great deal of support from the line ministries to implement, however, and the problem of selling prices for vehicles will likely slow the process down once again.

XVI. TRUCK TRANSPORT PRIVATIZATION - PROBLEMS

The problems for truck transport privatization and writing off are still unknown, since the process has not started fully yet. However, certain problems can be anticipated.

Price will once again be a problem, most likely. Since the resolution specifies that trucks should be written off or sold, enterprise managers will probably be blamed or accused if they write off trucks, or if they sell them for low prices. Thus, once again, price will be an issue and the Government will risk losing IMF and World Bank credits because of some rusted vehicles.

Reporting will certainly be an issue. There is no centralized reporting system, and it will be very difficult to keep track of how many trucks have been sold or written off. Forms are being developed, but implementing of these forms is not certain.

Dissemination of information and mobilization of resources will be important problems. In order to complete this huge volume of work, it will be necessary to organize directors of all transport companies, many directors of farms and other organizations, and explain the procedure to them.

XVII. TRUCK TRANSPORT PRIVATIZATION - RECOMMENDATIONS

In order to implement the truck transport program, and overcome the problems mentioned above, certain steps need to be taken immediately.

   a. The Ministers of Transport and Agriculture must be informed of the signing of the decree, and be required to inform their enterprises of the decree and the need to implement it.
   b. Regional seminars must be organized with staff of the Ministry of Transport, Agriculture, State Property Committee and Carana Corporation giving consultation on how to implement the decree.
   c. Reporting on the number of trucks written off and sold should be implemented through the ministries and seminars.

Unfinished Construction Privatization - Current Status, Problems and Recommendations

There are currently 343 unfinished construction sites remaining to be privatized. In 1998, 11 enterprises were sold, after 6 announcements were made for tenders. The last attempt to see unfinished construction sites was made on 9 October 1998.

It may be the case that, under current circumstances, there are no buyers for an unfinished construction site. However, that is rare, since for 0 dollars, someone would take the site and simply strip the building materials. Obviously, this is not the best result economically, but a crumbling unfinished construction site is also economically useless and only loses value.

Therefore, unfinished construction sites must be offered, in a well publicized announcement, with minimum starting prices. At first, conditions to complete the object may be attached, but in a second offering, no conditions should be attached.

XVIII. CONCLUSION

In spite of good progress on small scale privatization in 1998, the process not even half finished yet. Over 1000 objects remain to be sold, and this process should be completed in 4 months, which will mean a pace of small scale privatization almost as fast as than the period before the 15th of May deadline. Incorporation is also critical, and more enterprises now must register their shares emission each month than did in all of 1998, which was a fast year, in order to meet the World Bank and IMF conditions by March 1999. Sales of companies must accelerate also, and for this to happen, prices will have to drop dramatically, but there is no political will to do this at this time.

Most importantly of all, however, the privatization of the cotton ginneries, through international tender, must take place in the coming months, and this will require a concentrated effort in even in the next two weeks, in order to prepare the advertisement for the international tender. Carana Corporation is locating a consultant to advise the Government and SPC on the international tender, whom we hope will be able to travel immediately.

In the middle of 1998 there was the chance to keep the pace of privatization up, and meet the targets. That chance was lost, and unless a concentrated effort is made, the second tranches could slip further and further into the future

For additional analytical, business and investment opportunities information, please contact Global Investment & Business Center, USA at (202) 546-2103. Fax: (202) 546-3275. E-mail: rusric@erols.com

GLOBAL BUSINESS, RESEARCH AND POLITICAL LIBRARIES

RUSSIA BUSINESS LAW HANDBOOK

SOUTH AFRICA INVESTMENT & BUSINESS GUIDE

JAPAN BUSINESS & INVESTMENT OPPORTUNITIES YEARBOOK

BAHAMAS OFFSHORE INVESTMENT & BUSINESS GUIDE

LIBYA A "SPY" GUIDE

CHINA FOREIGN POLICY GOVERNMENT & GUIDE

RUSSIA A COUNTRY STUDY

INDIA BUSINESS INTELLIGENCE REPORT

US-ISRAEL POLITICAL & ECONOMIC COOPERATION HANDBOOK

ARMENIA EXPORT-IMPORT & BUSINESS DIRECTORY

Guides, reports and handbooks are available for the following countries:

Albania	Central African	Gabon	Lebanon	Niger	Solomon
Algeria	Republic	Gambia	Lesotho	Nigeria	Islands
Andorra	Chad	Georgia	Liberia	Norway	Somalia
Angola	Chile	Germany	Libya	Oman	South Africa
Antigua and	China	Ghana	Liechtenstein	Pakistan	Spain
Barbuda	Colombia	Greece	Lithuania	Palau	Sri Lanka
Argentina	Comoros	Grenada	Luxembourg	Panama	Sudan
Armenia	Congo,	Guatemala	Macedonia	Papua New	Suriname
Australia	Democratic	Guinea	Madagascar	Guinea	Swaziland
Austria	Republic	Guinea-Bissau	Malawi	Paraguay	Sweden
Azerbaijan	Costa Rica	Guyana	Malaysia	Peru	Switzerland
Bahamas	Côte d'Ivoire	Haiti	Maldives	Philippines	Syria
Bahrain	Croatia	Honduras	Mali	Poland	Taiwan
Bangladesh	Cuba	Hungary	Malta	Portugal	Tajikistan
Barbados	Cyprus	Iceland	Marshall	Qatar	Tanzania
Belarus	Czech Republic	India	Islands	Romania	Thailand
Belgium	Denmark	Indonesia	Mauritania	Russia	Togo
Belize	Djibouti	Iran	Mauritius	Rwanda	Tonga
Benin	Dominica	Ireland	Mexico	Saint Kitts &	Trinidad &
Bhutan	Dominican	Israel	Micronesia	Nevis	Tobago
Bolivia	Republic	Italy	Moldova	Saint Lucia	Tunisia
Bosnia &	Ecuador	Jamaica	Monaco	Saint Vincent	Turkey
Herzegovina	Egypt	Japan	Mongolia	& Grenadines	Turkmenistan
Botswana	El Salvador	Jordan	Morocco	San Marino	Tuvalu
Brazil	Equatorial	Kazakhstan	Mozambique	San Tome	Uganda
Brunei	Guinea	Kenya	Myanmar	and Principe	Ukraine
Bulgaria	Eritrea	Kiribati	(Burma)	Saudi Arabia	United Arab
Burkina Faso	Estonia	Korea, North	Namibia	Senegal	Emirates
Burundi	Ethiopia	Korea, South	Nauru	Seychelles	United
Cambodia	Faroe Islands	Kuwait	Nepal	Sierra Leone	Kingdom
Cameroon	Fiji	Kyrgyzstan	Netherlands	Singapore	United States
Canada	Finland	Laos	New Zealand	Slovakia	Uruguay
Cape Verde	France	Latvia	Nicaragua	Slovenia	Uzbekistan

Please send your order to
International Business Publications, USA, P.O. Box 15343. Washington, DC 20003
Download the catalog or purchase our products on line at Global Markets on Line: http://world.mirhouse.com
Ph: (202) 546-2103 Fax: (202) 546-3275 E-mail: rusric@erols.com
All guides are available in electronic format on CD-ROM

Doing business in newly developing Central Asian Markets

by
Fuat Berk Kırlı

International Technology Transfer Management
TFH-University of Applied Sciences
Berlin, April 2005

Introduction

- Goal of the Study
  - Overview to trade and investment climate of the Region
  - Focuses key challenges and opportunities
  - Provides a projection for home appliances market

- Methodology
  - P.E.S.T. Analysis (Qualitative analysis)
  - Mc Kinsey/GE Matrix (Quantitative analysis)

Analysis of Business Climate

- □ Politics
- □ Economics
- □ Socio-cultural
- □ Technology

Kazakhstan

Uzbekistan

Turkmenistan

Kyrgyzstan

Tajikistan

Politics

	Kazakhstan	Uzbekistan	Turkmenistan	Kyrgyz Rep.	Tajikistan
Political Stability	●	●	●	●	◕
Major political issues affecting business climate	◕	◕	◕	◑	◑
Trade barriers and import tariffs	◕	◕	◕	◑	◑
Intellectual Property Protection	◑	◑	◑	◑	◔
Infrastructure	◕	◕	◑	◑	◑

	Kazakhstan	Uzbekistan	Turkmenistan	Kyrgyz Rep.	Tajikistan
Recent Economic Performance					
Macroeconomic Outlook					
Openness to foreign trade and investment					
Distribution and sales channels					
Finding partners					
Advertising and trade promotion					
After sales service and customer support					
Selling to the Government					

Socio-cultural

	Kazakhstan	Uzbekistan	Turkmenistan	Kyrgyz Rep.	Tajikistan
Population	◑	●	◑	◑	◔
Area	●	◕	◕	◑	◑
Population below national poverty line	◕	◕	◕	◑	◑
Income Distribution	◕	◕	◕	◑	◑
Education	◕	◕	◕	◕	◕
Consumer Behaviors/ tendencies	◑	◑	◑	◔	◔

	Kazakhstan	Uzbekistan	Turkmenistan	Kyrgyz Rep.	Tajikistan
Telecommuni cation infrastructure	◕	◕	◔	◑	◑
IT Sector	◕	◔	◑	◑	◑
Government support on technology effort	◔	◔	◑	◑	◑
E-Commerce facilities	◔	◔	○	○	○

Home Appliances Market Analysis

- Introduction
  - Information about home appliance Industry
  - Market for home appliance industry in Central Asia
  - Market Size and Growth
- B/S/H/-PEG in Central Asia
- Mc Kinsey / GE Matrix for B/S/H/-PEG
  - Determination of Drivers
    - Market Attractiveness Factors (Vertical Axis)
    - Competitive Strength-Factors (Horizontal Axis)
  - Calculations & The Graphs

Kazakhstan

Kyrgyzstan

Uzbekistan

Tajikistan

Turkmenistan

B/S/H/-PEG in Central Asia

Central Asia Sales

Sales vs. Population

Desired market share

Market shares

Euro

Kazakhstan

Uzbekistan

Turkmenistan

Kyrgyzstan

Tajikistan

Mc Kinsey / GE Matrix for B/S/H/-PEG

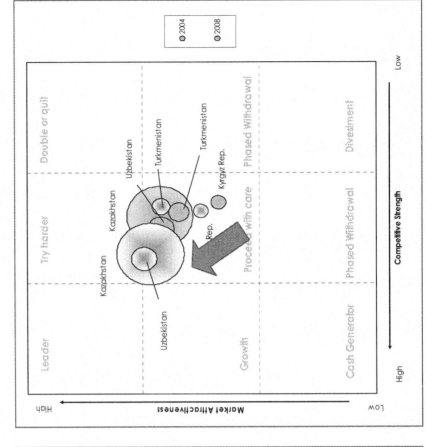

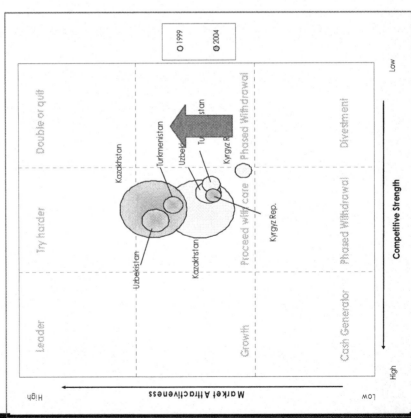

Conclusion

☐ Strengths & Weaknesses

☐ Key Opportunities & Constraints

☐ Challenges for the future

Kazakhstan

Uzbekistan

Kyrgyzstan

Turkmenistan

Tajikistan

Strengths & Weaknesses

Weaknesses

☐ Trade barriers including legislations

☐ Intellectual Property Protection

☐ Infrastructure

☐ Income Distribution / Poverty

☐ Consumer behaviors / Tendencies

☐ Technological infrastructure

Strengths

☐ Political Stability

☐ Economic Performance

☐ Macroeconomic Outlook

☐ Openness to foreign trade & investment

☐ Business environment

☐ Natural resources

☐ Huge Marketing playground

☐ Human Capital

Kazakhstan
Uzbekistan
Kyrgyzstan
Turkmenistan
Tajikistan

Key Opportunities & Constraints

Opportunities

- The recent economic recovery

- The region's natural resources

- The countries' human capital

- The enhanced willingness of the countries' leaderships to push forward with reforms and regional cooperation

- The increased international attention to Central Asia

- Population

- Political Stability

Constraints

- Weak democratic institutions and social capital

- Lack of market access

- Limited commitment to reform, capacity building and regional cooperation

- Lack of resources for public investment and social spending (for some)

- Debt overhang (for some)

- Weak institutional capacity and investment climate (for some)

Kazakhstan

Kyrgyzstan

Tajikistan

Uzbekistan

Turkmenistan

Challenges for the future

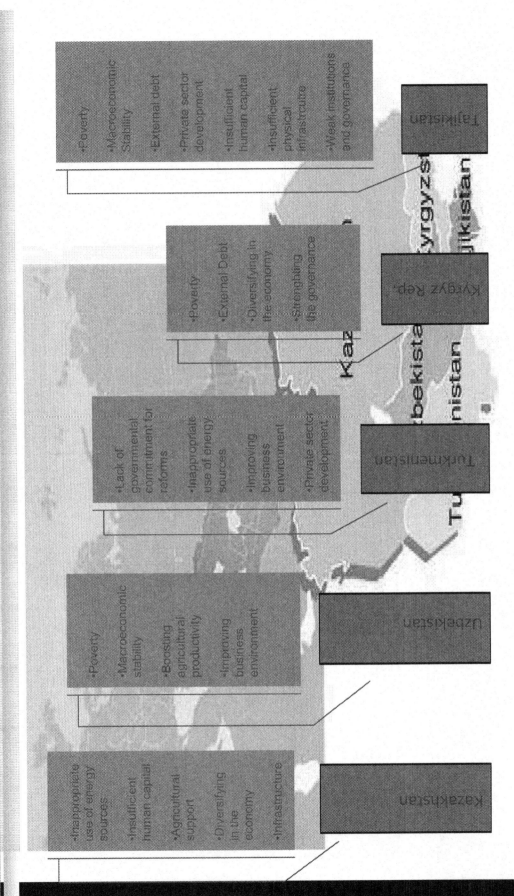

Thanks ...

Area: 143,100 sq km
Capital: Dushanbe
Population: 6,578,681
Population Growth Rate: 2.12% (2001 est)
Ethnic groups: Tajik 64.9%, Uzbek 25%, Russian 3.5% (declining because of emigration), other 6.6%
Life Expectancy: male 61.09 yrs; female 67.42 yrs
Birth Rate: 33.23 births/1,000 population
Infant Mortality: 116.09 deaths/1,000 live births
Per Capita Income: $286 (IMF World Economic Outlook; 2002 estimate)
Religion: Sunni Muslim 80%, Shi'a Muslim 5%
Language: Tajik (official), Russian widely used in government and business
Literacy: total 98%; male 99%; female 97%

President: Emomali Rahmonov
Prime Minister: Oqil Oqilov
Ambassador to the US: Rashid Alimov

Development Challenge

Tajikistan is a front line state in the War on Terrorism and, despite risks from its own Islamists, quickly gave the U.S. necessary access for the intervention in Afghanistan. Its role in the conflict and humanitarian relief has been essential. The most disadvantaged of the Central Asian republics, Tajikistan has limited resources, is landlocked with few transportation links, was ravaged by several years of civil war, and is one of the poorest countries in Asia. Lawlessness and trafficking in both arms and drugs remain a U.S. concern.

Notwithstanding its disadvantages, Tajikistan is successfully, if haltingly, making a transition to normalcy, civil order and democracy. Despite several potentially destabilizing events during 2001, such as the assassination of cabinet officials by unknown assailants, the various parties remain committed to peace even as they struggle for influence within the political landscape. The government continues to work to maintain a balance between various factions, including from the president's party and former opposition members integrated into the government following the 1997 Peace Accord. The peace process resulted in a unique coalition government (of Islamists and former Communists), and the Islamists are a vocal opposition. Yet, governance and rule of law remain weak. In 2001, Freedom House characterized Tajikistan as "not free", and its political rights and civil liberties ratings are both 6 out of 7, with 7 the lowest degree of freedom.

Corruption and local abuse of power are pervasive. Anecdotal evidence suggests that bribery is necessary for most transactions with the government, as well as for health services and training. Weak government institutions, deteriorated infrastructure and social services, and a largely subsistence (and criminalized) economy limit the pace of reform. Reforms are, however, moving forward, and economy grew modestly by about 10% last year. Since privatization began in 1991, Tajikistan has privatized nearly 5,500, an estimated 83%, of its small state-owned properties. The agricultural sector, which employs over 60% of the population, is seriously constrained by the deterioration of the country's irrigation infrastructure and a lack of quality inputs. The economy as a whole remains overly dependent on its two main exports, cotton and aluminum, the earnings from which are controlled by politically connected elites. Tajikistan has the lowest per capita GDP ($286) among the 15 former Soviet republics, and inflation in 2001 was 35.5%. Thus far, the government has not been able to establish the rule of law sufficiently to attract the domestic and foreign investment needed to spur economic growth. The perceived inability of the government to prevent either Islamic extremists or drug traffickers from transiting prompted the Government of Uzbekistan to severely restrict movements across their common border, effectively shutting off much of Tajikistan's international trade and migratory labor. Two successive years of drought have further set back the country's economic recovery.

Tajikistan's social indicators reflect the seriousness of the problem it faces: 80% of the population is below the poverty line, with 17% in extreme poverty. A recent national nutritional assessment found 17.3% acute malnutrition, with 4.2% severe malnutrition, and 37.9% chronic malnutrition. Tajikistan has the highest rates of infant mortality in Central Asia, with an estimated 116 deaths per every 1,000 live births. According to World Bank estimates, Tajikistan's total external debt is slightly over $1.2 billion, 129 percent of GDP, mostly to Russia and Uzbekistan. Debt servicing is expected to require 50% of total government revenues in 2002.

Contact Information

USAID/Central Asia Region (CAR)
Mission Director George Deikun
Park Palace Building
41 Kazibek Bi Street
Almaty, Kazakhstan 480100
Tel: 011-7-3272-50-76-12/17
Fax: 011-7-3272-50-76-35/36

Tajikistan Country Representative
Michael Harvey
Park Palace Building
41 Kazibek Bi Street
Almaty, Kazakhstan 480100
Tel: 011-7-3272-50-76-12/17
Fax: 011-7-3272-50-76-35/36

USAID/Washington
Central Asia Desk Officer Tim Alexander
Tel: 202-712-1669

USAID/CAR website: http://www.usaid.gov/regions/europe_eurasia/car/index.html

Overview of USAID's Focus in Tajikistan

Economic Reform and Private Sector Development Despite the government's willingness to reform its economy, political, and social instability remained a serious obstacle to the successful implementation of USAID reforms. In FY 2001, 735 Tajik entrepreneurs were trained in western business methods, and USAID training also helped 622 (49% women) bookkeepers become professional accountants, practitioners, and technicians. Similarly, EdNet watched network membership grow to 14 universities in less than a year, and supported two Visiting International Professors (VIPs). These VIPs helped develop their respective departments and delivered training and seminars to students and faculty in modern business principles and market economics. Tajikistan's leading accounting association qualified for membership in the International Council of Certified Accountants and Auditors (ICCAA). ICCAA is establishing an internationally recognized education, examination, and certification program in the Russian language. USAID worked broadly with the Tajik judiciary to create a more transparent and orderly system of justice. Advisors created a legal database of Tajik laws and normative acts that is the most comprehensive collection of its kind in Tajikistan. USAID advisors also assisted in the preparation of draft language for Intellectual Property Rights in the Tajik Civil Code. USAID played a key role in developing and implementing a successful examination process for prospective and sitting Tajik judges in FY 2001 and trained a core group of Tajik judges to establish an institutional judicial training mechanism. A court computerization program was launched at the City Court of Dushanbe, and training was provided to Dushanbe City Court and Council of Justice personnel which enables them to effectively use the legal database and computer equipment.

Water and Energy Management Up until now, USAID has had very few water and energy activities in Tajikistan due to security concerns and limited access to water and energy officials by advisors. Out of country training was the main focus of activities. With the easing of travel restrictions, we expect a significant increase in activities, especially in water. Staff of the Tajik National Hydromet Service are full participants in the regional snowmelt runoff committee that meets semi-annually to improve water allocations for the Central Asia region. They have begun collecting and processing water data for which USAID provided equipment and training. Several water courses were funded by USAID in cooperation with the Canadian Agency for International Development, through which Tajik water officials and managers better acquainted themselves with international water law, transboundary water management, and integrated water practices to improve irrigation efficiency. By the completion date of the activity, water managers should have the necessary tools and training to better collect, communicate and process water data resulting in improved allocations and overall management of the resource. Also, water and energy agreements will be based more on objective data and standards, thereby mitigating their potential for conflict.

Strengthening Democratic Culture and Institutions Despite the difficult travel situation to and within Tajikistan (and the security situation which demands restricted travel), support to Tajikistan's NGOs led to a marked improvement in NGO advocacy, service provision, and organizational capacity. The first independent radio station in Tajikistan, Radio Tiroz, opened in Khojand. Recommendations made by the Poverty Reduction Strategy Working Groups on public sector reform and improving parliamentary and judicial professionalism and independence were accepted by the President. USAID implementing partners ensured the participation of parliamentarians, judges, and NGOs in the process. This more participatory process resulted in recommendations including opening the parliamentary committee process and removing the judiciary from the control of the Ministry of Justice. Open meetings and seminars bringing together parliamentarians and NGOs on specific legislation are being held more frequently. Topics have included the family code, criminal procedure code, law on registering legal entities, and others. Three NGOs that received coalition-building technical assistance from USAID's local NGO resource center joined together to battle drug addiction among youth. Youth Initiative Center Ittifok, No Drugs, and Public Television SM1 created the coalition Youth Against Drugs to prevent further increases in drug addiction among youth. USAID-funded interactive training and roundtables by the coalition on the harmful effect of drugs has resulted in a marked decrease in drug addiction in the area. By working with political parties and the parliament, encouraging participation of and open meetings with NGOs in legislative decision making, USAID will help stabilize the post-conflict situation in Tajikistan. NGOs will have the necessary advocacy skills to help local communities address pressing social problems and mitigate the potential for conflict.

Quality Primary Health Care USAID's primary health care efforts in Tajikistan were strengthened with the opening of a new institutional partner under USAID's expanded health program – The Republican Training Center for Family Medicine in Dushanbe. In FY 2001 the USAID-funded partnership between the Ministry of Health and the Community Hospital in Boulder, Colorado provided equipment and skills-based training for primary care providers in family medicine and emergency medical services. USAID, in collaboration with the World Health Organization (WHO), conducted an assessment of TB prevention and control in Tajikistan to plan for a donation of TB drugs by the WHO Global Drug Funds (GDF). The assessment also led to the initiation of two pilot sites in Dushanbe for DOTS implementation. USAID helped the GOT successfully apply for funding from the Global Alliance Vaccines Initiative, which will extend universal Hepatitis B immunization at birth. Since independence, malaria in Tajikistan has reached epidemic proportions. Estimates are that the true number of cases is over 250,000. Since 1990, this is the first effort at reasonable estimation of malaria incidence in Tajikistan. WHO indicates that reported incidence of malaria dropped by 30 percent from 1997 to 2001, from 30,000 to 19,064. Research and training in HIV/AIDS surveillance have begun. USAID supported a study tour of government officials to a model Harm Reduction site in Lithuania; a Central Asian Condom Social Marketing Assessment and Workshop were conducted; and the Central Asian Initiative Conference on the Prevention of HIV/AIDS/STIs was held jointly with UNICEF and UNAIDS. Children and women of reproductive age in Varzob have benefited from improved reproductive health services for women. CARE's midwives and birth attendants see to the delivery of a high proportion of babies in Tajikistan, as hospitals and health facilities have fallen into extreme disrepair. Almost 5,000 women attended nurse-led education sessions on breast-feeding and infant feeding practices. USAID's efforts in child malnourishment surveillance and identification were supported through a new supplementary feeding center in Ayronom (with 16 more planned) using WFP food commodities.

TAJIKISTAN

TAJIKISTAN

Rank: 146

Score: 4.15

Category: Repressed

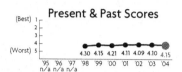

Present & Past Scores

(Best) 1
2
3
4
(Worst) 5

4.30 4.15 4.21 4.11 4.09 4.10 4.15
'95 '96 '97 '98 '99 '00 '01 '02 '03 '04
n/a n/a n/a

QUICK STUDY

SCORES

Trade Policy	3
Fiscal Burden	3.5
Government Intervention	4
Monetary Policy	5
Foreign Investment	4
Banking and Finance	5
Wages and Prices	4
Property Rights	4
Regulation	4
Informal Market	5

Population: 6,244,730

Total area: 143,100 sq. km

GDP: $2.6 billion

GDP growth rate: 10.2%

GDP per capita: $420

Major exports: cotton, vegetables, textiles, electricity, oil

Exports of goods and services: $603.6 million

Major export trading partners: Netherlands 29.8%, Russia 16.1%, Uzbekistan 13.3%, Switzerland 7.9%

Major imports: foodstuffs, machinery and equipment, petroleum, electricity

Imports of goods and services: $718.4 million

Major import trading partners: Uzbekistan 21.9%, Russia 18.8%, Kazakhstan 12.9%, Azerbaijan 4.9%

Foreign direct investment (net): n/a

2001 Data (in constant 1995 US dollars)

Tajikistan is one of the poorest countries in Central Asia. Its geopolitical location and proximity to Afghanistan have brought international development assistance, which has the potential to create jobs and increase long-term stability. Tajikistan has joined NATO's Partnership for Peace and is in the early stages of seeking membership in the World Trade Organization. The Islamic Renaissance Party of Tajikistan, which formerly spearheaded an armed rebellion, is the only Islamic group in Central Asia that has parliamentary and cabinet-level representation. The regime, however, continues to suppress other opposition movements, thereby increasing the likelihood of popular support for violence. Russian military forces continue to patrol Tajikistan's long border with Afghanistan. The economy is still half the size it was in 1991, and inflation remains high. Tajikistan depends heavily on foreign revenue from cotton. External debt and poor implementation of structural reforms have had a negative effect on macroeconomic performance. Tajikistan's government intervention score is 0.5 point worse this year. As a result, its overall score is 0.05 point worse this year.

TRADE POLICY
Score: 3–Stable (moderate level of protectionism)

According to the International Monetary Fund, Tajikistan's average tariff rate in 1999 (the most recent year for which reliable data are available) was 8 percent. Customs corruption is the most significant non-tariff barrier.

FISCAL BURDEN OF GOVERNMENT
Score—Income Taxation: **2–Better** (low tax rates)
Score—Corporate Taxation: **4–Stable** (high tax rates)
Score—Change in Government Expenditures: **4–Worse** (moderate increase)
Final Score: **3.5**–Stable (high cost of government)

According to the International Monetary Fund, Tajikistan's top income tax rate is 20 percent, down from the 40 percent reported in the 2003 *Index.* The top corporate tax is 30 percent. Government expenditures as a share of GDP increased 1.1 percentage points to 15.3 percent in 2001, compared to a 2.4 percentage point decrease in 2000. On net, Tajikistan's fiscal burden of government score is unchanged this year.

GOVERNMENT INTERVENTION IN THE ECONOMY
Score: 4–Worse (high level)

The World Bank reports that the government consumed 8.8 percent of GDP in 2001. In the same year, according to the International Monetary Fund, Tajikistan received 5.47 percent of its total revenues from state-owned enterprises and government ownership of property, up from the 3.43 percent reported in the 2003 *Index.* According to the U.S. Department of State, however, "Government revenue depends highly on state-controlled cotton production [and] the level of medium to large scale privatization is [low at] approximately 16 percent...." The Economist Intelligence Unit reports that "many of the enterprises in the...construction, transport, communications and agricultural sectors are still largely state-owned.... [M]ost of the labour force is still employed by the government...." Based on the apparent unreliability of reported figures for government consumption and total revenues, 2 points have been added to Tajikistan's government intervention score. Based on the higher reported percentage of revenues from state-owned enterprises, Tajikistan's government intervention score is 0.5 point worse this year.

 MONETARY POLICY
Score: 5–Stable (very high level of inflation)

Data from the International Monetary Fund's *2003 World Economic Outlook* indicate that from 1993 to 2002, Tajikistan's weighted average annual rate of inflation was 22.5 percent.

 CAPITAL FLOWS AND FOREIGN INVESTMENT
Score: 4–Stable (high barriers)

The government has opened some of the economy to foreign investment and has made some efforts to promote increased investment—for example, by offering two-year tax holidays on profits—but the bureaucratic procedure is arbitrary and restrictive. According to the Economist Intelligence Unit, "Although a few foreign entities have invested in Tajikistan, political and economic instability…have discouraged substantial amounts of foreign direct investment (FDI). Investors are deterred by corruption and the lack of democratic reforms, while the slow pace of the privatization process—in particular of medium- and large-scale enterprises—has also kept investment inflows low. Other factors deterring investors include limited access to finance and the weakness of the public administration." The International Monetary Fund reports that both residents and non-residents may hold foreign exchange accounts, although residents may hold them abroad only with the central bank's approval. Restrictions on payments and transfers include quantitative limits on wages for foreign workers and requirements on repatriation. Many capital transactions require the central bank's approval.

 BANKING AND FINANCE
Score: 5–Stable (very high level of restrictions)

The Economist Intelligence Unit reports that Tajikistan's banking system is weak and consists of the central bank and 16 commercial banks. Commercial banks have focused generally on channeling credit from the central bank to state-owned enterprises in the agricultural and industrial sectors. The state controls most of the financial system's assets. According to the EIU, "The combined capital of the banking sector was less than US$10m in March 2001, with most banks insolvent and hampered by non-performing loans. The three main private banks are Agroinvestbank, Orienbank, and Tojiksodirotbonk…with Sberbank being the only remaining state-owned bank. Although in theory most banks are privatised (having been transformed into joint-stock companies), they are still closely controlled by the state through the shareholdings of state-owned enterprises." The banking system is largely ineffective, and increasing numbers of people conduct business—including financial activities—in the shadow economy.

 WAGES AND PRICES
Score: 4–Stable (high level of intervention)

Wages and prices are greatly influenced by the large government sector. "Prices in many areas rose strongly in January–March 2003," reports the Economist Intelligence Unit. "This was attributable partly to the fact that the government is progressively raising fuel and energy tariffs in order to bring them more closely into line with world rates and to reduce the energy sector deficit—which the IMF has calculated as being some 5.5% of GDP." The government influences prices through extensive socialist-era collectives and state farms and state-owned industries and utilities. Since agriculture and electricity are the major economic output, such government intervention is significant. According to the U.S. Department of State, "The President, on the advice of the Ministry of Labor and in consultation with trade unions, sets the minimum monthly wage…."

 PROPERTY RIGHTS
Score: 4–Stable (low level of protection)

Protection of private property is weak in Tajikistan. According to the U.S. Department of State, "the Constitution provides for an independent judiciary; however, in practice judges do not function independently of the executive branch and the judicial system is subject to the influence of executive authorities. In many instances, armed paramilitary groups directly influence judicial officials…. Judges at all levels have extremely poor access to legal reference materials. Bribery of prosecutors and judges appears to be a common practice."

 REGULATION
Score: 4–Stable (high level)

The procedure for establishing a business in Tajikistan can be both tedious and time-consuming. *The Washington Post* reports that "corruption, overregulation, senseless tax policies and inertia have frustrated the development of a private sector beyond retail trade and simple services, according to business people, bankers and diplomats [there]." According to Freedom House, "Corruption is reportedly pervasive throughout the government…. Barriers to private enterprise, including limited access to commercial real estate and the widespread practice of bribe payments, continue to restrict equality of opportunity."

 INFORMAL MARKET
Score: 5–Stable (very high level of activity)

Informal market activity is present everywhere in Tajikistan, and despite laws to protect intellectual property rights, significant piracy of such goods continues. According to *The Washington Post*, it is calculated that drug smuggling represents about "a third of gross domestic product."

WORLD EXPORT-IMPORT AND BUSINESS LIBRARY-2006

Ultimate directories for conducting export-import operations in the country. Largest exporters and importers, strategic government and business contacts, selected export-import regulations and more...

Price: $99.95 each

TITLE *	ISBN
Armenia Export-Import and Business Directory	0739728830
Austria Export-Import and Business Directory	0739742124
Azerbaijan Export-Import and Business Directory	0739728865
Belarus Export-Import and Business Directory	0739742132
Belgium Export-Import and Business Directory	0739742140
China Export-Import and Business Directory	0749742159
Czech Republic Export-Import and Business Directory	0739728849
Denmark Export-Import and Business Directory	0739742167
Estonia Export-Import and Business Directory	0739742175
France Export-Import and Business Directory	0739742183
Georgia Export-Import and Business Directory	0739742191
Germany Export-Import and Business Directory	0739742205
Greece Export-Import and Business Directory	0739742213
Iran Export-Import and Business Directory	0739742221
Ireland Export-Import and Business Directory	073974223X
Israel Export-Import and Business Directory	0739739816
Italy Export-Import and Business Directory	0739742248
Kazakhstan Export-Import and Business Directory	0739742256
Kuwait Export-Import and Business Directory	0739742264
Kyrgyzstan Export-Import and Business Directory	0739742272
Latvia Export-Import and Business Directory	0739728857
Liechtenstein Export-Import and Business Directory	0739742280
Lithuania Export-Import and Business Directory	0739742299
Luxemburg Export-Import and Business Directory	0739742302
Mauritius Export-Import Directory	0739742310
Mexico Export-Import and Business Directory	0739742329
Moldova Export-Import and Business Directory	0739742337

**To order and for additional analytical and marketing information, please contacrt
International Business Publications, USA at:**
P.O. Box 15343, Washington, DC 20003, USA. Phone: (202) 546-2103. Fax: (202) 546-3275.
E-mail: rusric@erols.com
World Business Catalog on Line: http://world.mirhouse.com

TITLE *	ISBN
Netherlands Export-Import and Business Directory	0739742345
Pakistan Expoprt-Import and Business Directory	0739742353
Portugal Export-Import and Business Directory	0739742361
Russia Export-Import and Business Directory	073974237X
Spain Export-Import and Business Directory	0739742388
Switzerland Export-Import and Business Directory	0739742396
Syria Export Import & Business Directory	073974240X
Tajikistan Export-Import and Business Directory	0739742418
Turkmenistan Export-Import and Business Directory	0739742426
Ukraine Export-Import and Business Directory	0739742434
United Kingdom Export-Import and Business Directory	0739742469
US Export-Import and Business Directory	0739742442
Uzbekistan Export-Import and Business Directory	0739742450

**To order and for additional analytical and marketing information, please contacrt
International Business Publications, USA at:
P.O. Box 15343, Washington, DC 20003, USA. Phone: (202) 546-2103. Fax: (202) 546-3275.
E-mail: rusric@erols.com
World Business Catalog on Line: http://world.mirhouse.com**

WORLD INDUSTRIAL AND BUSINESS DIRECTORIES
LIBRARY 2005

Price: $129.95 Each

1.	Albania Industrial and Business Directory
2.	Algeria Industrial and Business Directory
3.	Andorra Industrial and Business Directory
4.	Angola Industrial and Business Directory
5.	Antigua & Barbuda Industrial and Business Directory
6.	Antilles (Netherlands) Industrial and Business Directory
7.	Argentina Industrial and Business Directory
8.	Armenia Industrial and Business Directory
9.	Australia Industrial and Business Directory
10.	Austria Industrial and Business Directory
11.	Azerbaijan Industrial and Business Directory
12.	Bahamas Industrial and Business Directory
13.	Bangladesh Industrial and Business Directory
14.	Barbados Industrial and Business Directory
15.	Belarus Industrial and Business Directory
16.	Belgium Industrial and Business Directory
17.	Belize Industrial and Business Directory
18.	Bermuda Industrial and Business Directory
19.	Bolivia Industrial and Business Directory
20.	Bosnia and Herzegovina Industrial and Business Directory
21.	Botswana Industrial and Business Directory
22.	Brazil Industrial and Business Directory
23.	Brunei Industrial and Business Directory
24.	Bulgaria Industrial and Business Directory
25.	Cambodia Industrial and Business Directory
26.	Cameroon Industrial and Business Directory
27.	Canada Industrial and Business Directory
28.	Cayman Islands Industrial and Business Directory
29.	Chile Industrial and Business Directory
30.	China Industrial and Business Directory
31.	Colombia Industrial and Business Directory

For additional analytical, business and investment opportunities information,
please contact Global Investment & Business Center, USA
at (202) 546-2103. Fax: (202) 546-3275. E-mail: rusric@erols.com

32.	Comoros Industrial and Business Directory
33.	Cook Islands Industrial and Business Directory
34.	Costa Rica Industrial and Business Directory
35.	Croatia Industrial and Business Directory
36.	Cuba Industrial and Business Directory
37.	Cyprus Industrial and Business Directory
38.	Czech Republic Industrial and Business Directory
39.	Denmark Industrial and Business Directory
40.	Dominica Industrial and Business Directory
41.	Dominican Republic Industrial and Business Directory
42.	Dubai Industrial and Business Directory
43.	Ecuador Industrial and Business Directory
44.	Egypt Industrial and Business Directory
45.	El Salvador Industrial and Business Directory
46.	Equatorial Guinea Industrial and Business Directory
47.	Estonia Industrial and Business Directory
48.	Falkland Islands Industrial and Business Directory
49.	Fiji Industrial and Business Directory
50.	Finland Industrial and Business Directory
51.	France Industrial and Business Directory
52.	Georgia Industrial and Business Directory
53.	Germany Industrial and Business Directory
54.	Gibraltar Industrial and Business Directory
55.	Greece Industrial and Business Directory
56.	Grenada Industrial and Business Directory
57.	Guam Investment & Business Guide
58.	Guatemala Industrial and Business Directory
59.	Guernsey Industrial and Business Directory
60.	Guyana Industrial and Business Directory
61.	Haiti Industrial and Business Directory
62.	Honduras Industrial and Business Directory
63.	Hungary Industrial and Business Directory
64.	Iceland Industrial and Business Directory
65.	India Industrial and Business Directory
66.	Indonesia Industrial and Business Directory
67.	Iran Industrial and Business Directory
68.	Iraq Industrial and Business Directory
69.	Ireland Industrial and Business Directory
70.	Israel Industrial and Business Directory
71.	Italy Industrial and Business Directory
72.	Jamaica Industrial and Business Directory

For additional analytical, business and investment opportunities information,
please contact Global Investment & Business Center, USA
at (202) 546-2103. Fax: (202) 546-3275. E-mail: rusric@erols.com

73.	Japan Industrial and Business Directory
74.	Jersey Industrial and Business Directory
75.	Jordan Industrial and Business Directory
76.	Kazakhstan Industrial and Business Directory
77.	Kenya Industrial and Business Directory
78.	Kiribati Industrial and Business Directory
79.	Korea, North Industrial and Business Directory
80.	Korea, South Industrial and Business Directory
81.	Kuwait Industrial and Business Directory
82.	Kyrgyzstan Industrial and Business Directory
83.	Laos Industrial and Business Directory
84.	Latvia Industrial and Business Directory
85.	Lebanon Industrial and Business Directory
86.	Libya Industrial and Business Directory
87.	Liechtenstein Industrial and Business Directory
88.	Lithuania Industrial and Business Directory
89.	Luxemburg Industrial and Business Directory
90.	Macao Industrial and Business Directory
91.	Macedonia, Republic Industrial and Business Directory
92.	Madagascar Industrial and Business Directory
93.	Malaysia Industrial and Business Directory
94.	Malta Industrial and Business Directory
95.	Man Industrial and Business Directory
96.	Mauritius Industrial and Business Directory
97.	Mauritius Industrial and Business Directory
98.	Mexico Industrial and Business Directory
99.	Micronesia Industrial and Business Directory
100.	Moldova Industrial and Business Directory
101.	Monaco Industrial and Business Directory
102.	Mongolia Industrial and Business Directory
103.	Morocco Industrial and Business Directory
104.	Myanmar Industrial and Business Directory
105.	Namibia Industrial and Business Directory
106.	Netherlands Industrial and Business Directory
107.	New Caledonia Industrial and Business Directory
108.	New Zealand Industrial and Business Directory
109.	Nicaragua Industrial and Business Directory
110.	Nigeria Industrial and Business Directory
111.	Northern Mariana Islands Industrial and Business Directory
112.	Norway Industrial and Business Directory
113.	Pakistan Industrial and Business Directory

For additional analytical, business and investment opportunities information,
please contact Global Investment & Business Center, USA
at (202) 546-2103. Fax: (202) 546-3275. E-mail: rusric@erols.com

114. Panama Industrial and Business Directory
115. Peru Industrial and Business Directory
116. Philippines Industrial and Business Directory
117. Poland Industrial and Business Directory
118. Portugal Industrial and Business Directory
119. Romania Industrial and Business Directory
120. Russia Industrial and Business Directory
121. Samoa (American) Investment & Business Guide
122. Samoa (Western) Industrial and Business Directory
123. Saudi Arabia Industrial and Business Directory
124. Scotland Industrial and Business Directory
125. Singapore Industrial and Business Directory
126. Slovakia Industrial and Business Directory
127. Slovenia Industrial and Business Directory
128. South Africa Industrial and Business Directory
129. Spain Industrial and Business Directory
130. Sri Lanka Industrial and Business Directory
131. St. Helena Industrial and Business Directory
132. Sudan Industrial and Business Directory
133. Suriname Industrial and Business Directory
134. Sweden Industrial and Business Directory
135. Switzerland Industrial and Business Directory
136. Syria Export Import & Business Directory
137. Taiwan Industrial and Business Directory
138. Tajikistan Industrial and Business Directory
139. Thailand Industrial and Business Directory
140. Tunisia Industrial and Business Directory
141. Turkey Industrial and Business Directory
142. Turkmenistan Industrial and Business Directory
143. Uganda Industrial and Business Directory
144. Ukraine Industrial and Business Directory
145. United Arab Emirates Industrial and Business Directory
146. United Kingdom Industrial and Business Directory
147. United States Industrial and Business Directory
148. Uruguay Industrial and Business Directory
149. US Industrial and Business Directory
150. Uzbekistan Industrial and Business Directory
151. Venezuela Industrial and Business Directory
152. Vietnam Industrial and Business Directory
153. Yugoslavia Industrial and Business Directory

For additional analytical, business and investment opportunities information,
please contact Global Investment & Business Center, USA
at (202) 546-2103. Fax: (202) 546-3275. E-mail: rusric@erols.com

CPSIA information can be obtained
at www.ICGtesting.com
Printed in the USA
BVOW03s1258210517
484730BV00001B/4/P